CONTENTION IN CONTEXT

CONTENTION IN CONTEXT

Political Opportunities and
the Emergence of Protest

Edited by Jeff Goodwin
and James M. Jasper

Stanford University Press
Stanford, California

Stanford University Press
Stanford, California

Printed in the United States of America on acid-free, archival-quality paper

Library of Congress Cataloging-in-Publication Data

Contention in context : political opportunities and the emergence of protest / edited
by Jeff Goodwin and James M. Jasper.
    pages cm
  Includes bibliographical references and index.
  ISBN 978-0-8047-7611-0 (cloth : alk. paper)--ISBN 978-0-8047-7612-7 (pbk. : alk.
paper)
  1. Social movements. 2. Protest movements. 3. Political science. I. Goodwin, Jeff,
editor of compilation. II. Jasper, James M., 1957- editor of compilation.
  HM881.C655 2011
  322.4--dc23   2011026604

Typeset by Bruce Lundquist in 10/14 Minion

In memory of Chuck Tilly

Contents

Preface

JAMES M. JASPER

I N COLLEGE I heard a charming story about George Santayana, that great thinker but forgotten philosopher. He was lecturing at Harvard one bright spring day, forty-eight years old and at the height of his fame, when he looked out the window and allowed his words to trail off. He walked out of the lecture hall, booked passage to Europe, and spent the last forty years of his life in Rome. I thought of Santayana when I had lunch one day with Jeff Goodwin in September 2008. We were sitting outdoors in what I think of as Roman weather when he pushed a manuscript across the table to me. He was leaving for Florence the next day, and asked me to help him finish this complex book project. (I expected him back in a year, but hey, you never know.)

Jeff had invited seventeen scholars to each read an important book on a revolutionary or social movement, asking what political opportunity structures contributed to its emergence. Then he asked the authors of the books to respond, and ten did. The response was so enthusiastic—and the exchanges so lengthy—that Jeff had more materials than any sane editor would accept for publication. It needed to be cut in half, something Jeff didn't have the heart to do. I ruthlessly suggested we publish only full exchanges, even though that meant losing several wonderful essays, and then ask the original critics to write a rejoinder to update the discussion and suggest new directions for research. (There was one exception: the U.S. civil rights movement, too important to skip even though Charles Payne declined to reply.) Two additional exchanges were withdrawn because the authors thought them outdated. Jeff and I would like to thank all the participants whose patient work did not end up in the published version: Said Arjomand, Nicola Beisel, Kathleen Blee, Chris Bonastia, Mark Chaves, Nina Eliasoph, Tina Fetner, Joseph Gerteis, John Glenn III, Doug Guthrie, Ernest Harsch, Charles Kurzman, Paul Lichterman, Rory McVeigh, Kelly Moore, Misagh Parsa, Kurt Schock, and Mark Thompson.

After languishing for nearly a decade (I knew, since I was one of the original contributors), the book also needed updating. For instance, Chuck Tilly, the great scholar of political process who had died only a few months before, had issued a torrent of books in his final years that touched on various dimensions of the external contexts for social movements and protest. Once we had the contract from Stanford University Press, we could ask the scholars to go back and revise their original contributions in light of subsequent intellectual developments like this.

We also asked Jan Willem Duyvendak (writing with Christian Bröer) to contribute a new chapter, since the tradition of political opportunity structures that his work represents differs from American use of the concept. Donatella della Porta was willing to contribute a piece showing her important extensions of political-opportunity theories. I would also like to thank Geoffrey Blank, Nico Legewie, and especially Kevin Moran for their editorial persistence in pulling the manuscript together, and the CUNY Graduate Center Department of Sociology for paying them to help me. Olivier Fillieule and Verta Taylor read the entire manuscript and offered extremely useful suggestions. At Stanford University Press, Kate Wahl was a model of efficiency as well as good judgment, and Joa Suorez was invaluable in directing the flow of paper and computer files during the final stages of preparation.

Despite its prolonged gestation, this volume should help us think about current trends in social movement theory. The concept of political opportunity structures is alive and well in journal articles, with many of the same conceptual problems it has always had. In social science broadly, however, there has been a marked swing of the intellectual pendulum from structure to agency in the past decade or so. In the field of social movements this has resulted in studies of meaning, emotions, and strategic choices. It is important not to forget the causal impact of structured contexts on how protest unfolds and in some cases even changes the world. Yet while recognizing the role of structural context, we can also rethink that role, casting structures in a new vision of the world around us as ever changing, ever open to human efforts. Structures and opportunities, we might say, neither enable nor constrain our actions. They *are* our actions, since we cannot have structures without action in them, or have action without the resources and channels through which it unfolds.

I think of myself as a writer as much as a social scientist, and so I care about how people use words. I devote a lot of time to editing other people's work, on the lookout for the abuse of words or ideas. Much of the debate over political opportunities and structures has been a battle over language, and as such it can never be fully resolved empirically. The most concrete predictions of any perspective are only testable if the concepts and words make sense. There is a tendency in studies of social movements to prefer empirical research to theory, but we need both. We need assessments of our language and concepts for their internal consistency, their logic, and their resonance with various audiences. Clearing the conceptual underbrush is a task that is never complete.

Chuck Tilly would probably smile at my Santayana story, knowing the truth behind it. There was nothing spontaneous in Santayana's decision to retire at forty-eight; he had been planning this for years. He had waited to come into the resources, namely a ten thousand dollar bequest from his mother, which allowed him to do it. And he didn't steam directly to Italy, but to Britain. He had not yet decided where to live, and he was kept from the Continent for four years as the nation states of Europe did what they had always done, wage war. Because Chuck helped us understand these processes, and so many more, we dedicate this book to his memory.

List of Abbreviations

ACLU   American Civil Liberties Union

AMIA   Argentine Israelite Mutual Association (Mutual de Asociaciones Israelitas Argentinas)

APDH   Permanent Assembly for Human Rights (Asamblea Permanente por los Derechos Humanos)

CELS   Center for Legal and Social Studies Centro de Estudios Legales y Sociales)

CGT   General Confederation of Workers (Confederación General de Trabajadores)

COFAVI   Committee of Relatives of Defenseless Victims of Institutional Violence (Comisión de Familiares de Víctimas de Violencia Institucional)

COFO   Council of Federated Organizations

CORREPI   Coalition Against Police and Institutional Repression (Coordinadora Contra la Represión Policial e Institucional)

CRH   Council on Religion and the Homosexual

CTN   Confederation of Nicaraguan Workers (Confederación de Trabajadores Nicaragüenses)

DOB   Daughters of Bilitis

EEOC   Equal Employment Opportunity Commission

ERA	Equal Rights Amendment
FBI	Federal Bureau of Investigation
FoE	Friends of the Earth
FMLN	Farabundo Martí National Liberation Front (Frente Farabundo Martí para la Liberación Nacional)
FSLN	Sandinista National Liberation Front (Frente Sandinista de Liberación Nacional)
HIJOS	Children for Identity and Justice and Against Forgetting and Silence (Hijos por la Identidad y la Justicia, Contra el Olvido y el Silencio)
IAN	Nicaraguan Agrarian Institute (Instituto Agrario Nicaragüense)
ISA	San Antonio (Sugar) Mill (Ingenio San Antonio)
MEDH	Ecumenical Human Rights Movement (Movimiento Ecuménico por Derechos Humanos)
MPVL	Mississippi Progressive Voters' League
NAACP	National Association for the Advancement of Colored People
NOW	National Organization for Women
POS	Political Opportunity Structure
RCNL	Regional Council of Negro Leadership
SCUM	Society to Cut Up Men
SERPAJ	Peace and Justice Service (Servicio de Paz y Justicia)
SMO	Social Movement Organization
SNCC	Student Nonviolent Coordinating Committee
WCC	White Citizens' Council
WEAL	Women's Equity Action League
WITCH	Women's International Terrorist Conspiracy from Hell

CONTENTION IN CONTEXT

Introduction

From Political Opportunity Structures
to Strategic Interaction

JAMES M. JASPER

If the enemy opens the door, you must race in.

Sun Tzu

Men who have any great undertaking in mind must first make all necessary preparations for it, so that, when an opportunity arises, they may be ready to put it in execution according to their design.

Machiavelli

T HE FRENCH TOWN of Poitiers lent its name to one of the most famous battles of European history, when England's Black Prince captured the French king in 1356, seventeen years into the series of sporadic campaigns known as the Hundred Years' War. At first light Prince Edward, commanding six thousand men in comparison to the French King John's twenty thousand, was pondering (and may have begun) a retreat in order to protect the many wagons of his booty that had already departed. The French, positioned on the highest hill in the vicinity, charged down when they saw the treasure escaping, and for most of the morning dismounted troops fought hand to hand around a thick hedge. Suddenly, a fresh contingent of French forces appeared, coming down the hill toward the now exhausted combatants. Many English soldiers began to withdraw, under the guise of escorting their wounded comrades. Edward's situation looked grim.

The French then decided to dismount and attack on foot, as they had ear-

The Politics and Protest Workshop at the CUNY Graduate Center, and especially John Krinsky, provided excellent suggestions on a draft of this chapter; I only wish I could have followed all of them.

lier, inadvertently offering an opportunity to the twenty-six-year-old Edward, who immediately recognized it, turning the tide and making a name for himself as a brilliant strategist. His soldiers, although dismounted, still had their horses nearby, a resource the French, having marched the final distance to the hedge, lacked. The English mounted and charged the large French army. Galloping horses are intimidating to men on foot, but equally important was the boost to English morale that came from going on the offensive rather than waiting to be attacked again. This restored the English soldiers' sense of agency.

In addition, Edward sent a small cavalry group down the back and around the side of the small hill where he was camped. When they suddenly appeared at the French army's flank, soon after the second engagement had begun, the startled French scattered. This was another opportunity for Edward, who pursued them right up to the walls of the town, where he captured King John. In the midst of several thousand corpses, he pitched his tent and sat down to dinner with John as his guest (before shipping him, with the rest of the loot, off to England to await ransom).

At dawn, King John had seemed to hold most advantages: good position, a much larger force, and the modest goal of preventing Edward from getting away with his slow-moving wagon train. And with the first engagement, the French seem to have shaken their main disadvantage, a forbidding sense of the superiority of English warriors. But by dusk, through vigilance and quick decisions, the Black Prince had pulled off one of the great victories of military history.

Central to strategic engagement of any kind is to be alert to changes that give you some new advantage. Opponents make a mistake, or circumstances alter in a way that suddenly favors your resources, skills, or position. In war, the fog lifts, the wind shifts, or a sudden freeze hardens the mud. In other contentious arenas, it may be new rules, a change in personnel, or some event, such as a scandal, that redirects attention and opinion. These temporary openings often make the difference in an engagement, and they are especially valuable for those with few stable resources. One side's mistake is the other's opportunity (Jasper and Poulsen 1993).

Other aspects of any field of conflict are more stable, encouraging certain kinds of action while discouraging or preventing others. You tailor your team and strategies to these structural features of the environment. These are long-run rules of the game or physical attributes of an arena, as distinct from short-run windows of opportunity within in arena. Rules advantage some players and disadvantage others, depending on their resources, skills, status, and position. (Holding a post in a hierarchy is like holding a position on a field of battle: different placements allow for different actions.) Both structures and opportunities impose costs and constraints on strategic agency, encouraging action to move in easier directions rather than harder ones (but rarely altogether determining that action).[1]

It has been called action and order, agency and structure, actors and their environments, players and games, and many more things: the mysterious interplay between intentions and outcomes in human action. Deep philosophical anxieties over determinism and free will lurk here, as well as unsettling explanatory challenges for all the social sciences. Observers of protest and social movements have always recognized these two sides of political efforts, acknowledging that protestors rarely get what they want, that social movements rarely succeed. But it is vital to understand why they sometimes do succeed (Ganz 2009). Diverse strategic arenas—such as wars, diplomacy, markets, party politics, and protest—exhibit the same complex interplay (Jasper 2006). This book aims at a better understanding of this interaction.

Political Opportunity Structures

The late Charles Tilly revolutionized the study of collective action in the 1960s by redirecting attention from the motivations and choices of protestors to their demographic, economic, and especially political contexts. In 1964 with *The Vendée*, in my opinion his best book, he showed that seemingly local mobilizations reflected broader changes in political institutions and who controlled them. For the next forty-four years he would elaborate on this idea that, as national political institutions developed in France and England, new struggles appeared over who would be represented and how, and whose interests would be served. In this way Tilly created what became known as the political-process tradition, centered on changes in the environments of protestors, in their external opportunities to act in certain ways. Let's take a look at the evolution of Tilly's views of the contexts of political action as he developed his *polity-centered approach.*

---

1. Vince Boudreau points out that I don't explain how the Black Prince managed to see his opportunity, a big gap for an approach that is intended to highlight decisions. If we had better evidence, we might be able to recount a discussion with his war council; we might see an adviser who had had similar experience before, for instance (Ganz 2009). But one reason that strategic approaches leave room for agency is that there is always a "vacant core" in which a choice is made, a choice that could have been different (Jasper 2006, p. 12).

Urbanization was the central process that, according to Tilly, explained why in 1793 rural communities of France's Vendée region erupted in resistance to the French Revolution while their more urbanized neighbors continued to support it. He lumped different processes under the heading of "urbanization," including economic and political integration with cities and especially Paris. Central were the religious, economic, and political elites who linked local with national: "The difference in apparent political affiliation [between pro- and counterrevolutionary areas] was less a matter of sharp disagreement in political philosophy than of differences 1) between an essentially apolitical electorate and a politicized one, and 2) between two different kinds of linkage between communities and the national political process" (Tilly 1964, p. 154).

Preexisting attitudes and ideologies mattered little, and Tilly's main target was grievance theories based on individual attitudes or emotions, or indeed any explanations that relied on mental states, which he considered "phenomenological individualism."[2] He stated the kernel of the political-opportunity model: "A set of circumstances which significantly weakened one or the other of these competitors [primarily bourgeois merchants and traditional nobles, vying for leadership over peasants and artisans], or transformed the external situation of the community, could give the bourgeois an opportunity to increase greatly his local power and, in the long run, his prestige" (1964, p. 157). The Revolution did just this. Nobles and bourgeois were both clear about their objective interests, and the emergence of a new, national arena centered on the Assembly gave an advantage to the latter.

In further research on France, Tilly would give less prominence to urbanization patterns and more to the rise of national markets and to the centralization of power in the national state, but the opening of new arenas remained central. In his grand summary of four centuries of popular contention in France, *The Contentious French* (1986), his basic framework consisted of interests, organization, and opportunity. He drew heavily on Marxism, which he admired for its stress on "the ubiquity of conflict, the importance of interests rooted in the

---

2. Robert K. Merton (1959, 1995) and others (especially his student Richard Cloward [1959], who emphasized that opportunities can be considered illegitimate as well as legitimate) promoted the term "opportunity structure" to stress that "deviants" and criminals were not inherently "bad," but had few opportunities to pursue legitimate social goals through legitimate, legal means, just as Tilly would show that protestors and revolutionaries—rather than inherently prone to violence—lacked opportunities to pursue their political goals through institutional, legal means. Merton placed equal stress on goals and on means, whereas Tilly focused only on the latter. Later "opportunity theories" in criminology, such as Felson's (1994) routine activity theory, also stress the opportunities that perpetrators face over their motivations.

organization of production, the influence of specific forms of organization on the character and intensity of collective action" (Tilly 1978, p. 48). What he claimed was missing from the Marxist tradition became Tilly's specialty, political processes. Simply put, "increasingly the action (or, for that matter, the inaction) of large organizations and of national states has created the threats and opportunities to which any interested actor has to respond" (1986, p. 77). Actors already have interests and are aware of them. The large organizations that intrigued him most were those of the state, which has become the ubiquitous context for contention in the modern world.

Despite Tilly's (1975, 1992) research on the state as an actor, especially in making war and taxing citizens, when it came to contentious politics the state tended to remain a "context" in his accounts rather than a player or set of players. Unlike Max Weber, for instance, who was interested in the intentions and ideologies of politicians, leaders, and officials (and the interactions among them), Tilly seemed content to read "interests" of state officials from their structural positions (as he did with non–state actors). They wanted territory, order, and especially revenues. His sensitivity to long-run historical change led him to focus on the emergence of the modern state *as a relatively unified player*, an explanandum that perhaps encouraged him to exaggerate the cohesion of the contemporary state. It is so much more unified than previous states, why look inside it for conflicts?

In one way, Tilly saw the state as a set of often-conflicting strategic players, since it was this conflict that opened opportunities for protestors to promote their causes, providing allies or distracting attention. Otherwise, this conflict within the state was never Tilly's object of interest. He did not examine the conflicting logics of different state institutions, the ideologies of parties or their leaders, the professional training of bureaucrats, the worldviews that might lead some officials to disagree with others, the contention between monarchs, nobles, parliamentary parties and factions, police forces, armies, judiciaries, finance ministries, and so on. All this remained "context," with the salient outcome either a divided state or a unified state. In his final book, *Contentious Performances* (2008), Tilly summarized the relevance of the state in just two variables: its capabilities and the political and civil rights it granted.

In his great project of the 1980s and 1990s, on British contention from the 1750s to the 1830s, Tilly (1995, 1997) deployed the same basic variables as with France to show how the expansion of capitalist markets and of the national state affected protest, now especially conceptualized and aggregated into repertories of action. This period saw the creation of a new arena, a powerful and accountable parliament, to which popular demands and displays were oriented—and remain oriented today in the form of social movements. Tilly (1995, p. 36) downplayed the language of opportunities here, but retained a strong focus on the "logic of interaction, of struggle itself," as opposed to scholars who seek "accounts of the actions of actors—individuals, communities, classes, organizations, and others—taken singly." He occasionally mentions goals, especially interests and rights, but these are scantily defined except that a gain for one group seems to entail losses for other groups. The influence of Marxism remains, in that economic classes seem to be the example that fits his model best. In this strongly contextual view, arenas define players' goals. (Just as for Alain Touraine [1981], in an unexpected parallel, the stakes of an arena help define a social movement.) In retrospect, Tilly's idea—developed in biting criticism of earlier theories—that one may study players or their interactions but not the two together seems both wrong and unfortunate.

By this time, others had adopted Tilly's contextual approach, defining it as a distinct paradigm of research and in the process extracting his concepts from their dense historical contexts to apply them to new periods and places. In 1982 Doug McAdam identified a new "political-process" model in sharp distinction to both collective behavior and resource mobilization. He especially intended it to highlight indigenous efforts more than John McCarthy and Mayer Zald (1977) did in their resource mobilization model, which McAdam thought overstressed elite resources and overextended the concept of resources into anything useful to a movement.

In McAdam's process model, four sets of variables explain the emergence of a social movement: broad socioeconomic processes, indigenous organizational strength (especially social networks and leaders), expanding political opportunities, and cognitive liberation (which includes both a sense that the current system is illegitimate and a belief that change is possible). Yet political opportunities tend to absorb the other factors. Citing Peter Eisinger (1973), McAdam (1982, p. 41) says, "*any* event or broad social process that serves to undermine the calculations and assumptions on which the political establishment is structured occasions a shift in political opportunities." In his empirical chapters on the U.S. civil rights movement he proceeds to adduce a wide range of opportunities: the decline of the cotton industry, the migration of African Americans out of the South, their electoral support for Democrats, America's Cold War struggle with the USSR, black organizations and networks and leaders, and more. These matter to the extent they lead to political opportunities. McAdam had moved away from Tilly's narrowly political type of opportunity. As James Rule (1988, p. 187) gently complained, "McAdam's work . . . illustrates some ambiguities in political accounts of militant action. It is difficult to draw falsifiable commitments from the explanatory factors he invokes." But falsifiability is always difficult in complex political settings; to me, the underlying problem is the inclusive vagueness of McAdam's variables. We needed more precise causal processes.

Perhaps because of its looseness, the word *opportunities* caught the imagination of scholars. Soon there were *cultural* opportunities (McAdam 1996), *organizational* opportunities (Kurzman 1998), *transnational* opportunities (della Porta and Tarrow 2004, 2007), *international* opportunities (Khagram et al. 2002), *discursive* opportunities (Koopmans 2004; Koopmans and Olzak 2004), *emotional* opportunities (Guenther 2009), and more.[3] Any advantage became an opportunity, and any scholar who needed some theory could easily adapt the term. I think the excitement over the concept reflected an awareness of the open-ended, sudden nature of strategic interaction, combined with an anxious desire to systematize the unsystematic, to predict the unpredictable, to tame agency by reducing it to structures.

Later, in the face of ever-proliferating lists of political opportunity structures (see Chapter 8, this volume), McAdam (1996, p. 27) returned to Tilly's narrowly political approach by offering this "highly consensual" list: (1) The relative *openness or closure* of the institutionalized political system, (2) The stability or instability of that broad set of *elite alignments* that typically undergird a polity, (3) The presence or absence of *elite allies*, and (4) The state's capacity and propensity for *repression*. (This is the list Jeff Goodwin originally asked our initial contributors to look for in their cases, presented in Chapters 1 through 8.) McAdam had apparently relaxed his objection to McCarthy and Zald's emphasis on elites. The list seemed sensible, although the factors often proved hard to define tightly or to observe independently of the actions they were intended to explain.

The world around us channels our actions in certain directions, or in Sidney Tarrow's favorite formula, it both enables and constrains us. This channeling takes many different forms, and the challenge of any book on political

3. I am intrigued by the idea of an "unwelcome opportunity," as Kirk and Madsen (1989, p. xxv) call HIV/AIDS for the gay community. An exogenous shift in cultural understandings allowed gay men to present themselves as sympathetic victims deserving protection and care— although not without rhetorical work to take advantage of the opportunity. Cultural opportunities of this sort do seem to fit the definition, and they can be either short- or long-run changes.

context is to sort them out. The risk of political-opportunity theory was to overextend its key concept and not distinguish sufficiently among different types of constraint. William Gamson and David Meyer (1996, p. 275) famously lamented, "The concept of political opportunity structure is in trouble, in danger of becoming a sponge that soaks up every aspect of the social movement environment—political institutions and culture, crises of various sorts, political alliances, and policy shifts." Elaborating on these risks, in 1999 Jeff Goodwin and I (1999/2004a) complained that process models conflated short-term openings and long-term structural shifts, implied "objective" shifts outside human interpretation, and ignored a number of important cultural and emotional factors. Why call something a structure, we asked, if protestors can change it, and especially when their main goal is to change it?

Only after political opportunity structures had come under attack, interestingly, did Tilly explicitly embrace the term, in *Contentious Performances* (2008). (He had mostly ignored them in his 2004 overview of social movements, where the central context is "democratization.") He addresses three of Goodwin's and my criticisms of the concept: "that analysts have used it inconsistently, that it denies human agency, and that it remains unverifiable because it only applies after the fact" (Tilly 2008, p. 91). He admits the charge of inconsistency but denies the other two. "POS can only shape contention through human agency," he says, shifting the way we should think about political opportunity structures. They are no longer independent variables, but dependent ones as well. A contentious campaign changes them, and they in turn change the context for future campaigns (which themselves can change the context, and so on, back and forth). Poignantly, this importance for particular campaigns opens the door to a range of topics—the sources of strategic creativity, the symbolic resonance of events such as foundings, the decision-making styles of powerful leaders, the rhetorical resonance of various tropes, and emotions and sensibilities—that Tilly had no time to explore. By finally acknowledging agency as inextricably tied to structure, however, Tilly left an enormous agenda for the rest of us.

The endless lists of opportunities, Tilly also argued, show that they can be specified in advance. In contrast to the four that McAdam had identified, he names six (2008, p. 91): openness of the regime, coherence of its elite, stability of political alignments, availability of allies for potential challengers, repression or facilitation, and pace of change. The generality of these, quite far from the concrete "mechanisms" that McAdam, Tarrow, and Tilly (2001) desire, suggests there is still work to be done. The first four are hard to recognize before insurgents attempt to take advantage of them: how do we know if elite allies are available before protestors do the strategic and rhetorical work of trying to align with them; and once they've done that work, how do we know what potential was really there beforehand? And how do we know just how divided elites are unless some segment decides to align with insurgents? How do we know a system is stable other than through its lack of change? Because the six factors are highly correlated, we need to be especially careful to specify the concrete mechanisms by which each operates. We need to replace catchall categories with *observables*.

To me, these opportunities are not independent variables. They arise out of struggles and challenges, through an interaction even more continuous than Tilly implies in his sequence of campaign-structure-campaign-et cetera. It would be simpler to see them as actions and reactions rather than as structures, to see them first as moves in a conflict and only second as (occasional) precipitates out of those moves. (Actually, they are complex sequences of interactions, not single actions: they need to be analytically broken down into concrete actions.) We cannot compare the agency of protestors with the structures of the state, since all players exhibit choices and thus agency. Chuck Tilly found remarkably few things to change his mind about in fifty years of research, so we should pay attention to those he did. It is typical of him to leave us, in his final book, a new formulation of old problems, causal imagery that should prove fruitful for research over years to come, even as we question and criticize it.

Can Political Opportunities Be Patched?

In *Dynamics of Contention*, McAdam, Tarrow, and Tilly (2001) seemed to abandon the whole system of political opportunities in favor of a mechanisms approach that specifies smaller causal chunks that can be concatenated to explain complex processes and outcomes (although, confusingly, they also retained "processes" as predictable concatenations of mechanisms).[4] Others have been pushing in the same direction, toward viewing political context in a more dy-

---

4. They again draw on Merton to see mechanisms as mid-range causal regularities. Most scholars who deploy the term *mechanism* mean instead a process at a lower level of reality: psychological or interactional instead of institutional, for example (Elster 1999). For "McTeam," a mechanism is like a mousetrap, which snaps shut in a predictable way when triggered. For me, the most useful mechanisms are things like emotions or "choice points" that are not deterministic.

namic, less structural way. Three years later, in a continuation of the 1999 debate, a number of other scholars joined the fray (Goodwin and Jasper 2004), pointing out emotional, cultural, strategic, and other directions overlooked by political-opportunity models. Richard Flacks (2004, p. 146), for instance, complains, "One of the defining characteristics of activists is that they are people whose actions are not interpretable simply in terms of situations; instead, they are people who act against institutionalized expectations, accepted belief, conventional values and goals." Like another contributor, Marshall Ganz (2004, 2009), Flacks finds strategy to be missing: "Surprisingly little attention is paid to examining, in a given movement situation, what activists themselves believe their strategic options to be and how these get evaluated and debated within the movement" (p. 147). Aldon Morris (2004, p. 246) similarly faults the process model for its "tendency to assign undue causal weight to external factors and its propensity to gloss over the deep cultural and emotional processes that inspire and produce collective action."

Reflecting on these debates, an astute French observer, Olivier Fillieule (2005), composed a "Requiem" for the concept of political opportunity structures. Admiring the concept when restricted to comparative research into the effects of national political structures, he complained about the lack of mechanisms to explain the effects of broad structures as well as about the inattention to the ways in which interactions affect the structures in turn. Accordingly, he concluded that the models remained static instead of dynamic. Fillieule added that the opportunities remained structural, rather than interpretive, due largely to the accompanying methods of research: "macro-comparisons based on quantitative analyses, statistical data, newspaper counts, surveys of organizations, etc." (2005, pp. 208–9; also Fillieule 1997). As Meyer and Minkoff (2004) also show, it is difficult to get at dynamic interactions through these kinds of data.

At the same time as Fillieule's requiem, David Meyer (Meyer 2004; Meyer and Minkoff 2004) tried to fix the concept, although partly by replacing political opportunity structures with the even broader term *political opportunities*. He reminds us (2004, p. 126) of the original point of the approach, "that activists' prospects for advancing particular claims, mobilizing supporters, and affecting influence are context-dependent." This is the kind of broad formulation that led Goodwin and me to call the perspective "trivial," but Meyer more usefully observes that political opportunities can be used to explain different things, including mobilization, tactical choices, and outcomes. But opportunities remain the primary independent variable. Meyer also claims that some protestors shift their tactics in reaction to opportunities more readily than other protestors (2004, p. 140), but this prototypology of players raises more questions than it answers—all of them outside the realm of political-opportunity models. Meyer is true to the Tilly tradition here, reading the players from their actions in arenas rather than developing an independent definition and account of players and their goals and actions.

Howard Ramos (2008) has taken up Meyer and Minkoff's challenge to specify how different protest movements face different political opportunities, as an alternative to the "cycle" model in which all insurgents tend to face the same opportunities and threats. Ramos points out that dynamic models, in which movements and countermovements interact (Meyer and Staggenborg 1996), and in which therefore protestors can create their own opportunities, make it even more difficult to assess the effects of changing opportunities on mobilization (because they are not seen as part of an ongoing interaction or strategic game). Interestingly, his most robust finding is that resources matter: available funding increases mobilization. This harks back to an older model of protest that political-opportunity theory was meant to displace, but with the twist that the relevant funding comes from the government. Funding is both a goal of mobilization and a means for it. By treating resources as a political opportunity, Ramos risks the "sponge" trap against which Gamson and Meyer (1996) warned. Something similar happened when scholars began to include grievances on their list of political opportunity structures (Meyer 1990; Smith 1996b; see Chapter 8, this volume). If political opportunities include everything, ends as well as means, then they no longer mean much of anything.

Opportunity versus Structure

Once we reach the point that political opportunities include both grievances and resources—the very factors that opportunities were meant to displace—then we need to make some distinctions where there has been too much conceptual lumping (Koopmans 2004). The most obvious distinction, which the term *political opportunity structure* unfortunately blurs, is between short-run opportunities and long-run structures. Oberschall (1996, p. 95) calls them events and institutional structures; Tarrow (1996, p. 41) contrasts dynamic and cross-sectional opportunities; Gamson and Meyer (1996, p. 277) observe that scholars compare opportunities either over time or across political systems.

Windows of opportunity open and close, often suddenly and unexpectedly; a rapid response is usually necessary to take advantage of them. Unsure of what others will do in strategic engagements, players cannot plan too far in advance, with the result that most strategy consists of responding to the actions of others, always looking for new opportunities (Jasper 2006). For example, in a devastating blow to game theory, behavioral economists have shown that game players typically anticipate only one or two moves in advance, rather than imagining the possible final outcomes and working back to select their moves (Johnson et al. 2002). This makes sense, since strategic interaction is simply too complicated to predict more than one or two moves in advance.

Our crisis is our adversary's opportunity, and vice versa.[5] The concept of windows of opportunity complies with the accepted definition of *opportunities* as something timely and favorable to some end or purpose. Opportunities are special because they are temporary.

Structures, in contrast, are relatively stable and difficult to change. People must adapt themselves to structures, much as the structure of a house forces us to walk through doors rather than walls. Herbert Kitschelt (1986, p. 58) saw this, using the term political opportunity structures to refer to "specific configurations of resources, institutional arrangements and historical precedents for social mobilization, which facilitate the development of protest movements in some instances and constrain them in others." He contrasted open and closed state structures for input into policy making, and strong and weak state capacities for implementing those policies. Protestors, he argued, would either confront the state or try to work within it depending on how open it was at each of these two stages. Perhaps because I started my scholarly career as a comparativist, I am sympathetic to Kitschelt's structural model. He wisely avoids the "historical precedents" part of his definition in favor of institutional arrangements, a conceptually crisp set of national laws for making and implementing decisions. I call these "arenas."

Like Fillieule (2005), I think that institutional political structures—or arenas—are a necessary concept to retain in our toolbox, even though I think they are easily reified. Hanspeter Kriesi, Ruud Koopmans, Jan Willem Duyvendak, and Marco Giugni (1995) have done the most to distinguish the relevant factors here. They claim to use political opportunity structures to explain the

---

5. I am told that a certain Chinese calligraphic character means both crisis and opportunity. Chuck Tilly would have known this: when I first got to know him, he used to go through Chinese flash cards while sitting in meetings.

effects of several new social movements, but these are both catchall phrases that do little of the analytic work. Instead, fortunately, these authors contribute by breaking political opportunity structures into more observable factors. They distinguish long-run and short-run factors. Among the former are institutional arrangements much like Kitschelt's, but Kriesi and his collaborators add traditional social and cultural cleavages (especially religion and class) that may or may not leave much room for additional conflicts to surface. New issues frequently emerge, but they are often twisted to fit the rhetorical frames of older cleavages such as partisan ideologies (Jasper 1992). They also add "prevailing strategies" that the state uses to deal with challengers, although they restrict this to various forms of inclusion or exclusion.

Kriesi and his collaborators also address short-run dynamics, conceived as whether a left-leaning party is part of government and whether it is open to a movement's demands. They recognize that movements gain these allies through elaborate rhetorical and strategic processes, and that these are fluctuating, short-run accomplishments. They also usefully introduce movement choices, arguing that waves of protest are due to these strategic decisions as much as to openings on the part of the state. There is constant interaction among various players. Unfortunately these authors retain the language of political opportunity structures, rather than developing a more open-ended, strategic, and interactive model. Opportunities are not usually structural, and structures are rarely opportunistic.

Edwin Amenta, in a series of articles and a book on the Townsend Plan (2006), has similarly laid out a number of political factors that lie between movements and their effects, ranging from long-run electoral rules to short-run alliances. In the structural tradition of Kitschelt and Kriesi, he rejects groups' stated goals and hence their success or failure as proper explananda, preferring to examine a variety of outcomes that might hurt as well as help the beneficiary population. Like those in the strict political-opportunity tradition, he can assume a group's interests or benefits as an unproblematic concept because he is interested in "disadvantaged" challengers. Although he presents his view ably in Chapter 9 of this volume, I am not altogether persuaded by his rejection of player goals, which he himself uses in characterizing politicians and bureaucrats who may share the movement's goals and hence be available as allies.

Without a careful catalogue of players and their goals (on all sides of a conflict), we cannot understand the defection of leaders from group projects to pursue their own agendas, or the basis on which alliances are formed. Nor can we distinguish between intended and unintended outcomes, a staple of political analysis. If we don't understand what players want, we can't comprehend what constrains them. As Koopmans (1995, p. 15) comments, "A basic shortcoming of all existing studies using the POS concept is that they lack a clearly stated motivational theory that would explain how these structural phenomena enter the strategic choice situations of individuals and organizations."

The Problems of Power

Political opportunity structures are parallel to the concept of power, which analysts have used to address the constraints and openings facing protestors. Power also "enables and constrains," depending on who has it. It channels action. We see power primarily in relations and interactions. Unfortunately the concept has inspired dense, unresolved debates, mostly of a philosophical sort, over what exactly power is, how we recognize it other than through its effects, and so on (Dyrberg 1997). It is as easy to reify power as it is to reify political opportunity structures, misrepresenting them as exogenous to strategic engagements in cases when they are not.

Like political-opportunity scholars, most analysts of power have focused on the ways it is used to constrain people; only occasionally do insurgents manage to break the bonds of power and change social arrangements. In contrast, Talcott Parsons and Michel Foucault both emphasized the enabling side of power, which allows groups to get things done—but there was a swing of the intellectual pendulum between these two famous scholars. Power allows "societies" to accomplish their various "functions," in Parsons' consensus-oriented eyes. He emphasized legitimate authority and the trust that it entails. For Foucault, power is far more sinister, although like Parsons he tended to see power as a structure operating behind people's backs. In between Parsons and Foucault the pendulum had swung toward Marxism, which in the U.S. academy reacted sharply against Parsons to emphasize the ubiquity of class conflict. Foucault, although in a very different national-political setting, led the subsequent reaction against Marxism. He showed that subjects have to be created, through a variety of disciplinary techniques, before they can enter politics, and that their economic class is only one kind of subject position (Laclau and Mouffe 1985). What he termed *disciplinary practices*, furthermore, do not line up precisely with states, weaving together various players inside and outside the state and thus breaking the state into a number of components.

Tilly, although a contemporary of Foucault, was part of the intellectual turn that was fashionable between Parsons and Foucault. He praised Marxists for seeing conflict everywhere, and his models largely accepted economic classes as the primary political groupings. Tilly's models go a little distance toward Foucault, recognizing that new political arenas help political players create new repertoires. But ever the structuralist, he was interested only in their actions, not their subjectivities. Political-opportunity models remain more Marxist than Foucaultian, assuming potential groups with preexisting desires and objective interests who only await the opportunity to pursue them (the "class in itself"), and giving no attention to the processes that might create the appropriate subjects and dispositions and desires. And like many Marxists, political-opportunity scholars tend to see the state or the polity as the only field of struggle that really matters; their models recrown the "sovereign" state that Foucault was so insistent on decentering. And so we see a key difference between Tilly and Foucault: for Foucault power does not simply constrain or enable preexisting projects, it entices and creates new goals, new subjects, new streams of action, new types of knowledge. For Tilly, a new institutional arena offers new means, not new ends or new subjects.

For the purpose of understanding protest, the most promising formulation of power comes from two scholars unusually sensitive to the perspective of the oppressed, Frances Fox Piven and Richard Cloward (1977). If poor people or ordinary people are going to win concessions from elites, they must disrupt things. Piven and Cloward have devoted their lives to demonstrating this stark insight. Recently, Piven (2006, p. 26) has added a structural layer to the act of disruption: *disruptive power*, "rooted in patterns of specialization and the resulting social interdependencies." Disruptive power lies in the threat of halting some process that one's opponents value—typically economic production but also the production of state legitimacy. Reinterpreting Tilly, she says (2006, p. 33), "industrialism meant the erosion of a power nexus between large landowners and the rural poor, and the emergence of interdependencies between capital and industrial workers." Disruptive power is a form of *veto power*, based on the holding of key positions in some economy, polity, organization, or network. We might also label it *positional power*, parallel to occupying a position in a field of battle.

Piven (2006, p. 26) says this form of power is not simply "there for the taking," as a pot of money might be. Rather, "the ability to mobilize and deploy contributions to social cooperation in actual power contests varies widely and depends on specific and concrete historical circumstances." This warning risks the problem facing all concepts of power and structure: a conflation of some preexisting potential with the action that supposedly realizes that potential. Something must be there before the strategy, even if as Piven suggests it is a necessary rather than a sufficient condition. We need to specify carefully what those preexisting advantages or disadvantages are: resources, laws, physical or bureaucratic positions, public opinion, and so on. Events and actions of *others* may then make some of these preconditions more advantageous or less, but so may one's *own* actions. (It usually takes both: the French left their horses behind, but the Black Prince had to realize that the value of his own mounts had suddenly risen.) The parallels with political opportunity structures are obvious.

What if we drop the oxymoron, "political opportunity structures" (and its companion, "power")? On the one hand, "political structures" seems a reasonable enough concept, as long as we remind ourselves of the metaphorical limits of the image of a structure as something fixed. But what about "political opportunities"? What does it add other than loose language? In the end, the word *opportunities* not only allows but also probably encourages vague overextension. Although an analyst may define it in a special, narrow way, the English word has a very broad, loose meaning that will always tend to incorporate too much.

Instead, we need to distinguish different kinds of advantages based on their sources, such as control over physical resources, legal rights to make certain decisions, reputations that inspire trust or sympathy, attention from others, moral resonance, cultural symbolism, the mistakes and vulnerabilities of opponents, political alliances, and more. Why not just talk about how challengers make alliances, how state players decide to repress or not repress them, how politicians respond, how state bureaucrats are playing various strategic games with each other, and so on? Why say that a player "makes an opportunity" for itself instead of simply saying what it does?

Causes and Consequences

In addition to structures versus opportunities, a confusion arises over whether political opportunities are causes or consequences of protest (independent or dependent variables). At the end of his life, we saw, Tilly (2008) claimed they are both: they are the outcomes of protest campaigns and the conditions for fu-

political opportunities dependent or independent var?

ture campaigns. While apparently dynamic, this model makes it difficult to sort out the various factors, as Ramos and others have argued. "Campaigns" and "contexts" are just too abstract to be of much help. Tilly's imagery simply repeats the same static causal model over and over, in the hope that the changing content of campaigns and opportunities provides sufficient dynamism. I would like to build more dynamism into the interactions themselves. In a Tillean perspective spanning hundreds of years we can see the connection between a new arena and repertoires of action; for a shorter time frame we need finer-grained, observable interactions before we can sort out any causality.

For complex strategic interactions, we may even need to abandon multivariate models that try to specify independent and dependent variables. If instead we can observe a series of actions and reactions, we can see how the contexts change rapidly, based on protestors' own choices and the actions they inspire in other players. We may need something similar to the extended forms of game theory that would allow us to follow long sequences of intentional and emotional actions by a number of players. When Bader Araj and Robert Brym (2010), for instance, operationalize shifting political opportunities/threats to account for Fatah and Hamas strategy during the second Intifada (2000–2005), all are in fact choices made by the various parties to the conflict: "when the Israeli security apparatus substantially increased or decreased the number of (1) assassinations of Palestinian militants and (2) violent deaths of Palestinians by other means (during riot control or Palestinian attacks), and when the governments of (3) the US and (4) Arab countries offered substantial inducements and/or made substantial threats that aimed to alter Palestinian strategy" (p. 846). Here, "context" usefully dissolves into a number of players reacting to each other.

We now see the limits to Meyer's effort to save political opportunity structures by distinguishing models for the emergence, tactics, and outcomes of protest. These are all part of a long series of interactions, not easily separable dependent variables or even distinct phases. This is no doubt why they are so often conflated in political-process research. Every action has potential effects on our allies and opponents, on bystanders, on the rules of arenas, and so on. Only in retrospect, moreover, can we say for sure which of these effects was decisive. One possibility is to focus more on choices as events, triggering other events (Jasper 2004, 2006). Most opportunities are the proximate result of players' choices and interactions; structures are the residue of more distant choices and interactions. Others' choices are our contexts, and vice versa, as we will see in a more strategic framework.

Note that the cases in parts 1 and 2 in this volume address the impact of political opportunity structures on movement emergence alone. If they are going to be independent variables, it is most likely at this stage, when movements do not yet exist. Yet even here they rarely appear suddenly out of the blue.[6]

A Strategic Alternative   *need observable mechanisms*

Several threads of our discussion point in the same direction: the need for observable mechanisms and factors aimed at explaining strategic interaction (Jasper 2006) or contention (McAdam, Tarrow, and Tilly 2001). A simple strategic vocabulary (drawn from Jasper 2004, 2006) should allow us to make better sense of players and their contexts. Players may be individuals, formal organizations, or informal groups and groupings; much political action consists of creating new players where only shared interests, intuitions, or values existed before (Polletta and Jasper 2001). I use the term *simple players* for individuals and *compound players* for teams, since the two often act differently.

Because players share some goals (never all), they can judge events as good or bad; they can construct grievances. These are complex cultural processes that often depend on moral entrepreneurs. Players also use a variety of means, due to expected efficacy, moral loyalty, and available know-how. Players interact with one another in various ways, which can range from well-intentioned cooperation to hostile conflict. Players also make decisions and act in arenas that provide stakes, rules, and often physical venues.[7] Players often shift from one arena to another to get what they want, and they typically seek arenas where their skills and resources offer the most advantage. Cultural and psychological meanings are fundamental because players are audiences for each other's words and actions, constantly interpreting what all the players (including themselves!) are doing. The "context" for any player consists of other play-

6. Political-opportunity models are plagued by the problem that cases are selected on the basis of the dependent variable, movement emergence. It is quite possible that just as many opportunities exist in situations where movements do not emerge. If we recognize that political opportunities are the result of struggles within arenas, then they are no longer independent variables and selection bias is less of a problem.

7. I prefer "arena" to the similar concept of "institution," since the latter includes not just concrete arenas in which action occurs, but also the cultural ideas that support the arenas. As sociologists use it today, "institution" also includes norms that support it, which are usually established in a circular way: for a debate over the term, see Jasper, Aboulafia, and Dobbin (2005). Hilgartner and Bosk (1988) use "arena" somewhat as I do. Lilian Mathieu (2009) compares *sector, field,* and *space* as concepts, although largely to grasp how activists and movement organizations are related to each other, rather than to other players.

ers and arenas, but it is simpler to think of players interacting with each other in a kind of "dance" (Boudreau 2004).

Just as the characteristic blindness of collective behavior models was to over-emphasize goals (and goals of a particularly murky, often unconscious kind), that of political-opportunity approaches was to give undue prominence to are-nas. Tilly tended to "read" the players and their intentions from the stakes in a given arena. The growth of an accountable Parliament in Britain in the late eighteenth and early nineteenth centuries (Tilly 1995) called forth social move-ments to make demands on it, created new repertoires, and eventually resulted in new policies and rules of the game. Tilly recognized some external influence of capitalism on the new arena of contention, but the arena was the big inde-pendent variable affecting almost everything else. In the same period, Meyer and Staggenborg (1996, p. 1633) presented political opportunity structures as the independent variables accounting for "emergence, development, and ultimate impact of social protest movements." Arenas metastasized into entire theories.

Strategic arenas are more open ended than political-opportunity models generally allow for. In one example, Meyer (2004, p. 137) concedes that, con-trary to political-opportunity theory, "Unfavorable changes in policy can spur mobilization, even at times when mobilization is unlikely to have much *notice-able* effect on policy." Meyer is recognizing some role for interpretation here, as well as acknowledging the awkward (perhaps even fatal) fact that closing windows of opportunity often spur mobilization rather than discouraging it (through emotional dynamics that political-process models do not address).

In a more open-ended strategic model, however, we could recognize more than the fact that mobilization sometimes fails. We could recognize that mo-bilization can provoke a strong reaction from other players that actually leaves the original player worse off than before it mobilized. Jane Poulsen and I (Jas-per and Poulsen 1993) pointed this out for American animal rights and anti-nuclear activists: their own initial successes led to countermobilization, which in turn made their own later campaigns less likely to succeed. The strategic Engagement Dilemma suggests there is always some risk, often considerable, to starting a fight: you never entirely know how it will turn out (Jasper 2006, p. 26). The blunt model of the "environment" that remains the core of political-opportunity theory has little place for such strategic contingencies, or for the many interactions that would help us explain one outcome rather than an-other. As Flacks (2004) complains, political-opportunity theory tells us nothing about how players grapple with such dilemmas. ✳

This strategic perspective, and especially the concept of arena, reminds us of some degree of symmetry among players. Corporations, the state, and other powerful players look for strategic opportunities just as much as protestors do; they solicit allies, accumulate resources, avoid resistance, and so on. Symmetry does not imply equality, and in fact by looking at both sides we can see how much easier it usually is for states and corporations to mobilize resources and gather information than it is for protestors.

This commonsense strategic vocabulary, derived inductively from re-search into a variety of institutional arenas (Jasper 2006), fits in many ways with Pierre Bourdieu's more jargon-ridden arsenal of concepts (Crossley 2002, Chapter 9). His idea of a "field" of contention, in particular, is close to an arena, which I prefer because it reminds us that there are audiences watching most of the action. "Field" often conflates players and arenas.[8] To deal with the many advantages that players can bring to the field, Bourdieu discussed a number of types of capital. In addition to economic capital, we deploy cultural, social, and symbolic capital in strategic projects. Capital is a useful metaphor, since it belongs to players, but its value depends on how others respond. Like power, the concept which it can displace or explain, capital mediates between players. Finally, Bourdieu used the idea of habitus to get at ingrained dispositions to act in certain ways, showing how these work their way into our very bodies, gestures, and stances. For my taste, the habitus, like Tilly's repertoires of con-tention, tends to focus on the conservative constraints, telling us little about the occasional innovations.

We can reformulate process theory armed with this strategic vocabulary. The best candidate for the label of "political opportunity structure," and the one most true to Tilly, seems to be changes in the rules of arenas. Players jostle to take advantage of any new rules (which amount, in varying degrees, to new arenas). Amenta (2006, p. 17) calls arena changes "the highest level" of benefits, since they "give a group greater leverage over political processes and augment the impact of future collective action." Second, the arenas themselves may use-fully be seen as structured: as Kitschelt and Kriesi analyze them, they are struc-tures, not opportunities. One lacuna of the political-opportunity tradition is to

---

8. In comments on this manuscript, Olivier Fillieule pointed out that Bourdieu assumed that all the players in a given field are pursuing the same prize, and that all other fields are dominated by the political field. Bourdieu's fields are closer to institutions than to arenas. In the Players or Prizes Dilemma, I have tried to identify the tradeoff for a strategic player between pursuing the rewards available in a given arena and punishing opponents in that arena—a dis-tinction not available in the concept of a field (Jasper 2006, p. 149).

forget that contention always continues over those rules, especially in their interpretation and application. A more strategic approach can show us tradeoffs, for instance, between the direct pursuit of goals within arenas using existing rules and resources and the pursuit of indirect objectives meant to change arenas and the distribution of resources. Changes in arenas are usually the result of contention, but they sometimes create new players to take advantage of the new rules.

Most of the "events" that get swept under the rubric of opportunities are actions by other players, including changes in arenas. These actions are strategic choices and moves intended to have various effects (they do not always have the intended effects, but that need not change our explanation of the moves or of their effects). Some of these choices become grievances for other players, around which they construct outrage and threat in order to mobilize supporters or sympathizers. Grievances are perhaps the worst candidates for political opportunities, which were intended to displace grievance-based models in the first place (Snow, Soule, and Cress 2005). Grievances tap into players' goals rather than their means, whereas opportunities should provide new means to pursue those goals.

We can recast McAdam's four opportunities in more strategic language. The first (openness) is about which players are allowed to play in what arenas, according to the official rules. (Although much of the action is about how excluded players influence arenas in unofficial ways.) Numbers two and three (elite alignment and potential allies), which are often difficult to distinguish, are choices made by other players (unhelpfully lumped together as "elites") that help or hinder protestors. The fourth factor (repression) consists of two nested factors: the *capacity* for repression is mostly due to resources (tear gas, tanks, guns, and so on); the *propensity* for repression reflects the strategic decisions and perspectives of those with the capacity.

By distinguishing players from arenas more carefully, we can see that political-opportunity models tend to conflate three concepts: the creation of a new strategic arena, different players' access to that arena, and their relative success in the arena once they have access. This tradition usefully emphasizes weaknesses in the state, but fails to distinguish the state as a set of arenas for conflict from the state as a set of players in those arenas. By assuming a kind of zero-sum competition between those in the polity and those trying to get in, the model also fails to appreciate the many arenas that comprise the state, and thus the ways that a player can maneuver these against each other.

We can assert that a "social movement" faces its "environment," but this formulation tends to reify both elements. A social movement is never a uni-

SM is

fied player, but a shifting coalition of players (groups and individuals) who come together for occasional events based on perceived overlapping goals. The idea of the "context" or "environment" of a given movement is even more of a conceptual stretch. What matters most are the many players out there, each with their own goals, choices, and actions. Often perceived as the opponent of movements, business, for example, is not some structural force but rather a set of organizations that make decisions and act to pursue their interests—and they should be analyzed in this way (Silver 2003; Chorev 2007; Gates 2009). Similarly, Rojas (2007) emphasizes the decisions made by university administrators (often based on individual idiosyncrasies) in their interaction with black power and black studies movements. If the rules of arenas matter, it is because a player is interpreting, enforcing, and creating them. There are other factors in a given environment, such as physical resources, cultural meanings, and rules (Jasper 1997), but they matter primarily when they are put into action—into play—by other players. (These factors can exert influence through an implicit or explicit threat that they will be used, but this is also a form of action.) It makes a difference that a law or rule is on the books, but mostly because players can refer to it in eliciting or preventing action from other players.

Ruud Koopmans (1997a) discusses exactly this, contrasting two sources of repression (the best studied of McAdam's four opportunity structures). Koopmans found that structural repression, especially legal bans on organizations or demonstrations, effectively suppressed the German far right in the 1990s, while strategic reactions such as police violence actually increased mobilization. Structural repression (he calls it institutional repression) prevented organizations and networks from forming in the first place, and was considered more legitimate because it was more consistently applied.[9]

We know a lot about players and how they are formed, how they operate, how they make decisions; about different kinds of actions and their implications; and about players' goals. The phraseology of political opportunities hides much of this, although it may be elaborated to tell us about arenas and their rules, and the impact of changes in those rules.

Many authors have moved in a more strategic direction while dragging the empty shell of political opportunity structures along with them. Valentine Moghadam and Elham Gheytanchi (2010) try to meld strategic choices and political opportunities—the latter being McAdam's list of four. In practice,

---

9. Thanks to Sun-Chul Kim for reminding me of this article.

they categorize opportunities as open, closed, or semi-open, although they also distinguish opportunities at a local and a global level. The real action takes place in a string of decisions by protestors and especially the state, mostly based on election results. Intriguingly, repression raises the stakes of action, it does not simply close it off: action in these circumstances "could lead to further government repression but it also could win widespread sympathy" (p. 272). We need to know more about the emotional and cognitive dynamics here, a case of the Engagement Dilemma of high risk.

Moghadam and Gheytanchi are not the only authors to point out differences in levels of governance, especially local, national, and international or global. The increasing influence (and recognition) of global politics casts further doubts on political-opportunity models, which focus on the actions of the nation state. In a strategic perspective that clearly distinguishes players and arenas, we can see these different levels simply as different arenas. Some of the players are the same as in national arenas, and others operate primarily in international arenas (Bob, in press). The scope of the arenas differs, but similar strategic interactions yield decisions and laws in all of them.

Once we dig beneath images of a "social movement" and its "environment" to the strategic interactions that compose them, we simply see a number of compound and simple players engaged in a variety of actions and interactions, in the course of which they refer to laws and other rules, deploy physical resources or coercion, and rely on new and existing understandings. A social movement comes to life as various individuals, formal organizations, and informal networks and groupings coordinate events and share some goals and know-how about tactics. These entities no longer have strict boundaries with the rest of the world, but instead shade off through networks and interactions into potential recruits, tacit supporters, bystanders, and others. Even more strikingly, the "environment" for a movement is no longer a set of structures, but rather other players who also use resources, meanings, rules, and so on as tactical tools. They may help or hinder protestors.

Knowledge, Vigilance, and Mistakes

If opportunities are not objective openings, neither are they simply insurgents' interpretations of the world (even though those interpretations can arouse mobilization and create opportunities). One way to mediate between these extremes is to recognize that protestors interpret their surroundings—and the openings these offer—based on knowledge they have of what others have done. We react to other players' actions in a certain context, not to the context itself. Instead of the reifying question of whether opportunities are there if no one sees them, we move to a strategic perspective as we see players reacting on the basis of what they believe about the world. A large part of strategic engagement consists of gathering and processing information about what others are doing; knowledge contains both information and interpretation.

Many or perhaps most opportunities arise because our opponent makes a strategic mistake upon which we can capitalize, such as sending his army forward on foot. A mistake may not even be directly related to the engagement at hand. The most obvious "blunder" in Jasper and Poulsen's (1993) discussion is to be caught in a lie, an embarrassment that undermines an organization's credibility in all arenas. Some mistakes are glaring, so obvious that any opponent could capitalize on them. At the other extreme, some moves are not really mistakes at all, but nonetheless allow or inspire opponents to react brilliantly to snatch victory from defeat. Most lie in between these extremes: whether they are seen as mistakes in retrospect depends on how the other side responds. King John's decision to send his troops on foot became a mistake only when the Black Prince decided to mount his in response. Opportunities are what you make of them in the give and take of strategic interaction. As Machiavelli (1965/1521, p. 122–23) put it, "Some advantages may result from the enemy's negligence and misconduct, and others from your own vigilance and good conduct." Most result from the interaction between these.

In other cases, something happens or comes to light that undermines an adversary's ability to act. A fiscal crisis or defeat in foreign war leaves a state open to revolutionary movements (Skocpol 1979), or at least to the electoral advances of the opposition. A scandal discredits a player, opens the way to reform efforts, or destroys a player's power to maneuver. Depending on who makes public the damning information, it becomes either an explicit *denunciation* or, if the media are simply doing their job, a *revelation*. Ari Adut points out that avoiding scandals "is an essential motive and ongoing activity of individuals, groups, and institutions" (2005, p. 213; 2008). (A *potential scandal*, on the other hand, opens the way to opportunities for blackmail, when we have damning information that we can use to our advantage.)

In some cases, *accidents* reveal operations or publicize conditions that would otherwise remain hidden. Often these are literal accidents, such as an oil spill that reveals the risks oil companies take every day (Molotch 1970). A "normal" nuclear accident reminds us how fragile these technological systems are (Perrow 1984). A military failure allows us to examine chains of command and normal operating procedures. Accidents can be more figurative, such as the inadvertent disclosure of damaging information. All such events bring un-accustomed attention and scrutiny to the activities of one or more players, frequently damaging their reputations.

Vigilance, with sufficient resources, can be systematized, as when governments tap phones or corporations send spies to protest meetings. Unions and protest groups also gather information about their opponents, despite fewer resources for the task. It takes time and funding to be vigilant, to watch one's surroundings carefully for opportunities, and to then move into action. People must be contacted, press conferences called, lawyers hired, legal documents filed, and so on. With sufficient resources, you can hire people with little notice; without them you must be capable of mobilizing other people or doing the necessary work yourself.

At the extreme, systematic vigilance is more like harvesting a resource than opening a window of opportunity—as in military "intelligence gathering." Obtaining information that is not widely available may give you an immediate opportunity to act, or you may simply store it away for a later chance to use it, like a police interrogator looking for inconsistencies in testimony. Information provides an advantage much as money or technological resources do.

There is a strategic Planning Dilemma or tradeoff between advance planning and flexible opportunism (Jasper 2004, p. 13). This holds that you can make plans in advance and endeavor to stick to them as closely as possible through the heat of strategic interaction, or you can flexibly respond to an unfolding situation in order to take advantage of any opportunities that come your way. Opportunism may entail advance preparation, such as training and practice, just not the planning out of your moves. While allowing more room to maneuver, opportunism also presents the risk of obscuring your main (or original) goal in favor of subsidiary ones, or allowing subteams to pursue their own agendas (a form of defection).

Strategic players may or may not recognize when windows of opportunity have closed: when the other side has regrouped, when the moment has passed for a statement to the press, when a confession of misdoing will no longer arouse sympathy but taint you with a cover-up. Nothing is more disastrous than trying to climb through a closed window. Reflecting the Engagement Dilemma, some apparent opportunities are actually traps. Windows of opportunity are temporary and must be recognized promptly. Good strategists see ways to take advantage of events and information that poor strategists do not. Many different responses are usually possible to any given opportunity.

With strategic processes like these, even though I have expressed them tersely, I think we can better understand some of what has been grouped under the catchall rubric of "opportunities."[10]

Empirical Tests *cannot be directly measured*

The political-opportunity debate has been tangled because it involves a number of concepts that cannot be directly measured. Structures, opportunities, and agency are concepts or presuppositions, not observational statements (Alexander 1982). Scholars end up operationalizing broad ideas such as opportunities in their own ways, formulating their own lists that suspiciously fit their own cases. And they rarely find measures adequate to the theories they hope to test. Much of the debate has necessarily been about whether the language of political opportunities is useful, not whether it is accurate. And much of the criticism has been that the language is too loose to be useful. In my view, it was extremely fruitful in the past, but the time has come to replace it with alternatives that might prove more useful in the future—a more progressive research program.

One mistaken way to proceed is to try to measure metaphorical or conceptual entities such as structure versus agency or context versus strategy, and then to compare their causal impacts. Structure and agency are present in all actions and engagements, and their salience depends on our point of view. Goodwin and I originally criticized political-opportunity models because they ignored the agency dimension. Araj and Brym's (2010) work on Hamas and Fatah is a model of how to account for decisions, as they sort through the actions by the many players, examining how these shift the incentives for other players, who then weigh their options and react accordingly. They are especially good on how leaders of the different compound players try to balance pressures from outside and inside the teams, acting in an "intentional, anticipatory, self-reflective, and self-reactive" manner, and "making plans in

---

10. Karl-Dieter Opp (2009, Chap. 6) cogently argues that political-opportunity theory relies on mostly unacknowledged micro-level incentives, and that much of the theory is superfluous when these are well specified. I highly recommend Opp's discussion, which focuses on Eisinger's, McAdam's, and Tarrow's formulations.

anticipation of future contingencies and regulating and correcting their actions in light of their current and past effects" (p. 864). They try to compare the influence of culture, political opportunities, and agency, defining *agency* as "truly creative breakthroughs," which they reasonably assert are quite rare. Yet creativity is only one special form (or possibly even a result) of agency. In the end, even these careful researchers cannot separate agency from context in a way that can be measured.

Contexts matter to strategy because strategic choices are made with a context already in mind; choices are not somehow prior to or independent of the context. Actions take place within arenas, geared to those arenas. (This was Tilly's great insight.) Strategy matters to context not only because it changes contexts, but because the contexts are contexts *for* something, namely strategic action. Action and context cannot be compared to each other at this level. What we can see are players engaged with each other, pursuing goals and having effects (even when these are unintended). Players and their actions are observable; structure and agency are not. We must drop to a more concrete level of reality, closer to empirical observations, in order to measure and compare.

One possible solution to the empirical challenge is to say that political opportunities are useful for understanding some types of regimes and not others. In *The Art of Moral Protest* I argued that Tilly developed political-process models to understand French and British movements for citizenship rights, as the repressive old regimes changed. When McAdam adapted the model to the United States, he applied it to a case that fit this model especially well, the Southern black civil rights movement (see Chapter 5). Here was a group, well-defined legally and culturally, that was excluded from political participation and economically oppressed. They needed new opportunities for political advancement. The collective players in such cases are well aware of their identities and interests, which contrast with those of most social movements in democratic nations, in which participants enjoy basic civil and political rights. They must do considerable cultural work in order to see themselves as a collective, as the "animal protection movement," for instance. Political opportunity models, I argued, apply better to "citizenship movements" than to "postcitizenship movements" (Jasper 1997). As a polity-centered approach, they naturally work best for movements demanding access to the polity.

In *Dynamics of Contention*, McAdam, Tarrow, and Tilly (2001) seem to argue the opposite, that existing political models reflect the movements of the 1960s in the industrialized nations. This "classical social movement agenda," which they had helped to formulate, was too static, too centered on individual movements, and too focused on the origins of movements (p. 42). In addition, "Its genesis in the relatively open politics of the American 'sixties' led to more emphasis on opportunities than on threats, more confidence in the expansion of organizational resources than on the organizational deficits that many challengers suffer" (p. 42). My view, in contrast, is that those who lack opportunities need them most.

The contrast between these two sets of scope conditions was the original intuition that led Jeff Goodwin to commission the discussions in Parts 1 and 2 of this volume, organized around the contrast between authoritarian regimes and the (normally) less repressive American context. He began with a test of 50 cases, asking scholars to make their best judgments about which of McAdam's four opportunities were present. He summarizes this work in the conclusion, finding that expanding opportunities matter in only 19 of the cases (and that contracting opportunities seem to have spurred mobilization in another 12).

Goodwin finds that opportunities matter more in repressive contexts than in democratic ones. In repressive contexts, it is almost tautological that protest movements can benefit from some lessening of repression. Yet even this depends on the kind of repression, the emotional reactions to it, and many other factors. In less repressive regimes, this factor will be less important. There, elite allies are perhaps more important, especially in helping protestors achieve their goals rather than in emerging as a movement. Strategic engagements unfold across a number of arenas in which your allies can help you win. The most common pattern of helpful opportunities was a combination of elite allies and elite cleavages (there may be some correlation between the two: if some elites defect to support insurgents, that will itself cause a cleavage if one did not already exist).

There is some potential circularity here. If dissatisfaction and protest appear, there are often some individuals or groups among political elites who see an opportunity to advance their goals by taking charge (or credit) for this mobilization. Rather than elites presenting an opportunity for protestors, the latter present an opportunity for elites. The real problem, however, remains the vagueness of the word *opportunity*.

At first glance the contrast between repressive and democratic polities partly appears in the subsample of Goodwin's cases that are analyzed in detail in parts 1 and 2. Among the repressive contexts, Jack Goldstone found most of them (in three different mobilization efforts), Anthony Pereira found two, John Hammond found all four but concluded they were unimportant, and

Citizenship mvmnts

Amy Risley found none. In the American cases, Francesca Polletta and John Skrentny found several, Adam Green found none early in gay rights mobilization but all four later, and I found none.

In fact, the cases seem to push beyond a simple dichotomy toward three kinds of regime. At one extreme, protestors can enjoy full citizenship rights, as with Smith's movement for peace in Central America; at the other, they can live in a dictatorship in which no one has rights and only a few have privileges. In between, protestors can live in a putatively democratic nation but still be excluded from full citizenship. This final status seems the one best suited to explanations through political opportunity structures. Tilly said this, more or less, seeing the social movement as the creature of democratic systems that did not yet live up to their own ideals.[11] These citizenship movements can face different forms and mixes of exclusions: political and legal as well as cultural and economic. The categories get even more complex, since some protests are primarily against state action (such as Reagan's intervention in Central America), while others are largely directed against corporations and other targets. Although these latter types of cases are not represented in this volume, we should keep them in mind.

In Chapter 1, Jack Goldstone reads John Markoff's extensive data on the complaints and actions of French peasants during the revolution as demonstrating that threat motivated as much action as opportunities did; opportunities are neither sufficient nor necessary for protest. What makes the most sense of Markoff's data, they agree, is to follow the interaction among the various political players, and to watch the peasants respond to others' actions. In his reply, Markoff adds the pressures of war on the old regime as a kind of opportunity. He also points out the broad extent to which opportunities involve culture, as players constantly watch and interpret each other's actions. An interpretive, interactive context requires far more attention to detail than McAdam's four broad opportunities. Goldstone ends with his concept of a relational field among players (see Goldstone 2004) as a way to understand these complex interactions.

For movements in rural Nicaragua, in Chapter 2, Anthony Pereira and Jeffrey Gould agree that there is an interaction of movement capacities with the opportunities in their environment. Pereira says further that we need much

---

11. The famous u-curve relationship, in which very high or very low levels of repression discourage mobilization while middling levels encourage it, was developed to explain changes within a nation over time, but might also explain differences across regime types. I again thank Sun-Chul Kim for pointing this out.

more specification of the kinds of opportunities that exist, while Gould insists on the consciousness of workers in the flow of action. Movement leaders face choices about what kinds of alliances to make, presumably facing dilemmas as well as structural constraints. Like Markoff, Gould additionally points to international players putting pressure on local political players.

Alison Brysk and Amy Risley agree in Chapter 3 that the human rights movement in Argentina emerged in spite of—in fact triggered by—extreme repression, without any of the four political opportunities. Instead, the movement managed to create opportunities for itself. International factors again mattered, this time in the form of support for the rights movement, but this support emerged only after the the movement itself had. Both scholars point to the cultural work that the Mothers of the Plaza de Mayo (Madres) did in order to persist as a movement, with Brysk emphasizing the new roles and identities they created for themselves out of maternal expectations and Risley focusing on the emotional dynamics. Although they disagree over the adequacy of Brysk's critique of rationalistic models, they both use that critique as a path toward more cultural, microlevel mechanisms.

In Chapter 4, John Hammond digs below the surface to conclude that political opportunities, which he carefully identifies, do not explain the emergence of rural unions in Brazil, except for some redirection of organizing after the military dictatorship was imposed in 1964. More important were the continuing efforts at mobilization, which was itself affected by local agrarian class structures. Pereira largely agrees, although he observes that political opportunity structures do not constitute a clear theory and so are hard to test.

All four of the cases in authoritarian regimes show that the efforts of the oppressed to mobilize create opportunities as much or more than they respond to them; we need to know more about the work they do and the choices they make. All the authors prefer to follow interactions among players directly, including international players, without the supposed intervening political opportunities.

The case that fits the political-opportunity model best is the U.S. civil rights movement, as refracted through Francesca Polletta's analysis of a book by Charles Payne in Chapter 5. This is not surprising, since Doug McAdam (1982) derived his version of political opportunities from his research on this movement. It is a sharp case of a citizenship movement by those deprived of all sorts of material benefits, political and human rights, and cultural recognition. Polletta extends the political-opportunity apparatus downward, suggesting that local networks filter how national opportunities are interpreted locally, that both challengers and elites are always internally differentiated in important ways, and that "elites" appear in the challenging community as well as outside it. She also continues a theme from other chapters: state repression can ignite mobilizing anger and indignation as well as demobilizing fear, suggesting the need for greater attention to emotional processes.

Anne Costain enthusiastically adopts a political-opportunity approach in her book on the U.S. women's movement, and in his essay on her work John Skrentny accepts much of that framework. While Polletta shows how the categories of movement and elite need to be broken down more finely, Skrentny similarly finds the state and the movement interwoven with each other. The implication is that players must be defined at a different level, perhaps that of networks of individuals, or of professions (Dobbin 2009). In his own work, Skrentny (2002) has shown the importance of the perceptions of political elites concerning other groups or players. Their views obviously affect how they react to others.

Adam Green and John D'Emilio, while not entirely rejecting political opportunities as part of an explanation of the homophile and gay liberation movements, point to some limitations. More influential, they agree, were long-term cultural shifts. Different factors unfold over different time scales, more complex than a contrast between short-run windows of opportunity and long-term structures. I believe that a strategic perspective, in which various time frames are filtered through the perceptions of decision-making players, is the best way we might integrate such diverse factors in the future. As with the women's movement, gay and lesbian rights movements demonstrate that a dichotomized view of a movement versus the state obscures many players. The other protest movements of the 1960s and 1970s, and individuals who moved across them, provided know-how and emotional encouragement without necessarily joining a new movement. Most of all, D'Emilio points to the immense complexity of movement emergence, making it hard to explain such an imprecise "timing." A carefully documented series of actions and reactions may be a focus that a strategic approach and a historian's approach share.

In Chapter 8 I interrogate Christian Smith's *Resisting Reagan*, about the U.S. movement to end Reagan's murderous support for repressive regimes in Central America. Whereas Skrentny accepts Costain's labeling of party competition as "elite division," I question whether this aspect of normal electoral politics is in the spirit of political-opportunity theory. The women Costain studied and the activists Smith studied all had normal voting rights, middle-class incomes, and no ongoing repression. These groups were not excluded from political arenas, they simply were not able to use those arenas effectively. I try to recast Smith's rich case study in strategic language, as various players (both new and preexisting) pursue their goals across many arenas. Political-opportunity language becomes redundant, and perhaps misleading, as a way to characterize fairly typical political interactions.

Most of our authors, having been asked to evaluate the presence of political opportunities, conclude something like "Yes, but." One or more political opportunities appear in most cases, but no one seems satisfied that these explain movement emergence.

Three final chapters further the work of specifying strategic processes beneath the political opportunity structures, all by authors close to the political-opportunity tradition. Edwin Amenta and Drew Halfmann defend the importance of context—who would not?—but suggest that political opportunity language is not the way to analyze it. They find the European structural approach more persuasive than the American windows approach. One of the developers of the European approach, Jan Willem Duyvendak, writes with Christian Bröer about ways that cognitive and emotional processes allow new players to emerge. They defend the idea of opportunities, especially those that lie somewhere between long-term structures and short-term windows. Finally, Donatella della Porta examines protest as a series of events that can themselves reshape the political landscape, taking advantage of Tilly's late recognition that campaigns shape context as much as context shapes campaigns. To understand such outcomes, we need the kind of fine-grained concepts that authors like these are developing. In the conclusion, Jeff Goodwin presents the empirical tests—not especially favorable to political opportunities—that originally launched this project.

· · ·

Charles Tilly forever changed the study of protest. No one will ever be able to ignore state players or reduce political contention to psychology. Just as others established the economic context of protest or its cultural context, Tilly did the most to demonstrate its political, institutional context. But we need to think about that context in the most useful manner, remaining true to Tilly's insights but perhaps cleaning up some of the language of the political-process approach.

One limit to Tilly's approach to context is that he tried to downplay the players, whether protestors or state agents, in favor of their "relationships." But the processes through which they engage each other took on an odd, reified reality. Without a sense of goals or decisions or biographical backgrounds, players are reduced to their participation in a particular interaction, like a kind of tar baby from which they cannot extricate themselves. Structures migrated, over the course of Tilly's career, from the economy and the state, as external realities to protestors, into the engagements themselves. He even defined repertories as peculiar to the pairs of actors who were engaged, with little left over to travel to new arenas.

I began this introduction with a Tillean historical vignette, meant not only to introduce some ideas but to show that the discussion of opportunities and environments applies to more arenas than protest. It is also a nod to Tilly's insistence that war making is a central process that creates states. Chuck might agree that we need to develop causal mechanisms that apply across many arenas. Because to me a more strategic perspective, focusing on arenas and on players with ends and means, seems the best means to accomplish this, my vignette differs from his stories in a crucial way: Edward's quick decisions mattered crucially to the outcome. In strategic rather than structural models, individual actions can make a difference.

PART 1
AUTHORITARIAN CONTEXTS

1   Peasant Revolts in the French Revolution

John Markoff's *Abolition of Feudalism*

JACK A. GOLDSTONE

MORE THAN two hundred years later, the French Revolution of 1789 remains pivotal for the study of social protest and revolution. The complex intertwining of noble resistance to the Crown, nonnoble elites' resistance to the privileges of the nobility, urban and regional resistance to centralized rule, revolutionary resistance to the power and perquisites of the Catholic Church, popular resistance to the suppression of that Church's role in society, and peasant resistance against a host of seigneurial, economic, and political practices, still resists our efforts to unravel its secrets. Why particular groups acted in particular ways at particular times remains controversial.

John Markoff's remarkable volume offers a wealth of evidence about why French peasants acted in the manner they did during the prime revolutionary years, 1789–1793. As one might expect from the tangle of events involved, he has provided an extremely complex answer, attributing the events to at least eight different kinds of peasant actions, each with its own distribution over time and across French regional space. Moreover, the timing and frequency of peasant actions cannot be determined simply from looking at the long-term structural characteristics of particular regions and their peasantries—rather, the kind of actions peasants took, and when and where they acted, was the result of a dynamic interaction between peasant communities and various elites and institutions.

Markoff's main conclusion, somewhat surprising from either a Marxian or Tocquevillean viewpoint (his two primary foils), is that the destruction of seigneurial privileges was not strongly sought by the peasantry at the outset of the revolution in 1789; instead, anti-seigneurial actions grew in response to the proclamations and actions of the elites in their national assemblies in Paris. At the start, peasant communities seemed more concerned about traditional issues of contention: taxes and access to food. It was the representatives of the Third Estate who were most vocally concerned with the privileges of the nobility. Only after the Third Estate's attack on the nobility during the campaign for the Estates-General, and during the ensuing debates on feudal privileges that reached its dramatic peak in the National Assembly's sessions of August 4–11, did anti-seigneurial actions dominate the agenda of peasant protests.

Markoff's evidence comes from two distinct data sets. The first is an extensive computer-coded log of the contents of the *cahiers de doléances* (the lists of grievances written by the nobility, the Third Estate, and rural parishes for submission to the Estates-General in the spring of 1789). Although *cahiers* were also prepared by the clergy, these are not examined in this volume. Of course, the *cahiers* that were submitted by the Third Estate were supposed to incorpo-

---

MAJOR EVENTS IN THE FRENCH REVOLUTION, 1787–1793

1787–88: Ministers Brienne and Necker plan a meeting of the Estates-General over the rejection of their financial reforms by the Parlement of Paris and an Assembly of Notables

February–April 1789: Elections held across France for representatives to the Estates-General

March–August 1789: Wave of mainly subsistence and panic actions by peasants

May 5, 1789: The Estates-General meets in Paris

July 14, 1789: Civilians and army members storm the Bastille in Paris

August 4–11, 1789: The Estates-General (reconvened as the National Assembly) announces the abolition of many feudal rights without compensation; declaration is not ratified by Louis XVI

October 5–6, 1789: Palace of Versailles stormed; Louis XVI ratifies August decrees

January–February 1790: Wave of mainly anti-seigneurial peasant actions

March 5, 1790: Feudal committee report to the National Assembly delays the abolition of feudalism

June–August 1790: Wave of mainly anti-seigneurial peasant actions

June 1791: Wave of rural insurrections, mainly anti-seigneurial

June 20–25, 1791: Royal family seeks to flee Paris

rate the views of the rural parishes that sent their representatives to the urban centers where the Third Estate *cahiers* were composed. However, Markoff justifiably takes the Third Estate *cahiers* to represent mainly the views of the urban notables and professionals who dominated the national representation to the Third Estate, and relies on his sample of *cahiers* from rural parishes to assess the views of France's peasantry.

The second data set consists of a list of rural actions by peasant groups (minimum of 15 persons) in France from 1788 to 1793. This astonishing tabulation—whatever its flaws, no doubt the most complete survey we have of peasant actions during the first part of the French Revolution—is divided among various types of actions (panic, subsistence, anti-seigneurial, and so on), located by region, and dated by day, month, and year. The result is a panoramic tableau of what Markoff calls the "rhythms of contention" by the peasantry.

Combining his analysis of these two data sets with an examination of the debates and actions that occurred in the National Assembly, the Legislative Assembly, and the Convention, Markoff claims that the destruction of seigneurial

---

September 13–14, 1791: Louis XVI formally accepts the Constitution

Spring 1792: Wave of rural insurrections, mainly but not entirely anti-seigneurial

April 20–28, 1792: France declares war on Austria, invades Austrian Netherlands (Belgium)

July 30, 1792: Army suffers major losses, Prussia and Austria invade France

August–November 1792: Wave of rural insurrections, both anti-seigneurial and counterrevolutionary

August 10, 1792: Louis XVI is taken into custody during the storming of Tuileries Palace

August 25, 1792: Feudal rights and tithes are abolished unless lords can show contractual arrangements of mutual consent

September 2, 1792: Fall of French fortress at Verdun to Prussian troops

December 11, 1792: Louis XVI formally charged with treason

March 1793: Wave of rural insurrections, mostly counterrevolutionary (War in the Vendée)

April 6, 1793: Committee of Public Safety established

June 2, 1793: Jacobins take control of National Convention

July 17, 1793: All feudal dues and tithes abolished without indemnity or compensation

dues, monopolies, and rights was neither the primary initial goal of the peasantry, nor the inevitable outcome of the Third Estate attack on noble privilege.
Rather, the peasantry and the Third Estate forced or encouraged each other to
go further in a give-and-take of insurrection and legislation from 1789 to 1793,
until in the end the surviving feudal seigneurial rights were wholly abolished
without any compensation. It was the course of this give-and-take, rather than
any structural predisposition or enabling factors, and not the simple breakdown of coercive authority, that determined the timing and nature of peasant
protests during the Revolution.

Origins of the Peasant Movement

Markoff establishes the initial goals and actions of the peasantry from 1788
through the summer of 1789—what we might call the insurrectionary ideology of the peasantry—from the targets of complaint in the *cahiers* of the rural
parishes. The initial actions, the practical aspect of peasant insurrection during
this period, are classified from the survey of actions by rural groups.

Despite the massive attention given to the French Revolution as bringing
about the "end of feudalism," in the spring of 1789 this was hardly the peasantry's main concern. Of the complaints in the rural *cahiers*, only 10 percent
of the listed complaints focus on payments made under the seigneurial regime,
and merely 4 percent on the clerical tithes and church exactions (*casuels*), while
32 percent focus on taxes (Table 2.2, p. 41). Of the eleven topics most often
mentioned in the rural *cahiers*, seven are explicitly about taxation. Taxation in
general is mentioned most frequently, followed by the salt tax, the tax on alco-
holic beverages, the tax on legal acts, the *taille* (land tax paid by commoners),
the tax advantages of the clergy, and the tax advantages of the nobility. The
salt monopoly, the royal *corvée* (compulsory labor services on roads), and the
Provincial Estates round out the top ten. The top-ranking seigneurial right, the
lord's right to raise pigeons for hunting, even though they fed voraciously upon
the peasants' fields, is only fourteenth (Table 2.1, pp. 30–31).

What is striking is not only the small weight given to seigneurial exactions
by the peasants, but the contrast with the *cahiers* of the Third Estate. Many of
the parish *cahiers* (23 percent of them, to be exact) make no mention of seigneurial rights at all, about the same as the *cahiers* of the nobility. In contrast,
grievances about seigneurial rights are mentioned in 98 percent of the *cahiers*
of the Third Estate. Among the peasant *cahiers* that do complain of seigneurial

impositions, the mean number of complaints per document is only 5.7; but among the Third Estate *cahiers* making such complaints, the mean number of complaints per document is more than triple, at 17.4 (Table 2.3, p. 41). In short, the Third Estate is much more concerned than the peasantry about the privileges and exactions of the nobility, stressing how the latter weigh upon commerce, liberty, and opportunities for improvement. The main articulation of anti-seigneurialism at this time clearly comes from the bourgeoisie. This is remarkable given the modern claim that the financial interests of the nobility and the upper Third Estate were almost indistinguishable (Taylor 1967).

If peasants seem more concerned with taxes than with seigneurial impositions, however, their attitude toward the latter is more radical than that of the urban notables who dominated the Third Estate. Among all the demands for actions on seigneurial rights contained in the sample of peasant *cahiers*, 36 percent called for the abolition of those rights without compensation. This is more extreme than the peasants' position on taxes (where only 24 percent of demands for action called for abolition without compensation), or the position of the Third Estate on seigneurial rights (where only 27 percent called for abolition without compensation.) In the peasant *cahiers*, 45 percent of demands for action regarding seigneurial dues recommended abolition (either outright or with indemnity), and only 15 percent suggested their reform, while only 24 percent of demands regarding taxes called for their abolition and 42 percent called for tax reform. Apparently, Tocqueville (1955) was correct in noting that to a substantial degree, peasants by 1789 saw the seigneurial regime as something they could do wholly without, unlike taxes, which might need reform but were likely to stay in some fashion.

If the flow of words shows that anti-seigneurial goals are not the primary element in peasants' written grievances in 1789, the flow of peasant protest events confirms that anti-seigneurialism was also not primary in peasants' actions. Overall, from 1788 through 1793, only 36 percent of all events were classed by Markoff as "antiseigneurial." These included attacks on chateaux, on the lord's rabbit warrens or pigeons, symbolic destruction of the lord's property or insignia, destruction or denunciation of manor rolls detailing feudal rights, collective and public refusals to pay dues, attacks on the lord's agents, and, rarely, attacks on the person of the lord. Subsistence events (grain riots or stoppages of grain carts), land conflicts, and panics together comprise 47 percent of all events, with anti-tax, religious, and counterrevolutionary events making up most of the rest (Table 5.1, p. 218).

The temporal pattern is even more striking. During the peak of the peasant insurrection in the summer of 1789, only 31 percent of events were anti-seigneurial; the rest were mainly panic and subsistence events. Anti-seigneurial actions by peasants *did* become dominant later in the Revolution: they form 81 percent of events during the peak of peasant actions in January–February 1790, 54 percent of events during the peak of June–August 1790, 69 percent of events during the peak of June 1791, and 47 percent of events during the peak of February–April 1792. They then recede after the onset of war with Austria and Prussia, forming only 29 percent of events during the peak of August–September 1792, while subsistence events rise to 77 percent of all events in November 1792, and counterrevolutionary events dominate (87 percent of all events) in March 1793 (Table 6.3, p. 297). In short, anti-seigneurial events are not the primary movers of peasant actions during the Revolution as a whole, or in its early stages in summer of 1789. They become primary only during the height of the debates about the abolition of seigneurial rights, and about whether indemnities will be paid to the holders of those rights (1790–1792).

Markoff's conclusion regarding the peasant anti-seigneurial movement runs as follows: although anti-seigneurial ideas were in the air in the late 1780s, they were far more important to the Third Estate, for their link to other privileges that blocked social and economic opportunity for nonnobles, than to the peasantry. The Third Estate, not the peasantry, identified seigneurial privileges as at the heart of what was wrong with the old regime. In 1789, although considerable anti-seigneurial actions by peasants existed, the majority of peasant mobilization (69 percent of events) consisted of grain riots and panics. It was the National Assembly that chose to respond to this peasant action by offering to abolish seigneurial rights on August 4.

Once these rights were challenged by the National Assembly, peasant attacks on seigneurial privileges intensified, growing from 1790 to 1792. The peasants' actions then spurred bourgeois legislators to react in turn, so that following each of the insurrectionary waves of 1790 and 1792 the National and Legislative Assemblies addressed the dismantling of the feudal regime. However, the Assemblies' actions were not always in the same direction; in 1789 the Assembly considered the abolition of seigneurial dues mostly without compensation, but in 1790 they turned back and sought extensive compensation and indemnities. This provoked more anti-seigneurial peasant protests, which in fact dominated peasant actions from 1790 through the winter of 1791 and spring of 1792. This led the Assembly to consider more radical concessions on abolition without compensation in the summer of 1792. Finally, following another wave of peasant actions in spring 1793, this time primarily counterrevolutionary, seigneurial rights were wholly abolished without any indemnity or compensation in July 1793. By this time, the elites of Paris had become accustomed to projecting their own concerns about feudalism onto the peasantry, responding to any peasant actions with further actions on seigneurial rights. As Markoff puts it, "for peasant insurrection to lead to concessions to the countryside on seigneurial rights, it was not necessary for the insurrection to have anti-seigneurial themes, only that it be large and widespread" (p. 511).

Markoff has thus overturned one bit of false reasoning—that because the Revolution's legislation on rural matters was primarily anti-seigneurial, the insurrectionary actions of peasants were also mainly anti-seigneurial. But we now have to explain several different forms of peasant action that contributed to the French Revolution, with panics, subsistence actions, and anti-tax actions, as well as anti-seigneurial reactions being the predominant ones up until the counterrevolutionary period beginning in 1793.

Here Markoff helpfully dismisses many of the structural verities about peasants and revolution. Using both regional mappings and a list of characteristics of rural communities, Markoff engages in what he calls "using France as a laboratory" to test various theories of rural mobilization. Most striking are his largely negative findings; none of the standard sociology-of-peasant-rebellions stories seem to apply. Whereas Skocpol (1979) and Stinchcombe (1983) see peasant mobilization against rural authorities as rooted in the communal life of open-field villages, Markoff's "data suggest that this theory is mistaken. . . . The role of open field settlement was actually to inhibit mobilization against the lords" (pp. 386–87).

The classic locus of peasant uprisings for the French Revolution, the open-field villages of the Northeast, actually was widely involved in peasant insurrection only during the summer of 1789; at other times other regions were more active. Overall, in the years 1788–1793, the northeast had the lowest rate of participation in anti-seigneurial events of any region in France, and indeed was among the least active for all kinds of peasant actions, with the north-center region (from the Orleannais to Burgundy) also lower in rebellious actions than other regions. For the Revolution as a whole, just as in the seventeenth century, the most active regions of peasant rebellion were in the southeast, Normandy, and the Paris region (Table 7.3, p. 347).

· · ·

The northeast had a slightly higher than average percentage of anti-seigneurial events among its total peasant actions, but the Mediterranean region (south-center, southeast, and southwest) showed an even higher proclivity to anti-seigneurial events. The north-central region, stretching across open-field plains from Chartres and Tours to Burgundy, had one of the lowest proclivities to anti-seigneurial events. Where the northeast (but not the north-center) does stand out is in the proportion of its events dealing with land issues: conflicts over the commons, enclosures, and woodlands. Although these were only 8 percent of all events in Markoff's sample, they were especially concentrated in the northeast and the southeast (Table 7.4, p. 353).

Regional differences are common. As noted, anti-seigneurial events are overrepresented as a fraction of total peasant actions in the northeast and throughout southern France. Counterrevolution is overrepresented in the west and to a lesser degree in the southwest. Subsistence events are overrepresented in Normandy, and for anti-tax actions, both Normandy and the far north stand out. Wage conflicts in rural areas are essentially limited to the area around Paris and the far north, while religious events and panic events are fairly evenly distributed, except that the south was less prone to panics and more prone to religious-oriented actions (Table 7.4, p. 353).

The problem with these regional differences is that they tell us little or nothing about the causes of different kinds of protest. The northeast and southern France are generally treated as widely different ecological, social, political, and economic zones, the northeast being an area of large estates, rentier peasants, and commercial grain farming, the latter an area of small farms, owner-cultivators, and olive-wine-grain production; why should both these regions be more inclined to anti-seigneurial protests? Subsistence events are overrepresented in Normandy because it was a granary from which much grain was shipped out; rural wage conflicts were concentrated in the zones of rural textile industry around Lille and Paris.

These observations are perhaps obvious and unilluminating for theorists of peasant action. Markoff therefore tries to link the frequency of rural protest to regions that are higher or lower on such factors as literacy, grain yields, proximity to towns, type of agriculture, population density, and so on. Markoff finds that neither higher nor lower density of settlement predicts peasant rebellion, that higher literacy warded off panics, and that efficient grain-producing areas had fewer subsistence events. Areas with high wheat prices in 1789 were more likely to experience the panics of the Great Fear, but otherwise, local prices had no relationship with other kinds of peasant actions. Arable regions were more vulnerable to subsistence events and to panics, but grassland areas were more prone to anti-seigneurial events (perhaps because of heightened conflicts over grazing rights). Almost all areas near major roads or cities were more prone to all kinds of peasant actions than more isolated parishes—perhaps because news regarding national issues penetrated more readily, or because there was greater involvement with regional and national markets. Neither richer rural areas (areas of in-migration by job-seekers) nor poorer rural areas (areas of out-migration by job-seekers) showed any greater disposition to peasant actions.

In sum, neither the "misery thesis" nor the "communal village thesis" adequately explains the location of anti-seigneurial actions, or the frequency of peasant actions in general. Most strikingly, it is hard to see how any long-term structural factors at all can explain the rather sudden shift from anti-seigneurial events being in the minority in 1789 to being dominant in 1790. For this reason, Markoff stresses the key role played by the National Assembly and its shifting efforts to address seigneurial rights as changing the context for peasant actions. Instead of structural factors, he sees contingent historical events and ideological factors (the latter reflected through the actions of the Assemblies in Paris) as the main motivators of peasant protest in the first five years of the Revolution.

Expanding Political Opportunities

Markoff frequently alludes to the changing conditions in 1788–1793 that favored increased peasant protest. "Peasant communities . . . are making judgments of danger and of opportunity" and actions were likely when "the country people experienced favorable opportunities, safety in action, and opportune targets" (p. 273). He mentions that the synchronicity of revolts in summer 1789 was "surely [rooted in] the very breakdown of the Old Regime" (p. 412), and that the collapse of coercion helped open the way for peasants to act.

All of this seems to support the notion that peasant protest actions in the French Revolution were highly opportunistic, responding to heightened opportunities to take action when the risks of reprisal declined and the probability of gain had greatly increased. Yet I do not believe a close reading of Markoff's data supports such a position. Quite the opposite. While a solid case can be made that anti-seigneurial events were a response to increased opportunity, most of the peasant insurrectionary events were not. Instead of being a response to increased opportunities, most panics, subsistence or religious events, and above all counterrevolutionary events, were taken in the face of actual or perceived threats to the well-being of peasant communities—mobilization to defend the community against dangerous and coercive outsiders. Insofar as such defensive actions, particularly subsistence events or panics, generally preceded anti-seigneurial actions, it can be argued that rather than increased opportunities and opportunistic actions, it was defensive mobilizations against threats, in part due to the breakdown of the central authority of the state, that initiated what Tarrow (and Markoff following him) calls a "protest cycle," which only later came to include anti-seigneurial protests (Tarrow 1994; Markoff 1996, p. 322).

The definition of opportunities that facilitate protest mobilization and/or its success has always proved elusive, but the editors of this volume have asked us to concentrate on four (drawing on the definitions of Tarrow [1994] and McAdam [1996]): (1) increasing popular access to the political process, (2) unstable elite alignments or intra-elite competition and conflicts, (3) elite allies who encourage popular protest, and (4) a decline in the effectiveness of repression that lowers the likely costs faced by protestors.

The first two elements apply to all forms of peasant protest in the French Revolution, the third applies to anti-seigneurial and counterrevolutionary protests, and the fourth to anti-seigneurial and perhaps to some panics and subsistence events. However, to understand how these elements did or did not create opportunities, we need to place them in the temporal and regional context of the various kinds of protest events charted by Markoff.

Peasant protests in the French Revolution begin in 1788, before the Old Regime has broken down, with a few dozen mostly subsistence events. These mount through early 1789, until in March through May of 1789 several hundred protest events occur, of which 70 percent are subsistence events. No doubt, peasant awareness and sense of community, as well as a sense of uncertainty and perhaps even fear for the future, grew with the elite mobilization and conflicts over the Provincial Estates and the campaigns for the Estates-General, and the gatherings to deliberate on and prepare the *cahiers*. Elements (1) and (2) are thus active. In the period up through May 1789, however, it seems unlikely that elites encouraged subsistence actions, or that the potential penalties for attacks on grain merchants and bakeries were sharply reduced. Rather, the failed harvest and dramatic increase in the cost of grain led to a familiar pattern of subsistence protests throughout France as arable peasant communities sought to prevent the movement of grain out of their reach. Just as the Flour War of 1775 saw a widespread mobilization of peasant communities over the availability of grain prior to the breakdown of the Old Regime, a similar tableau, perhaps on a more extensive scale, starts to unfold in 1788–89.

Things change after the fall of the Bastille, the emergence of the National Assembly from the Estates-General, and especially the decrees of August 4, amended and passed into law on August 11. These elite actions result in the condemnation of seigneurial rights as unjust and obsolete, and—condition (3)—undoubtedly encourage anti-seigneurial actions by peasants. Nonetheless, in the July-August peak of rural events, anti-seigneurial events have increased only slightly from the spring: panics (42 percent of events), consisting of mobilizations of peasant communities to arm and defend themselves in order to protect their grain against real or imagined marauders, predominate over anti-seigneurial events (31 percent) (Table 6.3, p. 296), and are less a reaction to opportunities for country people to seize gains than a provocation to defend one's community out of fear. Panics were no doubt spurred by uncertainty over political events, fears of conspiracies, concerns that the central government was no longer capable of maintaining order, and anxieties about grain supplies, the result of the joint harvest and political situation unfolding over the spring and summer. Yet they cannot be seen as the result of opportunities in the positive sense of a greater chance of gains at lower risks. Instead, they result from perceived heightened risks of being prey to violence in consequence of the state's paralysis and breakdown.

The discovery that the state was less able to act in response to subsistence actions and panics most likely paved the way for anti-seigneurial actions. Markoff demonstrates that parishes that experienced one kind of event were more likely to experience another (Table 7.12, p. 414). But this occurs more as part of a sequence, or cycle, of events, with earlier defensive actions occurring in response to fear and threat, and the success or nonpunishment of those actions leading to more actions seeking to create positive gains.

Interestingly, the cycle did not stop in 1789 with the progression from subsistence to panic to somewhat increased (but still in the minority) anti-seigneurial events. After a pause for the fall harvest, peasants began in the winter of 1789–90 to engage in anti-seigneurial actions throughout France. In the January-February peak of peasant actions in 1790, fully 81 percent are anti-seigneurial, and such actions dominate through 1792. While in 1789 and early 1790 peasants may have been encouraged by the Assembly's surrender of seigneurial rights, however, in later 1790 and 1791 they were mobilizing in protest at the Assembly's foot-dragging and insistence on indemnities and compensation for rights to be abolished. Given a clear focus by the Assembly's debates and shifts on the issue of seigneurial rights, the latter became the focus of peasant actions, at least until winter 1792. At that point, with war having broken out, subsistence concerns again became dominant, and by March 1793, counterrevolutionary actions against initiatives of the new revolutionary regime move to the fore.

Thus the complex protest cycle of peasant actions in the first portion of the Revolution moves roughly as follows. In 1788–89, in the wake of harsh elite conflicts and concerns about a breakdown of royal authority, most peasant actions are motivated by fear and perceived threats; the resulting panics and subsistence actions galvanize much of France and help prod the National Assembly into the abolition of feudal rights. However, once the earlier peasant actions meet with some legitimation through a weak coercive response and the anti-seigneurial legislation in Paris, opportunities in the sense of taking advantage of paths that lay open or that receive elite encouragement result in a wave of anti-seigneurial actions. Threat withdraws as a motivation for action, replaced by opportunities for gain. But this period is short; in 1790 it appears that the abolition of feudalism will become slower and more costly, as the Assembly threatens to impose expensive compensation for lost seigneurial rights. This provokes more anti-seigneurial rights protests, and by 1792 the Assembly is again debating abolition without compensation. Then in 1792, peasant mobilization shifts. Weak harvests and fears of war again lead to widespread defensive mobilization for subsistence actions, and in 1793, following the new regime's revolutionary legislation on the Church, another wave of mobilization spreads from the west, this time defensive and counterrevolutionary and placing both elites and peasants in dangerous opposition to the revolutionary government. It is thus clear that peasants are mobilizing mainly in response to renewed threats, and the Assembly's principal response is to enact further concessions on feudal rights.

This brief summary points to two sources of peasant actions: defensive actions undertaken in response to perceived threats, and offensive actions undertaken in response to increased opportunities to seize positive gains at reduced cost. Interestingly, the latter are in the minority of all peasant protest actions in the years 1788–1793; both at the opening and close of this period, defensive mobilizations in response to threat predominate.

Criticism

The consistency of the ideological and practical parts of Markoff's data makes a compelling story. However, as Markoff acknowledges, it is at least possible that both parts are misleading.

The *cahiers* of 1789 were public documents, written to gain assent from public assemblies. Despite peasants' antipathy toward nobles and seigneurial rights, they may have hesitated to go too far in denouncing or calling for the end of the old regime. If Timur Kuran (1995) is correct about the prevalence of preference falsification in public presentations under authoritarian regimes, the degree to which peasants did seek abolition of seigneurial rights in the *cahiers* would naturally understate their true preferences. Markoff's content analysis, based on counting mentions of seigneurial rights versus taxes and other complaints, would then understate peasant hostility toward seigneurial rights in 1789.

Thus it is remarkable that roughly 60 percent of rural *cahiers* in Markoff's sample called for abolition without compensation of a goodly number of seigneurial privileges, such as monopolies, tolls, rights to raise pigeons and rabbits (those despoilers of peasants' crops), and compulsory peasant labor. Only in regard to the medieval harvest imposts collected by seigneurs (*cens* and *champarts*), which had been converted to cash payments and which the peasants treated more like market rents than privileges, and to the lords' right to bear arms, did the peasant *cahiers* say relatively little about abolition. Still, this might reflect partial self-censorship of a more universal and thoroughgoing peasant hatred of seigneurial rights.

In addition, the register of peasant actions is limited to public group actions remarked upon in historical and scholarly sources. Renunciations and refusals to pay seigneurial dues by private individuals, or quiet nonpayment by villages without any public renunciation would not appear in Markoff's register of events. Only public renunciations or refusals to pay by fifteen or more individuals were counted as anti-seigneurial actions. In the spring and summer of 1789, in addition to the subsistence and panic events Markoff noted, there were possibly a great number of private or silent collective refusals or small-scale public refusals to pay seigneurial dues. If so, Markoff's analysis of the late emergence of anti-seigneurial actions would be false. Instead, a growth in the magnitude of such events would have taken place, from initial private and small-scale refusals to pay, to larger public refusals and attacks on rabbit warrens and pigeon coves, to attacks on chateaux and manor rolls.

If these suppositions are true, then some of Markoff's key arguments would be invalid, such as the lesser significance of seigneurial rights among the rural populace at the onset of the Revolution, and peasants turning to anti-seigneurial actions only after the Third Estate's attack on privilege had fanned the flames.

Still, the veracity of these suppositions would not invalidate my argument that opportunity was not the mainspring of peasant actions in the French Revolution. Even if private, silent, or small-scale acts of noncompliance with the seigneurial regime were widespread in 1788–89, this would not change the fact that a large number of panic and subsistence events spilled across France in these years. Nor would it change the fact that after 1792, counterrevolutionary actions became the main focus of peasant mobilization against authority. In regard to panics, subsistence events, and counterrevolution, a large part of the motivation for such actions surely was defense against perceived threat and, in particular for the latter, action was often taken in the face of strong coercive repression.

Historical data surely have their limits. We cannot know, for example, what thoughts were concealed behind the public proclamations of the *cahiers*, nor can we know the degree to which quiet noncompliance constituted an attack on the integrity of the seigneurial regime. It is therefore reasonable for Markoff to analyze the data he was able to acquire. His exposure of the sudden emergence and escalation of anti-seigneurial action in response to the opportunities and encouragement afforded by the actions of Third Estate legislators is ingenious; it also supports the prevailing wisdom about the importance of opportunities for offensive protest action to produce mobilization and success.

Yet the aspects of Markoff's analysis that challenge the conventional wisdom on opportunities also resonate as true. A large portion of the peasant protests in the French Revolution, both at its outset and in 1792–93, did not take the form of people acting to seize new advantages under the greater security offered by a collapse of resistance or repression. Rather, many of these protest events were reactions to the negative side of the breakdown of central authority, including a collapse of local security, concerns about the security of food supplies, and resistance against an unwelcome radical and hostile new regime.

Conclusion

The kind of mobilizations involved in panics, subsistence actions, and counterrevolutionary actions force us to look at opportunity in a new light, and to think of popular protest mobilization not merely in terms of a monotonic response to a greater or lesser degree of opportunity. The timing, the frequency, and the types of peasant actions observed in revolutionary France cannot be explained by viewing opportunity and threats as converse forces expanding or contracting a linear space for revolt, in response to a simply more-or-less divided and repressive state. It would be a mistake, therefore, to simply say that a divided and less repressive regime means less threat and more opportunity and more popular protest, while a more unified and repressive government means more threat and less opportunity and less protest.

The actual relationships are less linear and more complex. A divided and less repressive state may create threats of physical insecurity, interruption of food and other supplies, and a collapse of local order, leading to defensive mobilization over subsistence and local security (panics). It may also become involved in ruthless factional struggles, leading to defensive and counterrevolutionary mobilization against threats from the regime. This was not only true of western France in the Revolution; one can also think of England during the seventeenth-century civil wars when local communities mobilized (Underdown 1987), or of Russia during its revolutionary civil wars of 1918–1921 when the Whites mobilized peasants to defend themselves against the communist regime (Chamberlin 1965). In short, what I have called "state breakdown" (Goldstone 1991) can produce a variety of forms of popular mobilization, most of which would not necessarily be considered revolutionary in the sense of aiming for new advantages for particular groups.

Of course, a divided and less repressive regime may also create opportunities for popular groups to seize new assets or advantages, particularly when some elites encourage and legitimize such actions. And threats against one portion of the elite by the regime (attacks on the nobility, or the Church), depending on popular sympathies and the constellation of forces involved, can open up further opportunities for popular mobilization against that elite segment, as well as creating threat-based mobilization for its defense.

In sum, opportunities can increase the likelihood of popular mobilization, but so too can threats. A divided state with diminished repressive capacity can open up opportunities for protestors, but it can also generate threats that lead to defensive mobilization. When a state with repressive capacities targets a portion of its elite, opportunities for popular action arise, principally by the exertion of state power rather than through its absence.

The lessons of Markoff's rich book is thus that opportunity alone, in the sense of "easier pickings" that increase the likelihood of successful seizure of new assets or advantages, is not sufficient or always necessary to explain the very complex variety of different protest events and their timing. Rather, a dialectic of threats and opportunities both producing protests, albeit of different types and at different times as state power and policies vary, plus temporal patterns in which one kind of protest action can lead to others by expanding opportunities and by provoking reactions, is a better model for understanding the varied forms of popular protest one finds entwined in the flow of actual historical events.

RESPONSE TO JACK GOLDSTONE
John Markoff

I find myself in agreement with Jack Goldstone's concluding call for students of popular contention to pay attention to the complex ways threats and opportunities may be intertwined, and may shift over time, including threats and opportunities created by popular mobilizations themselves. I agree with most of the specific points he develops from data in *The Abolition of Feudalism*. In identifying anti-seigneurial actions as responses to opportunity and other sorts of actions as responses to threat, he has been able to summarize the large number of tables I presented as a clear temporal sequencing in the significance of threat and opportunity. I admire the elegance of this formulation (but I'd be a tad more comfortable with a qualification or two about this identification, since nonseigneurial targets were sometimes opportune, and threats—by the armed agents of lords, say—could sometimes precipitate anti-seigneurial actions). He has identified some important limitations to the data, which allow for rival hypotheses.

So I will use this "Response" mainly to comment further on notions of threat and opportunity in relation to popular conflictual mobilization, particularly with an eye on elements of the overall contexts of threat and opportunity that may easily get left out; I will also comment on the data issues, since I think they are matters of general importance for students of social conflict.

Looking at the Revolution as an amalgam of threat and opportunity would have come as no surprise to some of the participants. In its *cahier* the Third Estate of Draguignan observes that "hope is reborn from the midst of calamity itself; the most dangerous period for the monarchy is becoming the most memorable" (Mavidal and Laurent 1862, v. 3, p. 255). The specific checklist for assessment of expanding political opportunities employed in this volume focuses attention on actions of national elites; I would hope we don't lose sight of the possible significance of transnational political circumstances as favorable or unfavorable conditions. Thanks to Theda Skocpol (1979), sociologists are likely to think of France's international position as an important context for understanding the Revolution. With regard to peasant mobilizations specifically, the increasingly polarized international situation surrounding the Revolution increased the bargaining leverage of France's peasants, as the revolutionary political elite found itself not only in greater need of the tax revenues furnished by the countryside, but also in desperate need of rural sons in large numbers on many fronts. It is when war is approaching, in the spring of 1792, that legislators begin to respond to the most recent great wave of rural mobilization by advocating a wholesale rethinking of the notion of a gradual and indemnified phaseout of the rights of the lords that had prevailed in the legislation up to that date (Markoff 1996, pp. 474–79).

To suggest that the war opened up new possibilities for peasant defiance (as indicated, for example, by mounting conflicts over wages staged by laborers whose bargaining position was enhanced by military demands on manpower [Markoff 1996, pp. 293–94]), is to suggest that rational peasant bargainers might have been making instrumental use of a new opportunity. And if we are to explain the dramatic, if temporary, success of collective actions by people in town and country in securing the most thoroughgoing regulation of food prices in French history, we would hardly restrict ourselves to the domestic side of political opportunity structure—since the revolutionary elites began their economic policy making profoundly committed to economic liberalization—but would want to take into consideration the enormous leverage created by wartime exigencies.

The international arena may have helped open up another kind of opportunity as well, one that spills over the boundaries of any strict reading of the adjective in "political opportunities". From a very early point, revolutionary publicists, most certainly including the legislators, framed the confrontational relationship with other European powers around issues of feudalism. The tone was set early on by the response of the National Assembly's Committee on Feudal Rights to complaints of various German princes about the unwillingness of Alsatian peasants to go on paying seigneurial claims held to be guaranteed by the Peace of Westphalia. It continued in many a legislator's interpretation that French hostility to and foreign support for feudalism was a core issue in interstate tension. It underpinned optimistic claims that the continental states would avoid war in fear that their own peasant armies would refuse to fight potential liberators. And it culminated in statements of war aims that included the abolition of feudalism wherever French forces prevailed.

We can, for example, follow the rhetorical trajectory of the legislator Jean-Baptiste Mailhe as he moves from the contention that France has a national mission to instruct its neighbors "about the natural rights on which the destruction of feudal rights in France was based," through supporting the liberation of French-occupied territory from feudal rights, and on to advocating the ending of legal proceedings against anti-seigneurial peasant rebels in France itself (Mavidal and Laurent 1862–, v. 53, p. 473; v. 55, pp. 72–73; v. 56, pp. 65, 74). All this constituted a powerful rhetorical opportunity for French peasants to truly liberate themselves, as legislators were beginning to realize with war imminent and increasingly inclined to acknowledge with war begun (Markoff 1996, pp. 469–79). Looking beyond revolutionary France, while some significant episodes of popular mobilization might prove to owe little or nothing to such favorable transnational circumstances, it is evident that others do (McAdam 1998), and I believe that sociologists will have to give such things more attention in the future and to rethink many past instances of mobilization.

When Doug McAdam (1996, pp. 25–26) usefully sought to clarify the forms of political opportunities so that this broad concept would be rescued from becoming "an all-encompassing fudge factor" (Gamson and Meyer 1996, p. 275)—that in explaining everything it explained nothing—he specifically urged distinguishing political from "expanding cultural opportunities" (a subject on which he had previously written).

This specification of what political opportunity might be, and its disaggregation into the four elements considered in this volume, is valuable in permitting analytic focus, as Jack Goldstone's essay demonstrates. But what is analytically separable may not come neatly distinguishable in empirical reality: French Revolutionary peasants were not, as in some laboratory, exposed to "political" opportunities while shielded from "cultural" ones. They were exposed to both, in complex intertwinings that do not nearly so readily admit of separation as abstract formulations allow.

We may wonder about, and attempt to explore, the degree to which we could speak of peasants "appropriating" elite discourse, suggesting an instrumental usage of elite conceptualization against those very elites (and if we are sensible historians, we would also wonder to what extent it was the elites who were appropriating popular discourse, just as the popular *mais* became the official trees of liberty [Vovelle 1993, pp. 44–55]). But we would also have to wonder about the degree to which concepts shape thought and thought action, well beyond issues of calculated deployment of rhetoric. And we would have to consider the issues raised by Gamson and Meyer's (1996) important point that the perception of opportunity can itself be thought of as a matter of cultural framing.

Now my methodological point: if one restricts the field of vision, as appropriate in an analytic exercise, to political opportunities as distinguished from cultural ones, I would read my data the way Jack Goldstone does, as supporting an explanation of French peasant mobilization in terms of an intertwined mix of threats and such political opportunities. But the experience of French revolutionary peasants did not so readily segregate political from cultural opportunities. From the moment the legislature proclaimed the abolition of the feudal regime in its entirety in the summer of 1789, the way was open for peasant action on behalf of what rural communities could claim to believe were meant by "abolition" and "feudal regime" a great deal more than was spelled out in detail in the legislation that followed a half year later. And this is to put it merely instrumentally, as if peasants were only pretending that *abolition* meant certain things and *feudal regime* meant certain things in order to deliberately enlarge the scope of legislative action. Yet not everyone who acted as if the abolition of the feudal regime in its entirety meant something considerably more radical than the legislatures' lawyers contended it meant was merely pretending. This ambiguity was neatly caught by Jean-Sylvain Bailly (1821, v. 2, p. 244), mayor of revolutionary Paris, commenting that a particular piece of anti-seigneurial legislation "was poorly understood by the multitude who perhaps did not want to understand it." The eloquence of revolutionary legislators stirred the passions at the same time that it invited new calculation of threat and opportunity.

I believe that the entire modern era of social movements has drawn tremendous energy from elite legitimations. In a nutshell, to the extent that elites have claimed that their rule reposes on the will of the people, challengers have had the opportunity to make claims on behalf of that very people. I will not attempt to defend such a claim here; but I will offer the methodological caution that we will often find that political opportunities do not come in neat packages, and before becoming convinced that we have explained mobilizations adequately by pointing to such strictly political opportunities, we want to try to understand what else might also be going on. Developing methodologies to sort all this out will require us to think in some other way than decomposing causes into separable, additive components, as Goldstone has aptly noted. Differently put, we have the problem of disentangling analytically what history has entangled practically.

The data on contention that we have to work with is always likely to be flawed. As Goldstone points out, and as I indicated in *The Abolition of Feudalism* (pp. 211–16), individualistic or surreptitious forms of resistance, passive refusals to pay one or another exaction, small-scale collective actions, and sending letters to officials (unless there was some sort of public demonstration of sending that letter) all fell outside my data-collection machinery. This is a common sort of boundary in contention data, and it is worth trying to learn all we can about how the forms of contention that are easier to measure are related to those whose measurement is less easy. French peasants were probably as adept as any at wielding what Scott (1985) calls the often hardly visible "weapons of the weak."

As for the *cahiers*, we must always bear in mind that they were public statements of collectivities and not confuse them with what those who wrote them might have said to each other off the record, or what they might have said to themselves and not even to each other, concerning both of which we cannot help but have hypotheses but are unlikely ever to have very much data. I agree with Jack Goldstone that we always need to consider the possibility that statements of wishes by those subject to coercive retaliation are in part shaped by prudence and that we often are lacking the evidence to be certain. In the case of the grievance data we at least know something about whether peasant subjects were inclined to mute their voices if an agent of the lord was in the room. Some of the parish assemblies that drew up *cahiers* were presided over by a seigneurial judge, in accordance with the convocation rules, and others were not, despite the rules. A survey of local studies by historians who have examined this subject, as well as a study of a sample of the parishes from the Shapiro-Markoff data set, show that peasants were as inclined to demand the abolition of the seigneurial rights they mention when the lord's judge was chairing the meeting as when someone else was, and were actually somewhat more likely to even discuss the seigneurial regime. This is despite the evident attempts of some of those seigneurial judges to keep anti-seigneurial grievances out of the documents and the success of some in that endeavor (Shapiro and Markoff 1998, pp. 151–55). Of course, it is still possible that cautious rural communities guarded their tongues even when a seigneurial agent was not present, depressing the level of anti-seigneurialism in the *cahiers* as a whole. An extended discussion of how the circumstances of their composition shaped the documents may be found in Shapiro and Markoff (1998, pp. 125–65).

REJOINDER TO JOHN MARKOFF
Jack A. Goldstone

John Markoff and I mainly agree, and I happily endorse his point, which I had omitted in my comments, that such international factors as the pressures of war, the desire to win popular favor abroad, and rhetorical attacks and political restructurings against France's enemies had major repercussions in France's own internal struggles. Indeed, Markoff's subtle examination of how international factors interwove with domestic events to create waves of threat and opportunity argues for a still more complex approach to understanding the motivation and success of protest.

The complexity of popular protest in the French Revolution is a good illustration of an argument I made regarding more modern protests (Goldstone 2004). Protest can rarely be understood as a response to movements along a linear scale of greater or lesser political opportunities. Rather, protest groups usually calculate their actions in regard to a diversity of threats and opportunities, which may be presented from different sources at different times. A given group (urban workers, rural laborers, land-holding peasants) may perceive threats from one set of groups or actions, while also perceiving opportunities in terms of elite encouragement, state weakness, or the emergence of local or national or even international allies. A threat to one contender (such as the military pressures faced by France's new revolutionary leaders) may lead to opportunities for others (such as the workers and peasants whose acquiescence was vital for the war effort). As well, threats to one group (as with the Revolutionary regime's attack on the clergy, especially in Western France) may be perceived by allies of that group as a threat severe enough to warrant mobilization even against a strong state.

Given these complexities, I argued that protest is best understood not simply in terms of "opportunity structures," but in terms of a "relational field" that plots the relationships (adversary, allied, neutral, potentially allied, threatening) among a large number of relevant actors that constitute the social field in which the protest occurs. In the case of the French Revolution, the relevant actors include different ranks of peasants in various regions, urban wageworkers, middling bourgeoisie, upper members of the Third Estate, local nobles, the National Assembly, and international actors (Goldstone 2011). Since many of these relationships are built on perceptions, which shift over time, the relational field needs to be drawn up with attention both to the cultural framework that shapes actors' viewpoints, and to how those relationships change over time. In this field, "opportunities" emerge in terms of increasing allies and encouragement for actions against specific other actors, while threats can arise from various angles and spur various strategies of defense, shifting alliances, or counterattack.

It is a tribute to the depth of Markoff's research in *The Abolition of Feudalism*, and the richness of his analysis, that he forces us to envision and develop such a relational field to understand his findings. He has given us an exemplary model for the empirical and theoretical analysis of protest in a diverse national landscape. After reading it, one can hardly conceive of analyzing social protest as simply a matter of protest groups versus the state ever again.

2 Rural Social Movements in Nicaragua

Jeffrey Gould's *To Lead as Equals*

ANTHONY W. PEREIRA

too broad POS

T HE CONCEPT of political opportunity structure (POS)—the opportunities provided to social movements by specific features of
the political system—has provided new and persuasive explanations of the
timing, form, and outcomes of social movement activity. However, some critics
warn that the concept is "in danger of becoming a sponge that soaks up every
aspect of the social movement environment," ultimately explaining nothing
in attempting to explain everything (Gamson and Meyer 1996, p. 275). I will
argue, in a slightly different vein, that the concept of political opportunity can *his argument*
offer only a general guide to social movements, and that it leaves unspecified
much of what is important in our understanding of what movements achieve.
In particular, one of the key dimensions of the political opportunity structure,
alliances with external actors, leaves unspecified the nature and costs of those
alliances, and these qualitative dimensions of alliance networks do much to
explain social movement impact.

In examining historian Jeffrey Gould's fine study of several Nicaraguan
rural labor movements, *To Lead as Equals: Rural Protest and Political Consciousness in Chinandega. Nicaragua, 1912–1979* (1990), my focus will be the sugar
workers' trade union movement of the 1940s, and the campesino and indigenous movements of the 1950s and early 1960s. Gould's emphasis on worker
consciousness tends to downplay structural factors in explaining differences
among movements. And while he charts the impact of changing political opportunities on the movements, this factor is not decisive in his analysis. Gould

may also have equated two political openings that were in fact quite different for the two social movements concerned.

A central theme of Gould's work, indicated by his title, is the search for autonomy on the part of rural workers and campesinos—the construction of movements that reflect the workers' own vision of politics and which carve out space for independent political action. Nicaraguan sugar workers failed to achieve autonomy in the 1940s, according to Gould, but the campesino movements of the late 1950s and early 1960s were more successful. The eventual achievement of autonomy occurred despite (and at least partly because of) prior failures, exclusions, and repression. This story is inadequately captured by McAdam's (1996) four-factor template of political opportunity structure, not because the latter is too inclusive, but because it simply leaves unspecified the most important characteristics of political opportunity.

To Lead as Equals is set mainly in Chinandega, a department in the far west of Nicaragua, bordered by Honduras to the north and the Pacific Ocean to the west. This department, which had 155,000 residents in 1971, contains Nicaragua's most important sugar, cotton, and banana plantations. Gould's research was done in the cities, towns, villages, and hamlets that lie within

---

MAJOR EVENTS IN THE NICARAGUAN RURAL LABOR MOVEMENT

1927–1933: August César Sandino resists U.S. Marines

1934: Sandino assassinated on orders from Anastasio Somoza, chief of the National Guard

1936: First strike wave in Nicaraguan history, including workers at Ingenio San Antonio (ISA)

1936: Anastacio Somoza García stages a coup d'etat, holds an election, and becomes president on New Year's Day 1937

1944: Student-led demonstrations against Somoza; regime promulgates Labor Code

1944–1946: Labor organizing at a peak

1947: Fraudulent elections are held; new president Leonardo Arguello charts independent course, is refused recognition by the U.S.; Arguello is overthrown by Anastacio Somoza García, who names one of his wife's uncles, Benjamin Lacayo, as president

1948: Anti-labor repression, over 100 leftists arrested, including ISA labor leaders; U.S. recognizes regime

1950–1954: In Chinandega, cotton acreage increases from 2,000 to 100,000

1956: Anastasio Somoza García is assassinated by the poet Rigoberto López Pérez in the city of León

a twenty-five-mile radius of the departmental capital of Chinandega; these were central to the development of the worker and campesino movements. The book is concerned with geographical variation within and across movements; using terminology suggested by McAdam (1996, p. 31), we can say that the book shows how an initiator movement that began in one village in 1957 spawned several spin-off movements in neighboring localities in the early 1960s (p. 13).

Gould conducted his research between 1983 and 1989, when the Sandinista National Liberation Front (Frente Sandinista de Liberación Nacional; FSLN) was in power in Nicaragua. The core of his research consists of interviews with sixty-five leaders of and activists in the movements, each interviewed more than once. This oral history was supplemented with documentary sources when these were available. The book covers the periods of the governments of Anastasio Somoza García (1937–1956) and his sons Luís (1957–1963) and Anastasio (1966–1979), following the movements up to the successful Sandinista revolution in 1979.

Gould is especially good at tracing the process of "framing," the "conscious strategic efforts by groups of people to fashion shared understandings of the

---

1957: Birth of Chinandegan agrarian movement; nationwide state of siege following Somoza's assassination

1961: FSLN founded

1961–1964: Campesino movement coincides with Alliance for Progress land-reform initiatives

1963–1966: Limited democratic opening under President René Schick

1964: ISA cane cutters strike

1972: Earthquake kills 15,000; mismanagement of relief funds leads to elite disenchantment with corrupt regime

1974: ISA cane cutters occupy factory

1978: Pedro Joaquin Chamorro, editor of *La Prensa* and a political opponent of the Somoza family, is assassinated

1974–1978: State of siege; massive repression in countryside; major strikes at ISA and land occupations in Chinandega coincide with insurrectionary movements, prompted by Chamorro's assassination

July 19, 1979: Sandinista Revolution triumphs

world and of themselves that legitimate and motivate collective action" (McAdam, McCarthy, and Zald 1996, p. 6). He is especially interested in how discourses justifying elite domination can be subverted by oppressed groups with their own projects of resistance and redistribution. As Gould writes:

> [E]xpressions of popular resistance . . . borrow from the symbols of elite cultural domination. . . . Although such borrowings place limitations on the popular resistance . . . this weakness can be partially overcome by "the experience of opposition [and] by the fact that counterhegemonic strategies can expose the contradictions within the existing hegemony" . . . [T]he agrarian struggle of Juan Suazo and his fellow campesino militants was a lengthy apprenticeship in the use of elite language and symbols not only to make their claims but also to conceptualize their world in different and new ways (pp. 6–7).

Gould thus attempts to trace how identities are culturally and normatively shaped, an enterprise recommended by analysts of social networks (see, for example, Emirbayer and Goodwin 1994, pp. 1445–46).

Gould studies with most affection and detail the campesinos in San José del Obraje in the 1950s and early 1960s, among whom Juan Suazo was a key leader. In a critique of mechanistic class analysis, Gould offers these campesinos as an example of a movement forged by ties of residence rather than occupation, and community rather than standard class categories. He also shows how this movement contributed to the creation of a revolutionary alliance "from the bottom up" (Gould 1990, p. 16), taking issue with accounts of the Sandinista revolution that focus largely on political elites.

The people in San José used the term *campesinos* to describe their own condition and identity. The word signified common residence in poverty-stricken villages, despite the fact that people had different class positions. The villagers used the term *campesino movement* to describe the agrarian protest organizations that struggled for land, higher wages, and improved working conditions on cotton and sugar plantations (Gould 1990, p. 7). Gould calls the campesinos a "relational" class. They had different class positions in objective terms, including rural wage workers, peasant proprietors, and tenants. By the end of the 1950s, the rank and file of the peasant organizations were largely landless, while the leaders were smallholders, but they defined themselves inclusively as a *clase campesina* (peasantry) in opposition to the *clase terrateniente* (landlords) (Gould 1990, p. 8). Class was thus consciously created, but under structural conditions that clearly limited the campesinos' political choices.

The Importance of the Movement

Gould suggests that the Chinandega rural labor movements had a considerable impact on Nicaraguan politics. Indeed, they engaged the attention of key national political figures, including all three Somoza presidents. In keeping with the observations of Sidney Tarrow and others, Gould offers several examples of how the movements changed the political opportunities the peasantry faced through their own actions. Some of these will be discussed later.

Political opportunities are clearly key in explaining movement emergence and behavior. This can be seen in Gould's discussion of workers at the Ingenio San Antonio (ISA), a sugar mill and adjoining plantation in Chinandega that became the most important and modern such complex in the country by the 1940s. In 1926, Liberal rebels attacked government troops in Chichigalpa; this triggered an uprising at the ISA in which workers burned the distillery and deserted the plantation (Gould 1990, p. 33). Here, as elsewhere, elite conflict provided a brief opportunity for workers to break into the charmed circle of national politics. While a trade union formed in 1929 at the ISA did not endure, National Guard chief Anastasio Somoza's competition with traditional political elites provided workers with another opportunity for action seven years later. Somoza's ambitions led him to reach out for working-class support, giving impetus to Nicaragua's nascent labor movement. His successful 1936 coup d'état was nonetheless followed by the first strike wave in the country's history, in which ISA workers took part (Gould 1990, p. 39). Not all of these strikes led to gains for labor, and the strike at the ISA was repressed by Somoza's Guardia. Here, Gould sensitizes the reader to the way in which political opportunities are uneven across space and sectors within a national territory, not just over time. Presumably, other strikers fared better than the sugar workers in the ISA, but despite government repression the ISA enjoyed the status of a state within a state, a protected enclave that the new president felt he had to protect. The union at the ISA ultimately accepted defeat because it felt it had no significant outside supporters other than Somoza himself; its external alliance was vertical (with a powerful patron) rather than horizontal (for example, with other workers). As we shall see, Gould sees a move away from vertical and toward horizontal alliances as key to the campesino success more than two decades later.

Another significant political opening for rural labor in Chinandega occurred in 1944 when President Somoza, still anxious for working-class support in the face of a variety of political challengers, legalized trade unions and promoted a worker-peasant congress (Gould 1990, pp. 46–47). Importantly, the majority of the Nicaraguan population was rural during this period, and this sparked the "greatest period of union expansion in prerevolutionary Nicaragua's history" (p. 48); by June 1945, militants (most of whom were on the left) had organized 17,000 workers in over 100 unions (p. 48). ISA workers formed a union that in 1946 affiliated with the leftist Confederation of Nicaraguan Workers (Confederación de Trabajadores Nicaragüenses; CTN), a labor confederation that was tolerated, but not legally recognized, by Somoza. Somoza sought to control the ISA's sugar workers as he, now a major landowner himself, competed with other members of the agrarian elite and maneuvered to elect his handpicked successor to the presidency in 1947. While the union endured a mass firing of its members from the ISA in 1945 and National Guard troops occupied the ISA in 1946 (pp. 51, 53), it still retained some capacity for labor representation under a regime that characterized itself as *obrerista* (workerist) and whose leader was the *jefe obrero* (chief worker).

Ultimately, the sugar workers at the ISA lacked the internal resources, external allies, and appropriate discursive "frame" to resist the closing down of political opportunities that occurred after the 1947 election. After his candidate won the presidency in a fraudulent election, Somoza, no longer dependent on labor support, became less tolerant of independent unionism. He stepped up Guardia repression of trade unions and in 1949 definitively repressed the CTN. The same year, an alliance between mill and field-workers broke down. Increased mechanization of the mill and recent immigration of cane cutters had widened the gulf between relatively skilled, well-paid, local mill workers and less skilled, poorer field hands who were often migrants and typically regarded as "Indian." The ISA union came to represent skilled workers and machine operators, and excluded field-workers (p. 64). For Gould, the potential for a rural labor movement with broader class solidarity, greater autonomy from capital, and more radical demands had been snuffed out. The existing movement had not been strong enough to resist a decline in political opportunities. It would take another ten years for a rural movement to emerge that could.

The second movement, to which Gould devotes most of his attention, is that of campesinos in the 1950s and early 1960s. New Chinandegan rural communities united around a sense of common rights to "the people's land" in this period, and eventually garnered support from powerful political actors in the national capital. The key events occurred between 1957 and 1961. Like the sugar workers' movement of the mid-1940s, the campesinos took advantage of elite competition. Unlike the sugar workers, however, the campesinos went further in driving a wedge between landowners and exploiting the resulting intra-elite conflicts for their own benefit.

San José de Obraje, the center of the campesino movement scrutinized by Gould, almost doubled in size between 1957 and 1960, growing from roughly 60 to 110 adults and more than 400 children (p. 119). Thirty-five adults moved to the community in this period. The number of wage laborers increased, while tenant corn farming was squeezed out. The paternalism of the landed elite declined and relations of production were monetized and capitalized; workers became a mere cost of production.

From 1955 to 1961 the San José campesinos occupied land and government buildings, and held rallies and demonstrations. These actions involved from dozens to several thousand people, often with the assistance of the General Confederation of Workers (Confederación General de Trabajadores; CGT), an urban labor organization. The struggle turned on the peasants' demand for *ejidos* (communal lands) and a new agrarian reform law. The land occupations, in particular, drew the campesinos into conflict with the National Guard, which was sent to evict them on more than one occasion (pp. 121–38).

In reaction to these demands, President Luis Somoza established a congressional commission to investigate Chinandegan land claims in 1961. The commission granted 340 acres of communal lands to campesinos to cultivate collectively while awaiting their formal distribution. Two years later, the Somoza regime established an agrarian reform administered by the Nicaraguan Agrarian Institute (Institute Agrario Nicaragüense, IAN), which redistributed some land in Chinandega. However, the failure of the IAN to do this on a large scale paved the way, in Gould's view, for later campesino support for the Sandinistas, eventually contributing to the success of the 1979 revolution. During and after the revolution, workers occupied the ISA sugar mill, which was later nationalized, and the campesinos of San José occupied land en masse, becoming independent proprietors. Gould's narrative on the peasants' collective action ends here.

The third movement studied by Gould is that of the Sutiava, an indigenous people who were also involved in land conflicts in the late 1950s and early 1960s in León, Nicaragua. The breakup of traditional peasant communities in the 1890s, Gould explains, had deprived most campesinos in the region of a strong indigenous identity. The Sutiava retained such an identity, Gould argues, which gave them a unique ability to forge a communal, multiclass alliance. Unlike the San José campesinos, who were largely landless, about 40 percent of the Sutiavas still owned land in the 1950s. Their claim to land was based on a collective, communal right, however, expressed in opposition to Ladino (non-Indian) society. In Gould's words, the Sutiavas' ethnic solidarity "enriched the movement ideologically, strengthened it organizationally, and made it extremely difficult for the regime to contain" (p. 110). The Sutiava also posed the threat of armed resistance more credibly than did most other campesino communities. Interestingly, the CGT at one point accepted an "Indian" identity for the San José campesino movement, in part because in Somocista ideology Indians had pride of place as bearers both of national identity and traditional rights to communal land (p. 109).

Origins of the Movement

Structural economic changes play a major role in Gould's explanation of the emergence of the new campesino movement in the mid-1950s. In the 1940s, *hacendados* (owners of large estates, or haciendas) had evicted thousands of laborers from subsistence plots. Municipal *ejidos* (communal plots) that had been used for subsistence farming, hunting, and wood gathering were turned into cotton plantations. There had been no unions to resist. In the 1950s, an agro-export boom further displaced peasants from the land. The mechanization of cotton production accelerated, including the use of tractors, displacing labor and making labor demands seasonal rather than year round. Seasonal laborers grew from a small percentage of the labor force in the late 1940s to over 90 percent of the labor force by 1960 (p. 134). High cotton prices from 1950 to 1955 induced landowners to evict tenants in order to plant more and more cotton. The evicted tenants formed new villages and expanded the size of existing villages.

Their resettlement in villages thus provided the campesinos with both a common grievance (loss of access to land) and increased capacity to engage in collective action (concentration in urban communities away from direct landlord control). However, this economic and spatial shift does not seem to fit within the rubric of political opportunity structure. The first element of political opportunity posed by McAdam, McCarthy, and Zald (1996, p. 10), the degree of openness of the institutionalized political system, does not include *economic* inclusion. Yet it could be argued that economic inclusion may also provide a kind of political opportunity to workers, for example, to make demands in the workplace, even when the larger political system that governs the workplace is closed to worker participation. The political system could usefully be expanded in some instances, therefore, to include workplaces such as private enterprises and state bureaucracies.

The other three elements of political opportunity—the stability of elite alignments, the existence of elite allies who can encourage or facilitate protest, and the level of state repression against opponents—plays a large role in Gould's explanation of the trajectory of the campesino movement that is his principal case. In explaining the emergence of this movement, however, political opportunities play a smaller role than does the growing organizational capacity of the campesino movement of the 1950s, caused mainly by the economic and spatial transformation of the cotton boom. This increasing capacity came about during an epoch in which political opportunities were fluctuating widely and regime repression was intermittent and unpredictable. The theoretical conclusions one can draw from the study is that the interplay between political opportunities and movement capacities is dialectical; movements can become more politically effective even if political opportunities decline, as long as their capacities for collective action increase. This can occur either through an intensification of participant commitment as a result of the creation of new perceptual frames, or through an increase in material or organizational resources. Similarly, the same levels of repression of social movements do not work uniformly for regime leaders; successful resistance against repression is possible for some movements with many resources and strongly resistant frames, even as other movements are crushed. Satisfactory generalizations about the impact of political opportunities are thus likely to be interactional rather than axiomatic.

Expanding Political Opportunities

Two dimensions of political opportunity seem to play an ambiguous or marginal role in Gould's explanation of the emergence of the campesino movement in Chinandega in the 1950s. First, there appears to have been no major change during this period in the degree of popular political inclusion, at least in the formal political arena. (A more systematic treatment by Gould of elections and the suffrage would have been helpful in assessing this variable.) As for the degree of state repression, this seems to have been highly variable during the movement's emergence. In 1956 Anastasio Somoza García was assassinated, and his son Luís succeeded him amid a wave of repression against opponents. According to Gould, the regime subsequently supported, ignored, and repressed campesino movements, at different times and places. If this was the general picture, at least one significant contrast appears at the local level: Gould shows how the Guardia *comandante* in Chinandega in the late 1950s facilitated the movement's emergence because he was relatively moderate and sympathetic to the campesinos, especially in comparison to his violently repressive successor, in charge between 1962 and 1964.

Elite competition is much more important than either political inclusion or repression in Gould's analysis. The agrarian bourgeoisie in Chinandega were divided between traditional landed oligarchs, urban professionals investing in cotton, and *arriviste* Somocista politicians and officers in the National Guard. These divisions seem to have increased over time, especially when the government initiated a land reform, with support from the United States. San José campesinos were able to exploit these divisions and "eventually learned to play one elite faction off against another" (p. 86).

Gould is initially skeptical about the element of the political opportunity structure consisting of elite allies who encourage or facilitate protest. Although members of the San José community were mostly illiterate, and thus especially in need of external allies, this made the villagers vulnerable to outside control. Gould argues that elite allies frequently imposed heavy costs on the campesino movement, in the form of lost autonomy. The sugar workers' movement in the 1940s, as we saw, was limited by its vertical dependence on Somoza and Somocista ideology. The rural workers in Chinandega, on the other hand, moved laterally in the 1950s. Rather than reach up the social hierarchy for an elite patron, they made a horizontal alliance with urban labor, in the form of the CGT. CGT leaders could best be considered as influential allies, in Tarrow's terminology, rather than elite allies. Their influence stemmed from their institution's organizational strength, their political connections, and their presence in the national capital, rather than their social origins or resources. The connection with the CGT, in Gould's view, resulted in some loss of campesino autonomy but resulted in a broadening of the movement and a deepening of its class perspective. This horizontal alliance with urban labor, for Gould, was superior to the vertical link with elite patrons forged earlier by sugar workers.

Even this horizontal alliance does not escape Gould's criticism. He attributes the San José campesino leaders' acceptance of CGT President Escorcia's leadership to their need for tactical advice and legal assistance in the face of Guardia repression. The campesino leaders "still could not conceive of an alternative to an alliance with an outside force" (p. 125). Escorcia's leadership partly reflected the *caudillismo* (rule of dictatorial local bosses or *caudillos*) of Nicaraguan political culture, tempered as it was by the rank and file. The leadership of the campesino organization thus tended to take on characteristics of its enemies—the Guardia and the agrarian bourgeoisie—by developing a military-style chain of command. Escorcia, an outsider, became a sort of field marshal who expected the automatic fulfillment of his orders by the Chinandegan campesinos.

The Sutiava indigenous movement, representing some eight to ten thousand cultivators of various social classes, is presented as the most autonomous of the three movements studied by Gould. This movement appears not to have ceded control of its organizations to outsiders, although its main organization, the Comunidad Indígena, did pay some obeisance to the Somoza regime for tactical reasons in the early 1960s. The movement also maintained a loose and sporadic alliance with progressive students and labor leaders in León (p. 265). Its armed mobilizations resulted in larger concessions of redistributed land from the Somoza regime in the early 1960s than those made to Chinandegan campesinos in the same period. Gould sees solidarity, a tradition of militancy, and independence as more beneficial than external alliances, especially vertical alliances.

Structure, Subjectivity, and Causality

The strength of Gould's book is his careful attention to perceptual, cultural, and discursive shifts within the rural movements that he studies. He is interested in "how a people came to a qualitatively new collective understanding of their social world" (p. 6). His story is about how campesinos, in their encounters and struggles with "politicians, businessmen, soldiers, and hacendados," and through a series of "practical and mental steps" that became "qualitative leaps" of consciousness, developed a "class-rooted" perception of themselves and their conflict with landowners that enabled them, eventually, to "achieve their goals of land ownership and dignity" (pp. 5–6).

This emphasis on perceptions and discourses allows Gould to highlight both frames and political opportunities. While attention to the latter is not systematic or presented in the abstract language of comparative-historical sociology, it is certainly present in the text. What commands somewhat less attention is the changing organizational and material capacities of the movements. When describing the series of actions of the San José campesinos in 1961, Gould tells us relatively little about how and when the demonstrators decided to embark on these actions, how they got to the cities and fields where they held their demonstrations, marches, and occupations, and how they sustained themselves in these places. He seems to imply at times that the rural movements' most important organizational resource was discourse itself.

Gould's explanation of the emergence of the campesino movement is based heavily on the delicate business of assessing campesino consciousness, of deciding at which moments "qualitative leaps" in perception occurred and when "feelings of ignorance and dependence on their superiors" (p. 5) were outweighed by confidence, independence, and a spirit of resistance. I believe this leads to explanations that can give too great a weight to consciousness and not enough weight to political opportunities.

Gould does not explicitly address why an autonomous radicalism developed in San José and not in San Antonio. But he suggests that this intriguing divergence of outcomes was produced mainly by different wills: the campesino militants were radical visionaries who "constantly chipped away at the rank-and-file tendency to accept paternalism and rationalize their oppression" (p. 86). They dared to hope for more than a slightly higher wage or the use of a plot of land from the patron, and they had the courage to fight. The leaders of the sugar workers' union, it is suggested, lacked such daring: they compromised, accepting labor division in place of solidarity, and dependence and subordination in place of independence and resistance. Ultimately, for all its emphasis on external events, the drama in Gould's book is internal: it concerns the inner war within rural workers' own hearts and minds, the tension between their desire to risk everything and rebel in the name of autonomy and dignity, and their all-too-human willingness to quietly accept paternal control.

Agency and discourse are vital to an understanding of social movements. However, Gould's particular account of agency may exaggerate the difference of consciousness within the two movements he addresses and underplay how agency interacted with certain kinds of structural economic and political constraints. These constraints can be considered political opportunities. This statement can be elaborated by looking more closely at differences in production processes and workplaces involving the workers in the two movements.

Although Gould does not describe the ISA in detail, we can probably assume that the mill was a highly capitalized factory with tight labor control over workers, at least compared to field hands and tenant farmers. A key component of the labor force was its relatively skilled, relatively well-paid machine operators and technicians who had made substantial investments in their own training in the specific production processes of sugar milling and (perhaps) refining. Their livelihood was thus tied up in the mill (and its owners and managers) in ways that are starkly different from the relations between peasant smallholders and neighboring *latifundistas* (large landowners). Furthermore, increased revenues for the mill could at least potentially result in pay raises and a division of surplus between labor and capital in the mill, a kind of positive-sum compromise that is less common in conflicts between smallholders or tenants and big landlords over land and its produce, which are frequently zero-sum. Given these large differences in the structure of production and the workplace, there appeared to be far greater barriers to fully autonomous labor strategies at the ISA than in San José. (Gould does not tell us about the communities of the employees of the latter, hence we cannot assess the role of community in their collective action.) Another way of putting this, if we are willing to expand the conventional definition of political opportunities, is that the local political opportunities of the campesinos were greater than those facing the mill workers.

Consciousness thus might not be the whole story in explaining the ISA employees' relative conformity. One could imagine sugar mill workers whose consciousness was just as radical as that of the campesinos but whose bases for independent action were far more highly circumscribed by their workplace situation. Equally, one could imagine peasant proprietors who were not politically radical, who might even have desired to emulate their *latifundista* neighbors and become big patrons themselves, but whose structural situation of independent land ownership provided them the latitude to engage in militant conflict over land with other landowners. (This insight is the basis of Wolf's [1969] well-known "middle peasant" thesis.)

Moving away from production to the larger political system, Gould is also too quick to equate the political opportunities facing the two labor movements at this level. We are told that the ISA in the 1940s had a privileged position in relation to the Nicaraguan state; it was exempt from many taxes and impositions, its owner was a member of the Conservative party, it was a "state within a state," and so on. Even when Somoza was mobilizing labor, his perceived room to move against the ISA was limited. The *latifundistas* of Chinandega in the 1950s and 1960s, on the other hand, while formidable foes of the local campesinos, were relatively small fish in Managua compared to the owners of the ISA. These may not have been, therefore, comparable openings in the political opportunity structure. If one accepts that workplace and larger political constraints on autonomy were more severe in the case of sugar workers than for campesinos, then what Gould identifies as the reformist *obrerista* consciousness and discourse of the former may have been, in part, a recognition of the far higher costs of full-scale resistance to paternal control. Conversely, the campesinos' radicalism, while the result of a painful and slow process of imaginative leaps of emancipation, could also have been a reflection of the greater latitude possessed by scattered peasant communities that existed outside the direct control of *latifundistas* and only some of whose members depended on landlords for cash or land; this autonomy allowed these communities to defy core landlord interests and engage in direct confrontation with them.

My concern here is to understand the obstacles to autonomous organization faced by the ISA sugar mill workers. For those workers, the costs of autonomy may have appeared to be too high, and their political opportunities too limited. We must be careful about how we use their apparent conformity to make inferences about their consciousness.

Conclusion

This is a book by a careful historian who, above all, wants to tell the story of the campesinos he talked to. Gould adopts an ethnographic approach in part to highlight the importance of the agency of specific individuals in various collective actions. The book is full of factual information yet provides ample material for theorists of social movements.

The book confirms that the concept of political opportunity structure is paradoxically both too broad and not specific enough. As stressed by Gamson and Meyer, the concept encompasses the most significant aspects of the political situation facing any social movement. To say that a movement's prospects for effecting social change is influenced by the political opportunity structure is, thus, irrelevant. At the same time, the concept of political opportunity structure is not specific enough. In particular, it does not differentiate between the different types of alliances that social movements can enter into with outside groups. Gould's book shows the importance of the nature of alliances—and not simply their existence—for understanding the political impact of rural worker and campesino movements. It was one thing for sugar workers to ally with Somoza in the 1940s, and something else again for campesinos to ally with the CGT in the early 1960s. In the former case, a vertical alliance with a powerful and dictatorial political leader and businessman limited union demands to certain material favors, cut mill workers off from solidaristic pacts with field-workers, and confined union discourse to "*obrerismo*," in which President Somoza himself was the *jefe obrero*. The later campesino alliance with the CGT did limit rural union autonomy to some extent, but it also allowed for the making of more radical demands and a deepening of rural workers' class perspective. It also tied the movement to a national urban labor movement, giving it much more political force than it would have had on its own. It was this second—horizontal—alliance that contributed to the achievement of greater autonomy in the later period. In Gould's words, "the Chinandegan campesinos first used elite notions to understand their reality and then overturned the meaning of those notions along with their associated forms of deference to the elite" (p. 301).

Gould's book is exemplary in its careful use of oral history to capture the meaning of social movements for their leaders and militants. However, I think that this method, and the heavy emphasis on consciousness and discourse, leads Gould to underemphasize the importance of structural factors such as production processes, workplace organization, and community location. (These factors could usefully be included in the notion of political opportunities.) Major differences between sugar workers' and campesinos' structural situations are relatively undertheorized, even though these might have played a role in producing the contrast between the movements that these workers created. While Gould skillfully demonstrates how opportunities expanded, contracted, and stabilized on various levels at various times during the course of the movements' emergence, ultimately, this factor is not decisive in his analysis, and he roughly equates (in my view, inaccurately) the political opportunities that the sugar workers and campesinos faced. The author himself stresses the nature and quality of external alliances in explaining the ultimate success of the campesino movement, compared to that of the sugar mill workers, which in turn were produced by a more radical discourse and consciousness. It is on this point that Gould makes his most important contribution. Consciousness provides both for the vividness and humanity of a very good book and for the explanatory limitations of a comparison of two quite different labor movements.

RESPONSE TO ANTHONY PEREIRA
Jeffrey L. Gould

I was extremely pleased to read Anthony Pereira's analysis of *To Lead as Equals*, by far the most serious engagement with the work by any scholar. His review enhances its value by drawing connections to a body of sociological literature with which I was unfamiliar. I concur with Pereira's analysis of horizontal and vertical alliances and with his derivation of a central methodological point from my book that "the interplay between political opportunities and movement capacities is dialectical—movements can become more politically effective even if political opportunities decline, so long as their capacities for collective action increase."

Pereira considers the central weakness of the book to be the comparison between the Ingenio San Antonio (ISA) sugar mill workers' movement of the 1940s and the campesino movement of the late 1950s and early 1960s. Yet the book eschews any comparison between the two groups and does not point to greater radicalism on the part of the campesinos (in fact, socialists led the mill workers in the mid-1940s and Somocistas dominated the campesino movement until the 1970s). Systematic and fruitful comparisons would have been difficult between these two sociologically distinct groups operating in sharply different political and economic environments. Moreover, my research on the campesinos, written up in over two hundred pages, far outweighed that on the mill workers in the 1940s that accounted for a mere twenty pages. The methodological injunction that Pereira culls from the study about the dialectical interplay between opportunity and movement capacity certainly does help us to understand how the Chinandegan campesino movement could survive a period of severe repression including assassinations and mass imprisonment, whereas the San Antonio sugar workers' union movement could not survive the firing and jailing of its leading activists in 1947–48. The book emphasizes the importance of the village community outside of the hacienda boundaries and its policing reach as a locus of organizing that favored the movement. In comparison the mill workers resided on the company's property adjoining the plant. The key difference between the historical conjunctures and political opportunities in which the two movements operated can be thus summarized: in the late 1940s the dawn of the Cold War with its concomitant anti-communist fervor impelled Somoza to ally with the largest and most powerful company in the country to crush the left presence in the ISA union. In the late 1950s and early 1960s, the campesinos, on the contrary, benefited from the divided agrarian elite and from the U.S.-sponsored Alliance for Progress that favored moderate land reform. Moreover, the rebirth and rise of an opposition political movement during that period pushed Somoza toward an alliance, however tentative, with the emerging campesino movement. At the same time, the CGT leader, Ruiz Escorcia's sui generis brand of Somocista populism, to some degree, inoculated the campesinos against charges of communism that the leftists in the mill could not repel.

Shows how SM theory can be applied to work that is not nec, sociological

The transition from World War II to the Cold War created an irrepressible force against which the small and incipient leftist labor movement in Nicaragua and at San Antonio could do little. Somoza cracked down on labor throughout the country in part to impress the U.S. State Department in order to achieve diplomatic recognition (which it lost in 1947–48). Structural factors during the late 1940s also posed severe impediments to labor organization, especially the increasing levels of mechanization that deepened the division of the workforce, creating a relatively privileged, stable workforce of machine operators. The field-workers, on the contrary, were primarily temporary migrants who lived in geographically separate and distant *colonias*. Without a horizontal alliance between mill and field hands, there was no possibility for the San Antonio union to survive. Union activists, prior to the repression of 1947–48, did try to extend their organization to the countryside. Somoza, for political and economic motives (as owner of a plantation-mill complex), and the sugar magnates agreed that the organization of rural labor would be disastrous for their common interests.

Two patterns of social and political relations that emerged in the mid-1940s intensified in the late 1950s and 1960s. Nationally, the political-cultural divide between the middle class and elite opposition to Somoza and the popular movements during the early 1960s opened up an important opportunity for campesino mobilization. Locally, within San Antonio the division between mill and field-workers, due to significant technological advances, became even more pronounced. Symbolic of the division and the need to breach it, in 1974, field-workers during a strike forcibly occupied the mill to lecture the workers on class solidarity.

As I suggested above, Pereira is correct that I afford a more in-depth treatment of the peasants than of the sugar workers. The reason for that imbalance is rooted in the context of my research. Originally, my research plan envisioned a social history of the San Antonio sugar mill and plantation, tout court. Two factors militated against this project. First, the San Antonio sugar mill, in the early 1980s, continued to play an important role in Nicaraguan politics, in part because of its traditional leadership role in the Conservative party, but moreover because of its existence as the largest privately owned business in the country made it a showcase of the mixed economy in revolutionary Nicaragua. As a private company, of course, it had neither the incentive nor the obligation to open its archives. Someone in mid-level management slipped up and allowed me to consult the archives in 1983. Two days after I started, a high-level employee

problems w/ data collection

approached me and offered the aphorism: "*empresa privada, empresa cerrada*" (private company, closed company). Thus I had to rely on oral sources more than I had anticipated.

Unfortunately, I found the oldest generation of workers fairly guarded. They were fearful less of the Sandinista government than of the management, which remained in private hands until 1988. They were anxious about losing their pensions if they criticized the company. Furthermore, most of those workers who had participated in union activities had been expelled long ago from San Antonio. In order to interview them I had to journey throughout the country (mostly in vain). I finally realized that most of the seasonal fieldworkers, the overwhelming majority of the labor force, were virtually impossible to track down. Therefore I could not adequately trace the story of labor relations and conflict into the 1960s and 1970s, years in which the field labors were the principal actors at San Antonio. In short, ideal conditions were lacking to research the social history of San Antonio from 1936 to 1979 with the same degree of thoroughness that I was able to obtain in my research of the agrarian protest movement of the 1950s and 1960s.

Pereira also suggests that I do not adequately explain the resources of the campesino movement. I agree that I should have been more explicit about the significant CGT material support for the movement. Yet the text does suggest that Andres Ruiz Escorcia and the CGT labor federation (nominally Somocista) provided support. For example, "the CGT organized" the May 1961 demonstration and Ruiz Escorcia personally "led" the campesino demonstration at the Chinandega courthouse in June 1961 (p. 135). In 1962, Ruiz Escorcia brought along a "huge wirecutter" to cut barbed wire as part of a land occupation (p. 218). He "personally protected" the campesino leaders in Managua in 1962–63, a particularly dangerous moment of repression in Chinandega (p. 241).

Pereira also suggests that another weakness of the book is an overemphasis on consciousness at the expense of structural determinants. I disagree, but rather than muster textual support, it might be more useful to sketch out the context of my research. One of my principal goals, one that grew firmer as I continued to research and write, was to demonstrate the fallacy of the crude kind of class reductionism that I believed had profoundly negative political consequences in Central America and obfuscated any intellectual effort to come to grips with the social and historical reality of the region. The FSLN was promoting deterministic sociological and historiographical forms of knowledge and I wanted to ensure that scholars and militants might glimpse the richness of subaltern knowledge and experience outside the bounds of Sand-inista organizational history. Admittedly, after many years of discourse about discourse, today such a goal may seem quaint.

Unlike the mill workers, the campesinos I worked with were eager to have their story told. Many of their demands had still not been met, despite their support for the revolution. Moreover, their stories had moral lessons for the village youth who only had ears for the heroic tales of Sandinista fighters. The deal we struck was that I had to faithfully record their version of events. I would then be free to step back and contextualize the development of their movement.

When I started my research in Nicaragua I observed serious problems that only intensified during my two-year stay during the mid-1980s. Most signifi-cant were the limitations on the autonomy of peasant and labor organizations: instead of fighting for material gains and greater quotas of political and eco-nomic power, they seemed almost entirely dedicated to military defense against the Contras and their U.S. sponsors.

From my vantage point in Chinandega, it struck me that the Contras gained ground to the degree that the popular movements lost their autonomy of thought and action. Beyond military exigencies and the Leninism of the leadership that militated against grassroots, ignorance about the origins of the popular movements contributed to the erosion of autonomy. It seemed to me that such ignorance of contemporary Nicaraguan history was both conscious and unconscious. It was conscious in the sense that the FSLN sought to pro-mote the history of Sandinismo as the history of the subaltern classes. All that did not coincide with the history of Sandino, his followers, of anti-Somocistas, and the actions of the FSLN remained outside of the emerging official his-torical narrative. It was unconscious in that the new generation of Sandinistas knew little about the labor and peasant movements due to a certain lack of interest and because such histories did not exist.

It was in this context that I began the research in Chinandega. Although I had little idea what I would find, I did know that the FSLN would not play an impor-tant role and thus in this limited sense the book would be politically suspect. As I walked along those hot and dusty paths, I motivated myself with the belief that one day FSLN militants and leaders would read the book and then gain greater respect for the veterans of the labor and campesino movements. Thus my efforts would help to halt the revolution's march into the abyss and avoid the squelch-ing of so many dreams embodied in the triumph of 1979. Retrospectively such a belief seems extremely naïve. Yet without it I doubt I would have persevered.

What I failed to understand was that the political opportunity structure that would have allowed for such critiques already had been closed down. My early writings in Spanish (1985–86) about San Antonio and the labor movement were not published in Nicaragua until years after the FSLN was voted out of power. The bulk of the book was published in Nicaragua only in 2008.

I want to reiterate my gratitude to Pereira for engaging this book seriously and for analyzing it as a contribution to the literature on social movements. Moreover, I am thankful that his criticisms compelled me to revisit *To Lead as Equals* and the bittersweet memories of my fieldwork.

REJOINDER TO JEFFREY GOULD
Anthony W. Pereira

My exchange with Jeffrey Gould reveals some interesting points. First, his emphasis on campesino consciousness (as well as structural determinants of mobilization) was a reaction to a vanguardist, mechanistic class analysis that induced many of the Sandinistas, in his view, to ignore campesino voices after the success of the revolution in 1979. (Gould finds *campesino* to be the best word to describe the members of the social movement; it is the self-descriptive word they use themselves, and it is broad enough to capture the variety of conditions and occupations of the activists; p. 7.) Second, Gould's detailed analysis provides a basis for identifying more specific causal mechanisms involved in mobilization that are alternatives to the rather broad categories of political opportunities and political opportunity structures. These include the notion of a relational class identity; the ethnic solidarity of indigenous activists; and a social constructivist approach to the formation of movement participants' dispositions, desires, and interests. I will touch on each of these points.

I faulted Gould for giving too much weight to consciousness and not enough to the organizational and material bases for collective action in his account of campesino mobilization in Chinandega. I was insufficiently aware of the mechanistic view of class prevalent within Sandinismo to which Gould was reacting. Gould's emphasis on "how a people came to a qualitatively new collective understanding of their social world" (p. 6) is an identification of exactly the kind of "emotional, cultural, strategic, and other directions overlooked by political opportunity models" called for in the introduction to this volume. The interests of Nicaraguan campesinos cannot be read off from their "objective" class position, thus the Foucaultian issue of how desires and interests are formed rightly preoccupies Gould. In that sense Gould's book fits well with the aims of the present volume to more precisely specify social movement activists' ends, means, and interactions and thus escape the confines of a structural analysis of opportunities. The latter is a quixotic sort of analysis in the first place, as Jasper points out, in part because many opportunities are conjunctural rather than long term, open to interpretation and a variety of responses, and thus not structural at all. In that sense Gould's insistence on consciousness is posed as a counterweight to objective analyses of class that would obscure campesino agency.

Does Gould's book provide us with some concrete causal mechanisms that advance us beyond the generalizations of the political opportunity structure framework? I think it does, and one such mechanism is relational class identity. In the study of working-class movements it was E. P. Thompson (1963) who most clearly advocated for understanding class as a relationship and not simply as an abstract category defined by people's connection to the means of production. Gould describes Chinandega peasants as a relational class; that is, as bearers of a variety of different objective class positions (small landowner, tenant, wage laborer) who were united by their opposition to the large landlords and by their demands for land, as well as for higher wages and improved working conditions on the local cotton and sugar plantations. These demands led to large-scale occupations during the revolution, and the eventual redistribution of *terratenientes'* land to formerly landless peasants in the region.

The relational class approach is consistent with Jasper's invocation to accept that cultural and psychological meanings are important to strategic action, because "players are audiences for each other's words and actions, constantly interpreting what all the players (including themselves!) are doing" (Introduction, this volume). It also helps us to "distinguish different kinds of advantages based on their sources" (Introduction, this volume). For example, because landowners among the campesinos had physical and legal control over land, they could provide assistance to landless members of the movement. Similarly, the reputations of well-respected men such as Juan Suazo drew adherents to the movement. In addition, the "moral resonance" and "cultural symbolism" of the peasants' identity, consummated in the 1959 Cuban revolution and revered within the revolutionary left throughout Latin America in the 1960s, 1970s, and (to a lesser extent) 1980s, helped to cement the campesino-Sandinista alliance and make the revolution consequential in Chinandega.

Another mechanism that Gould identifies concerns indigenous ethnic identity. Gould's description of the Sutiava Indian community and its rebellion in the late 1950s in the area west of León emphasizes the power of ethnic identity in some forms of mobilization. Gould writes that the agro-export expansion in western Nicaragua in this period (a phenomenon spurred by government tax breaks and infrastructure projects) encountered resistance. One of the most pointed examples of this resistance was the Sutiava Indians' practice of destroying plantation fences at night. These acts were practiced by bands of several hundred Indians, who would cut the barbed wire under cover of darkness. A government attempt to mediate the conflict between the Indians and the plantation owners failed when the government representative, himself a landowner, was driven out of the community under a hail of stones (pp. 96–97).

While Gould does not analyze the strength of Sutiavan resistance in detail, it seems to have arisen from the Indians' shared use of land for hunting, the gathering of wood, and smallholder agriculture, as well as the bonds of ethnic solidarity. Furthermore, because Indian identity resonated in Nicaragua as a symbol of national independence and distinctiveness from the Spanish colonizer, Sutiavan resisters to the expansion of the large agro-export plantations found supporters among other Nicaraguans, including members of the elite. According to Gould, for example, the Conservative politician and newspaper owner Pedro Joaquín Chamorro wrote that Sutiavan demands were just (p. 97). Thus Sutiavan ethnic identity might have played an important internal and external role in the success of the movement's resistance. Internally, the Sutiavan Indians' special ethnic identity might have spurred their "cognitive liberation"—a belief that the social order is not legitimate, and that it is possible to change that order—since their outsider status already led them to question the reigning orthodoxy of the landowner-dominated social system. It also seemed to have facilitated their collective protests (Jasper, Introduction, this volume). Externally, the Sutiavans' ethnic identity seemed to induce a positive reception among others. The Indians were not mere vandals, but bearers of an identity with "moral resonance" (Jasper, Introduction, this volume) for the nation, and one that deserved respect and scrutiny.

From Gould's account we don't know exactly how these internal and external mechanisms worked, but they do bring us a long way past the rigid abstractions of the political-opportunity structure framework. It is also significant that Gould was intrigued enough by them to write a second book, *To Die in This Way* (1998), in which indigenous identity and mobilization play a much bigger role than they do in *To Lead as Equals*.

Gould also points out how the Sutiavans' success led campesinos in San José to reidentify themselves as Indian (pp. 110–11). Indian identity had been lost when communities were broken up in the 1890s, and many campesinos even considered "Indian" to be an insult. When one leader, Regino Escobar, decided to "rebrand" their movement as "Indian," however, the campesinos accepted the change. Once again, we see the protean power of cultural and psychological meanings in social movement activism, and how fluid the identification of the "we" and "us" expressed by movements can be.

A third and final mechanism that Gould's book identifies is what Jasper calls the "Foucaultian" analysis of the formation of social movement activists' dispositions, desires, and interests. Like critics of political opportunity structure models, social constructivists point out that structures are not objectively given, but have to be interpreted by actors; as Jasper writes, "Opportunities are what you make of them in the give and take of strategic interaction" (Introduction, this volume). This is why social movements could, under certain circumstances, become more politically effective even when political opportunities appear to decline. As with relational class analysis, the dispositions of social movement activists—including their willingness to fight—cannot be inferred from the outside, but must be verified through careful investigation.

Gould's book is based on meticulous investigation, thus it tells us quite a bit about where the Chinandegan peasants' fierce desire for land came from. The book covers roughly ninety years of Nicaraguan history, attempts to grasp the experience of at least six generations of peasant families in Chinandega, and expresses sympathy for the goal of peasant leaders to "make their history part of the cultural repertoire of their people" (p. 1). We learn about the breakup of peasant communities and the imposition of forced labor under the Liberal President José Santos Zelaya in the 1890s; Anastasio Somoza's coup d'etat of 1936, and the support given to Somoza by many peasants and workers; the slide into increasingly authoritarian rule by the Somoza dynasty; peasants' humiliating loss of access to land in the 1960s, as the large landlords, aided by the National Guard and the resources of the Somoza regime, expanded their agro-export plantations; and the revolutionary alliance between campesinos and Sandinistas of the 1970s that ended with the 1979 collapse of the Somoza regime (and the exile of Anastasio Somoza, the son of the president who came to power in 1936). While one individual could not have directly experienced all of these events (at least not as an adult), memory of them was passed on orally within the villages where Gould did his research, forming a "collective memory" of common struggle, partial victories, and temporary defeats.

Gould writes that "the ideological transformation of the Chinandegan campesinos involved the use of symbols drawn from Liberal rhetoric and from a dependent hacienda past rather than from the depths of village tradition" (p. 16). Their movement thus did not invoke some invariant, collectivist peasant "tradition" against modern capitalism, landlords, and the state; it emerged out of and was part of the capitalist transformation of agriculture. Gould is especially good on the recent past, as when he argues that a National Guard massacre of demonstrators in 1967 and the Somoza regime's misappropriation of international aid after the 1972 earthquake "sparked a realignment" of the anti-Somoza opposition (p. 271) of which the campesinos were a part. Gould shows how common religious sensibilities—another element of the cultural and psychological glue that can bind movements—helped to cement the alliance between campesinos and middle-class opponents of the Somoza regime. The religious sensibilities in this case came from Catholic liberation theology, in which the struggle for the revolution was seen as part of a quest for liberation, community empowerment, and individual spiritual salvation (pp. 276–77). In Gould's words, "Liberation theology played a vital role in fusing campesino and Sandinista ideologies" (p. 288).

Changes in consciousness led to action. In 1978 hundreds of campesino families invaded plantations in Chinandega. Gould shows how these actions "from below" ran counter to the political logic of the Sandinista National Liberation Front, which wanted to attack only those large landowners who opposed them (pp. 286–89). A tension thus existed between the campesinos' goals and the goals of the new regime, once it came to power in 1979. This tension remained throughout Sandinista rule (1979 to 1990), and led to campesino criticism of the regime's land reform.

In summary, Gould's book provides rich material for theorists of social movements anxious to move beyond the rigidities of an approach that sees movement "opportunities" as "structures." In emphasizing consciousness as well as structures; in seeing class in relational rather than objective terms; in recognizing the plasticity and power of ethnic identity; and in charting how movement activists' dispositions, desires, and interests are shaped over time in recurring protests, To Lead as Equals provides us with useful tools with which to build a more strategic perspective on the causes and consequences of social movement activity.

3   Human Rights in Argentina

Alison Brysk's *The Politics of Human Rights in Argentina*

AMY RISLEY

To INTERPRET arrests, torture, "disappearances," and other forms of state-sponsored terror as "expanding political opportunities" would seem counterintuitive at best and erroneous at worst. According to most political-opportunity models, decreasing levels of repression facilitate the emergence of social movements. In Argentina, however, the unprecedented violence that the military used to quell the popular sectors during the dictatorship of 1976–1983 gave rise to the human rights movement examined in this chapter. Indeed, the Argentine case reveals the weak explanatory power of political-opportunity variables as they are usually defined and operationalized. One may argue convincingly that the external political environment of systematic repression and its dramatic effects on people's lives partly explain the origins of human rights mobilization, but to suggest that this particular movement emerged in response to an "expansion" of political opportunities seemingly contradicts the underlying premise of political-process theory and obscures significant processes of collective identity formation.

The human rights movement arose in the aftermath of the 1976 coup and installation of the military regime. Participants included family members of the detained and disappeared as well as sympathetic members of Argentina's religious and professional communities.[1] At first the Mothers of the Plaza de

---

1. The "historic" organizations include the Argentine League for the Rights of Man, Grandmothers of the Plaza de Mayo, Mothers of the Plaza de Mayo, Relatives of the Disappeared and Detained for Political Reasons, Permanent Assembly for Human Rights (APDH),

Mayo (Madres) and members of other nascent groups limited their demands to information about the fate of their missing loved ones ("We ask only for the truth"), but soon the movement became the principal overt challenge to the regime. The "*raison d'être* of the human rights organizations was to oppose the logic of state terror" by emphasizing the sanctity of life and questioning the legality of the junta government (Mainwaring and Viola 1984, p. 31). The human rights discourse resonated overseas, and the movement quickly became an international cause célèbre.

During the democratic transition, activists enjoyed "enormous moral authority" for their bravery throughout the dictatorship and a sizeable audience for their "eloquent critique" of the regime (O'Donnell and Schmitter 1986, p. 52). Largely in response to their demands, a truth commission was organized in 1983 and *Nunca Más* (Never Again), a report detailing the human rights abuses, was published the following year. High-ranking members of the armed forces were tried for murder, torture, illegal detention, rape, and theft. However, soldiers fearing imprisonment rebelled on several occasions between 1987 and 1990, prompting the Full Stop and Due Obedience laws and President Menem's pardons, which precluded further punishment of those responsible for committing violations. Some Argentines began to perceive the activists' ongoing pursuit of justice as recklessly endangering the democratic transition.

Notwithstanding these setbacks, the Argentine human rights movement endured. More than three decades after its emergence, the movement continues to influence public policies, political discourse, and collective action. Newer groups have joined veteran activists in the struggle since the transition.[2] Although each organization tends to focus on particular issues, the movement as a whole has embraced a broad definition of human rights that incorporates civil, political, social, economic, and cultural rights. Participants include myriad issues under the banner of human rights advocacy and address challenges that at first glance seem only tangentially related to the dictatorship-era abuses: unemployment and poverty, intolerance and discrimination, police brutality, inhumane prison conditions, corruption, judicial irregularities, and Argentina's weak rule of law in general.

Center for Legal and Social Studies (CELS), Ecumenical Human Rights Movement (MEDH), and Peace and Justice Service (SERPAJ).

2. Examples of groups created during the democratic period are the Association of Ex-Detained and Disappeared, Children for Identity and Justice and Against Forgetting and Silence (HIJOS), Coalition Against Police and Institutional Repression (CORREPI), and Committee of Relatives of Defenseless Victims of Institutional Violence (COFAVI).

To combat these problems, activists have sought to influence state insti-tutions, elected officials, fellow civil societal actors, and the broader public. The creation of a Subsecretariat of Human Rights within the Ministry of the Interior, the inclusion of several human rights conventions in the nation's constitution, and the adoption of key laws are some of their more notable achievements. For instance, legislation passed in the 1990s assigned a legal identity (*ausencia por desaparición forzada* [absence by forced disappearance]) to individuals who had been involuntarily disappeared and provided repara-tions (*indemnizaciones*) to their families and to ex-detainees. In 2005, the Su-preme Court overturned the Full Stop and Due Obedience laws, opening the door to renewed prosecutions: hundreds of personnel in Argentina's security forces have been investigated, charged, detained, and/or convicted of torture, disappearances, killings, and other crimes. Meanwhile, the Grandmothers of the Plaza de Mayo have continued their efforts to identify and recover children of the disappeared. During the dictatorship, members of the security forces ar-ranged illicit adoptions of children who had been abducted with their parents or born in the detention centers. Hundreds of these (now adult) children have taken steps to find the "missing pieces of the puzzle" of their own identities with the Grandmothers' assistance.[3]

The groups also sponsor consciousness-raising activities to educate citi-zens about their rights, encourage a more tolerant political culture, and pre-serve the collective memory of the dictatorship and its victims. Efforts include organizing courses, roundtable discussions, lectures and cultural events, and publishing books, newsletters, and other materials. The Madres, who split into two distinct groups in 1986, continue to hold their famous weekly vigils in the Plaza de Mayo. Participants engage in additional forms of contentious politics, such as marches and *escraches*, which entail exposing and denouncing known torturers (and others accused of committing abuses) by demonstrating at their homes or places of work. The activists persevere in their demands for truth, accountability, and justice.

Movement participants have also framed social exclusion as a human rights violation in the face of growing unemployment, poverty, and inequality, which many attribute to neoliberal economic reforms. Some have referred to jobless and marginalized people as the "socially disappeared" or "the system's new

3. Interview with member of HIJOS, 7/31/97, Buenos Aires (All translations from the origi-nal Spanish are my own).

disappeared" (Risley 2006, p. 589).[4] A number of groups have offered support and solidarity to movements organized by unemployed workers (*piqueteros* or "picketers") and workers who seized control of factories abandoned by their owners in the depths of Argentina's economic crisis of the early 2000s.

Moreover, participants have made lasting contributions to repertoires of collective action (Tarrow 1994; Tilly 1978), and human rights is a "master frame" with broad resonance both within Argentina and beyond (Friedman and Hochstetler 2002; see also McAdam, McCarthy, and Zald 1996; Snow et al. 1986). For instance, the loved ones of the eighty-six people killed in the 1994 bombing of the AMIA (Argentine Israelite Mutual Association), a Jewish community center in Buenos Aires, have used similar collective action repertoires and framing strategies to denounce terrorism and demand justice (Risley 2006). During one demonstration, a speaker identified the victims' mothers as "the Mothers of Pasteur Street," where the building was located. After describing impunity as "a tragedy that recurs," she concluded the speech with the customary message of "*nunca más*."[5] Similarly, on the third anniversary of the attack, family members marched carrying photographs of the victims, read their names and ages aloud so that the victims were "present," and demanded punishment of those responsible for the crime. In short, various civil societal actors have drawn on human rights symbolism to legitimate their protests.

Due in part to its continued relevance and vibrancy, the movement has attracted the attention and, in some cases, admiration of scholars around the globe. The analysis presented in this chapter is based on this body of work as well as on field research that I conducted in Argentina.[6] Much of the discussion that follows will focus on Alison Brysk's (1994) book, *The Politics of Human Rights in Argentina: Protest, Change and Democratization*. In this comprehensive study, Brysk traces the movement's development during both the authoritarian and the democratic periods. The author's findings are the result of extensive research in Argentina. In addition, Brysk builds on rich theoretical

4. Interviews with members of HIJOS, 7/31/97, and the Argentine League for the Rights of Man, 7/10/97, Buenos Aires.

5. Speech delivered on 7/21/97, during Active Memory's weekly demonstration in Buenos Aires.

6. This research consisted primarily of interviews with human rights activists; participant-observation of meetings, protests, the Madres' weekly vigils, and other events; and the examination of the organizations' own publications. The Center for Latin American and Caribbean Studies at New York University provided funding for this research, which was completed between June and August 1997.

and conceptual frameworks used in existing scholarship on social movements, democratization, and human rights published in both Spanish and English. Brysk evaluates the extent to which the human rights discourse has been institutionalized and whether activism has encouraged change within civil society. She finds evidence of the movement's influence in each of these realms but also underscores a number of limitations. Instead of romanticizing activists, she concludes, "social change does not require heroes; it requires some small group . . . to behave courageously on some days—and simply to persist on others" (p. xii). The crux of her argument is that "citizens have an unexpected road to resistance: symbolic politics" and that "truth and values can create their own kind of power" (p. 171). For Brysk, this "pathbreaking" case offers salient lessons for other countries, especially those confronting the legacies of past human rights violations and undergoing the challenging process of democratization. Research on the Argentine movement does indeed generate opportunities for comparative analysis of social movements in both nondemocratic and democratic environments.

Origins of the Movement

The human rights movement originated in the midst of military dictatorship, when the armed forces unleashed the euphemistically named National Process of Reorganization (Proceso Nacional de Reorganización) on a highly mobilized citizenry. By the early 1970s, economic, social, and political instability plagued Argentina, which was experiencing an escalation of violence due to the rise of leftist insurgent groups and right-wing death squads. In 1976, the military ousted President María Estela (Isabel) Perón and seized power. The junta invoked national security doctrine, common in most Latin American military establishments at the time, and emphasized the threat of internal subversion. The consequences of regime change were much more calamitous than those of previous military interventions: the security forces tortured suspects in clandestine detention centers and forcibly disappeared tens of thousands, throwing drugged prisoners into the sea from airplanes or disposing of bodies in anonymous graves.

The category of "subversive" included people with varying partisan affiliations, ideological leanings, occupations, and class backgrounds. Brysk notes that the process of annihilating enemies "simultaneously reflected the regime's bureaucratic-authoritarian mission, the methodology of state terror, elements of a totalitarian apparatus, and personal caprice" (p. 39). In fact, the "decentralized and unaccountable repressive apparatus soon assumed a 'life of its own': victims were persecuted merely for social connections with other victims, or for affiliations with organizations erroneously labeled as guerrilla front groups" (p. 40). Argentines who escaped the fate of being detained or losing a loved one were forced to relinquish their civil liberties and political rights. The *Proceso* thus victimized all citizens through the politics of fear. Given the far-reaching

---

MAJOR EVENTS IN THE ARGENTINE HUMAN RIGHTS MOVEMENT

March 24, 1976: Military junta seizes power in a coup d'état that ushers in the National Process of Reorganization

1976–77: Several family-based groups emerge to protest the disappearances of family members

April 28, 1977: Las Madres hold their first Thursday afternoon demonstration in the Plaza de Mayo in Buenos Aires

August 5, 1978: Grandmothers publish a paid newspaper ad in *La Prensa* requesting information on missing children abducted with their parents

May 22, 1979: The Permanent Assembly for Human Rights (APDH) publishes a list of more than 5,400 cases of disappearance since 1975

August 10 and 14, 1979: Security forces raid the offices of APDH, Argentine League for the Rights of Man, and the Ecumenical Movement for Human Rights and confiscate files

December 10, 1980: Adolfo Pérez Esquivel, ex-detainee and member of the Peace and Justice Service (SERPAJ), is awarded the Nobel Peace Prize

April 15, 1983: An estimated 15,000 people participate in a human rights march for the disappeared in Buenos Aires

December 10, 1983: Raúl Alfonsín is inaugurated as president of Argentina; civilian, constitutional rule is restored

September 20, 1984: *Nunca Más* (Never Again), the report detailing the dictatorship-era abuses, is published by the National Commission on Disappearances (CONADEP)

April 22, 1985: Dozens of officers and accomplices are put on trial for murder, torture, illegal detention, rape, and theft; Generals Jorge Videla and Roberto Viola are among those who receive prison sentences

1986: The Mothers of the Plaza de Mayo split into two distinct groups: Línea Fundadora (Founding Line) and Asociación Madres de Plaza de Mayo

December 24, 1986: The Full Stop Law (Punto Final) is passed, imposing a time limit on redress of dictatorship-era human rights violations

and horrific nature of the repression, Brysk emphasizes the ways in which terror struck at the very core of society by penetrating the cocoons of people's homes, neighborhoods, and places of work.

Denial, suspicion, and social atomization accompanied this growing fear. Citizens would not learn the scope of the repression until later. And when they did hear about the disappearance of an acquaintance, people often assumed that he or she was guilty of something, as captured by the sentiment *"por*

June 4, 1987: The Due Obedience Law (Obedencia Debida) is passed protecting lower-ranking members of the armed forces from prosecution

October 7, 1989, and December 29, 1990: President Menem issues pardons to individuals not covered by prior legislation as well as convicted junta members, members of guerrilla forces, and members of the armed forces involved in the military rebellions that occurred between 1987 and 1990

November 27, 1991: Law 24.043 is passed, offering compensation to ex-detainees

December 7, 1994: Law 24.411 is passed, extending compensation to family members or spouses of the disappeared

May 11, 1994: Law 24.321 is passed, assigning a legal identity (absence by forced disappearance) to individuals who have been disappeared

1995: Children for Identity and Justice and Against Forgetting and Silence (HIJOS), a group of children of disappeared, imprisoned, and exiled persons, is created

March 24, 1996: An estimated 100,000 Argentines march under the banner of "Never Again" to commemorate the twentieth anniversary of the coup

August 12 and 22, 2003: The lower house of congress and the senate vote to nullify the Full Stop and Due Obedience laws, respectively

March 24, 2004: A "Museum of Memory" is created at the site of the Navy School of Mechanics (ESMA), a notorious detention center in Buenos Aires during the dictatorship

June 14, 2005: The Supreme Court overturns the Full Stop and Due Obedience laws, opening the door to renewed human rights–related prosecutions; hundreds of personnel in Argentina's security forces are investigated, charged, detained, and/or convicted of torture, disappearances, killings, and other crimes

December 11, 2009: Former navy captain and intelligence officer Alfredo Astiz goes on trial for the kidnapping, torture, and disappearance of several people, including founding members of the Mothers of the Plaza de Mayo, who were targeted in 1977 (Astiz allegedly posed as the brother of a disappeared person to infiltrate the Mothers of the Plaza de Mayo group) *algo será"* (translated loosely as "there must have been some reason"). Even if people sympathized with families or friends of the detained/disappeared, maintaining social ties with them (or anyone) was dangerous: members of the security forces were said to arrest citizens simply for appearing in another victim's address book.[7]

Victims' families who sought assistance from institutions of the state and society encountered innumerable obstacles. According to Brysk, the military left the judicial system intact but "dismissed all judges, replaced the Supreme Court and appeals courts, and subjected lower-ranking members of the judiciary to reconfirmation and a loyalty oath" (p. 43). Writs of habeas corpus and demands for detainees' rights to exile were met with silence. Other scholars have noted that mothers of the disappeared were taunted by the authorities, who suggested that they should have kept a closer watch on their "subversive" children (Bousquet 1983). Some officials went so far as to threaten family members in pursuit of information, warning that they were endangering their own lives and that of the missing person (Navarro 1989). Not surprisingly, the most common response was to deny that forced disappearances were occurring. Meanwhile, many Church leaders feigned ignorance and gained notoriety for their collusion with the military. Brysk explains how Church officials supported the regime's ideological positions and, more clandestinely, its tactics: "members of the clergy were seen at torture centers, in at least one case performing a Mass for shackled and hooded detainees—and urging them to confess" (p. 44).

Confronting these various forms of complicity and acquiescence and experiencing "intolerable uncertainty" and "personal anguish," affected individuals were transformed into activists (p. 42). They "turned to protest because their families and communities had been shattered, their neighbors were silent, and their own government had denied their existence" (p. 42). Several groups mobilized in support of essential rights to "life, liberty and personal security" (p. 7). Some demanded information about the military's practices and the fate of the disappeared; others clamored for greater accountability for the abuses. Brysk characterizes the human rights message as "morally coherent and internationally salient" and describes the bearers of this discourse as "legitimate, credible, and charismatic" (p. 11). The author discusses three main categories of groups that formed the backbone of the movement: civil libertarian,

7. Interview with member of the Argentine Section of Amnesty International, 7/18/97, Buenos Aires.

religious, and family-based. The first category included the Argentine League for the Rights of Man (Liga Argentina por los Derechos del Hombre; La Liga) and the Permanent Assembly for Human Rights (Asamblea Permanente por los Derechos Humanos; APDH), created in 1937 and 1975, respectively. These organizations, which predate the dictatorship, served as "mobilizing structures" for the incipient movement (McAdam, McCarthy, and Zald 1996): Brysk notes that some groups, such as the well-known Center for Legal and Social Studies (Centro de Estudios Legales y Sociales; CELS), founded in 1979, underwent a period of incubation in APDH or La Liga before becoming autonomous organizations. Participants typically refer to these groups as the "technical" arm of the movement; Brysk calls them "civil libertarian" to highlight their "appeal to universal principles and respect for legal norms" (p. 46). All played a role in uncovering, analyzing, and disseminating information about violations. They also attempted legal actions on behalf of detained and disappeared persons.

The second category of social movement organizations included religious and faith-based groups: the Ecumenical Movement for Human Rights (Movimiento Ecuménico por Derechos Humanos; MEDH), the Jewish Movement for Human Rights (Movimiento Judío por Derechos Humanos), and the Peace and Justice Service (Servicio de Paz y Justicia; SERPAJ). SERPAJ, created prior to the *Proceso* as a regional organization with a Christian humanist perspective, stepped up efforts to assist the "grass-roots sectors most affected by the repression" (p. 51). Like APDH and La Liga, SERPAJ facilitated the creation of other human rights groups. MEDH attracted dissident Catholic and Protestant clergy and offered "a source of alternative theological interpretation and religious legitimacy for the . . . movement" as well as aid to victims (p. 51).

Finally, family-based groups included the Madres de Plaza de Mayo, Abuelas de Plaza de Mayo, and Relatives of the Disappeared or Detained for Political Reasons (Familiares de Desaparecidos y Detenidos por Razones Políticas). People directly affected or victimized by the regime (*afectados*) formed these organizations in 1976 and 1977, when the repression reached its zenith. Brysk describes how the Madres, many of whom lacked any previous political experience, first met one another while searching for answers about their missing children. As their numbers swelled and their marches in Buenos Aires' most significant public space became more routine, the Madres "moved from a desperate search for their individual children to an identity-based social movement" that embraced all of the disappeared (p. 48). The Abuelas, united by their shared identity as both mothers and grandmothers of disappeared persons, focused their efforts on locating the children of the disappeared. Given the lack of a historical precedent that could guide their struggle, the Abuelas devised innovative strategies for investigating the whereabouts of their grandchildren.[8] The Familiares group differed from the others; it "included male relatives and did not engage in ritual protest centered on female identity" (p. 49). Moreover, members of Familiares took up the cause of political prisoners whom the military officially acknowledged in addition to that of the disappeared.

The boundaries separating these social movement organizations were fluid. A number of family- and faith-based groups had members with legal or other professional expertise; the "technical" organizations did not have a monopoly on such resources. Additionally, *afectados* sometimes joined or led organizations that do not fall into the family-based category. More important, the groups worked together toward common goals. The human rights movement was in fact a movement, not a loosely connected assortment of smaller movements or groups. Activists collaborated extensively as they gathered information about the ongoing abuses, provided assistance to victims and their families, and exhausted the limited legal options available in what was essentially an illegal regime. They tried to find the disappeared—who at the earliest phase of mobilization were not yet presumed dead—and the "stolen" children of the disappeared. Participants also gave much-needed moral support to each other. Brysk analyzes the movement's efforts to raise awareness through "the public projection of symbols, messages, and stories" and its relative success in carving out political space in an environment where political expression, debate, and participation (in trade unions, political parties, universities, and the press) had been squelched (p. 11). They struck a balance between "instrumental" behind-the-scenes work and more "expressive" public demonstrations (Foweraker 1995). Symbolic politics proved quite effective at garnering international support and inviting scrutiny of the military regime.

Any examination of the movement's origins must begin with an analysis of the unbridled repression of the authoritarian period. Understanding its terror, massive scope, and devastating impact on many Argentines is essential for grasping the motivations behind activism. Members of the human rights organizations stepped into the political and social void created by the closure of traditional avenues of participation, the attempted erasure of political identities and allegiances, and the silence or collusion of powerful actors. The movement

8. Interview with member of the Grandmothers of the Plaza de Mayo, 6/30/97, Buenos Aires.

grew out of the grief, pain, and outrage that people felt as a result of violence and terror. Its participants ultimately challenged the legality of the military's tactics and organized around a core of ethical demands that resonated both at home and abroad. Their discourse shaped politics during and after the democratic transition.

Expanding Opportunities

Do expanding political opportunities help explain the movement's origins and/ or development? Political opportunities usually refer to "dimensions of the political environment that provide incentives for people to undertake collective action by affecting their expectations for success or failure" (Tarrow 1994, p. 85). McAdam's "highly consensual list of dimensions" includes the relative openness or closure of the political system; the stability or instability of elite alignments; the presence or absence of elite allies; and the state's capacity and propensity for repression (1996, p. 27). Scholars tend to operationalize the variables by emphasizing relative opening rather than closing (for example, increasing popular access to the political system, elite instability, and elite allies, and decreasing repression). How useful are these for understanding human rights activism?

Brysk includes political process, resource mobilization, and other rational actor-based frameworks under the rubric of "economistic models" and suggests that such approaches fail to account for the "normative and expressive realm" of social movements. "Theorists within the economistic tradition are eventually forced to recognize this symbolic 'something else'; they attach it to their model as a resource, a repertoire, or a dimension of disruption—but they cannot *explain* it" (p. 8; emphasis in original). Brysk draws instead on the broadly defined "new social movement" approach and welcomes its emphasis on identity formation. I argue that expanding political opportunities fail to convincingly explain this movement, which burst onto the political scene under extremely inauspicious circumstances.

Access to the political system. The only "institutions" opening their doors to the popular sectors during the period in question were clandestine detention centers. The military actively sought to roll back the gains in political participation and representation that working-class Argentines had experienced in the heyday of Perón's populist rule. Congress, political parties, and civil society organizations shut down, retreated into the realm of the clandestine, or survived under strict military supervision. As noted previously, some of the movement's participants had been turned away, insulted, and threatened by the authorities. The postcoup crackdown made alternative forms of political organizing necessary but certainly did not facilitate mobilization.

Furthermore, if state, Church, or other officials had made some effort to listen to the *afectados*, it is likely that fewer people would have joined the movement. Instead, sympathetic lawyers and dissident clergy risked their lives to assist victims' families who had reached a dead end. The authorities' refusal to address their concerns merely served to legitimate the activists' claims. To illustrate, a member of CELS describes how participants in the movement presented a writ of habeas corpus for more than three hundred disappeared persons: "It was a fight to the death. We lost, but with honor. . . . We succeeded in showing that the judicial power at that time was an accomplice of the dictatorship."[9] Activists were convinced that theirs was an urgent task that could not wait for an eventual liberalization of the regime. No such political opening seemed forthcoming: the junta in Argentina did not compare favorably to other military governments in the region that eventually allowed certain political parties to function and eased other restrictions. Stated briefly, the movement's origins and development cannot be traced to any increasing access or political opening.

Unstable elite alignments. Political pluralism and partisan competition had vanished, but do we find evidence of factions or rivalries within the military or among its collaborators? Although bureaucratic authoritarianism differs from a personalist dictatorship in that the military governs as an institution, the leadership is not always unified. In Argentina, the armed forces enjoyed considerable internal cohesion during the initial phase of dictatorship, fostered by institutional strength, hierarchical structure, and dogmatic embrace of national security and anti-communist doctrine (Norden 1996; Pion-Berlin 1987). Long-standing rivalries between various branches, ranks, and individuals did not resurface until later (and especially after the military's defeat in the Malvinas/Falkland Islands War against Great Britain in 1982). In addition, the military's cordial relations with the Church precluded any significant rift. Even if cracks had appeared early on, it is not obvious that emergent social movements would have benefited unless certain factions succeeded in decreasing the use of repression against the citizenry.

9. Interview with member of CELS, 7/29/97, Buenos Aires.

Elite allies. The notion that an alliance might have formed between "soft-liners" within the armed forces and activists borders on the absurd, considering the military's war on all forms of mobilization. Yet how else might we operationalize the concept of "elite" in authoritarian environments? Shall we characterize the lawyers, medical doctors, psychologists, and other professionals who got involved in the human rights cause as "elite allies" who provided indispensable technical expertise to activists in desperate need? Such an interpretation is problematic for at least three reasons. First, determining who formed part of Argentina's social elite is not a straightforward task; the country had a well-educated population and a sizeable middle class during this period. Second, if these actors are nonetheless deemed elites, it is not clear that they assisted the movement in the manner envisioned by political-process theorists (for example, by lending material resources or legitimacy and encouraging participation in the existing system). The third and most glaring problem is that the professionals in question are widely considered to be full participants in the movement rather than outside allies.

Perhaps a focus on the domestic authoritarian context is misleading. According to McAdam, "movement scholars have . . . grossly undervalued the impact of *global* political and economic processes in structuring *domestic* possibilities for successful collective action" (1996, p. 34 [emphases in original]; see also Schock 1999). Brysk (1993, 1994) concludes that pressure from foreign governments, the United Nations, the Organization of American States, and transnational networks of nongovernmental organizations managed to save a few lives and prevent a dramatic escalation of violence. Sympathetic actors overseas disseminated information about the abuses, brought the de facto regime under scrutiny, and provided additional forms of material and logistical support to domestic groups. In 1980, Adolfo Pérez Esquivel, a well-known advocate and ex-detainee, was granted the Nobel Peace Prize, while the junta engaged in "defensive diplomacy" and other public-relations efforts (Brysk 1993, p. 247). Moreover, the Carter Administration viewed Argentina as an important test case for its human rights agenda. Wright notes that during "a November 1977 visit to Argentina, Secretary of State Cyrus Vance handed [General] Videla a list of 7,500 names of persons alleged to have disappeared" (2007, p. 123). As assistant secretary of state for human rights and humanitarian affairs, Patricia Derian visited the country on several occasions and met with human rights activists.

Are the movement's influential overseas allies best conceptualized as elites? Officials in the Carter Administration obviously qualify, but what about members of INGOs or student affiliates of Amnesty International who mobilize letter-writing campaigns? Even if we include them as "elites," the movement had already emerged prior to most of their assistance; as Brysk notes, activists "reached out successfully to the international system" (1993, p. 266). Brysk underscores the importance of this help during the movement's early stages but credits the movement's own initiative, not the UN or the Carter administration.

Declining repression. The military's apparatus of terror remained intact despite the international scrutiny. The repression, peaking from 1976 to 1978, continued until the regime collapsed in 1982–83. Few would disagree with the observation that participants in the human rights movement engaged in "high-risk" collective action (Loveman 1998). The military never indicated that it would curb its use of violence against citizens or treat the nascent human rights movement with kid gloves. On the contrary, numerous activists were detained, tortured, and/or disappeared, and thus subjected to the standard techniques of repression. The Madres' public presence and social status as "defenseless," middle-aged women sheltered them to some extent from brutal reprisals; yet even they were not protected from violence. Brysk provides a telling overview of the assault carried out against activists:

> Many of the original leadership of Las Madres (nine people) "disappeared," while the Movimiento Ecuménico lost two nuns, several priests, and a Protestant minister. The co-founder of the Asamblea . . . was kidnapped, tortured, and imprisoned for several years . . . while the leadership of CELS were arrested but then released. Several Liga lawyers disappeared, and a secretary of the Familiares was kidnapped, tortured, and forced to give false statements to the press denying her disappearance and alleging connections to guerrilla forces. Rank and file members of Las Madres were arrested repeatedly following demonstrations, and various *afectados* were detained to prevent their contact with human rights organizations (p. 56).

In short, participants were given "little or no protection from state persecution" (Loveman 1998, p. 516).

The fact that some Argentines were compelled to take such tremendous risks leads scholars to conclude that human rights movements in the Southern Cone "emerged despite (or because of) a severely unfavorable political opportunity structure" (Loveman 1998, p. 516). In cases such as Argentina, severe repression and state-sponsored human rights abuses actually created new "constituencies in a particularly dramatic and terrible fashion" (1998, p. 485). Franco argues similarly that "by attacking the family and destroying the home as a region of refuge, the military unwittingly unleashed powerful elements of resistance" (1992, p. 113). Specifically, Franco explores how the Madres' struggle transcended their individual circumstances and feelings of grief and outrage, which fostered immense solidarity. Human rights activists identify this as the "pain that was transformed into a struggle."[10] Participants also succeeded in conquering their fear. One of the Madres explained, "ever since they took my sons away I have never thought about myself. . . . It is as if lions grew inside of me and I am not afraid" (Chelala 1993, p. 69).

Without a doubt, the loss of a loved one resulted in a "schism of realities 'before' and 'after' the disappearance" (Schirmer 1989, p. 20). A member of Abuelas concurred: prior to the Dirty War, she (and other women like her) "lived in a different world" characterized by the "normal" routines of wage laborers and housewives; henceforth, their lives were defined by a quest for truth and justice.[11] They were no longer grandmothers, but grandmothers of stolen or missing children and mothers of disappeared persons. The Abuelas and Madres transformed motherhood into a collective, public, and politicized identity, with new expectations. The Dirty War decimated families, violated fundamental cultural norms, and gave rise to glaring contradictions between the military's practices and its ostensible mission to save Western, Christian civilization. In a departure from the conventional political opportunities model, McAdam (1994, 1996) has identified these suddenly imposed grievances, contradictions between cultural values and social practices, and increasing system vulnerability and illegitimacy as examples of "cultural opportunities." In summary, repression was essential for the emergence of the movement and the formation of collective identities among activists, but it had almost the opposite effect than the one posited by many proponents of political-opportunity models.

So far, we have seen that the framework of expanding political opportunities cannot explain the origins or timing of the human rights movement. It does not account for the urgency with which activists mobilized. These actors did not wait until the regime liberalized, the use of repression dwindled, elites

10. This slogan appeared on a poster displayed in the office of the Grandmothers of the Plaza de Mayo.

11. Interview with member of the Grandmothers of the Plaza de Mayo, 6/30/97, Buenos Aires.

offered encouragement, or some other opportunity arose. Instead of responding to external cues such as these, participants did what they thought was necessary and right, in the process carving out a political space under duress and
seizing opportunities (including international support) that subsequently materialized. The factors motivating collective action included emotions—especially love, pain, and outrage—and moral convictions regarding the sanctity of
the family, the rule of law, and justice. The methods used to eliminate perceived
subversives and quell dissent clashed with prevailing religious beliefs, cultural
values, and socially constructed identities. Following the movement's emergence, human rights activists created political opportunities for themselves and
for other civil societal actors.

Criticism

The Politics of Human Rights in Argentina has many strengths. Brysk draws on
diverse theoretical and empirical studies, analyzes several years of political history, and tackles a number of important and controversial issues pertaining to
human rights. On the other hand, some potential weaknesses in the book have
complicated the present effort to investigate the relationship between expanding
political opportunities and the emergence of the human rights movement. First,
Brysk oversimplifies when she classifies political process, resource mobilization,
political economy, and rational choice frameworks as "economistic models."
Although these approaches differ from one another, an endnote explains, they
all assume "individual, rational actors, material and structural bases of power,
and the predominance of political process over content" (p. 185). Instead of
considering each model individually and demonstrating how it fails to account
for human rights activism, she sacrifices complexity and nuance by lumping
them together. Brysk also appears to conflate some theories. While scrutinizing
resource mobilization theory, for instance, she brings in elements from other
frameworks when she suggests that the theory "situates the rational individual
in a context of group resources and a social structure that presents political constraints and opportunities" (p. 7). Moreover, she refrains from explicitly addressing the political-process model, despite its prominence at the time, and misses
an opportunity to assess its usefulness. Her critiques—and ultimately her rejection—of rationalist perspectives are not as convincing as they might have been.

Brysk concludes that new social movement and identity-centered approaches are more persuasive. Yet her own analysis of collective identity forma-

tion is surprisingly limited. She judges the human rights movement to be a case of identity-based mobilization but neglects to carefully examine the impact of the external political environment on individual and collective identities. Brysk seems satisfied with the attention given by the new social movement literature to factors both internal and external to the movement; she suggests that much of the debate "has centered on the conditions that give rise to expressive protest in diverse . . . settings," such as crises of legitimacy or a "lack of conventional political resources." Insisting that soon-to-be activists had nowhere to turn, Brysk argues that "the family emerged as a new kind of political actor in Argentina because state terror victimized the family as a unit, and because all other social institutions were repressed or acquiescent" (p. 8). The reader is left wondering why some people whose lives were turned upside down by repression joined the movement, while others did not, and why "lions" grew inside some of the mothers of the disappeared, while others continued to suffer silently. Whether the identities of clergy, lawyers, doctors, and other participants underwent a similarly abrupt change is left unexplored. Brysk mentions the politicization of social identities and the ways in which activists developed consciousness and overcame fear. Nevertheless, she is more interested in the "social legitimacy" of "mothers, clergy, and jurists"—a factor that made the movement persuasive and powerful—than she is in the actual process of identity formation (p. 10). Brysk could have deepened her analysis with a lengthier discussion of these processes.

A clearer indication of when the human rights movement gained sufficient momentum to be called a movement would have strengthened Brysk's study. The author describes how various human rights organizations were created while neglecting to provide details on how many people joined (although she does note that the Madres initially had fewer than fifteen members and eventually had several hundred). The founding dates of key groups lead us to believe the movement grew quickly early on, yet Brysk does not pursue the issue explicitly. She also contends that participants in a social movement "may belong to a specific organization, a set of organizations, or simply a community of values" but offers little evidence that such a community of values existed beyond the human rights organizations until later (p. 6). Regardless of its size, the human rights movement was the most important social movement that emerged during the dictatorship. In fact, Brysk's overarching goal in *The Politics of Human Rights in Argentina* is to analyze the movement's evolution and its impact, particularly during the country's eventual democratization. In fairness to the author, she does not promise a definitive account of the movement's origins.

Conclusion

Political opportunities were contracting rather than expanding on the eve of the human rights movement's emergence, demonstrating that social movements can originate even during the most dangerous periods of authoritarian rule. Activists mobilized due to the power of human emotions, the transformation of personal pain and grief into a collective, political struggle, and the relationship between external political circumstances and identity formation. These motivations are hardly unique to Argentina. Motherist movements have surfaced in a variety of political and cultural contexts; human rights advocates have worked in dire conditions across the globe; and women, youth, shantytown dwellers, and a host of other actors have engaged in high-risk, contentious politics under repressive regimes.

Movements like these raise a vital question: should scholars reconceptualize political opportunity to enhance its applicability to collective action that occurs in countries not typically classified as liberal democracies? Is it meaningful to compare movements that arise under regimes in which freely and fairly elected governments generally allow peaceful protest and respect other citizenship rights to those that emerge under dictatorships that brutalize the populace, put the legislature into indefinite recess, and prohibit the existence of certain political parties? In the latter regime type, citizenship is utterly trivialized: "a matter of holding a passport, obeying national laws, cheering for the country's team, and, occasionally, voting in choreographed elections or plebiscites" (O'Donnell and Schmitter 1986, p. 48). It is therefore not surprising that scholars have encountered myriad obstacles while extending the political opportunities framework to social movement activity in nondemocratic and developing countries (Boudreau 1996; Noonan 1995; Osa and Corduneanu-Huci 2003; Osa and Schock 2007). Foremost among these challenges is the paradox of protest in the face of repression (Osa and Schock 2007, p. 134). While violence and repression frequently decrease mobilization, they can also promote mobilization under some circumstances (Francisco 1995; Khawaja 1993; Moore 2000; Olivier 1991, Schock 1999). No consensus appears to have emerged as researchers sort through the contradictory empirical findings of existing literature. Nor is there a single theoretical approach for reconciling the political-opportunity model with these findings.

By the mid-1990s, it appeared as though advocates of political-process theory had reached a proverbial crossroads. On the one hand, they could rely on the conventional approach of searching for expanding political opportunities, acknowledging that the model was simply not relevant to all contexts and types of movements. Alternatively, they could insist that the concept was widely or even universally applicable, because any and all political changes, whether auspicious or unfavorable, were to be subsumed under the rubric of "opportunity." The second path was fraught with obstacles. The conceptual precision to which the theory's proponents aspire would be sacrificed (McAdam, McCarthy, and Zald 1996, p. 10), making political opportunity structure the "sponge" that Gamson and Meyer warned would absorb "virtually every aspect of the social movement environment" (1996, p. 275).

Since then, some of the model's staunchest defenders have acknowledged the wide array of factors grouped under political opportunities, the different concepts and measures being employed, and the competing (and/or conflicting) hypotheses being proposed (Meyer 2004; Meyer and Minkoff 2004). These researchers call for more explicit conceptualization and specification of political-opportunity variables, reject overly simplistic models positing a positive relationship between openings in the political structure and mobilization, and seek to clarify the dependent variables being explained (such as the formation of social movement organizations and movement outcomes). Yet they have surprisingly little to say on the subject of repression and nondemocratic regimes, though Meyer (2004) does concede that empirical tests that have incorporated cases of mobilization in such contexts have not lent much support to the theory.

Other analysts have relied on the conventional model of expanding opportunities to shed light on periods of political opening or liberalization within nondemocratic states. For instance, studies of communist regimes, as illustrated by the case of Poland in the late 1950s, have demonstrated that decreasing repression and divisions among elites help explain mobilization (Osa 2001). In her research on the Southern Cone, Hipsher likewise suggests that as authoritarian leaders "liberalize the political process and permit greater freedom of action, selected social movements emerge in protest" (1998, p. 153). Brockett's (1991) examination of peasant mobilization in Central America similarly achieves a better "fit" with the conventional model of expanding opportunities. To illustrate, in Guatemala, the government of General Kjell Laugerud (1974–1978) was "considerably less repressive than those preceding" it, which encouraged peasants to organize. At the same time, however, he notes that "indiscriminate repression can antagonize as many people into action as it neutralizes" (1991, p. 263). State violence in El Salvador, Guatemala, and Nicaragua in the 1970s "stiffened the resolve of many who were already in opposition and delegitimized the regime for many others," causing more peasants to support or join revolutionary groups (1991, p. 263).

In an effort to account for this seemingly paradoxical relationship between repression and organizing, some researchers have proposed changes to the model. For example, in his analysis of "people power" movements in the Philippines and Burma in the 1980s, Schock (1999) urges scholars to examine overall configurations of political opportunities, because violent, indiscriminate repression produces different effects depending on whether other opportunities are present (see also Osa and Schock 2007). In addition to adopting this "configurations" approach and suggesting that opportunities are not independent of one another, Schock (1999) finds it necessary to add two variables to the "consensual" list of opportunities: the international context and press freedoms/flows of information. Osa and Corduneanu-Huci (2003) likewise propose additional independent variables while applying the model to dissent in nondemocracies. Drawing on a data set of twenty-four cases, they identify social networks and access to media as sufficient conditions for mobilization in nondemocratic environments. Interestingly, social movement activity in Argentina circa 1977 is one of three cases included in the analysis that exhibit "more restrictive conditions" for activism: increased repression, a unified elite, a dearth of influential allies, and access to media or social networks (2003, p. 619). Osa and Corduneanu-Huci also suggest that the "strong impetus for mobilization" in such cases "stemmed from the communications media informing the public of extensive injustices and the ability of oppositional groups to use the media for organizing" (2003, p. 619). Exposés of regime violence in the foreign press were crucial in the case of Argentina, they argue. But were these variables really more significant for human rights activism in Argentina than emotions, family bonds, glaring contradictions between state-sponsored violations and religious convictions, cultural values, socially constructed identities, and other sets of factors discussed previously? It is difficult to accept the conclusion that access to media or social networks provided a stronger impetus for mobilization.

More recently, Osa and Schock have sought to defend the model by arguing that five political-opportunity variables are relevant in nondemocratic states: divided elites, influential allies, repression "dynamics," media access and information flows, and social networks (2007, p. 129). Indeed, they contend further that political opportunities are "*more* important for initiating mobilization in non-democracies," whereas "openings" of political opportunity are *not* always necessary in democratic settings (2007, p. 141; emphases added). In closed polities, it is hard to "motivate people to protest in the absence of political op-portunities," they conclude (p. 142). Although these scholars are generally satis-fied with the theoretical approach and its applicability to nondemocracies, they must nevertheless supplement political opportunities with other variables. For Osa and Schock (2007), that critical "something else" that explains mobiliza-tion is access to social networks. This addition muddies the conceptual waters, considering that political-process theorists usually include such networks in the category of mobilizing structures rather than the category of political op-portunities. The authors also propose that in nondemocracies, opportunities for organizing arise either "from outside of formal institutions, e.g., from social networks" or "from the failure of institutions, such as bureaucratic dysfunction or disingenuous government actions to increase legitimacy by reforming insti-tutions" (Osa and Schock 2007, p. 141). The concept of political opportunities once again resembles a sponge that absorbs too many features of the environ-ment in which movements emerge (Gamson and Meyer 1996).

A closely related strategy for keeping the model afloat is to construe both increasing and decreasing repression as opportunities (Osa and Schock 2007). Flexibility is maintained, because changes in either direction can encourage mobilization. Thus some scholars continue to include repression and other major obstacles under the rubric of opportunities in the "Alice-in-Wonderland world" of political-process theory (Goodwin and Jasper 1999/2004b, p. 116). In contrast, Almeida (2003), building on Tilly (1978), Goldstone and Tilly (2001), and other works, differentiates threats from opportunities and includes repression in the first category. Although threats usually increase the costs of collective action, well-organized groups that formed during prior periods of expanding political opportunities in authoritarian contexts may respond to threats with greater levels of mobilization or more radicalized forms of dissent. This approach has its limitations, however; the Argentine case does not fit the proposed sequence, given that the majority of human rights organizations were created in the midst of threats rather than opportunities.

In his final book, Tilly suggests that "any full conception of POS includes both opportunity and threat" (2008, p. 91). Instead of examining threat-induced contention, he argues that increasing threat, which entails the closing down of a regime, increasing stability, growing coherence or solidarity among elites, the loss of potential allies, and escalating repression, is likely to produce "declining extensiveness and effectiveness of contention" (2008, p. 91). Tilly (2008) then proposes that regime types and the capacity of the state matter.

To illustrate, in an undemocratic regime with a high-capacity state, we should expect stringent limits on (and control over) collective action. He illustrates this pattern with the case of increasing authoritarianism in Venezuela under President Hugo Chávez, whose government has controlled, banned, or monitored various forms of contentious politics, co-opting and repressing collective actors. In authoritarian Argentina, also a high-capacity, undemocratic regime, we observe similar patterns. This leads us back to the question of why and how Argentine movements emerged under such circumstances (and without expanding opportunities).

Recent efforts to apply the political opportunities framework to dissent in nondemocracies are certainly welcome, but the studies discussed here have not overcome the challenges noted earlier. A number of frustrating contradictions and competing hypotheses remain. Some scholars continue to identify a diverse array of factors as political opportunities and propose "broad and tautological" claims instead of "narrow and falsifiable" ones (Goodwin and Jasper 1999/2004b, p. 120). Finally, analysts trying to advance the political-process research agenda have not solved the conundrum of repression and contention.

RESPONSE TO AMY RISLEY
Alison Brysk

The debate over political opportunities is far from a purely academic exercise. While the identification of political opportunities can help to explain muted response to grievances and may guard against premature mobilization that triggers crippling repression, it offers little guidance for challengers facing closed political systems and intolerable oppression. Yet political opportunities, and even political structures, change in part through the agency of challengers against the odds. For this reason, my own research agenda centers on explaining when and why movements arise and succeed without sufficient political opportunities. To paraphrase an early theorist and activist, "people make their own history, although they do so under conditions not of their own choosing."

In order to continue this conversation, first I will explicate the conclusions of *The Politics of Human Rights in Argentina*, since Risley's essay correctly notes that I do not treat the concept of political opportunities explicitly in the text. Then, I will offer some refinements of my earlier treatment suggested by subsequent research. Finally, I will consider recent developments in Argentina and their implications for the debate on political opportunities.

Since my task in the 1994 text was to show that identity, grievances and agency mattered, I merely noted the closure of political opportunities due to repression, political deinstitutionalization, and the failure of all social structures outside the family. However, there are elements of the research suggesting a more nuanced view of political opportunity that may be helpful in addressing these kinds of cases. Political-process models do suggest a shifting scenario over time, and different degrees and dimensions of political opportunity may be relevant through the phases of movement mobilization: identity-building, recruitment, projection, and impact (see p. 38 for a general model). Thus some of the ironies I document, such as initial emergence under repression with declining movement impact during the consolidation phase of democratic transition, may be partially explained in terms of the increasing relevance of political opportunities during later stages of movement mobilization, and in "normal," institutional settings. But this reading of opportunity is more structural than an incentive or expectation-motivating agency.

As Risley points out, my findings also suggest that the opportunity structure must be treated as a multilevel process that includes international actors. Although in the Argentine case these latter offered mainly protection and projection, the literature on transnational networks and social movements shows that sometimes international opportunities can actually foster the emergence of challengers (Keck and Sikkink 1998). However, as my subsequent work on international indigenous movements demonstrates, this role is also connected to transnational grievances and identities, not just to the strategic alliances implied by the political-opportunity concept (Brysk 2000).

Turning now to extensions of my perspective that address Risley's critiques, she contends that I inappropriately conflate political-process, resource-mobilization, and rational-choice frameworks. In order to ground and situate my broader rejection of these economistic models, I subsequently wrote a general analysis of symbolic politics as a basis for both mobilization and projection of social movements (Brysk 1995). Analysts from the political-process tradition itself continue to extend their treatment of identity factors, notably through the concept of "framing" (Morris and McClurg Mueller 1992; McAdam, McCarthy, and Zald 1996). While both the literature and my own understanding have evolved to encompass more subtle and interactive relationships among the various alternative approaches, I will reiterate a fundamental distinction between political behavior based on strategic rationality and a politics of persuasion. Much of my symbolic politics approach in this study was prematurely constructivist, and many subsequent works on transnational social movements grant a leading role to "hearts and minds." The interaction between domestic and international "naming and shaming" has become almost the dominant explanation for the emergence and success of human rights movements (Keck and Sikkink 1998; Burgerman 2001; Hawkins 2002; Anaya Muñoz 2009).

This leads to Risley's most telling point, the need to elaborate the process of identity formation and to distinguish active from potential participants in the movement. The work under review did concentrate on documenting the impact rather than the formation of the movement, and can usefully be supplemented with more testimonial works such as Bouvard (1994), Fisher (1989), and the movement's own publications. Moreover, we now have Michelle Bonner's (2007) study that shows how maternalist identities as rights defenders were constructed in Argentina and then extended to new issues such as socioeconomic rights.

I touch on several elements of consciousness-raising in *The Politics of Human Rights*, which have been reinforced by my own subsequent work with other social movements and wider reading of the secondary literature. The first factor is role; participants form new identities more readily when grievances threaten a fundamental role such as mother, teacher, lawyer, or priest (including the subjective perception of that role; protective or passive mother? crusading or careerist lawyer?). A second factor is Other-identification, which inspires both altruistic risk taking and the formation of collective consciousness (such as "protesting for every mother's son"). Certain roles, previous experiences, and even ideologies promote higher levels of Other-identification. A third factor is the galvanizing effect of crisis and resistance and the later loss of purpose by some activists under objectively more favorable conditions. The immediate aftermath of repression may thus ironically generate more mobilization than the more peaceful lull that follows. Finally, as movements come to replace the families and communities shattered by repression, stigmatized identities become a source of pride and activists reinforce each others' resolve. Density of ties to the movement and a sense of mission will also inspire some to mobilize. I know of one family in which the victim's sister's mother-in-law took over the protest role, after years of assisting her in-laws' attempts and following the death of the victim's own mother, his sole remaining advocate. Although factors such as these can help us to identify probable precursors of mobilization at the macro level, they will seldom predict the microlevel behavior of individuals. For movements, it does not matter precisely which individuals mobilize, as long as some do.

In closing, I would like to expand on Risley's observation that the Argentine human rights movement survives a generation after its emergence. The movement's persistence and expansion into new areas of human rights struggle testify not only to the durability of identity-based mobilization, but also to the long-term potential of the opportunities created by that movement. Twenty years ago, only some of the seeds planted by the movement had sprouted: an international model for family-based protest and information-gathering, the healing power of investigations and "truth commissions," diffuse experiments in civic education, a citizens' lobby for military reform. One of the movement's key initiatives, widespread trials for military officers accused of human rights violations, appeared to have been stalemated, and the administration of Carlos Menem promised a diminished form of corrupt and unaccountable "delegative democracy" (O'Donnell 1994).

Today, although challenges persist, the movement's contributions to the Argentine political system and international human rights standards continue to generate new fruit. In the changed social climate, several middle-ranking officers finally confessed to their participation in the repression, acknowledging its scope and lack of military rationale, and solidifying social support for significant military reform. The longest-serving military ruler, General Videla, was rearrested in 1998 for kidnapping the children of detainees, while judiciaries in France, Spain, and the United States continue to call Argentine officers to account for crimes against humanity. In 2003, the Argentine Congress finally annulled the Due Obedience legislation that had shielded officers from prosecution if they were "just following orders." The Argentine Supreme Court overturned all of the various trial limitations in 2005, and systematic trials recommenced in 2009. To date, 1,400 military officers have been charged and sixty-eight convicted, including the last former military president and a group of officials responsible for one of the most notorious military concentration camps where dissidents were tortured and killed.

Because the Argentine movement made its own opportunities, it created new opportunities for those who would follow. A more dynamic, situated view shows that above and beyond policy change and political resources, movements produce social capital, symbolic capital, new repertoires of collective action, and legitimacy challenges to state power. Each of these facets of a movement's agency changes the game in the next wave of contention. Social movements are both subjects and agents of their own history.

REJOINDER TO ALISON BRYSK
Amy Risley

As Brysk suggests, human rights activists in Argentina did not merely respond to existing opportunities; they created their own. My research also supports these conclusions. Given the absence of political opportunities, what factors contributed to the movement's emergence? In this brief rejoinder, I continue the dialogue by identifying causal variables and mechanisms relevant to human rights mobilization in Argentina and to other movements, as well. A careful examination of human rights activism certainly entails scrutiny of the external, structural, and macro-level factors that help explain the movement's origins. However, micromobilizational factors ultimately provide more analytic purchase. Cultural, ideational, and emotional variables are especially salient. I will therefore focus on the emotions that fueled contentious politics in this case and propose that ordinary people whose personal lives were turned upside down by political violence subsequently transformed their pain and outrage into a collective struggle for truth and justice.

All investigations of protest movements that erupt under authoritarian rule begin with a discussion of political context. In Argentina, this environment was characterized by systematic and severe repression, the loss of traditional political institutions and spaces, and the silence or collusion of powerful actors. The social and cultural transformations that accompanied regime change, including growing fear and suspicion and the weakening of social bonds, were also significant. Of course, these contextual factors do not tell us *who* mobilizes under these circumstances or, for that matter, *why* they turn to collective action. We must trace the impact of external events on people's lives, families, and communities, as well as on individuals' psyches and identities. While performing this microlevel analysis of the Argentine case, we discover that emotions—love, sympathy, empathy, pain, grief, desperation, and outrage, for example—are undeniably important. Indeed, it would be nearly impossible for researchers to remain oblivious to this dimension of human rights mobilization during interviews with activists or participant-observation of their protests. Decades after the dictatorship, emotions remain intense.

According to Goodwin and Jasper's (2006) overview of the structural turn in the study of social movements, as sociologists embraced rational actor models and organizational theory, they became more concerned with *how* people mobilize than *why* they do so. Scholars often understood grievances (and individuals' emotions) to be pervasive and thus less "causally important or interesting" (2006, p. 615; see also Goodwin, Jasper, and Polletta 2000). In contrast, following the cultural turn, more researchers began to explore the "deep cultural and emotional processes that inspire and produce collective action" (Morris 2004, p. 246; see also Gould 2004, 2009; Aminzade and McAdam 2001).

Analysts have found emotions to be especially illuminating in cases of high-risk collective action (see Goodwin and Pfaff 2001). Wood (2001), for instance, suggests that peasants in El Salvador's opposition movement in the 1970s experienced pride and pleasure in their exercise of agency; they derived "emotional benefits" from participation even when facing the threat of violent reprisals. Similarly, human rights advocates in Southern Cone countries enhanced their sense of self-worth by assisting victims of state-sponsored abuses under difficult circumstances. A Chilean activist explained that "the suffering of the people I was helping was intolerable. . . . I would have lost my own dignity and self-respect if I hadn't done the work I did" (Loveman 1998, quoted in Einwohner 2003, p. 492). This quotation also captures the tremendous compassion and empathy that compelled individuals to participate in the movement. These emotions are equally relevant to the case of human rights activism in Argentina, where numerous professionals overcame their fear to assist the people most affected by repression.

The two principal types of emotions that Jasper (1998) delineates are likewise germane. "Affects" can include love for and loyalty to one's children, spouse, and other family members. These profound, abiding emotions shape the somewhat more fleeting emotions awakened by external events or changes. In the Argentine case, shock, grief, and anger accompanied the loss of loved ones amidst generalized fear and terror. Families of the detained and disappeared in particular suffered unbearable anguish and uncertainty; they were, in a word, "shattered" (Brysk 1994, p. 42). When this anguish was so great that it began to outweigh a person's fear for her own safety, when her sense of urgency overwhelmed any arguments against getting out and doing something, she was more likely to join the movement.

The death, disappearance, or suffering of a loved one is a fitting example of what Jasper refers to as a "moral shock," which occurs "when an unexpected event or piece of information raises such a sense of outrage in a person that she becomes inclined toward political action" (1998, p. 409; see also Goodwin and Jasper 2006). Moral indignation is a predictable reaction when one's family, home, community, or other objects of affection are threatened; it can be the basis for an initial step toward recruitment into a movement (Jasper 1998). The human rights movement also included people who had not lost a loved one but who nevertheless felt similar outrage. When state actions collide so forcefully with prevailing cultural values and deeply rooted identities, we should expect a strong emotional response. The practice of disappearing people violated the sanctity of the family as well as the basic tenets and rituals of Catholicism. Women and men who had internalized traditional gender roles experienced extreme contradictions when they were unable to protect loved ones—especially their children—from harm. Professionals who had pursued legal careers suddenly found themselves in a country without any semblance of due process or rule of law; and members of the clergy and other people of faith had to reconcile the military's stated goal of saving Western Christian civilization with its repressive policies. Similarly, Nepstad and Smith (2001) describe how cultural and social beliefs made members of religious communities "subjectively engageable," prone to experience moral outrage, and thus more likely to be recruited into the Central American peace movement in the United States. Many people of faith "embraced social teachings that emphasize peace, justice, and political engagement as essential expressions of religious commitment" (2001, p. 166). Their fidelity to these teachings created a sense of urgency and a need to respond to the atrocities being committed in Central American countries. Both cases underscore the necessity of considering broader cultural patterns, including preexisting identities, norms, and beliefs, that shape emotional responses to external events.

Additionally, participants in the emergent human rights movement recruited others by successfully transforming "emotional raw materials into specific beliefs and suggestions for action" (Goodwin and Jasper 2006, p. 619). Activists invented new forms of symbolic protest and political theater and used persuasive rhetoric. Collective action resulted in part from the "narrative structuring, interpretive resonance, and projection of affective information" that Brysk discusses in her work on symbolic politics (1995, p. 561). Their frames, much like "injustice" frames, entailed the "righteous anger that puts fire in the belly and iron in the soul" (Gamson 1992, p. 32, quoted in Goodwin and Jasper 2006, p. 617).

Targeting the military and its accomplices for this "righteous anger" helped human rights advocates recruit others into the movement. Brysk suggests that mobilizing messages identify and denounce a source of suffering and "redefine friend and foe" (1995, p. 577). These categories were clear cut for participants, who would create (and re-create) narratives about villains, victims, and heroes during their decades-long movement. For moral shocks to trigger collective action, something or someone must be blamed: the process of assigning blame involves "moral judgment" and an emotional change from dread to indignation (Jasper 1998). Whereas depression and resignation are said to inhibit political action, emotions such as outrage encourage it (Goodwin and Jasper 2006). Members of veteran human rights organizations have made similar observations about the grief and anger that put "iron" in their souls. Reflecting on her experiences during the dictatorship, one Madre noted that engaging in protest also allowed them to grieve publicly and collectively. They could (momentarily, at least) "unburden themselves of their pain." In contrast, most of the fathers of the disappeared were unable to experience the cathartic aspects of collective action; "*machismo* did not give males the right to cry, to scream." In her opinion, this helps explain why some of these men passed away prematurely or committed suicide.[12]

Stated briefly, the process of blaming the security forces and their collaborators for the atrocities of the Dirty War, casting judgment upon them, publicly expressing emotions, and arousing moral indignation in other people were all important factors facilitating mobilization. Outside observers would eventually criticize participants in the movement for clinging to these emotions long after the democratic transition; they viewed human rights advocates as too intransigent, fixated on the past, and invested in the politics of blame. Because many activists continued to make nonnegotiable, ethical demands in their pursuit of justice, critics charged that the movement was uncompromising and incapable of adapting to democratic politics, which reward "the logic of bargaining" (Brysk 1994, p. 20).

Outsiders began to challenge some of the narratives that identified the villains, victims, and heroes of the authoritarian period emanating from human rights organizations. In particular, simultaneous representations of the disappeared "as innocent victims of cruel and unwarranted repression and as heroes fighting for a just cause" raised doubts (Norden 1996, p. 98). Some participants

12. Interview with member of the Mothers of the Plaza de Mayo (Founding Branch), 7/8/97, Buenos Aires.

in HIJOS, for example, have sought not only to preserve the memory of their disappeared parents but also to continue the struggle of an entire generation of idealists who fought (both figuratively and literally) for a "more just" Argentina. Members of the Association of the Mothers of the Plaza de Mayo likewise have worked to vindicate the "beautiful youth" of that lost generation.[13]

Human rights activists were not alone in disseminating such narratives. Throughout the 1990s, family and friends of victims regularly published brief eulogies for the disappeared in major newspapers; some were identified openly as guerrilla fighters and praised for their dreams of "building a better world."[14] Nevertheless, the discourses used within certain human rights organizations provoked suspicion that their members were essentially apologists for armed revolutionaries on the far left.

Critics also thought that activists' lingering mistrust of state authorities, especially the police and the military, was unreasonable given that a constitutional regime was in place. On the other hand, it is not uncommon for civil societal actors in Argentina to hold adversarial attitudes vis-à-vis the state. Participants in social movements (and ordinary citizens) sometimes regard the state as "inherently authoritarian and corrupt" (Armony 2004, p. 149). Such views have a firm basis in reality; police using excessive force have shot and killed thousands of citizens, and scores of people have been subjected to torture, beatings, and ill treatment in police custody, as well as arbitrary arrests, disappearances, and executions (Armony 2004; Brinks 2003). According to victims' advocates, the authorities continue to employ dictatorship-era tactics through the "application of updated methods" (CORREPI 1995). Human rights activists often frame this violence as institutionalized forms of "illegal repression" and enduring legacies of authoritarianism (CELS 1997, p. 19; Risley 2006). They also conclude that some "agents of the state do not defend the public interest" (CELS 1997, p. 19). Thus the human rights movement still mobilizes people by identifying certain state authorities as targets for "righteous anger." Indignation is a strong and pervasive emotion that has fueled myriad protests in Argentina.

• • •

13. Interviews with members of HIJOS, 7/31/97, and Association of the Mothers of the Plaza de Mayo, 7/4/97, Buenos Aires. Although some of the interviewees' loved ones were members of armed revolutionary groups, others were involved in nonviolent causes.

14. *Página 12*, issue dated 7/16/97.

I have suggested that emotional variables such as pain, grief, outrage, love, and compassion must be included in any explanation of human rights mobilization in Argentina. Taking these factors seriously and, in the process, moving from the macro to the micro level would also deepen our understanding of other cases of contentious politics. By continuing to investigate cultural, ideational, and emotional variables, scholars can perhaps remedy some of the shortcomings of existing studies, including structural biases, an overemphasis on factors external to a movement, and a curious neglect of agency (Goodwin and Jasper 1999/2004b; Morris 2004). In the process of developing and refining these causal mechanisms further, mid-range theories of the emergence and evolution of social movements will be generated. Analysts will hopefully avoid the Scylla of searching for one universally applicable set of causes and the Charybdis of concluding that each movement is unique in its origins and that the quest for theory is therefore futile.

4 Rural Unions in Brazil

Anthony Pereira's *The End of the Peasantry*

JOHN L. HAMMOND

ANTHONY W. PEREIRA'S *The End of the Peasantry* discusses farmworkers' unions in the sugar-growing region of the state of Pernambuco in northeastern Brazil between 1961 and 1988. The time span encompasses the end of a populist regime, twenty-one years of military rule, and the first three years of civilian rule after the dictatorship. This quarter century also witnessed a dramatic transformation of agriculture throughout Brazil. In the northeastern sugar zone, landholding became more concentrated and processing more capital intensive. Many precarious landholders were squeezed off their subsistence farms and entered the wage-earning proletariat. The military regime permitted them to organize unions within Brazil's corporatist system of labor relations, but some leaders learned to transcend the limits of the system and use the unions to serve the class interests of the farmworkers. As farmworkers came to recognize the unions' representation of their interests as wageworkers, Pereira argues, they surrendered their utopian dream of individual landholding.

The cultivation of sugar has played a major role in Brazilian history. The northeast coast was the area of earliest Portuguese colonization, and today's state of Pernambuco was its center. Europe's craving for sugar enriched the colony and set the pattern for subsequent agricultural commodity booms that, facing volatile demand, formed the basis of the colony's (and later the country's) always precarious prosperity. The northeastern sugar fields were the destination for most of the enslaved Africans whose descendants make up more than half of Brazil's population today.

Labor-intensive cultivation, the enrichment of landowners, and racism also set the pattern for Brazil's concentration of landholding, wealth, and income at levels of inequality that remain among the highest in the world. Though the importance of sugar to the world economy declined after the eighteenth century, the sugar-growing oligarchs are still the dominant economic and political force in northeastern Brazil. They continue to practice traditional clientelistic politics. Through their control of local political machines and their unequal political representation, they exert a disproportionate political weight nationally. Landowners have used their power, including extralegal means, to inhibit rural organizing and have left the mass of the population of the northeast suffering the worst poverty in the country.

Organizations representing peasants and farmworkers nevertheless began to form in the 1950s when relations of production in the sugar fields started to change. Changes spurred by technological advances were intensified by state intervention, and modernization and capitalist development ultimately deprived many subsistence peasants of their land. Traditionally, peasants without land of their own had scratched out a living on underutilized plantations. Some squatted on marginal land, others rented plots or performed labor services on the sugar plantations and cultivated clientelistic ties of dependence with landowners who granted them access to land, credit, and occasional favors. As landowners modernized their operations and invested more capital, however, they concentrated their landholdings and expelled the tenants.

As a result, rural unrest grew in the 1950s. It took two forms. Its most radical expression was the Ligas Camponesas (Peasant Leagues), which arose in Pernambuco and spread to other states, calling for a radical agrarian reform that would redistribute land to those who worked it. Inspired by the Cuban revolution, a wing of the Leagues prepared for armed struggle. Unionization offered farmworkers an alternative model. President João Goulart sponsored a Rural Labor Statute, passed in 1963, that was intended to channel rural labor unrest into trade unions within the existing corporatist labor relations system. The Communist party, the Church, and supporters of the Goulart regime competed to organize new unions.

Brazil's landowning class responded to rural unrest with alarm. Suppressing peasant agitation was a key objective of the 1964 coup that brought to power the military dictatorship that ruled until 1985. The new government immediately dealt a crushing blow to rural organizing, outlawing the Leagues, restricting the unions, and persecuting and jailing the leaders of both. The successive military governments also initiated a process with more long-term consequences: they stimulated the conservative modernization of Brazil's agrarian economy (as well as its industrial economy). Until then Pernambuco had been losing ground to the newly emerging sugar-cultivating areas of the southeastern state of São Paulo. At first the regime favored the newer, more highly capitalized São Paulo growers, but in 1975 it adopted a major program to promote ethanol-powered cars in order to reduce the country's dependence on imported oil. The state provided incentives to manufacturers to produce the vehicles and to landowners in both regions to increase sugar production.

As the sugar plantations modernized, the demand for unskilled labor dropped. Peasants declined in numbers and were replaced by a diversified labor force. The new labor force cannot be called a proletariat, because even today not all its members live exclusively from wage labor. Pereira calls them a "peasantariat," because they share "characteristics of both peasants and

---

MAJOR EVENTS IN BRAZIL'S NATIONAL POLITICS AND THE RURAL UNION MOVEMENT

1889: Abolition of slavery

1955–1964: Peasant League organizing

1962: Miguel Arraes elected governor of Pernambuco

1963: Rural Labor Statute stimulates union organizing

April 1, 1964: Military coup topples Goulart government (and Arraes government in Pernambuco), outlawing the Peasant Leagues and restricting the unions

1975: Proálcol program founded to stimulate manufacture of ethanol from sugar cane, resulting in the modernization of sugar cultivation and a drop in the demand for unskilled labor

1979: *Abertura* (political opening) permits resumption of rural union organizing

October 2–8, 1979: Strike in Pernambuco sugar zone

1982: Direct elections for governors allowed in Brazil

1985: Civilian president Tancredo Neves named (died before taking office; his vice-president José Sarney assumes presidency)

1986: Miguel Arraes elected governor of Pernambuco

1988: New constitution promulgated with weak agrarian reform provisions

workers . . . seasonal and temporary work, migration, informal (and illegal) work, occasional ownership of small plots of land, and kinship ties with other smallholders" (pp. 60–61). Nevertheless, as field-workers came increasingly to depend on wage labor, he argues, they had more interest in higher wages and improved working conditions than in land ownership.

The dictatorship did not outlaw unions. Urban unions of industrial and service workers continued to operate under the corporatist labor relations framework created during the so-called "New State" of President Getúlio Vargas (1930–1945), following the Italian fascist model. That framework was extended to rural areas by Goulart's Rural Labor Statute. Though the statute was a product of the regime they had deposed, the military rulers recognized its promise of incorporating rural labor and containing unrest. It provided for the creation of unions of small farmers and farmworkers; the unions would give them access to the labor court system and be a conduit for welfare benefits. (There is a *sindicato* [union] in place in each *município*. I refer to these county-level unions in the plural, but individual farmworkers are eligible to join only one union, determined by the location of the workplace.)

The government hemmed in the unions with restrictions. It had the power to intervene and unseat elected union leaders, and did so whenever they threatened to use their office to organize political opposition. At the same time, however, the government co-opted the unionists with privileges for the organizations and benefits for their members. The Federation of Agricultural Workers of Pernambuco (FETAPE), founded in 1962, and farmworkers' federations in other states, grouped in the national Confederation of Agricultural Workers (CONTAG), expanded during the military dictatorship.

The corporatist system was set up to ensure the subordination of the unions to the government and to deny them autonomy to represent workers' interests. As French (1992) argues, however, industrial workers were often able to use the system to their advantage. At times they have dramatically broken through its limits; in the late 1970s, industrial unions became the key element of opposition to the dictatorship. In 1979 the military government declared an *abertura* (opening), which began the slow transition to a restored democracy. Unions seized the opportunity. Organizing metalworkers in the São Paulo industrial belt, the "new unionists" conducted illegal strikes and won some major concessions, not only increased wages but the de facto right to circumvent the legally mandated centralized bargaining at the level of the entire industrial sector and to bargain with individual employers.

Unrest spread to the sugar fields as well. Unions found ways to use the state-sponsored structure and the resources it had allowed them to accumulate, just as urban unions had done, to challenge the repressive regime. The rural unions of Pernambuco struck for a week in 1979. They won some important concessions, including collective bargaining. In contrast to the metalworkers, the farmworkers' unions did not favor decentralized bargaining; bargaining with individual growers would have weakened them. Using the existing system of labor relations to their best advantage, the rural unions in Pernambuco and elsewhere became a "powerful political force" (p. xvi).

As rural unions grew stronger, leaders and activists were targeted for violence paid for by landowners, despite the union's moderate, reformist posture. Landowners have long used hired guns to intimidate farmworkers from organizing. They resorted to violence more as the country edged toward democracy and government security forces no longer reliably suppressed worker organization. The readiness of landowners to use violence, Pereira shows, depended on the degree of modernization of agriculture. In those parts of the country where unskilled labor was no longer a major factor of production, paramilitary violence was rare. Where there was still a large unskilled labor force so that growers' profits depended on keeping wages down—as in Pernambuco, which despite some progress was still backward relative to the southern agricultural regions—landowners did not hesitate to deploy it. Outside Pereira's scope is the vast agricultural frontier where land speculators were unhindered in organizing paramilitary bands to attack squatters.

Pereira shows that the unions were weak actors in partisan politics—partly because the union leaders had little power to sway the votes of their members, but mainly because the party system was fragmented and clientelistic: national parties were weak and candidates typically traded favors for votes at the local level rather than subscribing to a programmatic party platform. Unions too found that engaging in electoral activity to defend general union interests achieved less than clientelistic trading with those who won office. Such dependence governed the unions' access to political spoils just as it governed peasants' access to land. The establishment of a civilian (though still not elected) government in 1985 changed little in the sugar zones. Pereira ends his study with the Constituent Assembly, which was elected in 1986 and produced the new democratic constitution of 1988. Advocates of agrarian reform hoped that the drafting of a new constitution would provide a crucial opportunity. President Sarney presented a proposal with a strong plank sanctioning land expropriations, and supporters and opponents mobilized public demonstrations and lobbying efforts. Some organizations of the rural poor, notably those supported by the Church's Pastoral Land Commission, took direct action, occupying farmlands around the country. While CONTAG and its affiliated unions promoted parliamentary pressure, they rejected direct action and viewed the Church-inspired militants as rivals. Landowners, meanwhile, lobbied against the reform provisions. They also stepped up the violent attacks on farmworkers and land occupiers; according to the Pastoral Land Commission's annual tallies, killings in land conflicts peaked in the late 1980s, reaching 161 in 1987 (Comitê Rio Maria, n.d.).

Opponents of land reform mobilized more effectively than supporters, and won. The 1988 Constitution contains only weak provisions for agrarian reform. In essence, land can only be expropriated if it is not producing. Landholdings that are productively farmed, however large, are not subject to expropriation. Criteria for expropriation were actually more restrictive than those of the land statute that the military government had decreed in 1964.

For Pereira, the unions' lukewarm position on land reform confirms the transformation of rural unionism from militant support for agrarian transformation to business unionism. FETAPE leaders, like the national CONTAG leadership, publicly demanded land reform but did not support other groups that occupied idle farms in Pernambuco and claimed the right to farm them. The unions' priorities were with the farmworkers, not with winning land for the tillers. CONTAG called for agrarian reform rhetorically because it had a greater base among smallholders nationally than its Pernambuco state affiliate had. But even the national federation put most of its energy into working within the much-changed agrarian system of Brazil to win its members advantages that nevertheless did not challenge the hegemony of big agricultural capital, such as better wages and working conditions for workers, and credit and marketing facilities for small producers. It accepted the domination of landlords and agribusiness. Rank and file members of the union, Pereira argues, no longer aspired to land of their own.

Pereira presents a clear, concise account of the transformation of rural labor and its organizations during this period. He makes good use of a variety of data sources: survey research, fieldwork, and archives. While his explanation is rooted in political economy—changes in the production process gave rise to changes in the agricultural labor force, which in turn altered the unions' potential base—he gives due credit to the role of the state in stimulating the changes in production and in establishing the corporatist framework within which rural unions organized.

He also pays attention to the role of popular culture in forming peasant identities and thereby affecting the possible scope of union action; he examines the preservation of a peasant cultivator consciousness in *literatura de cordel*, the Brazilian equivalent of pulp fiction, and in popular music. In a tantalizing but brief discussion, he compares the almost yearly strikes to carnival. In both, social hierarchy is inverted and people act in ways that are normally forbidden. During a strike, field-workers lay down their tools and stop working, they can challenge foremen, and union leaders can move freely about the plantations (p. 65).

Pereira says the union became a powerful political force in the 1980s, but that characterization is not entirely borne out by his own evidence—or, perhaps, "powerful" is a relative term and the union can be called that only in comparison to its weakness in the 1970s and the almost complete lack of effective representative structures before that. Clearly unions had some successes in representing worker interests. They gained somewhat improved wages and used the corporatist labor system to channel some government welfare benefits to workers. Pereira nevertheless portrays them as ambivalent ideologically, weak in relation to the party structure, and relatively powerless to resist landlord violence. Their strength lies in their adhering to and accepting the existing system, taking advantage of it and conveying its benefits to their members rather than challenging it.

Pereira sees this essentially as acceptance of the inevitable or, at least, the best possible deal for members. To continue to pursue land redistribution, he suggests, would be to pursue a utopian vision in the face of the irresistible advance of the big landowners. Some might question this implication of inevitability.

Agricultural Modernization and Union Growth

The consolidation of the power of the farmworkers' union in the sugar zone between the coup and the end of the military regime, Pereira argues, was due to the modernization of agriculture and state incentives for rural union formation.

First, the military government sponsored a conservative modernization of agriculture throughout Brazil. In sugar, the ethanol program provided a particular stimulus to adopt new, capital-intensive technologies. The composition of the labor force changed as precarious landholders lost their land and the salaried labor force grew in both the fields and the sugar mills. Peasants were replaced by a wageworking labor force, heterogeneous in skills and salary levels. Pereira calls this process *de-peasantization* in preference to *proletarianization* because most peasants did not become stably employed salaried workers, the number of small farmers grew, and many wageworkers were semiproletarians, retaining some access to land (pp. 13, 60–61). Many others, of course, abandoned the countryside entirely and migrated to the cities.

These changes expanded the potential base of the unions. The extension of the corporatist labor framework to the countryside and the state regulation of organized labor made the unions privileged instruments, gave them institutional resources, and thus affected their ability to recruit and mobilize. The legally mandated union structure directly conditioned the possibilities for union expansion. Labor laws dictate that unions are organized at the county level. They have a monopoly of representation, so that the union that has been recognized by the Ministry of Labor organizes all the workers in a given occupational category in a county, and no competing unions can be created. Union members pay compulsory dues, known as the *imposto sindical* (union tax), through a checkoff system. The national system of labor courts is the principal mechanism to resolve grievances; collective bargaining takes second place. Unions provide legal, medical, and dental services, and in some cases administer pensions, for their members (p. 81). Under this structure the local unions have an automatic claim on membership. They play a major role in welfare service delivery, especially in rural areas where few alternatives are available, and are responsible for administering large budgets.

This description applies to all categories of unions nationwide. In the rural unions, monopoly of representation means that salaried farmworkers and small farmers are members of the same union. Because farmers do not receive a salary, there is no checkoff for them, so their contributions are in effect voluntary; if they join, it is generally to take advantage of the welfare benefits. In Pernambuco, local unions in the sugar zone had mostly farmworkers as members, whereas union members in the poverty-stricken interior of the state were more likely to be small farmers with access to land as owners (de jure or de facto) or renters (under various cash and noncash arrangements). Both groups, with rather different interests, belong to the same union in any county.

This system makes the unions vehicles of incorporation and discourages worker militancy, and not only by putting different categories of workers with potentially conflicting interests in the same unions. Administering health-care delivery fills unions by bringing in government revenue and thus makes local union office attractive, but it places a heavy administrative burden on elected officers. Monopoly of representation minimizes political competition for union office. Because local officials play no significant role in statewide collective bargaining, they have little incentive to organize their members for union activism. As a result, unions rarely take militant action to assert workers' demands, though exceptions do occur, such as the 1979 strike.

On those exceptional occasions, unions take advantage of the very structure the state established to contain them. During the military dictatorship, they became virtually the only representative of rural workers, and they have remained so since. In Pereira's argument, their predominance was due to the changes in sugar production that expanded the base of the unions, and to the legal structure and incentives that stimulated union organization to incorporate that base. The dictatorship not only repressed other forms of farmworker organization, but also gave the unions facilities that enabled them to increase their membership and ultimately to challenge the dictatorship itself. The unions developed a solid base from which they could mobilize once the 1979 political opening or *abertura* gave an opportunity, and urban unions led the way in taking advantage of it.

Expanding Opportunities?

In explaining how the unions were able to mobilize farmworkers, Pereira emphasizes structural factors:

> The argument made here is that opportunities for action are explained mainly by macropolitical factors at the level of the national regime; capacities to act are influenced primarily by large historical processes—changes in social structure and the institutional form of representative institutions; and ideology and strategy are explained by the members' and especially the leaders' learning through experience and through local traditions and institutions (p. 11).

Opportunities thus find a place in Pereira's argument, but his emphasis is on capacities, determined mainly by economic and institutional structure. Can the experience of the farmworkers' unions in the sugar zone of Pernambuco nevertheless be taken as a test of the claims of political-opportunity theory? That theory suggests that at any given time a polity can be characterized by a specific political opportunity structure (POS), and that different POSs can be compared along a series of dimensions as more or less conducive to one or another outcome. The theory has many variants. Different authors offer different definitions of the POS, identify different dimensions, analyze its effects over varying time spans, and use it to explain different outcomes. I adopt the dimensions of political opportunity structure McAdam proposes (1996, p. 27): political access, elite competition, elite allies, and (negatively) repression.

For Brazil, the POS is best defined at the federal level. Although Pereira mentions politics at the state and local levels, he finds them relatively unimportant. Local-level politics is dominated by clientelism; state politics, although it is somewhat independent of clientelism and offers some potential allies, is nevertheless still largely organized by traditional elites who do not offer clear programmatic alternatives.

Between 1961 and 1988 Brazilian politics went through four distinct periods, each with a specific POS: 1961–1964, the presidency of João Goulart; 1964–1979, the first fifteen years of military rule following the 1964 coup; 1979–1985, the period of *abertura*, the lengthy, sponsored transition to democracy; and 1985–1988, the first years of civilian rule before the adoption of a new constitution. The conduciveness of the POS to mobilization varied significantly across this time span.

The changes from each period to the next include one deep rupture and two significant evolutionary changes. The new regime instituted in 1964 was fundamentally different from its predecessor. The post-1964 period is marked by two breaks, in 1979 and 1985, and thus three different POSs (1964–1979, 1979–1985, and 1985–1988), but the breaks were not nearly so decisive as in 1964. Political opportunities for organized labor changed little between the end of military rule and the period of restored civilian rule from 1985 to 1988, when Pereira ends his case study. The same labor legislation prevailed, and the structure and activity of the trade unions remained fundamentally the same.

McAdam treats the dimensions of POS quantitatively: they are more open or more closed according to the degree to which they permit protest or impede it. In examining the POS faced by the rural unions, I argue, one must also recognize qualitative variation. Conditions in the sugar zone became drastically less conducive to mobilization in 1964 and improved at each of the two subsequent inflection points, 1979 and 1985. The dictatorship quashed all mobilization—a severe quantitative decline—but the change from democracy to dictatorship in 1964 also brought a qualitative change in opportunities for unionization. The new opportunity structure was less conducive, but the opportunities it did offer were of a different kind. Unions gradually organized to take advantage of these new opportunities.

I take as the dependent variable the level of mobilization, departing both from McAdam, who claims that the POS should predict the timing, outcome, and form of protest—though it is not clear whether by "outcome" he means the substantive change that may result or the way in which a protest ends (McAdam 1996, p. 29)—and from the other essays in this volume, which focus on the emergence of movements. (By including *movement form* among the dependent variables, McAdam acknowledges qualitative as well as quantitative variation.) In Brazil during the period under examination, farmworkers mobilized in different structures and for different objectives. Between 1961 and 1964 two main types of organizations competed to represent rural workers in the sugar zone: the Peasant Leagues, which fought for land redistribution, and the unions, which worked for improved conditions of employment. After 1964 the Leagues were wiped out. All mobilization was channeled into the unions, and the ideological competition between unions sponsored by the communists, the Church, and the regime was no longer visible.

Nonetheless, predictions of the form of movement activity that will follow from a particular change in the POS have an ad hoc, unsystematic character. That is the case for McAdam's predictions (1996, pp. 29–31), and, admittedly, for my own observation of the changing form of farmworker mobilization following the 1964 coup. I will therefore focus on quantitative variation and examine the level of farmworker mobilization in relation to changes in the dimensions of POS that McAdam identifies.

In Table 4.1 I indicate schematically the strength of each of these factors (impressionistically estimated) during each of the four periods noted above. These

TABLE 4.1 Brazil's National Political Opportunity Structure, 1961–1988

	Second Republic 1961–1964	Dictatorship (1st period) 1964–1979	*Abertura* 1979–1985	Post-military 1985–1988
Political access	++	-	+	++
Elite competition	++	-	+	++
Elite allies	++	-	+	+
Repression[1]	+	--	+	+
Farmworker mobilization	++	--	++	+

[1] + means less repression: POS more conducive to mobilization

characterizations reflect shifts in opportunity structure at the federal level. Pereira, I should note, does not specifically examine them. We can nevertheless see that the opportunity structure that the Pernambuco unions faced changed over time in tandem with the rest of the country's. Conditions were most favorable to mobilization during the Goulart regime, declined precipitously with the installation of the military government, improved somewhat with the *abertura*, and improved even more with the end of military rule. The most dramatic break is between the first and second periods: access, elite competition, and elite alliances all fell sharply, while repression increased dramatically.

These assessments must be qualified, however. First, while the level of official repression declined significantly with the return of a civilian regime in 1985, the level of covert repression increased. Violence by hired guns, paid for by landowners, escalated in many rural areas across the country, including the Pernambucan sugar zone. (It is admittedly a moot point whether the behavior of private parties should be considered part of the POS, but in the present case paramilitary violence cannot be ignored.) Second, the availability of elite allies in Pernambuco varied somewhat independently of the national level. The Brazilian Democratic Movement Party (PMDB), a moderate left-wing party, won the governorship of Pernambuco in 1986, but as Pereira shows, its rule was not as favorable to farmworker interests as union leaders had hoped.

. . .

Do these variables, representing the different dimensions of POS, accurately predict the outcome that interests us, namely, the level of farmworker mobilization? At first glance they do. Mobilization virtually disappeared with the dictatorship, and rose again with the *abertura*. Examined more closely, however, the relationships shown here fail to correspond to those emphasized by political-opportunity theory. While the conduciveness of the political opportunity structure increased steadily from 1964 to 1988, mobilization did not. The break from the military regime in 1985 did not bring any particular upsurge of mobilization, which seems to have peaked in the 1979–1985 period and was a stimulus to, rather than a result of, the change in political regime. Thus the POS influenced levels of farmworker mobilization, but the relationship appears to be curvilinear, with mobilization rising as opportunities improved, but only up to a point.

The fact that mobilization rose for a time as opportunities increased and then fell or leveled off even though opportunities continued to grow more favorable can be explained in two different ways, not necessarily inconsistent with each other. First, it might reflect success. Farmworker mobilization may have declined after 1985 when the formal structure of opportunities appeared more favorable because the unions achieved a stable bargaining relationship with the sugar growers, one that brought some improvements in wages and conditions with each new contract. Achieving a stable place within the polity, a movement may adopt more conventional and less costly forms of organization. Whether one regards this shift as a sign of success or of cooptation, it means that mobilization is superseded by institutional action (Gamson 1990; Meyer and Minkoff 1997, p. 9; Oxhorn 1994; Piven and Cloward 1977).

A second possibility has more profound implications for political-opportunity theory. Mobilization may depend on preparatory organization that occurs under distinctly unfavorable opportunity structures such as prevailed in Brazil during the 1970s. Opportunities for organizing rural unions became more favorable than they had ever been, even though they were circumscribed by the official union structure. The opportunity structure in most of Brazil was not at all conducive, however, as the dictatorship regularly discouraged and repressed public mobilization. New movements nevertheless arose, recruited members, and accumulated resources. New methods of organizing spread through the country mainly under the auspices of the progressive Church and, at first, without an overt political program.

Outbursts of public protest that appear sudden and spontaneous to outsiders often depend on a lengthy but invisible process of preparation (see Morris 1984). Movements of workers, neighborhoods, and women that formed in urban Brazil in the 1970s could not draw on even the modest resources that the Rural Labor Statute had offered the rural unions, and they acted cautiously because activists were rightly afraid of infiltration and repression. When the farmworkers of the sugar zone went on strike in 1979, their unions tagged along behind these movements—especially the new industrial unionism. Most versions of POS theory define political opportunity by rather volatile elements of the political system (though there are exceptions; see Gamson and Meyer 1996, pp. 277–79). Farmworker mobilization was part of a national pattern of more gradual change that did not depend primarily on short-run changes in regime behavior and for which a POS explanation is therefore inappropriate.

In broad strokes, then, demobilization and mobilization of Pernambucan farmworkers correspond to the closing and reopening of the opportunity structure; examined more closely, opportunity structure and mobilization diverge. Farmworker mobilization in 1979 was part of a countrywide movement far out of proportion to the change in opportunity structure represented by the *abertura*. It declined after 1985 when the political opening became even more favorable. So while the organization of unions during the 1970s depended in part on the opening of a specific opportunity structure, the later course of mobilization cannot be explained by POS theory.

In summary, what POS analysis tells us about the specifics of the farmworkers' movement in the sugar zone of eastern Pernambuco is limited. Variation in the opportunity structure accounts less well for changes in farmworker mobilization over time than does variation in the class structure and the extent of farmworker organization. Opportunity may be determined at least as much by shifts in underlying structural factors, and movements can organize quietly and lay bases for later public activity even when opportunity structures are highly unfavorable.

RESPONSE TO JOHN HAMMOND
Anthony W. Pereira

I found John Hammond's analysis of my book to be careful, balanced, and concerned with big questions. It is probably the most detailed review the book has received. I agree with John Hammond that the Pernambuco case suggests that underlying structural factors can be as influential as the political opportunity structure in shaping the degree and character of social movement mobilization. Overall, my disagreements with Hammond's arguments are minor. Perhaps most important, by pointing to the issue of land redistribution, Hammond suggests that my book mistakenly assumes that certain structural elements (as well as the POS) in the sugar zone were permanent rather than conjunctural. With hindsight, I think this criticism is accurate.

Hammond divides up the periods of my study and argues that there were four distinct political opportunity structures facing the rural labor movement in Pernambuco. I think that overall, his characterization is accurate, and reflects a careful reading of the events described in the book. However, I disagree that the 1985 inauguration of a civilian president, José Sarney, represented a major political opening for the Pernambuco trade unions. My interviews with the labor leaders revealed that the majority did not see it in such terms. Of much greater significance to them was the reinstitution of direct elections (and hence interparty competition) for governor in 1982, and the election of Miguel Arraes in 1986—both changes at the level of state, rather than federal politics. In addition, the rural trade unions probably had as many elite allies in 1985–1988 as they did in 1961–1964. Consequently, my case neither fully confirms nor denies the predictive power of the political-opportunity approach, although it does show that the unions were able to make the largest impact on local politics when opportunities were opening at the national level, due to the pressure of other social movements.

Such an outcome is probably rather common because, in my view, the political-opportunity approach is not a clearly specified theory that links a set of changes to the forms and impacts of social movements. In Meyer's defense of political-process research, for example, he refers to it alternately as "theories," an "approach," a "tradition," and a "theory" (Meyer 1999), reflecting some ambiguity about its status. It seems to me to be a loose collection of approaches that share common use of a template of significant variables. These variables are so inclusive that almost every significant aspect of politics can be grouped within them. Hence, it seems that the concept of political opportunity is a helpful way to start thinking about social movements, rather than a definitive resolution of the puzzle of what facilitates their mobilization and shapes their activities and political influence.

Hammond is right to emphasize that the rural trade unions in Pernambuco became powerful in the 1980s only in relation to their relative powerlessness and subordination in the 1970s. However, the 1979 strike showed that union militants had been working quietly behind the scenes to increase unions' capacity for coordinated action and demand making. Thus an unpromising POS that inhibits social union mobilization may furnish the conditions for long-term, grassroots organizing that can be drawn upon once the POS liberalizes. Similarly, a relatively open POS may not see sustained levels of movement mobilization, or at least effective mobilization. This is how I see the difference between rural trade union organizing in Pernambuco in 1985–1988 compared to the earlier period of 1979–1985. It is not really the case, as Hammond argues, that the level of mobilization declined. The 1988 strike involved tens of thousands of workers, as had previous strikes that decade. The difference was that the strike had been routinized and, in the context of high inflation, increasingly ineffective as a means of improving sugar cane cutters' wages and working conditions.

Hammond is quite correct to question the inevitability of the decline in demands for land redistribution in the Pernambuco sugar zone. In hindsight, I now realize that in *The End of the Peasantry* I assumed that the structural trend I had described—the rise and dominance of capital-intensive large estates producing sugar cane for both ethanol and sugar production, and the consequent decline of smallholder agriculture—was irreversible. But the 1990s showed that it was not. Instead, a crisis in the sugar sector led to the emergence of the landless movement as the most important social movement in the Pernambuco sugar zone, eclipsing the trade unions. Land occupations, organized by the Landless Workers Movement (Movimento dos Sem Terra; MST) and other groups, took place throughout the region, impelling the trade unions to become increasingly involved in that struggle. This structural change in the sugar sector and the patterns of land use in the region, combined with an opening of the POS at the national level, meant that in the late 1990s the landless movement was one of the most politically dynamic forces in Pernambuco, as well as Brazil (see Gabriel Ondetti, *Land, Protest, and Politics* [2008]).

Wolford argues that Pernambuco's rural workers, unlike their counterparts in southern Brazil, tended not to see land reform in terms of their right to an individual plot of land. Because individually owned small farms had historically never been prevalent in the Pernambuco sugar zone, workers who engaged in land occupations there were just as interested in regular employment as they were in land ownership per se (see Wendy Wolford, *This Land Is Ours Now* [2010]). This is perhaps another indication of the limitation of the POS framework. While Hammond argues that the POS can be used to explain both the quantitative level of social movement mobilization (number of collective actions, number of people involved in each action, and so on) and the more qualitative issues of the timing, form, and outcome of social movement protest, what it cannot necessarily do is shed light on the content of social movement demands. As many other chapters in this volume show, demands are shaped historically, in the articulation and rearticulation of claims on state authorities. If the POS framework can help us understand the "how" and "when" of social movement protest, different approaches are needed to make sense of the "what."

REJOINDER TO ANTHONY PEREIRA
John L. Hammond

My intention in discussing Pereira's book was not to review it, but, like other essays in this volume, to see what light his findings and analysis shed on political opportunity structure theory (POS). This examination shows the need to qualify that theory; I did not intend my essay as a complaint that *The End of the Peasantry* failed to fit the theory. Pereira says in his reply that POS is "not a clearly specified theory that links a set of changes to the forms and impacts of social movements," and that "it seems that the concept of political opportunity is a helpful way to start thinking about social movements, rather than a definitive resolution of the puzzle of what facilitates their mobilization and shapes their activities and political influence." I agree completely. As I said in my essay, "predictions of the form of movement activity that will follow from a particular change in the POS have an ad hoc, unsystematic character."

Our main remaining disagreement has to do with the precise periodization of change in POSs. Pereira argues that the turning point in political opportunity relevant to the Pernambuco sugar workers was not the return to civilian rule at the national level in 1985 but the 1982 and 1986 gubernatorial elections in the state (two turning points?). Then, however, he says the Pernambuco unions had their biggest impact "when opportunities were opening at the national level." In any case, the choice of dates does not affect the analysis of the changes in political opportunity structure during the democratization period.

PART 2
    THE NORTH AMERICAN CONTEXT

5 The Civil Rights Movement

Charles Payne's *I've Got the Light of Freedom*

FRANCESCA POLLETTA

I N THE FALL OF 1962, few would have predicted that Greenwood, Mississippi, was about to become a hotbed of civil rights insurgency. Located in the Mississippi delta, legendary for its intransigent racism, Greenwood was still dominated by a planter class determined to retain its grip on the black residents who made up two-thirds of the county's population and owned less than a tenth of its land. The notorious White Citizens' Council (WCC) had its national headquarters in Greenwood. Counting a membership of 80,000 within two years of its founding in 1954, the WCC relied on economic reprisals and physical intimidation to destroy state chapters of the National Association for the Advancement of Colored People (NAACP). Outright murder was also part of the segregationist repertoire. In 1955 alone, seven black activists were killed.

When in the summer of 1962, an organizer from the Student Nonviolent Coordinating Committee (SNCC) began to have some success in persuading black residents to attempt to register to vote, county officials responded by cutting off the federal surplus commodities—meal, rice, flour, and sugar—on which 27,000 mostly black residents depended to survive the winter.

Cutting off the food supplies proved a tactical blunder, however. Through its central office in Atlanta and support chapters around the country, SNCC put out a nationwide call for food, clothing, and medical supplies. In distributing the donations, SNCC workers gave preference to residents who were suffering reprisals for attempting to register to vote. Voter registration efforts

rose dramatically. On February 25 and 26, 1963, 150 local black residents attempted to register, the largest group at one time in the Black Belt. White harassment kept apace, but now arrests and violence against civil rights workers
only spurred more mobilization. Over one hundred residents protested the arrest of the original SNCC organizer, Sam Block. When another SNCC worker
was shot, fifty more organizers descended on the county, along with national
movement leaders and celebrities. Voter registration efforts continued, joined
by marches—sometimes two a day—and rallies. Food and clothing distribution reached 1,349 people in the first three weeks of March. Greenwood put
police officers on twelve-hour/seven-day-a-week shifts, brought in personnel
from surrounding counties, and filled the city jail, but they were unable to stem
the mass mobilization. They stopped using police dogs when SNCC provided
the national media with photos of civil rights workers being attacked.

How to account for the Greenwood insurgency? It is tempting to view it as
an extension of a movement that had begun elsewhere. In what Doug McAdam
(1982) describes as a second phase of civil rights insurgency, formal political
organizations such as SNCC eclipsed the local and often non-political organi-

MAJOR EVENTS IN THE U.S. CIVIL RIGHTS MOVEMENT

April 3, 1944: U.S. Supreme Court outlaws the white primary in *Smith v. Allwright*

1944: Activists begin to mobilize around Mississippi voter registration; registered black
voters rise from 2,000 in 1940 to 25,000 in 1954

1947: Mississippi Progressive Voters' League (MPVL) is founded and claims a membership of 5,000

1951: Regional Council of Negro Leadership (RCNL) is founded; its mass meetings in
the early 1950s are attended by over 10,000 people

May 17, 1954: U.S. Supreme Court unanimously outlaws segregated education in
Brown v. Board of Education, signaling the opening of political opportunities for
black collective action

1954: NAACP activist Aaron Henry organizes four hundred residents to petition for
school desegregation in Clarksdale, Mississippi; intimidation and threats cause almost every one of them to remove their names

1954: In response to the *Brown* decision, the White Citizens' Council is founded in
Indianola, with membership swelling to 80,000 within two years; its tactics to de-
mobilize black activists include economic reprisals and physical intimidation

1955–1958: NAACP loses 246 Southern branches and 48,000 members; the number of
blacks on voter rolls plunges from 25,000 in 1954 to 8,000 in 1956

zations (churches, black colleges, and NAACP chapters) from which the movement had sprung and were able to mobilize support from a national conscience constituency of Northern churches, white liberals, organized labor, and students. In *I've Got the Light of Freedom*, however, Charles Payne cautions against such an explanation. SNCC organizers would never have gained a foothold in Greenwood, indeed, would likely never have gone there in the first place, without the help and inspiration of an older group of local leaders who had come to prominence in the 1950s. Veteran Mississippi activists had developed support networks that extended through a variety of political organizations, reached outside the state, and pushed the limits of Southern white officials' tolerance for mobilization. Their "spadework" provided SNCC workers personnel, contacts, and tactical expertise. The 1963 Greenwood movement was not simply an extension of a national movement into previously impenetrable areas of the Deep South but rather was forged in the same period and context as the national movement. To understand Greenwood in 1963, we need to understand Greenwood in 1953.

Payne's study of the Greenwood movement follows in a line of community-

---

1955: Seven black activists are murdered, among them Belzoni NAACP founder Reverend George W. Lee (May 7), his death ruled a "highway accident"; one to two thousand mourners attend the funeral, amid shouts of "He was murdered"

1955: The Jackson *Clarion-Ledger* editorializes against the shooting of activist Gus Courts, and the Citizens' Council offers a $250 reward for information leading to the arrest of his assailants; racial terrorism is seen for the first time as creating bad press

1955–1960: Black defiance is channeled into political concerns by such groups as the Regional Council of Negro Leadership and the Citizen's League, which bolster the beleaguered NAACP; Northern black allies such as Congressmen Charles Diggs and William Dawson, as well as businessmen and black media provide financial assistance and publicity

1962: Leflore county officials cut off federal surplus commodities to black residents after initial SNCC success in voter registration drives; SNCC puts out a national call for supplies and sends more organizers to Greenwood

February 25, 1963: 150 black Greenwood residents attempt to register to vote, the largest group at one time in the Deep South; the arrest of SNCC organizer Sam Block provokes marches, rallies, and stepped-up voter registration efforts

based studies of the civil rights movement that have explicitly challenged the "King-centric" view of earlier historical scholarship, and have implicitly corrected accounts that assume geographically undifferentiated national movements. Rather than concentrating on national leaders, federal agendas, and high-profile confrontations, with local leaders portrayed as King's lieutenants or followers, historians in the 1980s began to document local movements with distinctive origins, aims, and trajectories. "Blacks in these communities developed their own goals and strategies which bore little relation to national campaigns for civil rights legislation," historian Clayborne Carson wrote in a 1986 survey of the scholarship. "There is much to suggest that national civil rights organizations and their leaders played only minor roles in bringing about most local insurgencies" (1986, p. 24).

Since Carson's article, several scholars have tempered the sometimes overly localist perspective of the first generation of community studies, calling instead for analysis of the "complex ways in which local and national movements fed off one another" (Payne 1995, p. 415; see also Lawson 1991). But the latter perspective still poses interesting problems for the political-process model that dominates sociological accounts of the civil rights movement. If civil rights insurgency was indeed a movement of many movements, were the same national political opportunities responsible for them all? Do national political developments signal new opportunities in the same way to people in regions where the national government has long been seen as a distant actor with little impact? Should we look for additional layers of political opportunities: elite allies, political access, and declining repression at state and local, as well as national, levels?

I've Got the Light of Freedom helps to answer these questions. It gives a central causal role to expanding national political opportunities in accounting for the emergence of the Mississippi movement. But it reworks the political-opportunity thesis in at least three crucial ways: by challenging its distinction between elite allies (typically considered part of the political opportunity structure) and indigenous organizations (typically considered mobilizing structures); by viewing voter registration efforts as protest rather than as a precondition for it; and by suggesting that repression under certain circumstances facilitates rather than discourages protest. More broadly, Payne's account helps to expose questionable assumptions made by political-process analyses about what counts as movement "emergence" and whether we can conceptualize challengers as unitary actors. Instead, it supports the notion that Jasper details in the Introduction of movements and the groups that compose them as strategic players, who share some goals and not others, who mobilize people on the basis of their emotional indignation as much as their perception of new opportunities for impact, who respond to the tactical blunders of their antagonists as well as to longer-term redistributions of political authority, and who engage and reengage in long-running games whose rules may change even though the stakes do not.

I should note from the outset that much of the argument I attribute to Payne is teased out from a narrative that is deliberately much stronger on historical detail than theoretical elaboration (I will argue later that, while largely effective, Payne's focus on individual experiences and relationships sometimes obscures his causal claims). Payne does not engage sociological theories of movement emergence directly. His purpose is not to account for the beginnings of the movement in Greenwood. Rather, he aims to document a community-organizing tradition that generated neither the media-worthy events nor the subsequent historical scholarship that its community-mobilizing counterpart generated, yet was responsible for opening up the most oppressive areas of the South and went on to influence the women's, anti-Vietnam War, and New Left movements. Still, Payne's close attention to the extralocal activist networks and local political shifts that preceded mass insurgency yields insights about the relations between national politics and local protest that should be instructive to students of this and other movements.

Origins of the Movement

Before addressing Payne's account of civil rights insurgency, I will briefly summarize Doug McAdam's *Political Process and the Development of Black Insurgency*, where the key tenets of the political-process model were worked out. Challenging both collective behaviorist and resource mobilization accounts of movement emergence, McAdam emphasized political opportunities over system strain and emphasized indigenous resources over elite support (the latter, he pointed out, followed mobilization rather than preceded it). Key to the development of black insurgency were the political opportunities afforded by a newly vulnerable national political structure, the growth of indigenous institutions that provided insurgents necessary organizational resources and, mainly a result of the first two, Southern blacks' new sense of collective efficacy.

While the Compromise of 1877—and the alliance between Northern industrialists and Southern planters on which it was based—effectively organized blacks out of national politics, the erosion of that same alliance helped to bring them back in. The decline of the cotton industry in the 1920s and 1930s ended Northern elites' receptiveness to Southern planters' interests. It also spurred a massive migration of Southern blacks to Southern cities and Northern states where they were able to exercise electoral clout. The importance of the black vote was evident in the presidential elections of 1944 and 1948. Both would have gone to the Republican challenger had blacks voted for him. The growth in the Southern black electorate after 1950 further contributed to the salience of the black vote, McAdam argues. At the same time, America's postwar struggle with the Soviet Union for the allegiance of third world nations made it sensitive to charges of racism within its borders. Together these trends resulted in a federal government newly amenable to black claims.

The 1954 *Brown v. Board of Education* decision capped twenty years of Supreme Court decisions that were increasingly favorable to the interests of black Americans (only 43 percent of Supreme Court decisions handed down before 1931 favored black litigants while fully 91 percent between 1931 and 1955 did [p. 84]). Roosevelt's 1941 executive order establishing the Fair Employment Practices Commission, a response to A. Philip Randolph's threatened March on Washington, broke with the former hands-off policy of the executive branch. It inaugurated a series of supportive executive actions that continued into the Truman and Eisenhower administrations, among them a Committee on Civil Rights in 1946, plans for desegregation of the armed services and a comprehensive civil rights package in 1948, pressure for the desegregation of public facilities in the District of Columbia and a Committee on Government Contract Compliance in 1951.

Concurrent with these national developments, the growth of key institutions within Southern black communities during the 1930–1954 period, namely black colleges, churches, and NAACP chapters, provided black activists the communication, organizational, and ideological resources necessary to mount a full-fledged assault on white supremacy. By 1955, black activists could exploit federal vulnerability, strong indigenous resources, and a newfound sense of collective efficacy on the part of black Southerners in order to launch the first wave of mass insurgency.

At first glance, Payne's description of Mississippi in 1955 seems dramatically at odds with this picture. While the 1954 *Brown* decision was initially met with what seemed grudging acceptance on the part of white officials, within weeks acceptance had ceded to a wave of repression. Clarksdale NAACP activist Aaron Henry organized four hundred residents to petition for school desegregation but intimidation and threats caused almost every one of them to remove their names. Quasi-official state-funded White Citizens' Councils officially eschewed violence, preferring campaigns of economic intimidation and legal measures to disenfranchise blacks. In practice, these were often accompanied by physical threats and actual violence. The effect was chilling. Over 20,000 blacks had been on the Mississippi voting rolls in the early 1950s; the number dropped to 8,000 by 1956. Belzoni NAACP founder Reverend George Lee was murdered after a series of death threats; his death was ruled a highway accident (and the bullets in his jaw reported as dental fillings). Lee's NAACP colleague Gus Courts was shot six months later; surviving, he fled to Chicago for safety. T.R.M. Howard and Dr. C. C. Battle, two leaders of the Regional Council of Negro Leadership, were also forced to leave the state. A. H. McCoy stayed but saw his home wracked by gunfire. With Courts and Lee, the three men had been named on a Klan death list. In Charleston, NAACP activist Robert Smith simply disappeared. Between 1955 and 1958, the NAACP lost 246 Southern branches and 48,000 members. In the second half of the decade, Payne concludes, there seemed to be far more defeats than victories (p. 55).

Yet, he goes on, the decimation of black leadership in 1955–56 "is misleading, obscuring the fact that the return on racist violence was actually diminishing" (p. 40), and political opportunities for activism were in fact opening up. This seems a curious conclusion, given that repression was mounting, electoral power was declining, and two indices of indigenous organizational strength in McAdam's scheme—the black Church and the NAACP—seemed respectively unwilling to get involved in political activism and about to go under altogether. But Payne argues that the wave of repression that followed the *Brown* decision concealed three longer-term changes. The stranglehold of violence had in fact been permanently broken. Mississippi activists had secured allies outside the state who supplied essential financial and political resources. And black residents were meeting white intimidation and violence with political action. These changes made possible the consolidation of a cadre of Mississippi black leaders and then a mass movement that depended on their tactical expertise, political resources, and personal contacts.

Relaxed White Repression

Figures on lynching do not convey its brutal and public character: the crowds, often alerted days before by ads placed in local newspapers, the victims' slow torture and mutilation, their bodies dragged through the streets and burned, with murderers posing for photographs and taking body parts as souvenirs. But the graphic brutality was essential for communicating to black residents the costs of challenging a system dependent on black labor. Those lynched were often innocent of the crimes for which they were murdered (robbery, assault, rape of a white woman in one-sixth of all cases), but they were judged guilty by the white community—of becoming too prosperous, of encroaching on occupations considered white men's turf, of having mobilized fellow residents or workers against white brutalities.

Lynching's decline throughout the South—by 1935 the number had dropped from the hundred per year prior to the turn of the century to eighteen, and in the next twenty years, it would not rise above eight per year—reflected in part the federal government's new willingness to intervene in Southern racial practices, and behind that, Northern blacks' growing electoral clout. It also reflected the fact that racial terror was simply less necessary. In the 1920s and 1930s mechanized cotton production displaced thousands of workers at the same time as competition from synthetics and cheap foreign cotton devalued the cotton crop. With the Depression, the bottom fell out of the cotton market. The average price of cotton plunged from 35 cents per pound in 1919 to 9 cents per pound in 1931. By the 1960s, the great plantations would be using one-fifth of their former workforce. State officials who had passed laws to arrest Northern labor recruiters charged with luring away black cotton workers now worked on schemes to drive blacks from the state altogether.

So far, this argument recapitulates McAdam's. However, the decline of the cotton industry also undermined the hegemony of the planter class, Payne goes on, and the rise of a competing business class was another reason for lowered white repression, something McAdam does not discuss. Anti-lynching activist Jessie Daniel Ames wrote in 1939 that "we have managed to reduce lynchings . . . not because we've grown more law-abiding or respectable but because lynchings became such bad advertising. The South is going after big industry at the moment and a lawless, lynch-mob population isn't going to attract very much outside capital" (p. 21). The cost of bad publicity was increasingly entering into the calculus of overt racial oppression. Greenwood planters still managed to get their candidate into the mayor's office in 1957, but it was, says Payne, a last hurrah. "By the 1960s, then, there was no politically meaningful class of whites for whom suppression of Blacks was the kind of economic necessity it had been in years past. As terrible as it was for its victims, the level of violence is not what one would expect from people defending a vital class interest" (p. 203).

The new calculus was evident in white response to the 1955 Lee and Courts shootings. Nine years earlier, the national NAACP had organized a series of hearings in Jackson intended to establish Senator Theodore Bilbo's role in systematically disenfranchising black citizens. County registrar after county registrar testified openly about their efforts to keep Mississippi blacks off the voter rolls. Their candor, Payne observes, was "a gauge of how little some Mississippians of that period worried about the opinions of the world" (p. 25). By 1955, those opinions mattered. The Jackson *Clarion-Ledger* condemned Courts' shooting, and the Citizens' Council offered a $250 reward for information leading to the arrest of his assailants (who, the sheriff seemed convinced, were light-skinned Negroes). Mississippi's governor warned of federal intervention: "If they can say that state law has broken down, there's no telling how much federal interference might be forced on us" (p. 39).

Federal involvement in the Southern way of life was becoming a real possibility, Payne shows, and its possibility—never certainty—tempered at least official segregationist response to black collective action. For example, when SNCC workers in 1961 mounted their first registration drive, in McComb, white response was initially disorganized and ineffective. This was a function, Payne surmises, of white officials' uncertainty about what role the federal government would play in prosecuting interference with voter registration workers. The Justice Department's policy in McComb, and throughout the South, was erratic. Suits were sometimes filed on behalf of beaten civil rights workers, but their complaints were just as likely to be ignored (and the information sometimes passed on to local law enforcement officials). Young civil rights workers experienced the Justice Department's callousness as a profound betrayal, and their radicalization dates from their earliest encounters with the federal government in Mississippi. But Payne points out that the uncertainty of federal action was enough to restrain racial terrorism: "from the viewpoint of local law-enforcement people, the mere possibility of federal intervention was probably enough to put some limits, however slight, on violence and blatant illegalities" (p. 124).

Those who formed Mississippi's black leadership cadre in the 1950s tended to be least vulnerable to white economic control. They were independent farmers, real estate owners, undertakers, dentists. But the relaxation of white terrorism enabled them to hold public gatherings and to begin to groom a new generation of young leaders.

Co-optable Networks

When the federal government threatened to intervene in Mississippi's affairs, it did not act autonomously. Rather it responded to an increasingly well-organized group of activists and influential supporters. The Lee shooting reveals this shift. Payne writes:

> Ten years earlier, a killing of this sort might have been put down as a "traffic fatality," and no word of it would have crossed the county line. By 1955, Delta Blacks were better organized, better connected to concerned audiences outside the state. Negroes trying to use the phones the evening of the killing were told by the operators that all long-distance lines were tied up, so drivers were sent to officials of the NAACP and the RCNL [Regional Council of Negro Leadership] across the state . . . [RCNL president] Dr. Howard called Congressman Diggs—who had headlined the RCNL rally a few weeks earlier—who called the White House. In Jackson, Medgar Evers, the newly hired state NAACP field secretary . . . immediately began gathering material for the national press (p. 39).

Mississippi's diminishing isolation from the rest of the country was a function not only of the federal government's greater scrutiny, but also of black activists' ability to draw on national sources of publicity, financial support, and organizational expertise.

Within the state, the NAACP was but one of several organizations supplying black leadership. The Mississippi Progressive Voters' League claimed a membership of five thousand by 1947 (Dittmer 1994, p. 25). The Regional Council of Negro Leadership (RCNL) was founded in 1951 in the all-black town of Mound Bayou. Led by the charismatic T.R.M Howard, it held mass meetings that were attended by ten to twelve thousand people in the 1950s. While the NAACP was under attack, a Citizen's League was founded in Greenwood in 1957.

The agendas of these organizations centered on voting rights. Contrary to McAdam's argument that the movement before 1965 was united around a goal of desegregation (1982, p. 137), for postwar Mississippi black activists the goal was electoral power (see also Dittmer 1994; Bloom 1987). SNCC organizer Bob Moses recalls that NAACP activist Amzie Moore "wasn't distracted by school integration. He was for it but it didn't distract him from the centrality of the right to vote" (p. 106). From that vantage point, the important Supreme Court ruling—and one often overlooked, Payne observes—was the 1944 *Smith v. Allwright* decision outlawing the white primary. An estimated two thousand blacks were registered in the state in 1940, twenty-five hundred in 1946, but five thousand in 1947, an increase of 100 percent. By 1954 there were twenty to twenty-five thousand registered black voters (p. 25). The importance of the vote was not lost on white Mississippians. While the White Citizens' Councils were formed in response to the *Brown* decision, they "quickly became involved in a broader defense of white racism" (p. 35), with white control of the vote its centerpiece. Councils successfully lobbied for a law requiring potential voters to be able to interpret any section of the state constitution to the satisfaction of the registrar (a practice widespread even before the law).

The legal and illegal strategies were successful in disenfranchising blacks, and the number of registered black voters in Mississippi plunged to 8,000 in 1956. The decline was a setback in a long and continuing battle, however. By 1959, voter registration was back up to 15,000. Recognizing the role of organizations other than the NAACP in black Mississippi communities in the 1950s thus foregrounds a voter registration thrust that extended back before the war. It also helps to explain how Mississippi activists were able to survive the 1955–56 wave of repression. With memberships in multiple organizations, they continued to operate under the rubrics of other organizations when the NAACP was attacked.

In addition, multiple ties allowed activists to maneuver around the NAACP, thus avoiding some of its more onerous mandates and organizational territoriality. Local NAACP heads were "restive under the tight reins of the NAACP's national office" (p. 32), Payne observes, and sometimes downright dismissive. Of Roy Wilkins, Executive Secretary of the NAACP, Amzie Moore said, "He'd fly down here and hold our conferences and hold our annual 'days' and raise our freedom money and be advised by different people outa the New York office. And that was it" (p. 33). Payne documents numerous instances in which local activists such as Moore defied national NAACP opposition to pursue broader agendas and to form coalitions with groups the national office perceived as competitors. For example, in 1962, Medgar Evers, Aaron Henry, and Amzie Moore brought SNCC activists into the Council of Federated Organizations (COFO) coalition that would later coordinate the Mississippi Summer Project. It was a move that sat ill with national NAACP headquarters. "Had the veteran Mississippi activists, with their credibility and contacts, taken the stance toward the other groups that the national organization consistently took, the movement of the sixties would have had more difficulty establishing itself. Instead, they chose to legitimate the outsiders" (p. 62). Overlapping memberships thus enabled activists to draw on the resources of the NAACP while maintaining the tactical flexibility and responsiveness to local conditions that strict adherence to national directives would have made impossible.

Another important feature of Mississippi activist networks in the 1950s was their inclusion of black elite allies. Political-process theories have analytically separated elite allies (considered part of the political opportunity structure) from facilitative organizations within the aggrieved group (considered indigenous mobilizing structures). But in this case the categories overlapped; elites were members rather than supporters of the aggrieved group. As Jasper points out in his Introduction, the concept of "elite" mistakenly assumes a unity of interest among all those in that category. In this case, influential black individuals and groups outside the state provided money, organizational expertise, and national publicity. NAACP and RCNL meetings in the early 1950s featured national speakers such as Congressmen Charles Diggs and William Dawson, and attorney Thurgood Marshall. Black magazines and newspapers like *Jet*, *Ebony*, the *Chicago Defender*, and the *Pittsburgh Courier* garnered Northern publicity and provided financial assistance, as did Northern black civic organizations, churches, and banks. When Amzie Moore faced bank foreclosure on his home as a result of his civil rights work, he survived on donations solicited by *Jet* and the *Pittsburgh Courier*, and on assistance from the black-owned Tri-State Bank in Memphis. With contributions from the NAACP and organized labor, Tri-State opened a loan fund for black activists, enabling them to withstand white economic reprisals. Reverend Aaron Johnson of Greenwood saw his congregation and salary slip away when he opened his church to SNCC activists in 1962. A $1,300 gift and a weekly stipend from his church headquarters in Indianapolis enabled him to survive.

These outside groups and individuals also served as communicative resources, conveying to people in Mississippi the existence of new political opportunities and national support. For black Mississippians, the federal government had long been a distant and ineffectual actor. Most of the Supreme Court decisions and executive orders favorable to black claimants in the 1940s and 1950s had little chance of being enforced in Mississippi. FBI agents, even when they appeared at victims' behest, did little but take notes, and White Citizens' Councils were able to get black leaders audited by the IRS after 1955. The message was not obviously one of federal support for racial equality. Mississippi's long political isolation meant that a central challenge for activists was to convince residents that political opportunities on the national scene had meaning for people in Mississippi. While Attorney General Herbert Brownell was unlikely to appear at a Mississippi mass meeting in the 1950s, Congressman Diggs did so, and was more likely to be trusted and believed when he described the federal government's new amenability to black claims. But the communicative role played by influential allies worked the other way, too. Black luminaries and organizations with national reach were able to stimulate the Northern attention that compelled the federal government to take a stand on abuses in Mississippi.

Defiance

Payne identifies a third transformation under way in the 1950s that was responsible both for the emergence of a powerful black leadership and for their later organizing successes. Mississippi blacks were increasingly unwilling to back down from racist violence. Between one and two thousand mourners attended George Lee's funeral in 1955, and services were interrupted by shouts of "He was murdered!" (p. 38). Belzoni black residents went on to boycott white stores to protest the killing. Angry protesters gathered at the trial of Emmett Till's murderers a few months later, some of them carrying weapons. Amzie Moore dated the beginning of the modern movement in Mississippi to that time. And NAACP regional head Ruby Hurley linked the Till killing to an increase in regional NAACP membership. Black Mississippians had a long tradition of standing up to white oppression, Payne notes. What was different now was the scale of resistance, and its channeling into political forms: people joined the NAACP, boycotted white stores, and withdrew money from white banks.

Payne sees the change in consciousness as generational: "Black Mississippians coming to adulthood in the late 1940s had a stronger sense of entitlement" (p. 21). He cites Hortense Powdermaker's (1968) study of the Indianola black community in the early 1930s: blacks born in the early years of the century were less willing to accept the codes of ritual deference than their parents, and those who were well educated were even less so. One young man, typical of the better educated, "recognized his inability to vote as the crucial point. For him the vote has become the symbol of the kernel of the inter-racial situation. He maintains that . . . only a need for the votes of the Negroes will bring justice to them in work, in conditions of living, in the courts" (quoted in Payne, p. 23). Veterans and those who had traveled outside the state tended to be even more militant, Payne argues. Most of the leaders who came to prominence in the 1950s were among the 83,000 black Mississippians who had served in the Second World War.

Payne attributes people's willingness to participate to their perception that collective action was eliciting a more restrained response, albeit one that was often still violent. He also notes numerous instances of NAACP membership rising or boycotts developing in response to the arrest, beating, or murder of those known to be involved in the movement, for example, in response to Lee and Courts' shootings, Sam Block's arrest, and Medgar Evers' murder. This suggests the operation of indignation and outrage more than a cool assessment of the prospects for participating unharmed. Although Payne does not broach this possibility, I wonder whether violence against people seen as putting their lives on the line for the community helped to create a powerful and mobilizing sense of collective identity, one that transcended divisions of class and status within black communities. These activists tended already to occupy an interstitial position in black communities. They were relatively well-off but not part of the status-conscious and sometimes accommodationist black elite, and thus were more able than others to mobilize people throughout the community. Violence against them may have crystallized a community stake in collective action (see also Wood 2003).

In the 1950s, then, a combination of relaxed white repression, new activist alliances and organizations, and a growing sense of entitlement set the stage for 1960s protest by generating a group of leaders and a citizenry increasingly open to their organizing efforts. How did these older leaders spur and shape the movement? By providing an agenda, contacts, an organizational framework, and financial support for young activists. Historical accounts of SNCC's move into voter registration in 1961 tend to attribute it to the persuasive powers of the Kennedy administration. But Payne makes clear the role that Mississippi activists, especially Amzie Moore, played in convincing SNCC workers to launch a voter registration campaign and, importantly, to do so in Mississippi's rural areas. These counties had been all but written off by the national organizations on account of their danger, but they also held the greatest potential for black electoral strength. Some of SNCC's best organizers in places such as McComb and Greenwood were young Mississippians who had been identified and politicized by older leaders such as Moore, Vernon Dahmer, and Clyde Kennard. In addition to providing financial support, places to stay, and tactical advice, older leaders opened doors that would have been otherwise closed to outsiders. By the spring of 1963, Payne observes, "Black Greenwood . . . [had] become an organized town" (p. 132). This remarkable transformation was the result of the effective if unlikely cooperation of young SNCC shock troops with activists who had begun the movement more than a decade earlier.

Had they begun a *movement* more than a decade before? That is, can one characterize the actions of the NAACP, RCNL, and the Progressive Voters' League in the 1950s as insurgency, rather than as expanding the indigenous organizations that facilitated later insurgency? Certainly, Mississippi activism in the 1950s was elite, low profile, and small scale. But if we define a movement as sustained contention with authorities, and distinguish it from the growth of indigenous organizations on that basis, then what occurred in the 1950s was an early phase of the movement rather than solely a precursor to it. Would the national movement have come eventually to Greenwood without this prior history of activism? Payne does not answer this hypothetical question explicitly, but his account suggests that if national organizations had attempted to make inroads in the state without the aid of Mississippi movement veterans, they would likely have focused on segregation rather than voting rights, and have attempted high-profile and short-term demonstrations rather than building enduring political institutions. Given the clear costs of movement participation, it is unlikely, following Payne's argument, that such efforts would have succeeded.

Expanding Political Opportunities?

To what extent, then, were expanding political opportunities responsible for the Greenwood movement? Payne's account revises each of the four components of political opportunity identified by McAdam, McCarthy, and Zald (1996) and, in the process, illuminates dynamics insufficiently developed by political-process accounts.

Increasing Popular Access to the Political System

Payne follows McAdam (1982) as well as Piven and Cloward (1977) and Bloom (1987) in arguing that the federal government's increasing willingness to threaten—if not act on—intervention in the South was a function of Northern blacks' growing electoral clout. McAdam (1982, p. 157) argues additionally that a sharp increase in voter registration in the South between 1950 and 1965 further strengthened the power of the black vote. But in Mississippi, the precipitous drop in the number of blacks on the voter rolls in the mid-1950s would suggest that opportunities had contracted. Rather than a precondition for black activism, Payne shows, voter registration was an important goal and accomplishment of Mississippi black activism, something that McAdam's account misses. The drop in the voter rolls during the wave of 1955–56 repression was thus a setback in an ongoing battle (registered black voters had increased steadily from 2,000 in 1940, to 5,000 in 1947, to 17,000 in 1952, and 20,000–25,000 in 1954 [p. 25]). The larger point is that in the repressive context of the South, voter registration—that is, an institutionalized form of political behavior—*was* activism.

Unstable Elite Alignments or Elite Competition

In emphasizing the importance of the Northern black vote in spurring new federal interest in the South, Payne supports McAdam's argument that national party competition created political opportunities. But he also suggests that competition within Mississippi communities between an increasingly obsolete planter class and an ascendant stratum of white businessmen opened up opportunities for black activists. Desirous of Northern investment and aware of the (literal) costs of continued racial terrorism, white industrialists styled themselves racial moderates. Publicly cautioning segregationist restraint, they were sometimes able to persuade law enforcement officials to investigate and try crimes against blacks. In other words, repressive social control was relaxed not only in response to fears of federal intervention but also in response to the efforts of a new class who saw its economic benefits. Bloom (1987) has shown that white moderates crumpled in the face of the wave of white repression that followed *Brown*, but the earlier thaw enabled black activists to forge the networks that could withstand the subsequent assault. The larger point is that elite competition may occur at state and local as well as national levels. Such competition may reflect larger-scale regional or national developments (in this case, the decline of the cotton industry was responsible both for new pressures on the national democratic party and the decline of the planter class in Mississippi communities), but it may also take distinctive forms and establish unique alliances and conflicts.

Elite Allies Who Encourage or Facilitate Protest

Influential black individuals and groups outside the state supplied essential support in the early years of the movement. With political, cultural, and economic capital, they provided the resources that enabled black Mississippi activists to survive the periods of harshest repression. Black elites' connections to national white elites and the federal government made them credible framers of national political opportunities. Furthermore, their capacity to bring news of the South to the North helped to spur the Northern liberal indignation that compelled federal involvement, however erratic. These individuals and groups blur the distinction that political-process theory posits between elite allies (considered part of the political opportunity structure) and indigenous institutions and leaders (considered mobilizing structures), because they were both elite (politically and economically influential) and indigenous (solidary with Mississippi blacks) before the movement even began.

A tendency to conceive of elite allies and indigenous networks as mutually exclusive obscures important dynamics in the process by which an aggrieved population takes advantage of national political shifts. People whom writers have termed variously "mediators" (Mische 2008), "bridging leaders" (Robnett 1997), and "brokers" (McAdam, Tarrow, and Tilly 2001) seem to play critical roles in mobilization. Mississippi's isolation from the centers of political power and currents of mainstream opinion meant that such interlocutors were essential both to the framing processes by which national-level opportunities were perceived as such by local insurgents and to the processes by which national attention was focused on Mississippi and with it, calls for federal intervention.

Declining State Repression

The economic and physical reprisals launched in the wake of the *Brown* decision virtually put the Greenwood NAACP chapter and others across the state out of business. However, repression had already declined before the *Brown* decision, and its character overall had changed. White violence was more surreptitious, more likely to be threatened than acted upon, and more likely to be publicly condemned and investigated by white officials. Payne attributes the change to several factors: white planters' lessening dependence on black labor; their own eclipse by businessmen and industrialists eager to recruit Northern investment and concerned about their racist image; and black residents' more systematic use of armed self-defense.

The thaw in repression enabled activists to organize publicly and thereby develop networks that would be crippled but not eliminated by the heightened repression following the *Brown* decision. Subsequent repression, particularly that directed against activists, seems to have actually galvanized action by unifying divided communities in outrage at violence directed against people who were seen as fighting for the community's interests. Charles Brockett has interestingly challenged the rational choice argument that official violence targeted to opposition leaders is most likely to discourage mass participation, since it will supposedly convey to nonelites the futility as well as danger of participation. Such an explanation obscures the collective rationality and powerful emotions fostered by strong social ties, Brockett points out. "[A] violent attack by the state on a member of the group (such as a parent, a close friend, a village elder) could provoke anti-regime activity from other group members, not necessarily out of self-defense but out of outrage and a desire for revenge (as well as justice)" (1995, p. 124; see also Brockett 2005). In Mississippi communities, the violence may have helped to make activists symbols of the group, thereby unifying the group (see Wood 2003 for a similar dynamic). The timing and targeting of repression not only establish the costs of participation but generate collective sentiments of anger and indignation that are sometimes more powerful than those of fear. Increasing repression may actually spur activism if it follows a period of declining repression, during which insurgent organizations and networks are developed.

Criticism

Payne's account focuses on the Mississippi activists who anticipated, experienced, and made far-reaching changes. His aim is to bring the movement down to the level of the maverick NAACP officials, activist families, and quiet organizers who were its real leaders. This makes for fascinating history and provides important correctives to sociological accounts of movement emergence. The risk of such an approach, however, is that illustrative episodes and compelling profiles substitute for fully fleshed out arguments. Indeed, causal mechanisms are sometimes only hinted at in the text, and some passages are inconsistent. For example, Payne argues that as a result of the wave of reprisals that followed the *Brown v. Board of Education* decision in 1954, the NAACP lost 246 Southern branches and 48,000 members between 1955 and 1958 (p. 43). He also quotes without comment NAACP official Ruby Hurley's report of an *increase* in NAACP memberships in 1955 (p. 41). The Greenwood NAACP chapter "couldn't have been formed at a less auspicious time" in 1952, Payne contends, but that year, "by Mississippi standards was a relatively peaceful year in terms of race relations" (p. 138). The chapter "fell on hard times after the Till murder" in 1955, but "within two years" of its founding, "active membership had fallen off so much that the chapter became inactive" (p. 139), that is, in 1954.

   Payne's too-brief discussion of the relations between repression and insurgency is disappointing because the narrative hints at important insights on the topic. For example, his provocative and plausible argument that white violence in Greenwood declined because "the targets were increasingly prone to shoot back" (p. 204) is undermined by his failure to explain that shift. "Mississippi has a long tradition of Blacks taking up arms to defend themselves or their communities," he says. "What happened in the early sixties seems to be a good deal more systematic" (p. 205). How so? SNCC organizers, while benefiting from locals' willingness to stand armed guard, were not actively organizing more systematic self-defense. How did black residents organize armed resistance? How does Payne's argument here square with his earlier claim that the crucial change in Mississippi was the easing of white repression? Could organized armed resistance on the part of black Mississippians have worked earlier? Another interesting point: NAACP branches in the Southwest "generally seem to have weathered the [1955–56] repression better than branches in other 'easier' parts of the state" (p. 113). Why?

The competition between an ascendant business class and a declining planter class that Payne identifies merits further examination. Payne attributes the relaxation of repression in Mississippi in large part to the fact that it simply was not necessary. With the decline of cotton, plantations could make do with far fewer workers, and planters were being eclipsed in any case by a new class of industrialists who were eager for Northern investment. But the planter class fought hard for an archsegregationist mayor in 1957 and fought tooth and nail against desegregation in the wake of *Brown*—and encountered little resistance from white moderates. If white planters were battling to retain their hegemony on the terrain of racial policy, it is hard to imagine any reason to fight harder. Just as we have to ask when repression spurs rather than prevents mobilization on the part of an aggrieved population, we have to explain when the motivations for repression transcend narrowly economic interests.

Payne's task in this book is doubly difficult: to explain dramatic change without giving short shrift to continuities in activist networks and oppositional traditions, and to highlight the contributions of individuals without ignoring the structural and organizational conditions that made individual agency newly effective. His solution is to privilege narrative over theory. That his causal arguments are sometimes unclear or truncated attests to the complexity of the story.

Conclusion

Was the Greenwood movement the result of expanding political opportunities? Yes. Payne's account, however, suggests several revisions to the political-opportunity thesis. First, shifts in national-level political structures and alliances may not be perceived as affording obvious opportunities for people in regions that are politically isolated. More broadly, we need a better understanding of the processes by which national-level shifts "cue" local insurgency. The Greenwood case suggests that members of the aggrieved group who nevertheless enjoy national influence can play an important role in conveying political opportunities to local activists and drumming up support for them nationally. Recognizing these dynamics requires, however, that we abandon a narrow construction of elite allies that places them by definition outside the aggrieved group.

Second, the prospects for insurgency are affected by local political structures and elite alliances as well as national ones (Kriesi [2004] makes a similar point). Local structures may mediate national-level political shifts, they may be transformed by the same underlying economic or demographic processes, or they may counter shifts perceived at the national level. The Greenwood case shows that the relaxation of repression reflected not only whites' fears of federal intervention, the latter a function of Northern black electoral clout, but also the efforts of a new class of racial moderates motivated by the possibility of Northern investment.

Third, key dynamics are obscured by viewing challengers in unitary terms, without internal divisions and as given rather than created through political processes. The Greenwood case shows the role played by influential black allies outside the state—people who were part of the challenging group by virtue of their ties of racial identification and yet had access to economic and political sources of power. It also suggests that a precondition for insurgency was bridging the class and especially status differences that characterized Mississippi black communities. Mississippi activists such as Aaron Henry, E. W. Steptoe, and Amzie Moore were uniquely qualified to do so by virtue of their interstitial social positions (attesting to the importance of dynamics of brokerage described by McAdam, Tarrow, and Tilly 2001). Violence against activists may also have served to unify black communities. A monolithic understanding of the aggrieved group misses both these processes.

Now that sociologists of social movements have successfully put to rest views of insurgents as apolitical bearers of system strain or as entirely dependent on the munificence of elite allies, we should be able to develop more complex models of the relations between opportunities and insurgency. Key features of that model, Payne's account suggests, should be more variegated notions of challengers, allies, and political structures.

6   The Women's Movement

Anne Costain's *Inviting Women's Rebellion*

JOHN D. SKRENTNY

I F THERE IS A WORK that could be characterized as an archetype for
the political-process approach to social movements, Anne Costain's
Inviting Women's Rebellion is it. In her introduction, Costain describes her
initial puzzlement over the women's movement, and the epiphany she experienced when introduced to the political-process model. The mysterious political dynamics of the movement suddenly clicked into focus. In her study of the
women's movement, she tests and uses the theory with enthusiasm. The result
is a brilliant book that is to the women's movement what McAdam's pioneering (1982) work is to the civil rights movement. Like McAdam, she uses the
concept of political opportunity to analyze the emergence, impact, and decline
of a social movement.

Her case, however, offers a sterner test for the approach and the very concept of political opportunity than did McAdam's. In this essay, I describe
Costain's work and make two main points. First, the civil rights movement
played an important but unrecognized role in creating political opportunities
for women. Second, this book forces social movement theorists to question the
very concepts of social movement, opportunity, and government action. The
case of the women's movement exposes problems and ambiguities in a theoretical model which assumes that social movements and the government are
separate and discrete entities.

Inviting Women's Rebellion covers the period from the 1950s through the
1980s to capture the emergence and impact of what Costain calls the "current

women's movement" or the "contemporary women's movement." The study concentrates especially on the period from the early 1960s through the 1970s, when political opportunity was the greatest. Focus on this period allows her to highlight the emergence of the more mainstream groups, principally the National Organization for Women (NOW) and the Women's Equity Action League (WEAL), and their relationship to the federal government.

A "women's movement," of course, existed before the 1950s and has encompassed a multitude of organizations and group goals. The prehistory to Costain's account adds important context and can be summarized briefly. In the late nineteenth century and early twentieth century, the women's movement had two major factions, each with its own model for reform. The hallmark of the first group, the classical liberals, was the famous 1848 feminist

---

MAJOR EVENTS IN THE STRUGGLE FOR WOMEN'S RIGHTS

July 20, 1848: Seneca Falls Convention

August 18, 1920: Women win the right to vote with ratification of the Nineteenth Amendment

December 10, 1923: Equal Rights Amendment (ERA) introduced in House of Representatives and Senate

June 10, 1963: Equal Pay Act passed to prohibit unequal wages based on sex

October 1963: President's Commission on the Status of Women issues report, *American Women*

November 1, 1963: President Kennedy creates the Interdepartmental Committee on the Status of Women and the Citizens' Advisory Council on the Status of Women

1963: Publication of Betty Friedan's revelatory study, *The Feminine Mystique*

July 2, 1964: Civil Rights Act passed, prohibiting sex discrimination in employment

1965: *George Washington Law Review* publishes Pauli Murray and Mary O. Eastwood's essay, "Jane Crow and the Law: Sex Discrimination and Title VII"

June 30, 1966: National Organization for Women (NOW) is founded

1968: Women's Equity Action League (WEAL) is founded

October 12, 1971: House of Representatives approves the ERA

December 4, 1971: Women included in the Labor Department's affirmative action regulations

March 22, 1972: Senate approves the ERA

June 23, 1972: Title IX of the Education Amendments passes, prohibiting sex discrimination by education programs or institutions receiving federal funds

June 30, 1982: States fail to ratify the ERA

convention at the Wesleyan Chapel at Seneca Falls, New York. Women demanded equal citizenship, including suffrage and the right to relate to the government as autonomous individuals, unmediated by husbands or children. In short, they argued there should be no "separate spheres" for men and women (Evans 1989, pp. 94–95).

When women won the right to vote in 1920, many believed this was all they needed; any desired gains could come at the ballot box. Interest in the movement dissipated quickly, but the National Women's party pressed on with the classical liberal agenda, drafting the Equal Rights Amendment (ERA) and submitting it to Congress in 1923. The amendment was straightforward in its goal to make it unconstitutional for the federal government or any of the states to deny equal rights on the basis of sex, yet many old allies worked against it. These opponents believed the amendment was misguided, based on their belief in a fundamental difference between men and women, and that it would take away the gains of the other faction, whose model of justice was based on "republican motherhood" (Klein 1984, p. 17; Rhode 1989, p. 35).

This more traditional faction also fought for suffrage, but did so on a basis different from the classical liberals. Republican motherhood was based on the sturdy cultural foundation of separate spheres for men and women. These women understood efforts at reform as extending their sphere yet not equalizing individuals; in their view, women's suffrage allowed society the use of their benevolent, housekeeping instincts (Klein 1984).

While republican motherhood converged with classical liberalism on equal suffrage, the two factions diverged on so-called protective legislation, which granted restrictions on how employers could treat women workers, and which would likely be struck down if the ERA passed. In the Progressive Era, many states passed regulations governing the maximum number of work hours for women at the insistence of republican motherhood activists, and efforts at regulating minimum wages and working conditions for both men and women also occurred (Skocpol 1992).

While the republican motherhood activists achieved some of their goals with protective legislation, there were clouds on the horizon. One problem was that male-dominated unions actually joined the women in fighting for women's protection because these laws sometimes worked to remove female competition for jobs. In half the states, women were banned from many jobs, from shining shoes to legislative service. Most exclusions were based on alleged threats to health or morals; typical were bans on women working in liquor establishments. Although the two factions of women's groups fought over these issues from their beginnings in the Progressive Era, the Supreme Court allowed the laws to stand through the 1940s and 1950s. The fight centered on the ERA. As Deborah Rhode explains, the mothers felt that "true equality" must take into account "actual biological, social, and occupational differences between men and women," and they saw classical liberals as laissez-faire types, lacking in compassion (see Rhode 1989, pp. 36–45, for a review; also see Becker 1981; Rupp and Taylor 1987).

The current women's movement dates from the 1960s, and has most closely resembled the Seneca Falls, classical liberal strand of the women's movement. It is difficult to estimate its size. Costain, following Freeman (1975), rightly distinguishes between the "older" and "younger" branches. These categories separate, first, the professional women who served in President Kennedy's President's Commission on the Status of Women and the state-level commissions that formed shortly thereafter, and second, the women who came to the movement from other movements (most notably, the black civil rights movement) and from college campuses. Many other participant groups are hard to categorize. As Costain puts it, "Clearly, there is no *single* unified women's movement, but there are a multitude of groups, organizations, and individuals that although diverse, identify with the goal of improving the status of women around the world" (p. 3; emphasis in original). Still, Costain does present data showing membership in "selected women's groups." This reveals steadily but slowly growing membership from 1958 to 1978, with an increase from approximately 450,000 members to 600,000, and then a rapid rise to more than 800,000 by 1982 (the last year the ERA could be ratified in state legislatures), and an equally quick drop-off to about 600,000 in 1986 (p. 96). In her study, Costain casts a wide net, concentrating on the professional women's branch and excluding from the current women's movement some conservative organizations, such as those led by Phyllis Schlafly. These organizations have resisted many of the goals of the current movement, such as the ERA.

By all accounts, the current women's movement contributed to a fundamental change in the ways Americans viewed women. In addition, its development coincided with a variety of laws and regulations: affirmative action, various administrative rulings by the Equal Employment Opportunity Commission (including the banning of protective legislation), Title IX of the Education Amendments of 1972 (outlawing sex discrimination from educational institutions receiving federal funding), a law qualifying pregnancy as a disability for employer health plans, and numerous other laws, administrative guidelines, and court rulings. The precise role of the movement in gaining this cornucopia of rights is the subject of Costain's study. Costain is a close observer of the feminist movement and deploys virtually every method in the social scientists' arsenal. She interviewed lobbyists for women's groups in four "waves" (1974–75, 1977, 1981, and 1984) and combines interviews with an examination of the historical papers of NOW and WEAL. Costain also "analyzed and coded the abstracts of news stories about U.S. women using the *New York Times Annual Index* for the period 1950 to 1986, concentrating on events that reflected agitation on behalf of women's rights" (p. xvii), following a procedure that McAdam (1982) utilized in his study of the black civil rights movement. To examine actions by the government, Costain also used the *Congressional Record* and *U.S. Statutes at Large* to code and quantify the introduction of bills related to women's rights and laws actually passed. She also examines the public papers of the presidents "for references to women and women's issues." "This mixture of event analysis, interviews, archival records, and content analysis of presidential rhetoric," explains Costain, "is designed to show both the public and some of the private faces of the women's movement. It also provides a picture of governmental involvement with women's issues in this period" (pp. xvii–xix).

Origin of the Movement

Costain believes the federal government is key to understanding the origins of the current women's movement. The exact nature of the relationship is not entirely clear (more on that below), but the important role of government makes this a distinctive and intriguing case for a political-process interpretation.

To make her case, Costain first dismisses resource mobilization theory. This approach, she argues, predicts that the current women's movement would emphasize innocuous, incremental demands for progress so as not to alienate potential allies in the crucial formation periods, and would gain new resources from allies partly because of this strategy. Specifically, the movement would build on the legislative gains of the black civil rights movement, and "[c]onsequently, moderate groups from the civil rights and women's communities would join forces with the new women's movement, providing resources to sustain it" (p. 9). Scholars Gelb and Palley (1982) and Mansbridge (1986) are proponents of this view. They argue that women fought for "role equity" and not the more controversial "role change" as a strategy to gain assistance for the new movement.

Costain finds little support for this view. In examining stories about the women's movement in the *New York Times*, she finds that their fight for equality came later in the game, in the mid-1970s. Her data show that the movement asked for the smaller reforms later, after opposition developed, rather than early on (pp. 8–11). Further, the *Times* stories show funds coming to the movement only after it already formed. Paradoxically, allies of the movement showed much support in the 1950s, yet no movement formed (p. 16). Costain concludes that resource mobilization theory misses the key dynamics of the movement.

On the other hand, the *Times* data show some provocative pro-women moves by the federal government. Costain argues that "the aggregate data suggest that political-process theory, with its emphasis on the relationship between government and a new movement along with the mobilization of indigenous resources, goes furthest in exposing what appear to be key factors underlying the timing and development of the women's movement" (p. 22). Costain's primary agenda is to use the concept of political opportunity to explain both the emergence of the current women's movement and its achievements in the area of public policy (pp. xv, 15).

Costain wishes to "clarify process theory," specifically by taking on Charles Tilly's (1978) notion of how the government may facilitate a social movement. Facilitation, following Tilly, includes publicizing a group, legalizing it, and paying it off. More indirectly, the government may facilitate by reducing movement costs through lending information and strategic expertise, or limiting movement opponents' actions.

Facilitation, in this view, is most likely when a movement is already powerful and movement actions are small in scale. This does not fit the women's movement, according to Costain, since the vast majority of women had little power or connection with the few women who wielded influence in the early 1960s. Costain argues that facilitation occurred because of two different factors relating to political institutions. First, following Piven and Cloward (1977, 1983) as well as Tarrow (1983, 1988), she emphasizes democratic politics and the instability of political alignments as factors affecting facilitation. Politicians and parties will seek to build winning coalitions, and a newly organized group will be a target for courting. Secondly, borrowing from political scientists James Q. Wilson (1980) and Andrew McFarland (1987), Costain argues that conflicts among government elites may lead to movement facilitation, especially in government

agencies. Specifically, government actors may encourage countervailing interest groups' lobbyists; intergroup struggle is in the interests of administrators
because it protects government agency autonomy (pp. 24–25).

Government facilitation would be crucial because through the 1950s, wom-
en's issues were still dominated by opposing factions of the descendants of the
pro-ERA classical liberals and the anti-ERA republican mothers. The former
included the National Women's party, National Federation of Business and
Professional Women's Clubs, the General Federation of Women's Clubs, the
National Association of Colored Women, the National Association of Women
Lawyers, the American Bar Association, and the National Education Association. On the protective-legislation side was the Women's Bureau (of the Department of Labor) coalition, including the Women's Bureau, the League of
Women Voters, the National Consumers League, the National Women's Trade
Union League, the Young Women's Christian Association, the National Councils of Jewish, Catholic, and Negro Women, and the American Association of
University Women (pp. 27–28). Government facilitation helped to upset this
factional alignment. In the 1950s and 1960s, she argues, the Democrats' usually
reliable New Deal coalition was crumbling, and "There is a great deal of evidence that both parties were working to solidify an electoral majority during
these years; it would have been hard for them to ignore as large a bloc of voters
as women" (p. 32). Eisenhower benefited from a "gender gap" in voting over his
rival Adlai Stevenson in both 1952 and 1956, and appealed to women's groups
during campaigns and when in office. He called for an equal pay for equal work
law in January 1956, and promised support for the ERA in that year's campaign. Eisenhower also went beyond Truman in the number of appointments
to federal jobs given to women (pp. 33–34). Costain does not describe organized pressure on Eisenhower during this period, but he did make appeals to
the National Conference of Republican Women. Kennedy would follow suit in
taking a pro-women stance, but he emphasized legislation over political appointments and created a special White House organization to study women's
problems and propose solutions (p. 34).

Kennedy's actions proved crucial for the emergence of the current women's
movement. His actions mitigated the old factional disputes in the movement,
allowing for the opening of political opportunity. How did it happen? Esther
Peterson, head of the Women's Board in the Department of Labor, "persuaded
Kennedy to establish a presidential commission as a way to thwart pressure for
the ERA" (p. 28). The President's Commission on the Status of Women would

argue that different interpretations of the Fifth and Fourteenth amendments would achieve much of what was desired by the ERA supporters, such as ending jury exclusions and limitations on property and contracting,—while still allowing the protective laws. This stance did not end the factional split, but it brought the factions closer together. The Commission would also put together a comprehensive package of legislation to help women that would further reduce factional strife. The Commission's final report, 1963's *American Women*, gave the old factions a consensus agenda and a way to work together. While Costain does not list its recommendations, these included "specific bills for specific ills," such as provision of opportunities for women to work and develop skills on a part-time basis while they attended to family responsibilities, minimum wages for men and women, equal wages for equal work, better employment insurance protection for women, better maternity benefits, more generous childcare tax deductions, childcare facilities financed both publicly and privately, and constitutional equality (Harrison 1988, p. 164).

By 1963, Congress passed the Equal Pay Act and the following year, the Civil Rights Act of 1964. Title VII of the latter law was the only title to deal with women, but it covered the important area of sex discrimination in employment. Shortly before he was assassinated, Kennedy eliminated the President's Commission and created the Interdepartmental Committee on the Status of Women and the Citizens' Advisory Council on the Status of Women. The two bodies would "monitor the implementation of the recommendations of the presidential commission" and "continue the process of building a unified body of support for women's issues and a network that would help give rise to a new women's movement in America" (p. 29). Meanwhile, many younger women, involved in black civil rights and New Left organizations, were finding themselves treated as second-class members in these groups. These already mobilized women would be a boon to the new women's organizations: "the simmering discontent of young women in the civil rights and the new left movements of the early sixties created a new group of potential movement recruits with skills in protest activities lacking in most members of older women's groups" (p. 30).

These forces came together in 1966 with the agency facilitation discussed earlier. The context was that year's Conference of the Commissions on the Status of Women, which brought together women's leaders from the many state-level commissions that had formed—all modeled on Kennedy's Commission. Sympathetic officials of the Equal Employment Opportunity Commission (EEOC), especially commissioners Richard Graham and Aileen Hernandez, teamed with

Mary Eastwood of the Justice Department and Catherine East of the Citizens' Advisory Council on the Status of Women to encourage formation of a new women's group. Specifically, they focused on encouraging Betty Friedan, whose influential *Feminine Mystique* had appeared in 1963, to head the new pro-women pressure group. At the conference, Friedan and Kathryn Clarenbach, of the Wisconsin Commission, along with thirteen other women, formed the National Organization for Women (NOW). NOW quickly became the pressure group for women that many had hoped for: "Within hours of NOW's founding, its leaders had sent telegrams urging the reappointment of Graham to the EEOC, mailed letters asking the EEOC to rescind its directive on 'help wanted' listings in the newspaper, which allowed private employers to specify 'male' or 'female' positions, and contacted House and Senate offices supporting legislation mandating equal federal jury service for women and men" (p. 45).

NOW originally tried to limit its goals to the recommendations of *American Women*, but by November of 1967, it had moved to the left, endorsing both abortion rights and the ERA. These actions prompted more conservative members to leave, allowing NOW to move even "closer to the women's liberation groups that were forming across the United States in the late sixties" (p. 46). NOW and other groups would experience various convergences, splinters, and reconvergences, but pressure for policy change and gaining new awareness of women's inequality and oppression would be constants.

Costain gives cursory attention to another factor that helps explain the emergence of the women's movement—the raising of a new consciousness. Like McAdam (1982), she describes objective changes in a group's status to explain new ways of looking at the world that catalyzed the desire for change. Starting in the 1950s, the rate of women graduating from higher educational institutions increased, the percentage of married women decreased as divorce became more common and women married later, fertility declined, and more women entered the workforce. "As women lived through a wider range of experiences, in the work world and at home, where they might be the principal wage earner, they began to see public issues differently from men," explains Costain (p. 41). Political interpretations of discrimination at work and problems of single parenting followed. She quotes approvingly from Piven and Cloward (1977, p. 12), who note, "For a protest movement to arise out of these traumas of daily life, people have to perceive the deprivation and disorganization they experience as both wrong, and subject to redress." Costain adds, however, that government played an important role in this cognitive liberation, as "the presidential and

state commissions on the status of women gathered and publicized information about the legal, social, and economic hardships faced by most women"
and the early legislative initiatives of Congress and the president suggested that
government was a plausible vehicle for bringing about change" (p. 41).

By the 1970s, a significant new women's movement had emerged, and the
federal government was moving right along with these developments. Without any notable increase in support from public opinion, favorable publicity,
or organized lobbying, members of Congress, led by Edith Green and Martha
Griffiths, led a drive to bring the ERA to the floor of the House. The key to this
effort, which also included Green's groundbreaking hearings on sex discrimination in education (employment discrimination was also discussed), was the
lack of opposition from the old opponents of the ERA, especially organized
labor. As Costain argues, "it was not so much the perception of pressure from
women or women's groups that got Congress to pass the ERA, as it did in 1972,
but the crumbling of organized opposition" (p. 58).

The government was not just supporting the demands of women's groups,
but shaping the agenda. In the early 1970s, women's groups balanced demands
based on equality with demands oriented toward women's special needs, according to Costain's data from *New York Times* stories. In fact, her *Times* data
show women giving some priority to special needs issues. Similar balance was
shown in NOW's 1968 Bill of Rights, which demanded the ERA, enforcement
of Title VII for sex discrimination, equal educational opportunities, and laws
that would provide job training and subsidies for poor women commensu-
rate with those provided for poor men. In the special needs category, NOW
demanded as matters of right maternity leave in employment and social security benefits, tax breaks for working parents in home and child-care expenses,
provision of child-care centers, and the right for women's control over reproduction. Interviews and a review of women's group newsletters from the early
and mid-1970s revealed that "none of the groups could be characterized as
pursuing an agenda driven exclusively, or even predominately, by pursuit of
legal equality for women" (p. 83). In the same 1970–1974 period, however, the
government strongly pushed equality issues and neglected special needs. By
1975, the movement itself began to initiate more events focusing on equality than on special needs" (p. 87). While Costain believes Nixon did not support women's issues (others disagree; see Hoff 1994), women's groups still
had many other "woodwork feminists" helping their case along: "Feminists
on congressional staffs provided vote-counting networks both for women's

groups and feminist members of Congress such as Martha Griffiths, Edith Green and Margaret Heckler (R, Mass.), who were rounding up support for women's rights legislation" (p. 75).

Inviting Women's Rebellion also describes the decline of the movement, beginning in the 1980s. One cause was the failure of the necessary number of states to ratify the ERA. The other was the election of Ronald Reagan to president, which led to a significant closing of political opportunity. Reagan was popular with men, decisively won two terms, and was generally opposed to government regulation, including that which might help women. He was specifically opposed to legal abortion and affirmative action. He wanted support from women but "was at a loss about what to say" to them (p. 112). Though NOW and other groups continued to generate news events, government-initiated issues and events declined (pp. 116–17).

Expanding Opportunities?

While "political opportunity" is the central concept in political-process theory and thus in Costain's story, it has been plagued by imprecision. In response, Doug McAdam (1996) added clarity by identifying four different types of political opportunity. How do these relate to the current women's movement?

First, consider the factor of increasing popular access. The ability of women's groups to gain an audience with government leaders and to be treated seriously is a type of political opportunity that is clearly a part of Costain's account. Increasing access to the system came as presidents sought women's votes, appointed increasing numbers of women, and put them in new positions of leadership.

The role of NOW initially was to make moves that women's advocates in the government could not make. As Costain explains the triggering event in NOW's formation, "delegate Kathryn Clarenbach, leader of the Wisconsin State Commission on the Status of Women, and other concerned delegates were told that Clarenbach could not introduce resolutions supporting the reappointment of feminist Richard Graham as an EEOC commissioner or stronger enforcement by the EEOC of the Civil Rights Act Title VII's ban on sex discrimination since these would be interpreted as criticisms of the Johnson administration, which had organized the conference" (p. 45). Recognizing "the limitations of various [existing] organizations," NOW began its wave of pressure (telegrams and letters to the executive branch) and protest (sit-ins, pickets, fasts, declarations, and demonstrations). NOW and WEAL also found sympathetic ears in Congress. Such access to the system gave such groups confidence that their activities were worthwhile, though Costain does not explicitly explore the leaders' subjective interpretations of opportunity.

Second, regarding unstable elite alignment and competition, Costain explicitly invokes the importance of elite competition to explain the opportunities for the movement to form and develop. As mentioned above, these are discussed in the context of "clarifying process theory," especially Tilly's notion of government facilitation of movements.

The main competition is between Democratic and Republican party leaders, and the goal is the support of women's groups and the votes of women in general. Citing Piven and Cloward (1977) and Lawson (1976) on the importance of party competition for black votes—which created political opportunity for the black civil rights movement—Costain maintains that "Women were similarly objects of interparty competition, although less has been written about it" (p. 33). As the New Deal coalition crumbled, party leaders sought possible new coalition partnerships. Eisenhower sought women's support, and "[w]hen John Kennedy was elected president in 1961, after winning by the narrowest of margins, he quickly consulted with advisers about how to gain support from women and women's groups" (p. 34). While Eisenhower appointed more women, Kennedy had his important commissions, and talked more frequently about women, though these gestures were symbolic and not linked to legislation or policy initiatives.

Costain also suggests important divides between Congress and the White House. The number of bills concerning women's issues introduced in the House of Representatives, for example, doubled between the Eighty-sixth Congress (85 bills) to the Eighty-seventh (168), and similar doubling occurred between the Ninetieth (about 150 bills) and the Ninety-first (about 300). "Clearly," she deduces, "this mounting pressure within Congress for an equal rights amendment was influential in pushing [Esther] Peterson and Kennedy to form the Presidential Commission on the Status of Women and to propose an equal pay act as a possible alternative to it. Congress, in turn, was pushed to greater legislative activism by the recommendations put forth by the Presidential Commission" (p. 38).

Inviting Women's Rebellion claims that elite competition at the EEOC was also crucial. While Commissioners Hernandez and Graham tried to make the EEOC take sex discrimination seriously and believed it to be an important problem, "[t]he rest of the commissioners did not, speaking facetiously of every man's right to have a woman secretary" (p. 39).

Costain does not discuss at any length how women's activists viewed these circumstances. She asserts but does not support the claim that "the early legislative initiatives of Congress and the president suggested [to women] that government was a plausible vehicle for bringing about change" and that with party competition for women's support, "the electoral arena became an outlet for women to make their interests felt, through running for electoral office and through voting for candidates who seemed to recognize their values" (pp. 41–42). It is not clear from the analysis how party competition affected the movement after Kennedy, since there is little evidence presented here that the new women's groups ever took the Republicans seriously as allies. The basic strategy to take advantage of elite competition would be to take a party-neutral stance, and try to play the parties off of one another (Frymer and Skrentny 1998). Pressure and protest in the late 1960s and 1970s seemed to be designed only to make the Democrats take their stated pro-women commitments seriously.

In fact, the early women's movement seemed hemmed in by its reliance on the Democrats, despite the fact that NOW was formed partly to enter pressure and protest areas where women's commissions feared to tread. It "took pains, initially, not to go further in their stated goals than the recommendations of the Presidential Commission on the Status of Women" (p. 45). Later, however, after Costain describes efforts by NOW to avoid being mired in controversy, the organization moved to the left, and there is no evidence in the analysis that women's organizations sought to exploit Democratic-Republican competition, at least in the obvious way of offering support to the party who promised the most. In 1968, NOW endorsed the ERA and legal abortion, which distanced the group from some Democrats but did not move it closer to Republicans or to any strategic neutral ground to invite more competition from both parties.

Indeed, as mentioned above, conservatives left the group, and "[t]hese desertions allowed NOW to move to the left politically, bringing it closer to the women's liberation groups that were forming across the United States in the late sixties." A year later, in 1969, Friedan urged NOW to pay more attention to critics who said the group was moving too slow, not those who said it was moving too fast (p. 46). Even NOW's less-progressive spin-off, WEAL, pushed for issues that mostly appealed to the Democrats' left wing, arguing for various nondiscrimination measures. There is no evidence presented in the book that they acted to exploit elite competition or to court Republican support. While Costain does demonstrate that the GOP was proportionally more likely to sponsor the ERA than the Democrats (p. 59), she also maintains that this occurred without the ERA being a major priority of the movement. Thus, even where Republicans gave support, there is little evidence in the book that women leaders (as Costain defines that term) cared for this support. While women's groups may not have strategically exploited party competition, party leaders certainly competed for women's votes, some competition between Congress and the White House increased the speed of government action, and Republican support likely increased the sense of movement power.

Third, regarding elite allies, Costain emphasizes the crucial role played by allies of the women's movement in positions of power or influence in the federal and state governments. Before the current movement emerged, Esther Peterson of the Women's Bureau pressured Kennedy to support women's rights. The more dramatic example is Graham, Hernandez and others at the EEOC, some of whom fought for women's rights in an organization hostile to that cause, and who strongly encouraged the future leaders of NOW to form an organization.

Inviting Women's Rebellion does not contain evidence that Graham and Hernandez or anyone else at EEOC sought to facilitate a women's movement in an effort to create countervailing pressures to increase autonomy. This is the claim that Costain introduces early on as an important clarification of process theory, but the evidence here suggests Graham and Hernandez were simply supporters of the cause of women's rights. Hernandez later became president of NOW.

Some Congress members were also feminists or sympathetic to that cause, especially Edith Green and Martha Griffiths, and congressional staffs also contained feminists. In addition, Costain relates that, "In the course of conducting interviews with congressional staff and lobbyists for women's groups in 1974–75, I was told the names of wives and mistresses of members of Congress who were active in conveying information from women's groups to the member" and that a legislative assistant told her that "girl friends of representatives were a greatly underutilized resource in lobbying campaigns" (pp. 75–76). Costain emphasizes this key role of elite allies, made up of persons who may have been sympathetic to women's rights for years. In her 1974 and 1975 interviews with "congressional staff members, women's rights activists, and some agency personnel, the most common off-the-record comments told of giving and receiving clerical assistance and inside information from government workers to women's movement groups." This allowed the groups "to achieve a political impact much more quickly than would otherwise have been possible" (pp. 39–

40). Costain asserts, but gives no examples, that this aid worked both ways. While government officials aided the women's groups, the groups, by virtue of their very existence and presence, aided the officials: "With the emergence of a popular women's movement, they could now claim a public demand for solutions to these problems" (p. 39).

Why were there so many friends in government, particularly Congress? "Part of the answer," explains Costain, "is ideological" (p. 133). Perhaps "moral" is a better word. Griffiths and some others repeatedly introduced the ERA, and officials in the EEOC fought for women's rights. Costain does not show any feminist ideology (in the sense of a coherent world view such as Marxism) that animated supporters, but we can conclude that many officials believed it was the good or just thing to do.

The other reason for elite allies according to Costain is that some politicians who may have been less morally concerned held ambitions for higher office, and "began to view equal rights for women as an innovative issue with the potential to further their presidential aspirations" (p. 133). Especially in the Senate, these "policy entrepreneurs" may support issues not so much because of moral commitment but because these issues "will attract majorities in Congress and build their national reputations" (p. 133). To a surprising and fascinating degree, then, Costain describes the allies that women's leaders found in the federal government.

The fourth factor to consider is declining government repression. Unlike many other social movements, there was rarely any serious threat of repression of women's movement organizations. Costain therefore gives this subject little attention. She explains that of the "major women's organizations already in existence" before NOW formed, all of them "refused to take the initiative in speaking out" not because they feared government repression but because "they were afraid of being labeled feminist" (p. 45). In the 1970s "several of the groups, including the United Methodist Women and some of the more active feminist groups, felt that the Central Intelligence Agency (CIA) was responsible for break-ins and phone taps in their offices during the Nixon administration" (p. 75), though these remain only allegations and unfounded fears that had no clear effects on movement strategy.

The women's movement rarely engaged in protest activities that could be seen as challenging government authority. Violent language from groups such as the Society to Cut Up Men (SCUM) and the Women's International Terrorist Conspiracy from Hell (WITCH) was treated sensationally but rarely seriously by the press (p. 47). Demonstrations such as NOW's pickets were peaceful, and radical actions often took a symbolic form rather than a violent one. For example, a protest in front of the White House featured a skit by the New Feminist Theater, while WITCH released mice at a Madison Square Garden bridal fair and also put a "hex" on Nixon's wife Pat. The famous Freedom Trash Can, in which bras were deposited, was never even set ablaze (pp. 47–49). Declining government repression of the women's movement, therefore, was not a factor in its development.

Criticism

Costain's account is all-encompassing in method and scope, making it difficult to utilize the critic's favorite strategy of taking a scholar to task for neglecting some factor in the universe of possible factors. But one important omission does stand out. *Inviting Women's Rebellion* discusses at various points the black civil rights movement, but that movement does not figure prominently in the account; specifically, it is not a part of the explanation of expanding political opportunities.

Indeed, some distinctive features of the women's movement actually recommend downplaying the black movement. The women's movement has its own history and milestones, such as the 1848 Seneca Falls convention. It has distinctive internal conflicts, and its tactics are unique. In the more recent period, women's groups have demanded women-specific issues that have no analogs with the black civil rights movement, such as maternity leave and sexual harassment laws.

Costain downplays the importance of the black civil rights movement primarily because she identifies its importance with a resource mobilization interpretation of the women's movement, which would assert the importance of the civil rights movement as a stepping-stone, for women leaders to build and attract resources, allies and goals. She argues that the theory would stipulate that the women's movement, "by urging the incremental extension of equal treatment to women, used legislative gains of the civil rights movement to add protection for women," and that the civil rights groups joined forces with women's groups. Costain rejects this view, since women's groups' "insistence upon passage of the ERA, day-care legislation, and the Equal Credit Opportunity Act reflected their view that women could not simply piggyback black civil rights issues," and they did not shy away from big issues to focus on incrementalism

downplays CRM b/c RM perspective

(p. 10). The civil rights movement is thus only a bit player in the story, and Costain ignores it altogether in a section on how women's consciousness was raised in the 1950s and 1960s (pp. 40–41).

The women's movement and the civil rights movements are certainly different, but there is no reason to relegate the civil rights movement's importance to a resource mobilization interpretation. A compelling argument can be made that fits it into Costain's political-process/political-opportunity model. Costain describes the value of the perspective in its emphasis on how the "political process" can become receptive to a new movement, both encouraging its growth and allowing it to make some policy impact (p. xv). On these dimensions, it seems clear in Costain's own account and in published works (including some she cites) that the black civil rights movement played an important role in increasing the receptivity of the government to the women's movement.

The politics of race discrimination and sex discrimination have intriguing and significant linkages. Women's leaders drew heavily on the linkage in publicizing injustices that women suffered, coining such phrases as "Jane Crow" (analogous to "Jim Crow"; Murray and Eastwood 1965), "Aunt Toms," and the idea of "chick as nigger" (Friedan 1991, pp. 95, 140). McAdam has labeled this a "diffusion process," maintaining it is a cultural or cognitive dynamic whereby members of one social movement organization creatively adapt and interpret the "frame" of another group (McAdam 1995, pp. 226, 229).

This race-sex linkage also had a role in gaining leverage with the government and more generally increasing political opportunity. It is misleading to study the women's movement in isolation from the black movement.

McAdam (1995, pp. 224–25) has suggested that expanding political opportunities have little relationship to the rise of spin-off movements, pointing out that the gay rights movement developed precisely when political opportunities seemed to be contracting (in 1969, the first year of the Nixon administration). Seeing no change in the "institutional features of the system" and no benefit from changing political alignments in this case, he concludes that the existence of a reform cycle does not improve the leverage of all organized contenders. The "late risers" confront a government that is preoccupied with the "early risers" (McAdam 1995, pp. 224–25). This may be true, but it does not preclude the possibility that initiator movements, such as civil rights, open political opportunities for later developing movements, such as the contemporary women's movement.

Costain follows other political-process theorists in arguing that unstable elite alignments and competition are factors in creating political opportunity.

weakened
dt ckm

She points to the weakening of the New Deal coalition as a factor leading to competition for women's votes. What is not explained is the important role that the civil rights movement had in leading to this weakened New Deal coalition. Liberal Democrats had neglected racial equality to avoid alienating Southern Democrats and some labor unions, particularly the building trades. It was the civil rights movement that forced their hand, leading both Democratic and Republican coalitions to go into flux (see, for example, Scammon and Wattenberg 1970; Edsall and Edsall 1991; Sugrue 1996, 1998; Skrentny 1996). This gave a new opening for women to press their demands.

The civil rights movement helped create opportunities where new women's groups could gain access and find allies. It must be remembered that perhaps the single most important law that "invited women's rebellion," the Civil Rights Act of 1964, was designed for blacks. Paul Burstein's (1985) research, also cited, shows that nearly all witnesses at hearings for Title VII and its precursors were representing black groups. A short-term coalition of women congress members and Southern opponents of black civil rights, who were ultimately at cross-purposes and had different hopes for the future of the bill, led the drive to amend Title VII to add sex discrimination protection (p. 37). Without the civil rights movement, however, this opportunity would not have existed at all.

The crucial result was that Title VII created the EEOC to fight discrimination on the basis of race, color, religion, national origin, and sex. This was its legal mandate, but the overwhelming source of support for (and resistance to) Title VII and the creation of the EEOC came because of race. It is not surprising that EEOC administrators gave priority to race discrimination, though this was clearly unjust, especially since a third of the complaints the EEOC received were from women (Skrentny 1998). The neglect of these complaints fired the consciences of EEOC commissioners Aileen Hernandez and Richard Graham, and "by 1966 virtually every women's organization protested the EEOC's cavalier attitude toward sex discrimination" (Harrison 1988, p. 192). Hernandez and Graham had key roles in encouraging NOW's formation, but the EEOC existed and received its budgeting because the civil rights movement had succeeded in pushing Title VII through an extremely reluctant Congress. Thus the civil rights movement helped create an institutional access point and base of influence for actors who shared the goals of NOW.

Further, the perception of the federal government's responsiveness to the civil rights movement—it was on record as being on the side of equal rights—was also a likely factor in the emergence of the current women's movement. This idea of government responsiveness may be included in the ideas of increased access or "openness" (as McAdam puts it; 1996, p. 27), or as part of declining government repression. The fit is not perfect, however, since the new movement is extrapolating and deducing from the experiences of another movement and not its own history or situation. Put simply, the perception of expanding opportunity (and increased leverage) can come with the success of another movement. Early on, supporters of the idea of a women's commission were asking Kennedy to give as much attention to women as to blacks, as Cynthia Harrison describes (1988, p. 111) in a work cited by Costain. NOW's organizers were impressed by the success of the civil rights movement, declaring in its Statement of Purpose, "There is no civil rights movement to speak for women, as there has been for Negroes and other victims of discrimination. The National Organization for Women must therefore speak" (Friedan 1991, p. 112). Friedan told an audience at Cornell University in 1969 that "women are going to have to organize just as the blacks and any oppressed peoples have had to, not to destroy or fight or kill men or even to take power away from men, but to create institutions that will make possible a real life of equality between the sexes" (Friedan 1991, p. 149). Therefore, though it is true that early congressional initiatives on women's issues provided the sense that "government was a plausible vehicle for bringing about change" (p. 41), Congress's higher-profile initiatives for blacks sent the same message sooner and stronger.

The civil rights movement had effects on political opportunity for women's policy success as well as group emergence. Costain documents that the government took the lead on women's issues, and pursued an equality agenda although the women's groups equally supported a special-needs agenda. But she also acknowledges that the civil rights movement had made government actors "comfortable" with (more receptive to) the equality agenda (p. 138), and that the ERA had a "logical link" to the civil rights movement, making Congress "ready" to move on it and other civil right–related bills (p. xv). These acknowledgments are only briefly noted, and their importance minimized. But did these links and this readiness not in some way increase opportunity, increase possibility or likelihood of access and successful outcomes? I would argue that they did, and thus were significant parts of the opening of political opportunity.

Inviting Women's Rebellion raises an important definitional question: What is the difference between a social movement and a government-initiated reform, and are there clear boundaries between the two? Social movement studies generally start with the assumption of movements and the government as discrete entities. A group with a grievance usually begins the process by seeking anything from legislative reform to total social revolution. The movement is assumed to be excluded from normal institutional avenues of political action, and the state for some reason refuses to address the outside challengers' grievance. Political-process theory allows that movements may have allies who are government officials and who may "facilitate" movement action.

The case of women's rights and policies may go beyond allies and facilitation. The government was infiltrated by "woodwork feminists," and many in leadership positions strongly promoted women's causes. Further, government officials strongly encouraged—essentially begged—the major women's group (NOW) to form. Government officials then proceeded to disregard much of the new women's agenda, and aggressively furthered their own idea of women's ends. But what precisely is the role of government in Costain's account? Who are the real activists? Where does the government end and the social movement begin?

While Costain's study is fascinating and empirically driven, ambiguities remain on these questions. For example, Costain is inconsistent and vague on the important point of just how social scientists should characterize the role of the government in the development of the current women's movement and political opportunity in general. The book, with many metaphors and a variety of verbs that dance around this issue, accepts the social movement/government separation and grants a leading role to the government. In the conclusion of the chapter on "The Opening of Political Opportunity for Women," for example, Costain says, "It is more accurate to assume that government officials anticipated the rise of the women's movement than that they promoted it" (p. 42). "The stage was set" because of government action for quick influence when the movement emerged in 1966 (p. 42). Government, therefore, was a "prime determinant of the timing and initial political agenda of the movement" (p. 43), "played a key role in determining the course" of the movement (p. 122), and "was willing to facilitate [its] emergence and early development" (p. 136). The title of the book suggests that the government "invited" women to rebel.

Did government recede from its leadership role on women's issues after its invitation was sent out? Costain's answer is no, at least until the election of Reagan. While the new women's groups and some professional groups undeniably exerted substantial pressure, they did not clearly take the leadership role. Based on her statistical analysis of the relative impacts that government, the women's movement, and public opinion had on each other between 1950 and

1986, Costain concludes, "At different times, Congress, public opinion, and the women's movement played a leading role in guiding policy affecting women" and that one cannot divide the period into stages or identify "a single dominant actor." Neither Congress nor the movement, however, will "willingly stray too far from public opinion" (pp. 131–34). This may be a point worth developing: political-process theory does not assign an important role to public opinion in the expansion of political opportunity. More immediately for scholars of the women's movement and social movement theorists, however, clarification of the nature of the government's key role is necessary.

The primary difficulty is that throughout the book, Costain (like other political-process theorists) continues to treat the new women's groups and the government as separate entities. The book makes clear that the government was shot through with "institutional activists" (Santoro and McGuire 1997). Indeed, while Betty Friedan gets much-deserved credit for starting NOW, it appears that the impetus for the current women's movement came from the government itself, not some marginal challenging group with a grievance. EEOC officials actively set out to create a new movement; other officials in the status of women commissions joined them. The House and Senate had feminists in elected positions and on staffs. Even the Nixon administration had officials strongly promoting feminist causes, such as Rita Hauser (Graham 1990). Often these individuals had close ties to the emerging women's movement or were members, but this was not always the case and in some instances advocates were acting before the current women's groups formed. Because these individuals often took initiative on behalf of women but did so independently of the women's movement, it is difficult to simply label them allies, or to say they were "in" the movement. As David Meyer has argued, the boundaries between the "power holders (the challenged)" and "activists (the challengers)" in a contemporary liberal polity "are often hazy at best" (Meyer 1997, p. 6). Political-process theory gives a misleading picture by portraying them as separate actors.

Conclusion

Inviting Women's Rebellion takes its place as must-reading for scholars of the women's movement and students of social movements in general. It is an exemplar for the political-process approach to social movements. The case of the women's movement is so challenging that it shows both the strengths of the theory and its limitations.

The concept of expanding political opportunities is central to Costain's story. I have argued that the civil rights movement had a role in expanding political opportunities for women. There are cursory references to the civil rights movement in *Inviting Women's Rebellion*, but no adequate recognition of its importance in disrupting political coalitions, creating institutional access points, imparting a sense of government responsiveness, and providing models of influence and legislation that women could exploit or adapt. This point, however, does not so much conflict with Costain's study as it is complementary to it.

Another potential area of concern is more abstract. So interwoven are "the women's movement" and "the government" that it is a strain to try to analytically separate them. The basic (and surprising) fact is that even before the modern women's movement formed, this incipient movement had advocates in positions of power. Indeed, the current movement arguably began in the government as officials, mainly in the EEOC, actually encouraged the extragovernmental women's movement to form. In analyzing the role of expanding political opportunities for the development of the women's movement, the concepts of "popular access" and "elite allies" may be nonsensical. The feminists in the government were not just allies, they were sometimes leading the movement.

The problem highlights ambiguities that are inherent in a concept of "political opportunity" broad enough to include such things as legislators passing laws without pressure from women to do so. This is not Costain's fault so much as a problem with political-process theory. At least in the late twentieth century United States, there is considerable overlap between the challengers and the challenged. Costain's book reflects the ambiguities in political-process theory, but also challenges us to respond to them.

RESPONSE TO JOHN SKRENTNY
Anne N. Costain

John Skrentny's chapter gives me the welcome opportunity to revisit two of the major issues that have both intrigued and troubled me since *Inviting Women's Rebellion* was completed two decades ago. The first is the extent to which the civil rights movement provided opportunities that were then exploited by feminists to mobilize a successful women's movement. The second is how to separate social movement initiatives from government measures facilitating the emergence and development of a new movement. Or, phrased differently, how do we determine where a movement begins and the formal processes of government end?

Considering first the role of the civil rights movement, I do not think it is possible to study any American social movement arising in the sixties or later without reference to it. The civil rights movement is both a pathbreaking and a defining movement, important not only symbolically for what it represents, but crucial because of the extent to which it transformed formal and informal structures of American politics. On the symbolic and ideational level, it developed a powerful language linking equality, freedom, and justice that succeeded in exposing the painful contradictions between national goals and practice (Huntington 1981). The movement revealed graphically how majority populations within the Southern states were denied the vote, access to adequate schooling, and a chance to advance economically at the same time as America was labeled "the melting pot" and a land of unparalleled opportunity. As Doug McAdam (1996, p. 37) has commented, the civil rights movement also unintentionally undermined "the electoral alignments that had served as the basis of liberal Democratic control of the White House since 1932." This led to a transformation in American politics that resulted in a resurgent Republican party in the South and Republican domination of the presidency from the late sixties on. Although this macrolevel impact of the civil rights movement greatly affected the structure of opportunity presented to the women's movement, it was no more or less defining for women than for many other movements of the period.

Other binding ties between the women's and civil rights movements also warrant acknowledgment. First, many of the earliest activists in the women's movement came to it following significant involvement with the civil rights movement (Evans 1979; Freeman 1975). Research on the life-changing impact of activism in a challenging political movement suggests that not only would these women have been less savvy about styles and techniques of protest without this earlier experience, but they may also have been slower to mobilize around women's concerns (McAdam 1989). Second, there can be little doubt both that the language of the Equal Rights Amendment was modeled on the Fourteenth Amendment and that the ERA was of critical importance in sustaining a women's movement (Kay 1988, pp. 161–73). Leila Rupp and Verta Taylor (1987) have stated that pursuit of the Equal Rights Amendment was the single touchstone representing feminism in the 1940s and 1950s, with the National Woman's party in the forefront of this effort. Also, as Skrentny and I both observe, Title VII of the 1964 Civil Rights Act was yet another instance in which paths broken by civil rights advocates directly advanced women's rights.

Beyond these visible ties between the two movements, it is important to recognize as well their shared discourse. Richard Braunstein, Heidi Berggren, and I analyzed the extent to which newspaper coverage of women and women's issues utilized the language of civil rights (Costain, Braunstein, and Berggren 1997). We took random samples of *New York Times* articles on women in the United States for the four decades spanning 1955 to 1995. Only during the first period of study (1955–1964) were fewer than half the articles framed in a civil rights context. During both second and fourth decades (1965–1974 and 1985–1995), half the articles featured this perspective. In the third decade (1975–1984), more than three-quarters of the articles dealt with civil rights. This period was the height of national and state efforts to ratify the Equal Rights Amendment (ERA).

After providing evidence that appears to undermine my own case, suggesting that I may have unreasonably neglected the civil rights movement in my effort to explain the timing, circumstances, success, and impact of the women's movement, I will now defend the emphasis within my book. First, because virtually every American social movement appearing after the civil rights movement learned from its experience and adjusted to the political opportunities available in its wake, I believe that to understand the women's movement, in contrast to other "post–civil rights" movements in the sixties, it is necessary to identify characteristics unique to that movement. Because of the long history of alliances between the abolitionist and woman suffrage movements before the Civil War, as well as splits that arose after the war, aspects of civil rights are an important part of the women's rights story. Yet, by the early 1970s, when I began to research Washington-based lobbying by women's groups, I was repeatedly cautioned to recognize the differences between black civil rights and women's rights. The two most striking were, first, what women regarded as a "star system" among the civil rights leaders. The tactical and strategic splits that had divided the leadership of what then barely seemed a single movement—with Martin Luther King, Stokely Carmichael, Rap Brown, and Malcolm X all having led adherents in different directions—solidified the resolve of women's movement activists not to permit hierarchical organization and national leaders to divide the movement. Second, the inability of the civil rights movement to sustain its sweeping legislative victories from the sixties into the seventies caused those representing women's groups to look for political tactics appropriate to a majority of the population rather than those effective for minorities.

More important than the preference of women's activists not to be folded into the broader analysis of civil rights, my downplaying of the connection to the civil rights movement was due primarily to the evidence I accumulated that Congress, presidents, and courts all preferred to deal with women's issues in a civil rights rather than in an interest-group/special-needs context. It often seemed easier for political institutions to legislate against discrimination in education, employment, and so on by adding a ban on sex discrimination than to commit resources to research and fund quality day care, effective health coverage for women, or access to drugs and procedures to control reproduction. While not meaning to deny credit to the civil rights movement for many of the most important gains of the women's movement, I believe it may have been the mediated influence of government that led these civil rights extensions to be delivered to women, as much as it was women's tactical choice to pursue them. This is part of the "invitation" to rebellion. By joining the push for legal equality in the sixties and seventies, women were able to gain a number of legislative victories rather quickly, while laws to benefit women as women were much slower in coming.

This leads directly to Skrentny's other major observation. It is indeed extremely difficult to draw the line between government and movement. This is not only evident from the women's movement, but from the civil rights movement as well. The assistance provided to movement activists by Robert Kennedy as attorney general and by other lawyers in the Civil Rights division of the Justice department are well documented. The women's movement benefited from Republican First Lady Betty Ford's adoption of equal rights for women as her special project. This suggests two things to me. First, it is very important to learn more about the relationship between established institutions of government and social movements. Traditionally, the relatively strong state and local government sectors in the United States and the robust interest group community have been seen as stabilizing politics by diffusing and transforming the efforts of political movements to pursue change. By contrast, Sidney Tarrow (1998b) holds that strong federal units historically and at present provide organizational opportunities for social movements ranging from prohibition and abolitionism to black civil rights and gay rights to build membership and gain strength. This disagreement within the literature on United States federalism deserves more exploration by social movement scholars, with the women's movement as an important case to assess federalism's role in shaping political change.

The second aspect of this social movement/government link is the language used to discuss each. Paul Burstein (1998) has asserted provocatively that interest groups, social movements, and political parties may not differ from one another sufficiently to warrant studying them separately. As an example, using the case of the women's movement, the gender gap in electoral politics may be viewed alternatively as a logical outcome, a single manifestation, or the institutionalization of the women's movement. To decide which it is requires an understanding of both the women's movement and institutional politics. After the suffrage movement, the long-awaited (and even feared) bloc of women's votes never appeared in sufficient numbers to reshape politics. Scholars now tend to view women's voting in that period as the institutionalizing and disappearance of the movement. But, in the case of the contemporary women's movement, the turnout gap, with women voting in larger percentages than men, combined with the persistent gender gap, in which women vote for different parties and candidates than men, suggest a different conclusion. In fact, it is possible to view the gender gap as the mechanism moving the women's movement into the government.

To conclude, it would be extremely useful to have a wide-ranging assessment of how much the civil rights movement provided opportunities for other movements in comparison with the women's movement. Undoubtedly, some will have profited more than others, but the relative debt has too long gone unmeasured. Second, both the language and the concepts applied to study social movements and political institutions should be revisited to see if a common language may reveal more about their relative contributions to political change. Finally, in the case of the women's movement, I believe that the extent of its political opportunities and the possibilities of its transformative impact lift it out of the category of average cases. As an outlier, I agree with John Skrentny that it can teach us a great deal about the complexity of movement and government linkages.

REJOINDER TO ANNE COSTAIN
John D. Skrentny

Anne Costain and I agree more than we disagree. What remains to be explored is what the women's movement in the late twentieth century can tell us about movements, opportunities, and how to think about and explain political and social change.

In my own research on the women's movement and its policy successes, I have compared this movement with others that were fighting for change at about the same time and were seeking similar goals of nondiscrimination and equal opportunity (Skrentny 2002, 2006). These included movements working on behalf of Latinos, Asian Americans, American Indians, the disabled, white ethnics, and gays and lesbians. Not all these movements were successful—white ethnics and gays/lesbians failed to win significant rights during the same period. Women struggled more for gains that came relatively easily for nonblack ethnoracial minorities.

The pattern of success/failure does not correlate with movement size or resources, nor does it depend on when the movement started. As I sought to examine political-opportunity variables to explain variations in success, I began to see that political opportunities need to be viewed as dependent variables as much as independent variables, as James Jasper notes in his introduction to this volume. Why do some movements gain more access, allies, or elite competition for their support than other movements?

I argued that understanding why some movements had an easier time achieving policy success than others requires understanding how policy-making elites perceived different movements. Even when seeking the same goal, such as rights to nondiscrimination, different movements face different challenges, as seen most clearly in the challenges faced by gay rights activists. Elites have been especially reluctant to grant this group rights and opportunities, and even today, gays and lesbians lack basic rights to nondiscrimination in the workplace in federal law. The historical record also shows that elites put up very daunting roadblocks to rights for both white ethnics and women.

The reason, I argued, had to do with the different meanings that policy-making elites perceived in different groups. These policy-elite perceptions were important in the development of minority rights, but I believe they are part of any case of policy making, or at least social policy making. In the case of the development of minority rights, including women's rights, these meanings had at least three different dimensions. First, there was the *definitional* dimension. This relates to the most basic identity of the social group that is the (potential) object of policy. Aspects of group definition include the salient physical characteristics of the group, what elites perceive the group's history to be (Is a particular group traditionally a focus of state concern? In what way?), and how elites expect that group to behave in the future (Will they reward us with votes if we help them?).

Analytically distinct from these definitional meanings are *moral* meanings. These refer to perceptions of how deserving a group may be for some kind of targeted social policy, which may in turn be related to perceptions of that group's suffering (How much? What has caused any group suffering or extreme needs?) and/or perceptions of that group's contributions to society (Have they done something special for us or contributed distinctively in some way?).

A third dimension of meaning is the perception of *threat*. Policy makers may view a group as undeserving and very different from past objects of solicitude, but if they also view that group as potentially very violent and likely to lead to a loss of state control or to threats to national security, they go ahead and create social policies to attend to that group. In this way, policy-elite perceptions of threat may override perceptions of, for example, unworthiness.

In the case of minority rights, variations in movement success depended strongly on how elites defined the groups (especially regarding how similar they were to blacks), and how morally deserving they perceived groups to be. A big part of the story of the women's movement in the 1960s and 1970s was the problems this movement faced because elites defined them as very different from African Americans. This meant that women's groups had to fight harder for the same rights that other groups, including Latinos, American Indians, and Asian Americans, were able to win more easily. Gays and lesbians faced even bigger challenges: elites saw them as very different from blacks, as morally suspect, and thus undeserving of help, and they did not see them in their disadvantaged state as a threat to government control or national security. Gay and lesbian groups fought hard, but policy-elite perceptions (either based on voters' perceptions or elites' own principles, or both) ensured that they had the fewest political opportunities.

Through careful comparative analysis, we can document the effects of policy-elite perceptions on social movement successes. I have not made it a point of focus to identify the origins of the perceptions, but this should not be terribly difficult. I have traced the linkage of Latinos, Asian Americans, and American Indians to African Americans at least back to the 1940s in the minds of policy makers intent on preventing discrimination. Elites were much less likely to define women as a group similar to African Americans until women's groups pressured them to change their perceptions in the 1960s. In effect, women's groups "rebranded" women with a new meaning: not identical to blacks, obviously, but similar enough that they should receive extensions of civil rights policies designed for blacks, including nondiscrimination rights and affirmative action.

Gays and lesbians today are still engaged in a struggle similar to that faced by women's groups decades earlier to change their group meaning. It is possible that the struggle for gay marriage may have the effect of changing the meaning of gays and lesbians in the minds of policy-elites from morally challenged or depraved to "folks like us" with the same sort of mainstream aspirations—such as a happy family life with a loving partner—and thus are deserving of access to these things. A change in the policy-elite perceptions of the meaning of gays and lesbians would lead to greater political opportunities.

Costain and I agree that the women's movement forces movement theorists to reconsider the movement versus state dichotomy that is so common in the literature. The women's movement did not only have allies in the state, or access to the state. In important ways, the women's movement was "in" the state: movement actors operated from positions of power and used that leverage to pursue ends for women's rights.

Jasper notes in his introduction that it is important to disaggregate the state and be aware of different policy styles in the state. Different state "players" (to use Jasper's term) will likely have different concerns and logics of action. In my experience, this is a valuable insight and I have used it in my own work, and it has important implications for political opportunities. Understanding the dynamics of different institutions in the state (each as a separate player) is an important part of understanding movement opportunities (or one might say probabilities) for success.

Here, sociologists can learn much from political scientists. Understanding the dynamics of different state institutions is exactly what political scientists do. When I did my research for my first book (Skrentny 1996), in which I sought to understand how affirmative action developed for African Americans in the face of great resistance, I soon discovered that different state actors came to see affirmative action as a rational policy choice for different reasons and following different institutional logics. Although there is some classic work in sociology on administrative agencies (Nonet 1969), other institutions, such as the presidency, had never been investigated by sociologists. Yet such a study was appropriate and necessary to understand why a Republican like Richard Nixon would support a policy like affirmative action.

In order to understand political opportunities as a dependent variable and better understand policy-elite perceptions, we must disaggregate "the state" and analyze its internal dynamics. While I did not find much variation in how different state institutions defined "women" or in the moral or threat meanings they attached to this group, it is highly likely that variations abound. For example, the history of immigration policy shows consistent variations in how the White House and the State Department, on the one hand, and Congress on the other, viewed immigrants (Skrentny 2002). Presidents and State Department officials tended to see immigrants as extensions or agents of foreign states with whom the United States sought to maintain friendly relations. Members of Congress, in contrast, often saw migrants (particularly in the early twentieth century) as economic competitors, as criminals, or as cultural contaminants. These varying perceptions led nativist movements to find allies in Congress (while advocates for Asians and for Eastern and Southern Europeans found enemies or resistance to their wishes in Congress), and Congress passed various immigration restriction measures, sometimes over presidential vetoes and the complaints of State Department officials.

What explains this intra-state, institutional variation in policy-elite perceptions? In the case of early twentieth-century immigration politics, I believe it is variation in the audience or constituency that separates the State Department/ White House from Congress. The former two institutions make foreign policy and are regularly engaged with a world audience and the perceived meanings and cultural boundaries of foreign lands. This leads them to see immigrants as factors that may allow the United States to win leadership of or curry favor from foreign states. Members of Congress, in contrast, focus on the parochial concerns of their districts or states. Different institutional orientations lead to different perceptions of the objects of policy (immigrants), and this in turn leads to different opportunities for success for different movements and in different venues of the state.

In summary, the case of women's rights helps us to see the importance of political opportunities in understanding the development and especially the success of a social movement. To truly understand how political opportunities work, we need to see them as a dependent variable. When we look at movements in a comparative framework, we can see that political opportunities can vary significantly from group to group, and they do in part because policy-elite perceptions vary between groups. Policy-elite perceptions, in turn, can be shown to vary among different players in the state structure. Though I believe these concepts help make social movement variations intelligible, they admittedly make the story more complex. On the other hand, political success is rarely simple.

7 Gay and Lesbian Liberation

John D'Emilio's *Sexual Politics, Sexual Communities*

ADAM ISAIAH GREEN

O N THE EVENING OF JUNE 27, 1969, in the course of a routine gay bar raid, New York City police became the targets of what was later called history's first lesbian and gay riot. Then, incensed patrons of the Stonewall Inn directed catcalls and boos at the officers, pelting them with coins, bottles, and assorted debris. When the police took refuge behind the bolted door of the bar, the angry mob gathered outside promptly shattered the windows, smashed the door open, and set the Stonewall Inn ablaze. That evening, and in the forty-eight hours following, rioters took to the streets of Greenwich Village, disrupted traffic, distributed literature condemning police harassment, and called out for gay civil rights. For many, Stonewall would ignite the lesbian and gay liberation movement in a key turning point for sexual politics in American history.

In the months and years that followed, lesbian and gay activism increased exponentially and with unprecedented visibility in the United States, accompanied by the efflorescence of gay newspapers, gay bars and baths, gay cinema, gay parades, gay niche marketing, and a wide array of openly gay-owned and -operated businesses and service organizations. Over time, gay liberationists gained powerful inroads to centers of political power, organized substantial voting blocs in urban centers, and acquired a gay rights plank in the Democratic party's national platform in that year. Equally significant cultural transformations are also attributed to gay liberation, including challenges to

cultural change –
framing

the dominant, heteronormative narrative that enshrined the reproductive, heterosexual nuclear family.

In the early twenty-first century, U.S. lesbians and gays find affirming representations of themselves in mainstream, prime-time television programming, and in the music and sports industries. So, too, gay and lesbian civil rights struggles have made substantial, if as yet incomplete, advances toward open participation in the armed services, an end to discriminatory practices in housing and employment, and the legal right to marry and adopt children. In the academic world, Lesbian and Gay Studies curricula have materialized at break-

---

MAJOR EVENTS IN THE HOMOPHILE MOVEMENT

February 28, 1950: Undersecretary John Peurifoy interrogated by the Senate Appropriations Committee about suspected homosexuals in sensitive national security positions; Senate subsequently releases a report condemning homosexuality

June 7, 1950: Senate Resolution 280 directs Senate Investigations Sub-committee to investigate the employment by the government of "homosexuals and other sex perverts"

April 1951: Emergence of the homophile movement in Los Angeles by founders Harry Hay, Bob Hull, and Chuck Rowland; establishment of the Mattachine Society

August 28, 1951: *Stoumen v. Reilly*, the first successful American gay rights case, regarding the right of the California Board of Equalization to suspend the liquor license of the Black Cat Restaurant for catering to homosexuals

June 23, 1952: First legal case backed by the Mattachine Society; the trial of Dale Jennings, arrested for lewd behavior in a Los Angeles public park and charged with entrapment, marks the first occasion of an openly gay man claiming his legal rights as a citizen within a courtroom setting

April 27, 1953: President Eisenhower's Executive Order 10450 is issued, causing thousands of suspected lesbian and gay individuals to be denied employment or fired by local and federal authorities

October 19, 1955: Emergence of the Daughters of Bilitis (DOB) in San Francisco when four lesbian couples gathered to create a social organization for homosexual women

November 15, 1961: Homophile Movement and Militant Activism: Frank Kameny forms the Mattachine Society of Washington D.C. to support his legal battle to maintain his employment with the federal government; which had been revoked solely because of his homosexuality

December 31, 1964: Police raid New Year's Eve fund-raiser for the new Council on Religion and the Homosexual in San Francisco

neck speed throughout the United States and Western Europe. In short, the homosexual—widely considered to be a human aberration less than fifty years ago—now occupies a profoundly transformed place in American society. To be sure, the issue of homosexuality in political, legal, and cultural arenas remains contested and will likely remain so well into the twenty-first century. Nonetheless, the lives and identities of lesbians and gay men have been refigured by gay liberation as the issue of homosexuality has been brought out of the closet and into the foreground of American culture and politics.

But the riot at Stonewall and the political movement that followed were not

June 7, 1965: *Griswold v. Connecticut* recognizes a right to privacy in the context of marital sex, providing grounds for lawyers to challenge the criminalization of homosexual conduct

June 16, 1965: *Scott v. Macy* complicates Civil Service Commission dismissals of homosexuals in federal employment; the New York Civil Service Commission begins hiring self-identified homosexuals

October 1965: San Francisco homophile militants, with the support of the Council of Religion and the Homosexual, establish Citizens Alert—a highly publicized 24-hour hotline that provides lawyers, photographers, and other services to victims of police brutality

August 1966: Homophile activists persuade Mayor John Shelley to secure anti-poverty funding for a highly populated gay area of San Francisco

November 2, 1965: Election of New York Mayor John Lindsay raises the spirits of homophile activists following his campaign endorsement of a police civilian review board

1967: Court cases of job discrimination and sodomy emerge as a product of gays and lesbians being aided by local and national chapters of the American Civil Rights Union

January 1, 1967: Increasing police harassment of the Black Cat and other gay bars in Los Angeles

1967: Highest courts in New York and New Jersey rule that a business license cannot be revoked solely on the grounds that an establishment caters to known homosexuals; substantial evidence of indecent behavior, beyond homosexual kissing, would have to be provided by the police before a bar could be closed

March 1969: Assemblyman Willie Brown introduces a Consenting Adults Bill in the California legislature following pressures from homophile groups

June 27, 1969: Stonewall Riot occurs in New York, as patrons of the Stonewall Inn resist police harassment

homophile mvmnt   1950s

the first organized lesbian and gay struggles in American history. In fact, as John D'Emilio makes clear in *Sexual Politics, Sexual Communities: The Making of a Homosexual Minority in the United States, 1940–1970,* gay liberation would not have been possible were it not for the homophile movement of the 1950s and 1960s and the transformation in consciousness it inspired. In this probing work, D'Emilio documents the formation and development of the homophile movement, situating its organizational and ideological evolution within the context of larger social, political, and economic structures and processes. From this bird's-eye view, D'Emilio analyzes the Stonewall riots and ensuing movement struggles, and links the explosive surge of gay liberation activities in the 1970s to the cultural and political infrastructure established by the homophile movement.

Guiding D'Emilio's analysis is the question of the timing and the course of the lesbian and gay liberation movement. D'Emilio suggests that gay liberation constituted a decisive moment in a much longer historical process of homosexual identity development. Marshaling a wide range of historical evidence, including, among others, newspaper articles, law enforcement statistics, interviews, and various organizational minutes, D'Emilio links local political moments to larger social and political contexts.   *links political*

Origins of the Movements

In explaining the emergence of both the homophile movement in the early 1950s and the modern gay liberation movement in 1969, D'Emilio emphasizes the process of gay identity formation and the social, political, and economic structures that shaped this process. Both gay movements were made possible because lesbian and gay individuals conceived of themselves outside of morally loaded psychiatric and psychoanalytic discourses that rendered homosexuality pathological. Changes in self-conception among homophile pioneers and the later radicalized identity politics of gay liberationists both served, to differing degrees, to transform homosexuals from a class "in itself" to a class "for itself."

D'Emilio's account begins with the shift to industrial capitalism and concomitant social transformations in the second half of the nineteenth century. At this time, the reproductive imperative of the agrarian family began to diminish as urbanization and the rise of independent wage labor drew sons and daughters out of the constraints of family life and into the cities. To the extent that agricultural production and human reproduction were no longer essential for economic survival, many men and some women were freer to fashion

frame

their lives around individual sexual preferences. In the late nineteenth and early twentieth centuries, individuals with same-sex attraction might find a small, hidden network of men and women like themselves in urban centers. Nevertheless, these networks were largely rudimentary and invisible, and incorporated only a very small percentage of homosexuals. Most homosexuals lived the better part of their adulthood in isolation, with little if any knowledge of urban homosexual subcultures.

It would take World War II to jump-start the formation of lesbian and gay subcultures, as young men and women from around the country relocated from their small hometowns to larger cities that housed defense-related industries. Then, the sex-segregated environments of the wartime effort offered unique opportunities for men and women in military units and in factories to explore same-sex attraction. What is more, for some military personnel, encounters with urban homosexual subcultures fostered the development of alternative sexual lifestyles. According to D'Emilio, by the end of the war, a sizeable number of men and women identified themselves as lesbian and gay and, thereafter, led sexual lives of their choosing in the context of homosexual networks from their hometowns and in metropolitan centers.

Concurrently, in the years leading up to and following World War II, Freudian psychoanalytic theory would gain popularity among a growing class of elite psychologists and psychiatrists, with the effect of consolidating a sex-object choice model that divided sexual orientation into binary heterosexual and homosexual categories. In this typology, heterosexuality was associated with physical and mental health and homosexuality with pathology. Law, medicine, *frame* and the criminal justice system invested these constructions with local institutional authority and the power of the state. The paranoia of the postwar, McCarthy era further stigmatized homosexuals in the dominant imaginary, which conceived of "the homosexual" as predatorial, pederastic, sinful, communistic, and psychopathic.

On the other hand, the Kinsey reports, which found that homosexual activities were far more prevalent than generally expected, gained circulation and *change* press in the 1950s. These findings began to chip away the psychiatric consensus *frame* that homosexuality was pathological. If more than a third of men reported homosexual activity to orgasm at some point in their lives, it became increasingly difficult to accept medicalized constructions of homosexual orientation. The Kinsey reports offered gay and lesbian individuals a sense that their sexuality was not as aberrant as the prevailing medical account implied.

It was at the intersection of these dual forces—the proliferation of homosexual subcultures and the intensification of anti-gay discourse and state repression—that the homophile movement emerged in Los Angeles in 1951. Its founders—Harry Hay, Bob Hull, and Chuck Rowland—had all been members of the Communist party at some point in their lives and, from this exposure, had extrapolated an analysis of homosexuals as an oppressed minority. Convinced that homosexuals needed to develop a sense of group identity and a politicized analysis of their marginal status, Hay, Hull, and Rowland formed the Mattachine Society. Following Marxist theories of social change, the Mattachine leadership mobilized a gay constituency for direct mass action. Weekly discussion groups examining the origins of homosexuality and the causes of oppression inspired a new gay consciousness as members of the Mattachine were challenged to reject the hegemonic sickness model in favor of an identity politics founded on sexual diversity. In the four years that followed, Mattachine membership would increase to over two thousand, spreading throughout California and to New York and Chicago.

The Daughters of Bilitis (DOB) emerged in San Francisco in 1955 when four lesbian couples gathered to create a social organization for gay women. Soon after, the organization produced a monthly publication for lesbians, the *Ladder*, addressing issues concerning female homosexuality from around the country. In founding DOB, its principal leaders—Del Martin and Phyllis Lyon—sought to create a safe social space for gay women to socialize outside of the bar scene. Ensuing group discussions of cultural and political issues led Martin and Lyon to expand the mission of the group to include the transformation of public understandings of lesbianism through education. Joining forces in 1956 with the Mattachine Society and the offshoot publication, *ONE, Inc.*, the homophile movement was well under way.

In D'Emilio's account, the homophile movement arose as part of a larger historical process that included industrialization and urbanization, World War II, the dominance of medical and psychiatric discourses, the growth and development of gay subcultures, and the repression of the McCarthy era. These converged to produce the conditions under which a gay identity could develop and become a rallying point for political change. Prior to World War II, gay identities and subcultures were simply too diffuse and isolated to produce a politicized gay constituency, no matter the conditions. However, following World War II, urban gay subcultures had matured to the point that the virulently anti-gay climate of the McCarthy era made homophile organization virtually inevitable. Inspired by the ideological innovation of Hay, Rowland, and Hull, which transposed the Marxist analysis of the plight of the working class to an analysis of the plight of the homosexual, the homophile movement and gay "consciousness" were born.

In the years following the formation of the homophile movement, seismic political and cultural transformations reduced the costs of a mass gay movement while facilitating a radicalized gay identity politics. The sexual revolution of the 1960s challenged the prior dominant, conservative, heteronormative sexual discourse with a progressive, sexually permissive discourse that characterized the era of "free love." New ideas about sexuality circulated in fiction, film, pornography, social science literature, and nonfiction exposés. These media brought the issues of nonprocreative and homosexual practices and pleasures to the foreground of American culture, with the effect of highlighting peoples and places where homosexuality was identified, accepted, and practiced. Additionally, the introduction and mass marketing of oral contraception and the circulation of norms affirming sexual exploration further liberated sexuality from a reproductive telos, opening the American cultural imaginary to new ways of conceiving sexuality and, especially, homosexuality.

framing not just pol.

D'Emilio points out that the cultural transformations that characterized the sexual revolution were necessary but not sufficient factors for the emergence of gay liberation. Once a collective gay identity acquired a critical mass, it would take other factors to produce a radical movement and to reduce the costs associated with participation in gay political struggle. According to D'Emilio, the larger culture of protest associated with the African American civil rights movement and the New Left were pivotal, as these movements radicalized gay youth and promoted an active, oppositional stance toward authority and the status quo. Identification with gay liberation connoted a timely political defiance rather than a stigmatizing medical condition. So, too, successful legal challenges to state-sponsored censorship, employment discrimination, and police harassment reduced further the costs and consequences of movement participation. Taken together, the sexual revolution, the culture of protest and legal advances in gay civil rights radicalized gay youth and homophile militants while significantly reducing the costs of movement participation. Hence, when patrons of the Stonewall Inn took to the streets in protest of police harassment in June of 1969, the conditions were ripe for a mass political movement. The Stonewall riot was the situational trigger that unleashed a much larger radicalized and radicalizing gay political consciousness.

like wmns mvmnt depend on CRM

Expanding Opportunities for the Homophile Movement

On the eve of the emergence of the homophile movement in the early 1950s, the national paranoia of the McCarthy era had reached its zenith. Any deviation from gender, sexual, or political convention was associated with immorality and, moreover, threats to national security. Indeed, in the years directly preceding and following the emergence of the homophile movement, homosexuals were all but excluded from access to the political system. The rise of a national moral panic brought on by state elites was then accompanied by efforts to weed out the presence of "sexual deviants" from all civil service positions. Toward this end, the FBI, in conjunction with the post office and local law enforcement agencies around the nation, constructed a massive multi-institutional apparatus for the identification, arrest, and conviction of homosexuals.

D'Emilio painstakingly traces these contracting political opportunities for homosexuals in the postwar era. Beginning in 1947, President Truman established the loyalty program for Federal employees, the Justice Department issued a list of "suspicious" organizations, and the House Un-American Activities Committee initiated highly publicized hearings concerning suspected subversives (p. 40). Early in 1950, Undersecretary John Peurifoy was interrogated by the Senate Appropriations Committee about suspected homosexuals in sensitive national security positions. Later that year, Governor Thomas Dewey of New York and the national chairman of the Republican party, Guy Gabrielson, made national headlines when they claimed that homosexuals were infiltrating the government and were "perhaps as dangerous as the actual Communists" (p. 41). Soon after, the Senate released a report condemning homosexuality and warning that "even one homosexual can pollute a government office" (p. 42).

Between 1950 and 1953, thousands of suspected lesbian and gay individuals were denied employment or fired by local and federal authorities. Following President Eisenhower's executive order 10450, suspected homosexuals were vigorously weeded out and dismissed from federal jobs. Those accused or convicted of illicit sexual behaviors, including individuals found associating in gay bars, saw their names, addresses, and places of employment printed in local newspapers, with often devastating personal consequences. By the mid-1950s, over 20 percent of the labor force had been given tests designed to identify "sexual perverts."

In nearly every realm of social life the homosexual in the 1950s had become the embodiment of moral aberration, psychic pathology, and a threat to

[handwritten margin notes: "even tho political climate was off, there was no", "way to establish strategic frame", "clearly diagnosed as a problem but no way to go about it"]

national security. The decade can thus be characterized as a time of dramati-cally decreasing political opportunities for lesbian and gay individuals, as they were actively marginalized from centers of power, faced increasingly pernicious and stigmatizing accounts of themselves by political and medical elites, and encountered a consolidated, repressive apparatus charged with weeding out homosexuals and subjecting them to persecution, surveillance, and control.

If expanding political opportunities cannot explain the emergence of the homophile movement, D'Emilio's research suggests that contracting political opportunities are equally insufficient as determinative causal factors. To be sure, decreasing access to political centers of power, growing anti-gay consensus among political elites, and increasing state repression shaped and structured the development and growth of the homophile movement, increasing the costs of mass mobilization. Nonetheless, D'Emilio traces out anti-gay traditions dating back to the Middle Ages in what he refers to as an "unbroken history of hostility toward homosexual behavior" (p. 241). Anti-gay sentiment was hardly new to the McCarthy era, but had taken various historical forms preceding the Cold War. What distinguished the 1950s was the particular confluence of processes and events characterizing the times—advancing industrialization, urbanization, the legacies of World War II, and the predominance of sickness models of homosexuality, for example—all of which had the dual effect of producing the growth of urban gay subcultures and gay-identified people, while marking them targets of state, legal, and medical surveillance and control. In this account, contracting political opportunities undoubtedly contributed to the impulse of homophile leaders to mobilize, but it was the convergence of other, larger historical processes that determined the timing and nature of the emergence of the homophile movement.

[handwritten margin note: "counter movmnt framed"]

Expanding Opportunities for Gay Liberation

By the time patrons of the Stonewall Inn took to the streets in 1969, considerable cultural and political transformations had occurred not only as a result of lesbian and gay militant struggles earlier in the decade, but also because of exogenous historical forces. The general political turbulence of the 1960s contributed to a sense among radical homosexuals that the traditional centers of power were weakening. Moreover, homosexuals had enjoyed some decline in state repression, with new legally protected rights to assemble and to be served alcohol. These expanding political opportunities, in combination with larger cultural transformations in sexual mores and in the self-concept of homosexuals more generally, provided the conditions for the modern gay liberation movement.

D'Emilio's research suggests that a series of events in the years leading up to Stonewall had lowered mobilization costs through small but substantial political and legal gains. These included reduced police harassment, legitimated rights to association and, in some instances, protected federal employment. For example, in 1965, with the support of the Council on Religion and the Homosexual (CRH), San Francisco homophile militants established Citizen's Alert, a highly publicized twenty-four-hour hotline that provided lawyers, photographers, and other services to victims of police brutality. Police brutality promptly halted, while the number of gay bars rose exponentially. In New York in 1967, the state's appellate court complicated the routine revocation of gay bar licenses, ruling that police needed substantial evidence of indecent behavior, beyond homosexual kissing, to close a bar. Subsequently, far fewer bar raids and bar closings occurred in New York.

In the second half of the 1960s, the number of gay-related civil rights cases reaching federal courts more than doubled as compared to the first half of the decade. In the years leading up to the Stonewall riots, New York, New Jersey, Pennsylvania, and California had all established the constitutional rights of lesbians and gays to assemble and to be served alcohol. The 1965 Scott case complicated Civil Service Commission dismissals of homosexuals in positions of federal employment, ruling that such dismissals must at least be accompanied by a specification of the particular immoral conduct at issue along with a justification as to why the conduct would impede occupational conduct. In the years that followed, the New York Civil Service Commission began hiring self-identified homosexuals. By 1967, aided by local and national chapters of the American Civil Liberties Union, gays and lesbians found the issue of job discrimination and sodomy taken up in discourse and court cases around the country, as this formerly anti-gay legal organization publicly declared its opposition to police harassment and job discrimination based on sexual orientation.

Some elite support appeared. While the majority of political elites during the 1960s retained their anti-gay commitments, a few adopted pro-gay positions. In San Francisco, in 1966, homophile activists persuaded Mayor John Shelley to secure anti-poverty funding for a heavily gay neighborhood. In the mid-1960s, San Francisco also witnessed annual "candidate nights" sponsored by homophile organizations. Local politicians took out ads in homophile publications and expressed support for the homophile movement. Similarly, in March 1969,

Assemblyman Willie Brown introduced a consenting-adults bill in the state legislature following pressures from homophile groups. And in New York, the election of John Lindsay in 1965 raised the spirits of homophile activists following his campaign endorsement of a police civilian-review board, which would provide a semblance of citizen oversight with respect to police action.

Elite legal organizations, too, such as the American Law Institute and the International Congress on Penal Law, supported sodomy law repeal during the 1960s. Both organizations drafted a model penal code, which, while largely ineffective in producing actual changes in legislation, nonetheless concluded that private homosexual sex between consenting adults was a protected personal liberty.

We should be wary of overstating the presence of elite allies in this period. Although the homophile movement had obtained some support from elites, this was mostly from lower-echelon bureaucrats and did not reflect the sentiments of the vast majority of political and legal power holders, who retained anti-gay commitments throughout the 1960s. More significant than these small gains was the general turbulence of the 1960s "culture of protest," which radicalized gay activists while providing a sense among many homosexuals that traditional centers of power were weakening. D'Emilio argues that the majority of participants in the gay liberation movement were young radicals recruited from the ranks of the New Left. These gay men and women had taken up activism either through the anti-war movement, the women's movement, or the black power movement. Adopting the countercultural, oppositional stance of their radicalized peers, gay liberationists were merely extending the political and social criticism of the New Left to the case of homosexual oppression. This extension was facilitated by the sexual revolution and the hippie counterculture. In short, the culture of protest of the 1960s paved the way for gay liberation.

Reducing the 1960s culture of protest to a political opportunity for gay liberation would obfuscate the primary way in which it catalyzed mobilization among homosexuals, which was—by generating widespread normative commitments to protest and to the struggle for civil rights. In D'Emilio's account, homosexuals became radicalized in the 1960s primarily through appropriating the anti-establishment and civil rights frames of the student and black power movements. While perceptions of a vulnerable state undoubtedly followed from small gains in elite support and from the proliferation of organized contention during the 1960s, it was changes in the cultural sphere—namely, normative commitments to protest and concomitant civil rights frames—that supplied the most critical impetus for homosexuals to initiate gay liberation.

In sum, militant homophile agitation and broader legal reforms improved the climate for lesbians and gays in the years preceding the Stonewall riots. Small gains in securing elite allies coupled with the political turbulence brought on by the 1960s culture of protest made activism normative while creating a collective sense of a weakened state. Decreased state repression, gains in civil rights and support from the ACLU all constituted an expansion in the political power and maneuverability of homosexuals in the latter half the 1960s. However, looking more locally to the political climate in New York City in the months prior to Stonewall, we find, to the contrary, a reinvigoration of state repression. The new commanding officer in the city's sixth precinct initiated a series of gay bar raids throughout the Village. Moreover, John Lindsay had recently lost his party's primary and, in the midst of a mayoral campaign—"always a bad time for the city's homosexuals" (p. 231)—had made a concerted public effort to "clean" the city of its sex deviants. In this sense, the Stonewall riots occurred in a local context of contracting political opportunities in combination with the more macrolevel expansion of political opportunities. These factors worked in tandem with cultural transformations to produce a mass, politicized gay consciousness. "Young gay radicals," D'Emilio concludes, "could act on the slogan `Out of the Closets and into the Streets' because they did not fear the consequences" (p. 246).

Criticism

D'Emilio's account of the rise of the homophile and gay liberation movements embeds microlevel events within larger, macrohistorical processes, locating the attitudes and actions of homosexual activists within the economic, political, and cultural contexts in which they occurred. In situating detailed events within broader historical and structural currents, D'Emilio provides a compelling sociological explanation for understanding the timing and developmental trajectory of the two movements. D'Emilio's work represents an ambitious and rigorous historiography, marshaling complex sets of actions and events in a rich and synthetic analysis. Nonetheless, looking more closely at the emergence of the Mattachine Society, Daughters of Bilitis, and gay liberation, some questions remain regarding the precise causal mechanisms of their development.

As I noted, D'Emilio's analysis of the timing of the emergence of the homophile movement in the early 1950s rests on a confluence of historical events and processes, including advancing industrialization and urbanization, World War II, and medicalized constructions of homosexuality. These factors provide the broad socioeconomic and cultural conditions under which the first politicized gay identities would take form: "Before a movement could take shape, the process [of self-identification] had to be far enough along so that at least some gay women and men could perceive themselves as members of an oppressed minority" (p. 4).

D'Emilio's account is complicated by historical work (including his own) on lesbian and gay communities, which provides evidence of the existence of substantial homosexual networks before the 1950s. George Chauncey (1994) and Lillian Faderman (1991) have documented homosexual subcultures in Harlem and Greenwich Village dating back to the turn of the century. Then, many urban homosexuals traveled and socialized in gay networks that were fairly well developed, albeit stratified by race and class, among other social characteristics. What's more, the rise of sex panics, censorship legislation, and state-sponsored anti-gay repression in the Prohibition and Depression eras make it clear that networks of homosexuals, then referred to as "inverts," were well known and generally poorly received in urban centers well before World War II. This evidence suggests that, at a minimum, other factors beyond the coincidence of homosexual networks and state repression are needed to explain why the homophile movement emerged in the early 1950s and not in earlier decades. To the extent that the early homophile movement did not involve a mass mobilization of homosexuals, and to the extent that most of the earliest homophile members had lived in gay networks in metropolitan areas prior to World War II (Murray 1996), it is unclear exactly how the postwar crystallization of gay subcultures contributes to an explanation of the emergence of the homophile political organization. D'Emilio's explanation of the birth of the homophile movement would seem to turn on an ideological innovation, mainly, a change in political consciousness among homosexuals that would bring gays and lesbians together into an organized opposition. Hay, Hull, and Rowland, drawing on their prior work within the Communist party, provided just such an ideological innovation, refiguring gay identity from a class "in itself" to a class "for itself." Still, we are left to wonder about the emergence of this ideological innovation and its possible relationship to the other causal variables in D'Emilio's model.

Similar questions about the precise causal mechanisms of gay liberation arise from D'Emilio's analysis of the Stonewall riots and the movement agitation that followed. Throughout the 1960s, political contention over lesbian and gay issues occurred in a host of locations throughout the United States in episodes as dramatic as Stonewall. For instance, on New Year's Eve, 1964, the police raid of a fund-raiser for the new Council on Religion and the Homosexual (CRH) in San Francisco resulted in prolonged media coverage, as the event provoked the wrath of the the ACLU, the lesbian and gay community and even the presiding judge at the trial of the police officers that followed. Subsequently, opposition to the anti-gay police action involved not only homosexuals, but highly respected professionals from the community, including heterosexual religious and political officials. And in 1967, stepped-up police harassment of the infamous Black Cat and other gay bars in Los Angeles provided another explosive run-in with police, leaving a bartender hospitalized with a ruptured spleen and numerous gay patrons viciously beaten by officers.

The event would set off the largest gay demonstration of the decade as several hundred homosexuals protested in the streets, espousing a radicalized, confrontational politics. Still, from these highly charged political moments, no national gay liberation movement emerged, even though these events were as highly confrontational and public as the Stonewall riots. From D'Emilio's account, we are to assume that these former episodes simply came too early in the development of a radicalized gay identity to ignite a mass movement. Yet other accounts (for example, Murray 1996), suggest that Stonewall ignited a mass movement less because of its novelty as a gay riot than because of its occurrence in New York City, the heart of the mass media in the United States. D'Emilio's analysis, in other words, may be missing key variables that explain the precise timing of the onset of gay liberation. In sum, while D'Emilio has elucidated the long-term economic, political, and cultural processes that produced the conditions under which the homophile and the gay liberation movements emerged, questions about the precise causal mechanisms of their onset remain unanswered.

Conclusion

In his study of the homophile and gay liberation movements, John D'Emilio's work demonstrates the emergence of two gay movements in opposing political conditions: the homophile movement emerged at a time of dramatic contraction in political opportunities, while the gay liberation movement arose in the context of their continuous expansion. To be sure, D'Emilio's research makes a strong case for seeing political opportunity structures as important variables that shape movement progress, but these structures produced no consistent effects. If both expanding and contracting political opportunity structures can give rise to a social movement, it would seem that other factors outside of the political-process model must be at play in causing movement onset.

D'Emilio's study urges us to consider the rise of gay social movements in the context of larger, cultural processes. In the case of the homophile movement, gays and lesbians had to first reject the sin and sickness models of homosexuality to embrace a political analysis of their position in society and organize accordingly. A decisive cognitive turn was required. And in the case of gay liberation, gays and lesbians, in sufficient numbers, had to see a direct-action approach as reasonable and effective. Reduced mobilization costs were important, and these surely came from the slow but steady expansion of the political opportunity structure in the 1960s. Nevertheless, it was only when mass protest became a normative part of the broader U.S. cultural fabric that a sufficient cadre of radicalized activists from other movements would join together to initiate gay liberation.

In this sense, the culture of protest that amassed during the second half of the 1960s was likely pivotal in raising the issue of gay liberation. It was in 1969—less than two years after the musical *Hair* first announced the coming of the "Age of Aquarius"—that the Stonewall riots ignited the modern gay rights movement. In short, in both the homophile and modern gay movements, factors other than the political opportunity structure were as, if not more, important in producing organized contention.

RESPONSE TO ADAM GREEN
John D'Emilio

At a time when the shelf life of intellectual work grows ever shorter, it is a great privilege to have a book of mine that was published many years ago be treated with the level of respect and seriousness that Adam Green affords it. It is also a treat to have it be used to evaluate a theoretical approach to social movements and to have my work in turn be evaluated against that theoretical approach. Unlike sociologists and political scientists, historians tend to wear theory very lightly, if at all. For all the innovations in the discipline of history over the last generation, the narrative tradition still holds the center. In my own work, which is very much embedded in that tradition, I try to think that theory informs, without constraining, my construction of the history of the gay and lesbian movement in the United States, and that my account can, in turn, inform the development of social movement theory.

In this brief comment, I have three points to make. The first will address the ways that political-opportunity theory and my account of the gay movement align with one another. The second will address an issue that political-opportunity theory does not. These first two points are very much consistent with Green's longer discussion. The third, however, will challenge the utility of political-opportunity theory altogether by suggesting the ways that our accounts of social movement history are both arbitrary and artificial.

Point 1. Political-opportunity theory does help us understand the initial emergence of a gay and lesbian movement in the United States (the homophile phase) and then its rapid transformation into a mass movement at the end of the 1960s (the gay liberation phase).

The fate of the homophile movement allows us to see the significance of both political opportunities and political constraints. One could argue that a number of elements in American public life in the mid- and late 1940s encouraged the beginnings of a gay movement. The experience of the nation, especially those who served in the armed forces, in successfully fighting a war against fascism placed on the table the ideals of democratic rights and fairness. The sense of political entitlement that military service gave to gay GIs, analogous perhaps to the experience of African American veterans, encouraged some few to organize for their rights. The publication of the Kinsey Report of male sexual behavior in 1948 and the relatively positive discussion in the press of Kinsey's findings on male homosexuality gave reason to believe that society was now readier to accept the gay people in its midst. Out of these elements came the impulse to found organizations with a political mission and the courage to pen the first major manifesto of homosexual rights published in the United States. But if a sense of expanding political opportunities allowed for these tentative beginnings, the rapid change in the political climate from the end of the 1940s through the next decade helps us account for how slowly the homophile movement grew and how little it was able to accomplish. The advent of McCarthyism and the climate of intolerance it bred, and specifically the aggressive anti-gay policies and practices of government at every level, left very little room for these first pioneering activists to maneuver.

By the end of the 1960s, the political environment had changed dramatically, and in ways both specifically and generally applicable to gay men and lesbians. For instance, a series of Supreme Court decisions between 1957 and 1966 on the issue of obscenity widened dramatically the boundaries of permissible sexual discourse and sexual representation. Other Supreme Court decisions, specifically in the areas of birth control and police behavior, elaborated the notion of privacy as constitutionally protected, constrained the arbitrary behavior of police, and strengthened due process rights. The judicial revolutions of the Warren Court, in other words, spoke in multiple ways to the situation of homosexuals. Meanwhile, the successes of the civil rights movement and the ability of student protest to shake the government made it seem plausible that collective action promised rewards, while feminism and the counterculture were arguing that issues of sexual behavior were very much the province of political action. Taken together, all these developments pointed toward expanding political opportunities, hence the explosive growth of gay and lesbian political action in the years immediately after the electrifying Stonewall riots in New York City.

Point 2. While political-opportunity theory can explain some things, it isn't rich enough to explain everything.

Green refers to my discussion of macrolevel structural changes in American life—the evolution of a capitalist economy, for instance, or the urbanization of the population, and certainly that kind of broad and deep change over time has to enter our theoretical calculations. These "big picture" elements help us understand why events occur in the last third of the twentieth century and not in the century's first decade. But my reservations about political-opportunity theory have more to do with issues of culture, consciousness, and social experience, topics that Green also raises.

As an example, the Supreme Court decisions referred to above can be understood within a political-opportunity framework yet might have more of an impact on how gay men and lesbians actually lived and, consequently, what they thought about their situation. Ready access to pornography or pulp novels, or the ability to read about gay experience and gay relationships in fiction or in the press, helps create a denser experience of being gay, which creates a stronger sense of group identification, and which in turn makes the leap to feeling the grievances of an oppressed minority easier to manage. Further, living through the (hetero)sexual revolution of the 1960s might affect the attitude of many gay men toward their sexuality. More willing to express it and to experience it as a right and a pleasure, they might also be more likely to engage in activities that bring them into conflict with the police, but in a context where the free expression of sexual desire seems natural and normal, not tawdry and depraved. And so, rather than be constrained by oppression, they choose to resist.

Take also the "culture of protest" that both Green and I comment on. Indeed, the proliferation of protest might lead some lesbians and gay men rationally to conclude that political-opportunity beckons, because protest seems to be working. Yet I suspect that for many students and young adults of that generation the so-called culture of protest functioned as a normative expectation: this is what we do, this is what makes us belong, this is what we get validation for. Put another way, in 1959, when the police raided a gay bar, patrons might cower, or they might camp it up; in 1969, rioting had entered the repertory of reactions.

Point 3. Beware the historical narrative out of which we construct our social movement theories, for it, too, is constructed.

Green raises the issue of the "key variables that explain the precise timing" of gay liberation, and the "precise causal mechanisms" that explain its onset. Encountering those phrases, I realized that a social scientist attempting to test something like political-opportunity theory needs something as solid as those terms imply.

But what if our histories of social movements, which are the raw material for building sociological theory, turn out to be far more tenuous than we usually admit? What if they are constructed narratives of a sort that, although not completely arbitrary, defy the search for precision—precise timings, precise mechanisms, precise anything?

For instance, Green's discussion of my book turns on the founding of the Mattachine Society in 1950 as the event marking the emergence of the homophile movement and on the Stonewall riots in 1969 as the event marking the emergence of gay liberation. In doing so, he is following faithfully the history of the homophile movement as I recorded it, and of gay liberation as virtually everyone dates it. But why these events? Why not the founding of the Veterans Benevolent Association in 1946, or the publication of *Vice Versa* in 1947, or Robert Duncan's essay, "The Homosexual in America," of 1944? Why use the Stonewall riots to date the beginnings of a new phase of the movement rather than the police raid of California Hall in San Francisco in January 1965, for example, which ushered in a dramatic new stage of the gay movement in that city? Or any one of several other events in the 1960s? As someone who has been both complimented for and accused of writing seamless historical narratives, I assure you that I could write a persuasive history of the gay and lesbian movement using any number of events. But doing so would require the sociological theorist to then cope with a different historical measuring point for evaluating the balance of political opportunities and political constraints. Rather than trying to claim that historical experience is so fluid as to make our narratives thoroughly arbitrary, I wish only to caution that political-opportunity theory places too much emphasis on clear beginnings, historical ruptures, and time-lines. The desire for dramatic events, for heroic characters, or for clear turning points might lead us toward the construction of narrative accounts that sustain such an approach. Yet we miss something vital if we fail to recognize the im-portance of continuities, the very subtle shifts that allow one era to shade into another, that make the moment when a movement emerges more ambiguous than is comfortable for our theory.

So I end where I began. Let's wear our theory lightly. Let's use it to inform rather than constrain our understanding of social movements.

REJOINDER TO JOHN D'EMILIO
Adam Isaiah Green

D'Emilio's consideration of political-process theory and its relation-ship to the Homophile and Gay Liberation movements offers students of social movements at least two suggestive leads for future study.

First, it may be necessary to reconceive how we define the onset of a social movement. Some movements, to be sure, would seem to have definitive begin-nings. But D'Emilio's comments suggest that movements may in fact have long gestation periods that are not necessarily visible in the form of a riot or the advent of a movement organization—a good example of Melucci's submerged networks. For example, while the onset of Gay Liberation can be identified with the Stonewall riots, D'Emilio points out that a new style of politicized gay or-ganization had taken place at least five years before Stonewall. It is not entirely clear why we should consider the Stonewall riots as the defining moment of the birth of the gay movement. Perhaps we need to consider social movements in more nuanced terms, with periods of gestation, uprising, formal organization, rapid mobilization, and dissolution, for instance. When we do, we may find different kinds of relationships between the state, opponents, and movement activities. The many "whens" of a social movement may be more effectively ana-lyzed in relationship to political opportunity structures, among other variables.

Even in light of the importance of political opportunities, D'Emilio offers the insight that changes in the opportunity structure are not necessarily deci-sive factors for movements or, when they are relevant, their effects might work less as state-level changes than through other social and cognitive processes that they encourage. That is, "political opportunities" may be relevant for social movements because of their symbolic implications or because they are correlated with changing normative expectations and cognitive frames around how to conceive of and address social ills. For instance, unstable and eroding elite alliances during the 1960s or the instability of the institutionalized political system may represent the "opening" of the political opportunity structure, but their primary significance in promoting gay liberation may have worked at other levels, such as inspiration for new kinds of activist identities centered on mobilization and direct action.

D'Emilio's remarks suggest that students of social movements need to be wary of attributing causal properties to political opportunities, when the latter may, in some instances, function as correlates, not causes, of more important explanatory factors of movement formation. In the case of gay liberation, for example, expanding political opportunities occurred at the same time as societywide normative transformations regarding how to conceive of oppressive political conditions—that is, the 1960s culture of protest. Moreover, during this period, future gay and lesbian activists were exposed to new, popularized repertoires of action through their involvement with the African American civil rights movement, the feminist movement, and the New Left more generally. To extrapolate from D'Emilio's remarks, the expansion of political opportunities was copresent with the 1960s culture of protest, but the latter, not the former, was decisive in getting the gay liberation movement under way. In short, social movement research will need to disentangle the many synchronous events and processes attendant to organized political contention. In light of D'Emilio's account of the contracting and expanding political opportunity structure in the homophile and gay liberation cases, both movements would seem to hinge on new cognitive frames made possible by, in the first instance, the U.S. communist movement and, in the second instance, the 1960s culture of protest. In fact, in these cases, political opportunities had contradictory outcomes.

8 The U.S. Movement for Peace in Central America

Christian Smith's *Resisting Reagan*

JAMES M. JASPER

I N 1981, when he was asked to help a Salvadoran hitchhiker who had been seized by the Immigration and Naturalization Service, Jim Corbett was raising goats near Tucson, Arizona. Corbett filed the proper form to prevent the hitchhiker from being deported without a hearing. Each time he tried to see the Salvadoran, though, he found that the INS had managed to hustle him off to another detention center just before Corbett arrived. The INS lied outright to Corbett, tried to intimidate him, and illegally deported the Salvadoran—something Corbett discovered only through the chance intervention of another detainee who had seen the man. He was stunned and outraged— and ready to fight back. He and his wife borrowed $4,500 against the trailer where they were living, and wrote to five hundred fellow Quakers and Quaker meetings around the country. They raised several hundred thousand dollars in two months, but in response the INS simply changed its policies, raising bail for each illegal immigrant from $250 to $3,000 and incarcerating Salvadoran applicants for asylum (whose requests, at any rate, were inevitably denied, since the Reagan administration would not acknowledge the torture and death squads linked to the regime it was supporting). Each new repressive action by their own government only stoked the Corbetts' indignation. When Jim began finding local churches that would shelter illegal immigrants in violation of federal law, the Sanctuary movement was born.

Corbett is typical of the United States citizens who became deeply involved in helping to bring peace to Central America, fighting the Reagan administration's support for the Contras in Nicaragua and its aid to brutal dictatorships essentially at war with their own people. This protest movement, in existence throughout Reagan's eight years in office, mobilized over one hundred thousand people, most of them motivated by religious and moral values. Unlike its larger contemporary, the movement against nuclear weapons, the Central America peace movement was eventually quite successful. It encouraged Congressional Democrats to oppose Reagan's insane adventurism and probably prevented a U. S. invasion of Nicaragua. Thousands of its members went beyond the usual protest repertory of rallies, marches, and civil disobedience, as they visited Nicaraguan war zones to document Contra damage and illegally housed refugees from the region. They acted in the face of severe harassment by U.S. federal agents and operatives of Central American governments, which went far beyond infiltration and break-ins to kidnapping and rape in their tactics of intimidation and oppression.

Once neglected in comparison to the well-researched movement against nuclear weapons, the Central American peace movement eventually found its

---

MAJOR EVENTS IN THE CENTRAL AMERICA PEACE MOVEMENT

December 23, 1972: Earthquake destroys most of Managua, capital of Nicaragua, after which dictator Anastasio Somoza Debayle siphons off most relief money to cronies

Late 1970s: Economic deterioration in Central America; rise of guerrilla movements in El Salvador, Nicaragua, and Guatemala; vicious military campaigns by these nations' governments

July 16, 1979: Somoza flees, Nicaraguan revolution succeeds

March 24, 1980: Murder of Óscar Romero, archbishop of San Salvador

December 2, 1980: Rape and murder of four American women, including three nuns and a lay missionary, by Salvadoran troops

January 20, 1981: Ronald Reagan takes office as U.S. president

March 24, 1982: Southside United Presbyterian Church declares itself the first public sanctuary for Central American refugees; within a year 50 additional churches have joined it, with more than 600 secondary groups offering their support

December 1982: As part of a military appropriations bill, the U.S. Congress passes and Reagan signs the Boland Amendment, prohibiting aid to those trying to overthrow Nicaraguan government

April 1983: Thirty Americans travel to Nicaraguan war zone in effort to document devastation by U.S.-supported Contras

October 25, 1983: U.S. invades Grenada after a coup ousts leftist government; first "Project Witness" visit

deserved chronicle and analysis in Christian Smith's extensive *Resisting Reagan: The U.S. Central America Peace Movement* (1996b). Smith smoothly recounts a series of stories: the deterioration of conditions and the rise of protest in Central America; the Reagan administration's mad obsession with the region; the initial involvement of individuals such as Corbett in the United States; the development of formal groups (he concentrates on Sanctuary, Witnesses for Peace, and the Pledge of Resistance) and a vibrant social movement; the battle over public images and opinion; and the intense repression, apparently orchestrated by the CIA, that made Nixon's burglars look like Boy Scouts. Of special interest to us, Smith tries to fit his stories into the framework of political opportunities.

Origins of the Movement

Smith describes Central America as a region wracked by state repression and periodic violence for nearly five hundred years. In the mid- and late 1970s

---

January–March, 1984: CIA mines Nicaraguan harbors, killing dozens

October 1984: Secret CIA training manuals are discovered in Honduras, designed to train Contra fighters how to sabotage government property and to kidnap and assassinate civilians and government officials

October 9, 1984: First mass public signing of the Declaration of Resistance in San Francisco, promising to go to Nicaragua in the case of a U.S. invasion

1984: Reagan administration pressures local INS officials to investigate and prosecute Sanctuary activists

1984–1990: More than 140 break-ins at offices and homes of U.S. Central America peace activists occur

October 5, 1986: American mercenary Eugene Hasenfus is captured while flying arms to the Contras, eventually leading to the Iran-Contra scandal showing illegal Reagan administration efforts to fund Contras

August 7, 1987: Esquipulas Peace Agreement signed in Guatemala

July 1988: Fourteen trucks of food and medical supplies heading for Nicaragua are stopped and eventually attacked at the U.S.-Mexico border

January 20, 1989: George H. W. Bush takes office as U.S. president

February 25, 1990: Sandinistas lose national elections

the situation deteriorated into a sizable economic and political crisis, with increases in poverty, malnutrition, protest, and repression. The governments of El Salvador, Guatemala, Honduras, and Nicaragua demonstrated "an astounding reactive intransigence in the face of moderate efforts toward economic, political, and military reform" (pp. 13–14), including campaigns of torture, death squads, imprisonments, and "disappearances." Despite Jimmy Carter's policy of promoting human rights, repression and opposition both increased, creating a situation, essentially, of armed warfare. Only Nicaragua had a successful revolution, in 1979, but "in most parts of Central America the pattern was similar: pressure for moderate reforms intended to rectify injustice and poverty met intransigent repression, which resulted in increasing radicalization, rebellion, and often revolution" (p. 17).

One result of the warfare and starvation in the region was a flow of refugees northward, most of whom had to cross only two or three borders to enter the United States. After Reagan took office in 1981, almost none were granted the political asylum they requested, and so they remained in the United States illegally. Perhaps the most memorable strand of the peace movement that emerged was the Sanctuary movement to house these homeless immigrants and shelter them from federal efforts to return them to the dangers of Central America.

Another development under Reagan was increasingly active U.S. policy in the region. Whereas past intervention by the United States had consisted mostly of aid for repressive regimes—support that had diminished under the Carter Administration—enthusiastic military advisement and supplies now blossomed. Reagan and his advisers saw Nicaragua as the first domino in the region's fall to communism. This view, along with Reagan's horror of the communist "evil empire," explains the administration's hysteria over Central America. As soon as Reagan came into office he revived assistance to dubious right-wing regimes in Central America linked to "antiterrorist" death squads and fostered "low-intensity warfare" in Nicaragua, where the Sandinistas were the anti-Christ inspiring U.S. policy. Eventually, hundreds of thousands of citizens would be killed or maimed, and several million would be made refugees—mostly (except in Nicaragua) by their own governments. Entire villages were destroyed, and the region's economy was devastated.

Several key events helped to crystallize the emerging outrage among North Americans. Two occurred in the year before Reagan took office: the murder of San Salvador archbishop Oscar Romero while he was saying mass, and the rape and murder of four American women (three of them nuns) by Salvadoran

government forces. Two others—the discovery of CIA efforts to mine Nicaraguan harbors followed by the entire Iran-Contra scandal—came to light at
the height of the movement, and possibly because of the movement. All these
events were powerful condensing symbols that neatly captured what the protestors were so outraged about.

A large number of the protestors were active church members whose religious faith and networks helped draw them into the movement (Nepstad
2004). A number of Christian denominations had members who had done
missionary and social work in Latin America, and so were attentive to developments there. Sanctuary, part of the broader movement, was first established by
Corbett's appeals to Quaker congregations across the United States. Eventually, grassroots interest led the leaders of many denominations to take stands
against Reagan's policies. The religiosity of the movement contrasted with the
secular tone of many other recent movements, including that against nuclear
energy (Jasper 1990), that for animal rights (Jasper and Nelkin 1992; Jasper
and Poulsen 1995), and much environmentalism. Yet the movement had considerable appeal to left-liberals alarmed by Reagan's aggressive militarism.

Although Smith does not offer anything like a simplified causal diagram to
explain the emergence of the Central America peace movement in the United
States, the elements of his account are clear enough. He describes the outrage,
anger, and shock of individual Americans as they learned about their own government's actions. He especially emphasizes the moral and religious principles
behind these emotions, which make nonsense of "rational choice" explanations
(Nepstad and Smith 2001). The initial activists capitalized on these principles
to create social networks, especially through their churches, to mobilize resources and arouse action. Finally, Smith describes a number of political opportunities that he claims opened for the emerging movement.

Expanding Opportunities?

Smith argues explicitly and emphatically for political opportunity structures as
crucial causal variables, calling them "of paramount importance," and describing political-opportunity theorists as having "hit the bull's-eye." Their influence even continues past the movement's emergence: "The case of the Central
America peace movement merely adds to the number of diverse movements
and campaigns whose births, lives, and passings appear best explained by
openings and closings in the structure of political opportunities" (p. 378). To

208 The North American Context

underline their importance, Smith makes the importance of political opportunities the first of his six theoretical conclusions. Moreover, he sticks close to the original metaphor of political opportunity structures that, like windows, open and close—a root metaphor that many political-process theorists have backed away from but which still, often implicitly, colors their models.

What kinds of things count as political opportunities for Smith? To explain why the movement appeared and flourished, he lists "President Reagan's obsessive preoccupation with Central America, the political vulnerabilities generated by the Vietnam syndrome, division and elite defection in the U.S. government, and repeated White House policy blunders" (p. 378). The "contractions" of opportunities that demobilized the movement include "the political effects of the Iran-Contra scandal, the Esquipulas peace accords, the ascent of President [George Herbert Walker] Bush, the electoral defeat of the Sandinistas, and the displacement by new political issues" (p. 379).

We can break both sets of factors into several categories. Reagan's obsession, and the support for despicable regimes or armies that followed from it, provided the *grievance* that inspired the movement, just as Bush's succession and the Esquipulas agreement removed it. As for the latter, signed in 1987, it led to peace accords between the Sandinistas and the Contras and between the Farabundo Martí National Liberation Front (FMLN) and the Salvadoran government. "Activists began to believe that they were witnessing the fulfillment of their ultimate goal, peace in Central America" (p. 353). As some of his informants said, it was time for them to move on.

Other political opportunities on Smith's list include *strategic choices* made by government officials and other elites. Many of these, such as the more than 140 documented burglaries of activists and their organizations, were made in response to the actions of the protest movement, and opened very temporary opportunities for further action by the movement. Some were part of normal partisan politics, as Democrats in Congress took advantage of Reagan's blunders in Central American policy. If this is an opportunity that arose independently of the Central America issue itself, then it is an opportunity that always exists in the two-party system of the United States, which always entails a division of elites to the extent that Democrats and Republicans vie for office. Instead, I would view the partisan attention and conflict over Central America as the result of the issue's and the movement's emergence, not a precondition for it. Of course, once they adopted the issue, national politicians may have reframed or channeled it in their own way—a different question (Jasper 1992).

Like efforts to suppress the movement, partisan attention would arguably not have existed were it not for the movement itself.

Other factors on Smith's list are what many would call *cultural* or *biographical* (Jasper 1997). The symbolic resonance of the Vietnam War, along with its diverse psychological effects on decision makers, is a good example. The rise of new political issues, here and elsewhere, is typically a combination of shifting cultural sensibilities and strategic choices by newsworthy opinion makers. Struggles occur over how to frame events and information; for instance, what lessons to draw from Vietnam. Presidents Carter, Reagan, Bush II, Clinton, and Obama had contrasting understandings of that war that could be explained only through careful attention to their own life histories. Suppose we were willing to accept Reagan's obsession with Central America as a political opportunity rather than the movement's grievance. How would we explain it? We would need to delve into Reagan's biography and psychology, adduce idiosyncratic factors from his past and from his mental world. We would need to look at his relationship to broader themes in American culture, such as images of manhood, national pride, and fear of communism (Rogin 1987). This is precisely the kind of mental apparatus that most political-process models were designed to avoid, but which Smith deploys to good advantage.

Surprisingly absent from Smith's list of political opportunities are factors having to do with *political structure*: electoral systems, laws and constitutions, and federalism in the United States, for example. These are structural in the sense that they are difficult to change, and thus change infrequently, and when they do change it is more by reinterpretation than by explicit transformation. They are missing because they were not very important to the rise and fall of Smith's movement. After all, as we all saw during the Iran-Contra scandal, Reagan's top aides were willing to ignore and circumvent laws and constitutional structures that got in their way. The CIA illegally orchestrated the mining of Nicaraguan harbors and published and distributed a "freedom fighters manual" to show Contras how to sabotage property and murder opponents. These activities were remarkably centralized in the White House, whose staff circumvented other branches of government until they were eventually discovered. Their activities became strategic opportunities for the peace movement to mobilize further outrage.

Everything that helps a movement tends to be counted as a political opportunity (Jasper 1997, p. 35). With this kind of expansive definition, the very existence of a movement is credited to political opportunity, leaving us with few cases of unsuccessful movements for comparison. What is more, there is little agreement among scholars over what counts as a political opportunity, so that each scholar compiles a unique list from the case she or he is studying. Any movement that has mobilized successfully is bound to have had opportunities to do so (studies of unsuccessful mobilization are rare, even though it happens every day). But if each list of causal factors is derived from the empirical case at hand, with those factors that are absent conveniently ignored, it becomes impossible to test the idea that certain political opportunities may be important in some cases, but not in others (Goodwin and Jasper 1999/2004a, b). By deriving his own list of political opportunities from his case, Smith has no trouble finding influential ones. What is the evidence, however, if we stick to McAdam's (1996, p. 27) "highly consensual list" of dimensions of political opportunities necessary for explaining movement emergence? As I read Smith's account, the evidence is almost entirely negative.

First, did the protestors gain new access to the political system in the early 1980s? These were typical middle-class American citizens, with the ability to vote, lobby legislators, bring lawsuits, contribute money to favorite organizations, travel abroad, and so on. None of these rights expanded during the period under question. But the question itself does not apply well to this movement. Before Reagan became president in 1981, there was no pool of potential protestors who shared the same goals and grievances that merely needed an opportunity to be expressed. We cannot compare 1984 with, say, 1974. Prior to Reagan's policies there was no "will" there to be thwarted or facilitated, no interests to be suppressed or advanced. Access for a group cannot change unless there is a group, relatively constant over time, that wants to use it in pursuit of its goals (Ringmar 1996).

This kind of movement differs from the civil rights or labor movements, which were based on preexisting communities with well-understood grievances and interests, and which existed prior to any mobilization. It makes sense to speak of the access of Southern blacks to the political system, since laws had created a distinct category and identity for blacks that functioned to restrict their freedoms. In many movements, however, the mobilization is about creating a sense of a grievance and an identity as much as about acting upon it. Southern blacks in the 1950s knew they were being mistreated, but in the case of the environmental movement, for example, potential environmentalists had to be convinced that the environment was an issue that mattered to them. Only when they formed a social movement did environmentalists begin to build a

sense of their own identity, the loyalties of a community, and the social networks to support them. Elsewhere (Jasper 1997) I have called the first type of
movement *citizenship movements*, because they consist of a preexisting (often
legally defined) group that is pursuing political, economic, or human rights in
order to advance the group toward full citizenship, full incorporation in society. I call the second type of movement *postcitizenship* because its members already possess those rights; they are full citizens but pursue other forms of social
change (sometimes for beneficiaries other than their own group).

As for the second item on McAdam's list: was something happening to political or economic elites that might have suggested that protest would be easier
or more effective, perhaps competition or a split among elites? Not before the
movement started forming. Reagan's very election would seem to have been a
signal that this was not a propitious time for liberal social movements. As the
movement grew, however, religious leaders in certain denominations became
critical of Reagan policies, so that a split soon formed. Religious leaders often
have the power of public opinion, but little political or economic power. What
they can offer, however, are the organizational resources to sustain protest; for
instance, to hire lawyers to defend actions on the edge of legality, or financial
resources to publicize the movement's complaints. But again, it was largely individual members of Protestant denominations who became involved first, and
who then pressured their church hierarchies to go along. At the start, there
was no religious elite ready and willing to encourage or support protestors.
Postcitizenship movements like this one attract attention only when they begin
to mobilize themselves into a movement, unlike excluded groups who already
suffer some clear deprivation.

This is also the answer to McAdam's third factor: the presence of elite allies
who encourage protest. Many religious leaders responded favorably to their
members' activities, but they had no initial reason to desire this kind of protest.
We should be clear, too, about their motivations. In cases in which leaders went
along with their congregations, they did so because they felt it was the morally
correct position, not because they could gain some advantage vis-à-vis other
elites or organizations (such as winning converts from other denominations).
In fact, they almost certainly acted against what they assumed were their organizations' own interests, butting heads with a popular president.

What, finally, is the evidence about state repression? It was not decreasing in
any way in 1981. If anything, federal agencies began to harass protestors once
they started their activities in opposition to federal policy, including a large

number of break-ins that activists rightly believed were the work of the U.S. government. This repression (admittedly mild compared to what was happening to protestors in Central America itself, or what happened to Southern black protestors in the 1950s) seems to have spurred greater mobilization rather than the opposite (just as the stronger repression in Central America itself increased mobilization).

On all these dimensions, political opportunities changed only once protestors began to mobilize, in strategic response to their mobilization. There were no changes—other than Reagan's policies themselves—that spurred the initial mobilization. But we can look at some of them as spurs to further mobilization of a movement already in operation. Here, it seems that efforts to repress protest organizations had the effect of increasing outrage and indignation and energizing the protestors, rather than dampening their spirits. If anything, repression had the opposite of the effect usually predicted by political-opportunity models.

Criticism

By creating a new list of political opportunities that might affect social movements, Smith would seem to be supporting and extending the concept. Yet his flexibility may represent a "conceptual stretching" that shows how tautological the concept of political opportunities can become (Jasper 1997, pp. 33–42; Goodwin and Jasper 1999/2004a, b). This is especially true when we discover that Smith's list contains virtually none of the factors on McAdam's list. McAdam's list represents the kind of factors (a slackening of repression, the need for powerful allies) that may aid a severely oppressed group in its fight to attain citizenship rights; Smith's list presents factors (media attention, blunders by opponents) that are relevant to a postcitizenship movement composed of citizens who already have those rights. Let me go through Smith's list again.

Because political-process models were developed partly to explain what, besides grievances, were important in explaining movement emergence, it seems odd to include grievances among the opportunities. This is a bit like saying that cardiac arrest gives a local ambulance an opportunity to come to your house, as though the driver wanted to do that anyway and was just waiting for an excuse. This kind of causal model ignores, or strongly downplays, the role of intentionality in human action. At the least, this conflation makes it impossible to compare the effects of grievances with those of opportunities. To me, opportunities should be thought of as opportunities for action, given a certain level of will. They are about the means, not about the ends. They should not be conceived as stimuli to develop the will itself. Even in citizenship movements, the will cannot always be assumed. In no case does it appear automatically when a potential opportunity arises.

Given the rapidity with which they change, it is difficult to see why strategic actions on the part of the federal government should be called structures, although opportunities they surely were. Most of these strategic blunders, including the break-ins, lies to the public, and arrogant attitudes, were additional grievances that fueled further outrage (what I have elsewhere termed "procedural grievances," when government agents who are expected to redress social problems actually cause more problems through their response [Jasper 1997, p. 276]).

In this case, the structural metaphor of windows that open and close seems less useful than a language of strategic game playing (Jasper 2006). The government does something that outrages a large number of people, who then organize events and promulgate emotions and arguments in response. The news media, government officials, targets of the protestors, and others react in turn in various ways. Some of their responses serve to quiet the protest, others only exacerbate it. The latter, especially in retrospect, we can call blunders (Jasper and Poulsen 1993). The structural language, which makes it seem as though windows of opportunity open and close themselves, disguises the interactive nature of these actions, especially the complex expectations each player has about what the other players will do, how they will respond, and how they expect the others to respond to their response. When another kid on the playground punches me, I either punch him back, run away, or crumple up in pain. In other words, I respond, and he will in turn respond to what I do. Perhaps each of our actions can be seen as an opportunity for the other to react in some way, but this metaphor takes the volition, motivation, and all the rest of psychology out of our interaction. For instance, the pleasures of the game itself (even of a schoolyard fight) disappear in the metaphors of structural opportunities.

Most of Smith's factors fall into this category. It was not determined (structurally or any other way) that the Sandinistas would lose the Nicaraguan elections of 1990; otherwise, the United States government would not have spent tens of millions of dollars trying to influence them. Elections present a perfect example of how prolonged strategic interaction and strategic posturing for the benefit of third parties come together in an unpredictable outcome. Elite defections are also calculated strategic choices, responses to the actions of both sides to a conflict. Even the rise and the fall of political issues result from complex strategic interactions among many different political players.

Additionally, government repression seems to have encouraged rather than discouraged this protest movement. Peace activists in the United States faced considerable intimidation, repression, and personal costs. Had they been looking for good opportunities for protest, they would probably not have launched and sustained the movement they did. Perhaps the Carter administration would have been sympathetic; Reagan's was viciously hostile. In 1988, for example, U.S. agents at the Mexican border stopped a fourteen-truck convoy of food and medical supplies heading for Nicaragua. After a twenty-five-day standoff, the agents maced and arrested the members of the convoy when they tried to cross into Mexico (p. 39).

This unexpected positive effect of intimidation (found in many movements besides this one) suggests to me that political-opportunity models are working with a flawed psychology. They assume, implicitly in most cases, that individuals act in a relatively calculating pursuit of interests (admittedly the interests of a group, not those of the self-interested individuals of rational choice models), so that lowered costs of repression lead to more action. Smith himself shows how unsubstantiated this kind of thinking is, since people also follow a number of moral and religious principles that often conflict with their self-interest: "the majority of activists became involved more because they believed it was the right and necessary thing to do, *whatever the outcome*, and not primarily because they calculated that the probable consequences of their individual participation warranted their involvement and justified the costs it would entail" (p. 195). When repression increases protest, it is typically because people's moral sensibilities have been shocked, not because their relative costs and benefits have changed.

The intimidation faced by North American protestors hardly compares to the murder and torture with which governments often repress citizenship movements. And yet increased military repression in Central America in the late 1970s and early 1980s does not seem to have worked, despite more than two hundred thousand murders. Indeed, in many cases this brutality seems to have driven peasants and others into armed rebellion, often in an effort to assert their basic human dignity (Wood 2003). Here again, the evidence seems to go against the dubious psychology of standard political-opportunity models.

Conclusion

There is considerable evidence in Smith's thorough study for a model of movement emergence that features moral shocks and grievances, emotions, and
psychology rather than political opportunities. In what twist of language can
we analyze violent repression as an "opportunity"? More often an inhibitor of
protest rather than an incentive, in that regard surely military or military-style
repression represents the most closed of political opportunities. But when violence spurs mobilization, we need to turn to emotions, a sense of threat, the
propulsion of shocks and outrage, and other psychological and cultural factors
for insight; "moral shocks" should be at least part of our explanation (Jasper
and Poulsen 1995; Jasper 1997). Cultural meanings and emotions are structured, of course, but not in the same way that political structures are, and they
are thus changed in different ways. Collapsing them to another political opportunity structure can be deeply misleading.

Smith theorizes about "moral shocks," calling them "epiphanal turning
points," which he in turn defines as "pivotal episodes, sometimes momentously
wrenching or awakening experiences, the repercussions of which seem to have
driven and defined the meaning of their lives as activists ever since" (p. 203).
Virtually all his stories of individual activists include such a moment, full of
powerful emotions and crystallizing moral intuitions, that creates an activist identity. They are clearly shocks that transform through a "jolt": "Whether
traumatic, exhilarating, or sobering, these critical moments all appear to have
unexpectedly broken into these people's lives. They all jolted their subjects'
basic perceptions of reality, elucidating for them a new awareness of what is
truly valuable in life" (pp. 206–7). These shocks can be related to grievances—
people are killed or harassed or lied to—but not so easily to political opportunities. Again and again, individual Americans were energized by their personal
experiences, a crucial process in the creation of the movement. Yet political-
process models frequently ignore all this on the assumption that people are
always ready to protest, needing only the opportunity (and the "cognitive liberation" of thinking that their protest could succeed [McAdam 1982]).

Political-opportunity theorists assume the will is there, requiring only an
opening to be expressed. But grievances themselves must be created, often
through negative emotions such as anger, outrage, indignation, and fear. A
sense of threat is a powerful motivation (Jasper 1997), whether the spur in
this case was the deterioration of the economy and government repression in
Central America in the 1970s or the harassment by U.S. agents in the 1980s.

Much human motivation revolves around what repulses, terrifies, or outrages us, rather than what merely attracts us.

Metaphors of political opportunity seem especially poor for understanding two important dimensions of social and political life: emotions and strategic choice. *Emotions* permeate social action and once dominated the study of social movements, but they were jettisoned in an effort to make protestors appear rational. Emotions and rationality are not opposites, but permeate one another in a variety of ways. Once scholars recognize this, they will be able to reinsert moral shocks and other emotional dynamics into the core of their models of social movements. *Strategic choice*—the subtle interaction between different sides in a conflict, the nuanced expectations they have of one another, the creative ways they try to catch each other off guard, and so on—is another psychological dimension of protest that fits poorly in the structural metaphors of political-process theory. And yet the outcomes of protest are never predictable just from preexisting resources or opportunities; they are shaped partly by the game itself, which is open-ended enough to encourage people to keep playing. Despite McAdam's favored term, *political-process theory*, process models remain trapped within the structural logic of forces that operate behind our backs. A fuller attention to process would examine the strategic dilemmas and choices that protestors, their opponents, the state, and other players face. We have seen that early mobilization of the Central America peace movement itself created most of its opportunities, which were hardly structural shifts that occurred without intervention. Strategic games are partly open ended in ways that structural metaphors ignore. The outcomes of most political processes cannot be known in advance.

Political-opportunity theories are derived from citizenship models, in which a well-defined group is aware of its interests, has extensive grievances, and faces severe repression, such as Southern blacks in the 1950s or the European working class in the nineteenth century. For them, the removal of a little repression is like a window that opens. But most groups of protestors, especially in the advanced industrial countries, are not sitting outside the window with a well-formed list of grievances in hand, just waiting for that window to open in order to squeeze through. In most cases people require a shock for them to realize that their basic moral sensibilities are being violated, that they even have a grievance to mobilize around.

One final hint that Smith's fine study is ill served by political-opportunity language: outside of the conclusion, in the actual case, the term *political opportunity* rarely appears. Instead, we have a cascade of emotions, shocks, moral sensibilities and principles, framing devices, strategic choices, blunders, and interactions. Smith acknowledges these elements in his theoretical conclusions, noting especially the importance of morality and religion (see also Smith 2003). But this insight is undercut by his lip service to political opportunities.

Political opportunities are a Procrustean framework that can be stretched or modified to fit any social movement. But what use is this flexibility, when, for instance, the political opportunities that fit the Central America peace movement and those that fit the civil rights movement have no overlap? There might be no harm done in using one term to cover everything, except to language. But I fear that our models also suffer, because other factors become distorted when seen through this lens. We could speak, I suppose, of cultural opportunities and emotional opportunities and even biographical ones (rather like biographical availability), but the passive language of structures, of openings and closings, hardly does justice to these other aspects and processes. At one time the metaphor of political opportunities may have expanded our vision; today the concept often seems to distort it.

RESPONSE TO JAMES JASPER
Christian Smith

First, some context. In my view, the most helpful general theoretical framework for understanding the dynamics of social movements is a revised version of the political-process model first advanced by McAdam in 1982. Not simply a one-dimensional political opportunities theory, this model also accounts for the importance of mobilizing organizational structures and what we can call grievances. What in McAdam's original model has needed revising, I think, is his concept of "cognitive liberation." In my 1991 book, *The Emergence of Liberation Theology: Radical Religion and Social Movement Theory*, I argued that McAdam's version of this factor was too cognitively oriented and calculating. I suggested instead the need to strengthen our understanding of the emotional, volitional, moral, aggrieved, and unstable nature of what I instead termed "insurgent consciousness" (1991, pp. 55–57, 61–64, 245). This need has been evident to many in the field, and much helpful work has been done in the 1990s to attend more closely to the role of culture, identity, emotions, and religious and moral commitments in social movements. Many chapters in my book *Disruptive Religion: The Force of Faith in Social Movement Activism* (1996a) have contributed to this effort.

My book *Resisting Reagan: The U.S. Central America Peace Movement* (1996b), which Jasper has critiqued, builds on this background and extends my claims about insurgent consciousness. In fact, the central theoretical argument of this book has nothing to do with political opportunities. Rather, the principal theoretical claim it advances is that the assumption of rational egoism, built into most versions of rational choice theory worthy of the name, is completely inadequate for making sense of my case; that some movement actors are motivated more by deontological moral commitments irrespective of pragmatic outcomes than by teleological considerations of achievable ends. Thus the issue I primarily engaged was not what political opportunities explain, but what human beings are like and what explains their actions. "Moral outrage, religious obligation, emotional passion, personal commitment," I concluded, "were the forces that drove the Central America peace movement for a decade" (p. 168).

Thus when Jasper argues that moral grievances "should be at least part of our explanation," I couldn't agree with him more, and was ubiquitously explicit about that in *Resisting Reagan*. In fact, the book devotes much more space and intellectual energy to detailing and theorizing the social sources of activists' moral outrage than to elaborating on political opportunity structures (the section on political opportunities consumes only twenty of the book's 464 pages).

Nevertheless, my explanatory account of the Central America peace movement added to my exploration of moral grievances an analysis of political opportunities and organizational structures as well. Political opportunities were important for the movement's emergence and subsequent success. Here is where Jasper's critique comes into play. Jasper's central charge is that what I described as political opportunities are really not political opportunities, but actually grievances, strategic choices, and cultural and biographical factors. He seems to want to define political opportunities as directly related to formal "political structures," such as "electoral systems, laws and constitutions, federalism in the United States." But this is a rather narrowly constructed version of political opportunities, linked most closely with the European comparative scholarship on political structures. If, however, we conceptualize political opportunities as changes in the institutional structure or informal power relations of a given national political system that make (what will become) a movement's adversary significantly more vulnerable to a political challenge (see McAdam,

McCarthy, and Zald 1996, p. 3), then the account in *Resisting Reagan* is entirely coherent and credible.

I argue that two kinds of political opportunities facilitated the Central America peace movement (McAdam 1996, p. 27): the instability of broad elite alignments that typically undergird a polity, and the presence of elite allies. I document in *Resisting Reagan*, for example, the importance of a major split among Washington foreign policy elites in 1981 and following, by which myriad important former diplomats, State Department, CIA, and NSC officials, academic political scientists, and think tank scholars came vehemently to oppose and prosecute their case against the president's Central America policy. I show how the U.S. withdrawal from Vietnam only eight years before Reagan took office fostered a deep division in Congress and among foreign policy experts, the U.S. military, and even the early Reagan administration about the president's Central America policy. I discuss how the late 1970s and early 1980s brought to Washington a "postelectoral era," a "dual sovereignty" pitting Congress and the White House in a contest for foreign policy jurisdiction, and the intensely rancorous partisan split that developed over the new "Reagan Revolution"—all of which aided the cause of the Central America peace movement in a way that Jasper's "normal partisan politics" never could have. I document how White House policy blunders alienated even some of Reagan's natural allies in Congress, making his Central America policy increasingly vulnerable to challenge. And I explain how Reagan's highly visible strategic approach to Central America created an enormously vulnerable political target against which nascent Central America peace activists were able to mobilize an unlikely but effective coalition of opposition forces.

Certainly, some of these factors also had the result of aggrieving incipient activists; few "variables" in the social world exert only one type of effect. But the political significance of these factors for the movement extends far beyond inciting grievances. As or more important, they offered an embryonic (and later thriving) peace movement political opportunities to act with some degree of success. And to try to explain the emergence and accomplishments of the Central America peace movement without accounting for them as political opportunities would significantly limit our analytical vision.

A simple "null hypothesis" thought experiment helps to clarify the matter: "controlling" for the high intensity of activists' grievances, consider the prospects of the Central America peace movement, had foreign policy elites, the Congress, the military, and the White House *not* been extraordinarily divided by the forces and events I document in the book, and had many important foreign policy elites and members of Congress *not* sided with the movement. The Central America peace movement would never have been able to mobilize anywhere near the number of activists or accomplish anything like the successes it ultimately did. These were in fact identifiable political opportunities external to the movement that made a big difference in the movement's experience.

Jasper, however, argues that at least some of these opportunities were themselves actually created by the activism of the movement. This is partly wrong and partly irrelevant. Many of the political opportunities I describe existed chronologically prior to the emergence of the peace movement. The proverbial political excrement actually began hitting the fan in 1981 when, for example, Alexander Haig gave his infamous speeches and press conferences about "drawing the line" and "going to the source," and when the new Reagan administration began ousting respected moderate and liberal foreign policy experts and diplomats from their government positions. This was happening long before anyone ever dreamed about Sanctuary, Witness for Peace, or the Pledge of Resistance, and it set the political stage for their emergence. Only later in the decade did movement actions act upon the political environment to generate more political opportunity.

Critical reflection on our theoretical constructs can be a valuable exercise. I find Jasper's distinction between citizenship and postcitizenship movements, for example, helpful for specifying the usefulness of the political-process model. And in my work I share Jasper's views on grievances, emotions, strategic interactions, and rational choice. Furthermore, the comparative view of individual case studies to determine under what conditions political opportunities work in what ways, which this book undertakes, is important as well. But it is a stretch to argue that political opportunities of the kind McAdam (1996) specifies were not important for the emergence of the Central America Peace movement.

Jasper concludes his critique of *Resisting Reagan* by arguing that its analysis actually supports "a model of movement emergence that features moral shocks and grievances, emotions and psychology rather than political opportunities." Knowing that we need not choose between one or the other, the task remains to figure out how to decide when some empirically important factor is an opportunity or a grievance, or both. The forces that I have called political opportunities may indeed also have had the effect of aggrieving incipient activists; but a complete analysis of the Central America Peace movement must recognize the critical importance of political opportunities that were afforded the emerging movement by the instability of broad elite alignments and the presence of elite allies that I documented.

Could I have restructured the argument of *Resisting Reagan* to be solely a story of moral community and moral outrage? Perhaps. Some (besides Jasper) have suggested in retrospect that I should have done just that, to give the book a more distinctive theoretical flair. But would this have either strengthened our understanding of the Central America Peace movement or advanced the general state of social movement theory? I think not.

REJOINDER TO CHRISTIAN SMITH

James M. Jasper

I leave it to the reader to decide whether Chris has fairly represented my argument or cogently replied to it. I shall also leave aside some obvious areas of agreement, such as the role of morality and emotions in political life and this movement in particular (Nepstad and Smith 2001; Smith 2003). Instead, I would like to sketch a brief account of this movement's rise and fall in the language of strategic engagement rather than that of movement and context. As I argue in the introduction, the way beyond the controversy over political-opportunity models is to specify all the players on all sides, their goals and means, and the interactions among them through various arenas.

Reagan's triumph in the 1980 electoral arena reflected his promises of a more aggressive approach to international arenas, especially to fight communism, and a less intrusive approach to domestic economic arenas. (Once he was in power, Republicans took control of the Senate and, in ad hoc alliances with conservative Democrats, frequently got their way in the House.) The Reagan administration set about doing both, although the highly visible symbols of bellicose diplomacy attracted unwanted attention and controversy from a variety of NGOs and members of the bystander public. Reagan's opponents, domestic and abroad, were able to promulgate a sense of threat in a range of issue areas. More important, many compound and simple players who had allied with Reagan for the election split from him over some of his extreme positions—including his Latin American policies. No large, compound player is ever unified, and the degree of unity varies across arenas and issues. Defections always occur, as they did in this case.

Shifting factions account for a large part of the explanatory power of political-opportunity models, especially the two variables called *elite allies* and *elite competition.* These terms imply that there is the elite on the one hand, and then there is everyone else, and that the elite tends to remain unified under normal circumstances. A more strategic perspective suggests that no state is fully unified, such that some factions and individuals are constantly scanning events for chances to defect or resist if they think it is to their advantage. In this case we see no changes in the U.S. state as arena—no institutional changes, that is—nor do we see any change in the underlying strength of the U.S. state as a player within any arena. Far from any weakness, we see it asserting its muscle in foreign arenas. The Republican administration tried to distinguish itself sharply from the Carter regime it had demonized in 1980. We see politics as usual.

Yet politics as usual frequently entails actions that arouse the attention and indignation of others. Any strategic arena is prone to actions that feel threatening to others even when they are not intended as aggression toward those others (Jasper 2006, p. 31). In this case, the Reagan administration's aggression was initially directed toward the Sandinistas and other "communists." One unintended consequence was to outrage enough American citizens to create a protest movement, operating in nonelectoral arenas but still normal enough in today's "social movement society." This movement was creative enough to invent some new tactics, which in turn attracted the press coverage that helps movements flourish. Protestors face dilemmas in dealing with the media: they want the attention, but they cannot control how they are portrayed (Gitlin 1980).

At that point, the more radical elements in the Reagan Administration began targeting protestors themselves, exacerbating the latter's own indignant energy for protest as well as generating even more media coverage and sympathy from bystander publics. Alliances always tend to fracture when one player pursues goals that its allies do not share, and the lawless extremism of some Reagan staff (think Ollie North) caused just this to happen. Those singled out for harassment might have left the protest alliance, facing too great a cost (this would be a standard prediction of political-opportunity theory), but their indignation often kept them in the movement despite the costs. Many reacted with exhilaration, taking the harassment as a sign they were getting through to the government (p. 322).

Dynamics like these are well described in the language of strategic players interacting with one another in pursuit of their conflicting goals across various arenas. We need a careful catalogue of players and alliances, showing why they had different goals or different tastes in tactics (for illegal versus legal tactics, for instance). We also need some biographical and cultural analysis in order to understand those goals, and we need some sense of strategic dilemmas and choices in order to grasp the means used. Smith includes all this in his extensive case study. I see no reason to add the extra layer of structural shifts represented by political-opportunity model language, which hides the players and their actions. From the micro perspective we can see the constant strategic efforts and choices and interpretations players make in interacting with each other. Attention to these small mechanisms prevents us from placing too much faith in overly simple dichotomies that are supposed to exist at some imagined macro level.

PART 3
NEW DIRECTIONS

9 Opportunity Knocks

The Trouble with Political Opportunity and What You Can Do about It

EDWIN AMENTA AND DREW HALFMANN

THE CONCEPTS "political opportunity" and "political opportunity structure" and their allied theoretical claims have caused much trouble among scholars of social movements. On the one side are those who hope to shore up the concepts by forging a consensus on a few opportunities (McAdam 1996; Tarrow 1996) or by developing well-ordered lists of opportunities (Gamson and Meyer 1996; Meyer and Minkoff 2004). On the other side are those who argue that the concepts and their theoretical claims are overblown, overly structural, and contain unrealistic assumptions about the knowledge and sophistication of movement activists (Goodwin and Jasper 1999/2004a).

We have colleagues and friends on both sides and have learned a great deal from all of them; for that reason should probably duck this debate, but that is not an option. Our own work focuses mainly on the influence of political contexts on the mobilization and, especially, the consequences of social movements (see, for example, Amenta, Halfmann, and Young 1999; Amenta 2006; Halfmann, 2011). We typically avoid the term *political opportunity*, for reasons that we outline below, yet even this often gets us into trouble. Reviewers and editors inquire: "Aren't you really talking about political opportunity structure

We thank Tina Fetner, Jeff Goodwin, James M. Jasper, and the participants in the NYU Sociology Department Workshop on Politics, Power and Protest for comments and criticisms on a previous draft of this chapter.

here?" And, "why use other terms when *POS* is already available?" We typically reply that other terms have specific meanings but we are less certain what *political opportunity* means and what it is supposed to explain, that we prefer more specific, better defined terms such as *states, bureaucracies, electoral systems, policies, political parties, and interest groups.*

In this chapter we assess the utility of the political-opportunity concept for research on social movements. Our criticisms are somewhat different than those of other scholars. If the concept is structural, that is no indictment in our view (more on this later). Nor do we think that the concept implies unrealistically sophisticated and knowledgeable actors. Still, we argue that the concept is far less useful than it might be.

The main problem is that scholars often conceptualize "political opportunities" in ways that are essentially ambiguous and peculiarly disconnected from other conceptual developments in social science.[1] In addition, they often fail to theorize connections between "political opportunities" and the phenomena they are supposed to explain. Finally, the concept of "political opportunities" allows for almost endless hypotheses and is employed in widely varying ways by researchers, making it difficult to appraise the theoretical arguments associated with it. Political opportunity is not so much a snarling vine, as Goodwin and Jasper (1999/2004a) suggest, as it is a long string of loopholes. Below, we first address general difficulties surrounding the concept and then criticize its allied theoretical claims. We finish by offering suggestions for research on the effect of political contexts on social movements and discuss the ways in which our own work implements these suggestions.

---

1. To ensure clarity, by "challengers" or "social movements" we mean politically disadvantaged groups engaged in sustained collective action to secure their claims (Jenkins 1995). In order to publicize their cause and gain support and influence, challengers in democratic polities typically mobilize participants more than pecuniary resources. We are less certain what it means for a social movement to "emerge." "Social movement mobilization" is the amassing of resources by challengers to engage in collective action; that is, action intended to gain collective benefits. Given their outsider status, challengers are likely to engage at least occasionally in collective action that is "unconventional" (Kriesi et al. 1995; Clemens 1997) as well as "non-institutional" (McAdam 1996) or "disruptive" (Kitschelt 1986), but they do not need to do so to fit this definition. The types of action themselves require explanation. By "social movement impact" we mean those collective goods—(group advantages or disadvantages from which nonparticipants in a challenge cannot be easily excluded)—for the group represented by the social movement that are achieved by the movement. These collective goods can be tangible or intangible and need not be anticipated by social movement actors (Amenta et al. 2010; cf. Gamson 1990).

The Trouble with the Terms *Political Opportunity Structure* and *Political Opportunity*

First things first: the terms *political opportunity structure* and *political opportunity* are too confusing to be useful. The first term fails on basic grounds. With all due respect to Merton, who originated the concept "opportunity structure," no concept should include both *opportunity*, which implies something happening in the short term, and *structure*, which implies aspects of a context that are slow to change. The term allows those who focus on short-term fluctuations in political contexts to close ranks with those who focus on long-standing and relatively unchanging aspects of political contexts. Though this may promote fellow feeling among scholars, it does not serve clarity.

Partly for this reason, scholars often employ the shorter alternative, "political opportunity." But this term has its own problems. According to the American Heritage Dictionary, *opportunity* means "a favorable or advantageous circumstance or set of circumstances." *Circumstance* means "a condition or fact attending an event and having some bearing on it," and this is usually "outside of willful control." Given these meanings, some have criticized "political-opportunity" arguments for implying that movement actors are on the lookout for opportunities and are thus likely to perceive them. If challengers do not react in a savvy manner, according to critics, then political-opportunity arguments are not supported.

Let us consider the words of the political operator George Washington Plunkitt, a minor cog in the nineteenth-century Tammany Hall patronage machine in New York City. Plunkitt said, "I seen my opportunities and I took 'em," (Riordan 1963, p. 3), referring to what he called "honest graft"—technically legal, but morally doubtful windfalls based on political-insider information. For example, he would learn of the city's plans to build on a parcel of land, purchase it cheaply from its unsuspecting owners, and later sell it to the city at a steep profit.

We parse Plunkitt's boast because he uses the term *opportunity* in a more defensible way than most social movement scholars. Plunkitt implies that money-making situations were created by others, not by him. His statement also implies that he perceived (or "seen") those chances. He might have missed them had he not been privy to useful information and known what it meant. The statement also indicates that he acted on his opportunities, or "took 'em." In other words, he acted in a way that produced favorable results for himself. He might not have acted quickly or effectively enough to get what he wanted, but he did.

Among scholars, however, the terminology of opportunity has prompted an odd debate about whether "opportunities" can be "missed." Critics of the concept (Goodwin and Jasper 1999/2004a) and supporters of it (Gamson and Meyer 1996) agree that if opportunities are not seized, they are not opportu- nities. Neither Plunkitt nor we agree with this position. If opportunities, as hypothesized and stipulated beforehand, do exist, then they of course can be missed. If Plunkitt had neglected to purchase the soon-to-be-valuable land after having learned of the city's plans, that would not mean the opportunity had never existed. If you did not invest in housing from 1997 to 2005, that does not mean the opportunity to do so did not exist. An opportunity implies only the potential to take advantage of it. Like anyone else, social movement actors might miss opportunities to mobilize. For our purposes here, "opportunity" is a concept invoked in causal statements about social movements. Thus any claim about the effectiveness of any specific hypothesized opportunity requires empirical demonstrations to ascertain its plausibility. In that way it is not any different from other hypothesized relationships.

A greater problem with the terminology is that the analytical possibility of missed opportunities offers an easy way out for scholars who employ political-opportunity arguments. Generally speaking, there is only one credible interpretation when a scholar hypothesizes that some factor has a causal effect but empirical research finds no such effect: that the causal claim is exaggerated. For an opportunity argument, however, there is a second possibility: that the opportunity would have mattered had it been correctly perceived. Such a claim might be supported by circumstantial evidence; for example, showing that a similar challenger took advantage of the postulated opportunities, or that challengers in similar circumstances at other times or places were able to take advantage of them. Then again, the claim might merely be asserted.

Another problem with opportunity arguments is that they typically do not address the question of what they provide opportunities for. Do activists mobilize because they perceive increased opportunities for mobilization or increased opportunities for impact on public policy and public opinion? These motivations are often conflated (Meyer and Minkoff 2004). The term *opportunity* is also lacking in what might be called conceptual range. As generally conceived, opportunities can "open" or "close," "expand" or "contract," implying that there can be anything from no opportunity to endless amounts of it. As employed in theoretical claims about the emergence of movements, the concept suggests that the polity is generally closed off to movements, but occasionally not. Yet for a concept meant to be translated into a theoretical independent variable, *opportunity* does not have enough room on its negative side. Conceiving of opening and closing of opportunities makes it difficult to think of the political context as having effects that are adverse to challengers.[2] Also, if "open" means merely the likelihood that movement activity is not going to be repressed, then it may mean little in most democratic societies, for which repression of most forms of citizen mobilization is not the norm.

The term *threat* (Tilly 1978; Koopmans 1997b) is sometimes posed as the opposite of opportunity, but using it that way also seems troublesome. The dictionary suggests that the term means "expressing the intention to inflict harm or punishment." Its opposite would be closer to "safeguard" than "opportunity." Another uneasy opposite to *opportunity* is *constraint* (McAdam 1996). This term implies a threat to restrict as well as actual restrictions. All in all, this means that using political opportunity as a causal term requires a parallel set of causal terms to distinguish aspects of the political context that discourage aspects of movements. Each of these terms, however, has conceptual range problems similar to those surrounding *opportunity*.

We advocate a substitute term, one we have been using already and that has been employed by others, who, perhaps to their advantage, are nonnative English speakers (see Rucht 1996; Kriesi 1996). Instead of political opportunities, it seems far better to speak of political contexts. From there it might be claimed, by those who want to make such arguments, that aspects of the political context encourage or discourage the mobilization of challengers, their forms, their types of action and the impact of their collective action, etc. (These influences are likely to differ according to the outcome being considered.) The advantages of this alternative are many: it is not particularly confusing; it does not indicate either long- or short-term aspects of situations, or, more important, both; and it leaves it up to the scholar to define these contexts—what they are expected to influence and why. It seems less likely to provoke needless debate over ontological issues.

Another advantage of using the term *political contexts* over *political opportunities* is that the former does not imply much specifically about social movement activity other than that it is likely to occur for any number of reasons. Although a few assumptions still prevail, there is no need to assume that social movement actors are Plunkitts with a cause. Political contexts can be seen as

---

2. This is analogous to the problem with using "success" and "failure" as standards to judge the impact of social movements. Movements can gain without succeeding and have effects that are worse than merely failing (Amenta and Young 1999b).

setting off selection processes in which some forms of activity—not necessarily initiated by the political context in the first place—are encouraged or discouraged by the political context. Employing the term and concept in this way does not make assumptions about the rationality of social movement actors. They do not have to perceive and seize opportunities. Instead, political contexts would have the influence of channeling activity that is constantly occurring or likely to occur on its own (Amenta and Young 1999a). It can be argued that those forms and types of activity that fit the political context will be encouraged by a cycle of increasingly productive collective action; those actors engaged in unproductive collective action will be discouraged by a process of defeat and discouragement or redirected elsewhere. Although this does imply that actors will notice whether their action is working and to what degree, they need not be particularly savvy to do so. All that is required of scholars is to specify important aspects of the political context and the aspects of social movements that they might affect.

The Trouble with Theories of Political Opportunity

Changing the term will not solve all its conceptual and theoretical difficulties. Some argue that political opportunity as a theoretical perspective is too structural to be able to explain social movement phenomena. But this is not the main problem. Many theoretical arguments, especially of the middle-range sort, are one sided or have specific emphases. If a political structural theory can explain a great deal of social movement phenomena that scholars deem important, what would be wrong with that? A complete account of any movement will no doubt need to go beyond structural explanations, but social scientists and their theories need not explain every single aspect of individual movements or movement organizations.

The problem with the concept is not that it is too structural, but that it is unclear whether it is structural or not. The concept is ambiguous in two main ways. The first is that political opportunity is seldom well defined and the set of factors deemed to constitute political opportunity are typically defined broadly. There is much discussion of factors such as institutional political systems, authorities, elites, input structures, and output structures but not enough discussion about narrower factors such as states, bureaucracies, political parties, and the like. Political sociologists and political scientists have offered refined distinctions about various aspects of democratic polities, such as party systems, the concentration of authority, and the capacities of state bureaucracies, but these are mainly ignored by political-opportunity theorists, making it difficult to connect studies of social movements to other work in political sociology or political science.[3]

The second ambiguity centers on what political opportunity is supposed to influence about social movements and why. Political opportunity has been claimed to explain the timing of the emergence of movements, their growth, decline, their level of mobilization, the form of mobilization, movement strategies and actions, movement "behavior," and the impact of movements. We see nothing inherently wrong with such ambition. If one theoretical argument explains much of what scholars want to know about a set of related phenomena, the argument is powerful. Yet scholars have not given enough thought to why political contexts would influence all these different types of outcomes, nor have they adequately conceptualized the outcomes themselves. Scholars have also failed to connect the various lists of opportunities to specific dependent variables or objects of explanation, ignoring the possibility that different outcomes may require different explanations (Amenta et al. 2010).

Ambiguities in the political-opportunity concept lead to several problems in empirical research. Translating the concept into specific causal statements and hypotheses susceptible to empirical analysis is not easy. Because researchers can define political opportunities as almost any aspect of the political context, they can apply the concept in various ways to multiple outcomes. Scholars claim that opportunities matter in many studies (see reviews in McAdam 1996 and Meyer and Minkoff 2004). Yet they cite opportunities that are often only loosely related to the conceptual categories that supposedly undergird the term "political opportunity." For that reason, such studies can be only remotely connected to one another. Because political opportunity is not connected to other conceptual developments in political sociology it is difficult for those working in the area of social movements to relate their own findings to studies of related phenomena.

Early articulations of the political-opportunity thesis (Tilly 1978; McAdam 1982), and many subsequent ones (Meyer 2004), argued that there is a curvilinear relationship between political opportunities (however defined) and protest frequency (and a variety of other outcomes). Theorists have also argued that political opportunities predict protest better than other factors such as resources or grievances. Empirical tests of this thesis have been mixed at best. Meyer (2004) suggests that this may stem from variations in the ways that po-

---

3. Perhaps this is because opportunity arguments were initially designed to explain both revolutionary movements and the typically more limited movements that appear in democratic polities (Tilly 1978).

litical opportunities are conceptualized and operationalized as well as the failure of scholars to distinguish between different types of outcomes. We agree, while doubting the existence of any consistent relationship between "open" political contexts and protest. It might be possible to identify such relationships between specific aspects of the political context and specific types of outcomes (such as party control of the government and the birth of new movement organizations), but it seems unlikely the thesis will hold in general. And we also doubt that it will hold for the policy impacts of social movements, because (as we argue below) these depend on an interaction between movement tactics and specific aspects of the political context.

What You Can Do about It

We believe that it is worth theorizing about the effects of political contexts on social movements, but we have a few suggestions for doing so:

Avoid the terms "political opportunity structure" and "political opportunities." The former term can be read as internally contradictory. The latter implies that actors perceive and seize opportunities and that political contexts are merely open or closed to movements rather than damaging to them. If you must employ the term, make sure that the political opportunities that you specify are in fact *political.* Also, bear in mind that in using the term you are implying something about the nature of social movements and the way in which they react to aspects of the political context. The more neutral term "political contexts" does not carry this baggage.

Don't worry about consensus. Some scholars hope to better specify the political opportunities by agreeing on a particular set of factors that constitute them (such as McAdam's "openness" of the political system, elite alignments, movement-elite alliances, and the repressive capacities of the state). This search for consensus is premature given the underdeveloped state of the concept and its allied theoretical claims, and the likelihood that different movement outcomes are affected by different elements of the political context. Such consensus will also be difficult to achieve, given the significant differences in the theoretical claims of scholars who use similar terms. Finally, any consensus on specific factors that make up the broader concept will do nothing to resolve the basic problems of the concept itself.

Be conceptually clear. It is probably best to stay away from vague terms such as "institutional political structure," "access," "elites," and the like—the terms most closely associated with the concept political opportunity. If you feel the need to use these terms, specify what you mean by them. In conceptualizing the political context it is probably best to start with terms already current in political science or sociology. That makes it possible to employ the conceptualizations, arguments, and research findings of scholars studying similar or related phenomena. This means referring to the state, political party systems, interest groups, constitutions, bureaucracies, policies, and so on. Also, make sure to distinguish factors that are structural or long term from those that are dynamic or short term and factors that are systemic from those that are local.

Theorize specifically and precisely. That is, connect your concepts in precise ways to important social movement outcomes and be specific about what you are claiming—on both sides of any causal statements. We are well past the point where it would be useful merely to list potentially important political contexts or to list yet more categories of social movement outcomes. Instead, more specific theorizing is needed about issues that have already received a lot of attention, such as the mobilization of movements, their character, and their potential impact. It seems likely that different aspects of the political context influence different social movement outcomes in different ways. It is also helpful to specify mechanisms for any theoretical argument: indicating why you think aspects of the political context are likely to have the postulated effects. It is worthwhile as well to set boundary limits for any theoretical claims, or at least to think about them. The vagueness of the political-opportunity categories possibly results from the necessity of applying them to any instance of collective action at any place or moment of history.

Appraise your claims as exhaustively as possible. In most social movement research, it is not easy to appraise claims in a rigorous way, as most studies are case studies. But even case studies can be expanded in ways that make it possible to appraise theoretical arguments (King, Keohane, and Verba 1994). If you cannot devise ways to appraise your claims, it is possible that they are not appraisable and thus may need reformulation.

Political Mediation and Political Institutional Models

In recent work, we have each explained aspects of social movements, notably their impacts on public policy, by reference to particular political contexts, in ways that reflect our suggestions. Amenta's "political mediation model" explains the political impacts of movements in terms of the interaction between movement tactics and political contexts (see Amenta, Halfmann, and Young 1999; Amenta, Caren, and Olasky 2005; Amenta 2006; Amenta, Caren, Chiarello, and Su 2010). He argues that the effects of particular movement tactics on political outcomes are mediated by long- and short-term contexts. To be effective, collective action must change the calculations of relevant institutional political actors, and movement organizations must match their tactics to political contexts.

The political mediation model specifies that combinations of political contexts and tactics are expected to lead to influence. Long-term political contexts include underdemocratization that produces elected officials with little motivation to aid have-nots, patronage parties that produce elected officials who deflect programmatic policies, political fragmentation that offers numerous veto points to powerful minorities, and a winner-take-all electoral system that makes it difficult to build third parties. Short-term political contexts include professional and powerful state bureaucrats with expansive domestic missions and control of the government by political parties supportive of social spending. Amenta arrays a series of tactics from highly assertive (electoral challenges) to unassertive (public information). When both elected officials and state bureaucrats are supportive, minimally assertive tactics are sufficient, but when they are not supportive or hostile, more assertive tactics are necessary. Moreover, if elected officials are supportive but bureaucrats are hostile, or vice versa, movement organizations need to assertively target the hostile parties. The model indicates the conditions under which policy influence is possible and when it is possible, which combinations of contexts and strategies will produce influence, as well as the combinations expected to lead to extreme influence.

In each instance, the concepts are readily operationalized, and Amenta and his coauthors appraise their arguments empirically, mainly by way of the Townsend Plan and the old-age pension movement of the 1930s and 1940s. This direct appraisal contrasts with the standard way the social movements literature deals with politics: identifying influence and working backwards in search of a political opportunity. The proving grounds include large-scale regression analyses across all states over time, across counties in California, and across members of Congress; some small-N "most similar" comparisons across a few states in which one tactic or short-term context varies slightly at different times (such as before and after the Social Security Act and in the early and late New Deal); comparisons across policies (the movement-contested old-age assistance program versus the non–movement-contested aid to dependent children program); and comparisons across challengers with different approaches (veterans and Huey Long's Share Our Wealth). Further, to address the combinations of characteristics leading to influence, Amenta et al. (2005) deploy fuzzy-set qualitative comparative analyses to identify which states and legislators took the most radical approaches to the old-age policy; these analyses appraise the combinational aspects of the model and advance theory regarding the conditions under which extremely high influence is likely.

Most movement scholarship deems all movements to be alike and thus suggests that claims or findings for one movement should apply to all of them, regardless of context or movement characteristics. Although the political mediation theory was meant to apply widely, it remains unclear whether some conditions specific to the United States are scope conditions of the theory. For instance, there is no real variation in the electoral system either across units or time, and political fragmentation is fairly constant. Similarly, not all movements are the same. The Townsend Plan and the old-age pension movement sought far-reaching policy changes. The movement was highly influential but unsuccessful, and later took new organizational forms. In these ways, it bears a resemblance to several other movements of the mid-twentieth century, notably the anti-alcohol, anti-war, (first) feminist, and nativist movements. It was less similar to several other movements that not only gained influence, but sustained long-term leverage and a continuous organizational presence, for example, the civil rights, environmental, (second) feminist, and labor movements. Perhaps generalizations from the mediation theory may apply best to far-reaching, influential, short-lived movements and require modification to apply to influential movements that sustain consistent and long-term leverage.

Halfmann's (2011) book takes a stronger political institutional position and seeks to explain both the demands of social movements and their policy impacts. This work also addresses conditions that vary cross-nationally, in its focus on abortion politics and policy in the United States, Britain, and Canada. The main explanatory political contexts are two medium-term characteristics of national political institutions: the concentration of decision authority in particular policy areas (federalism) and the nature of electoral systems. These conditions influence both the demands and the results of movements. Halfmann appraises these arguments by examining variations in tactics and political contexts across countries, policies, policy-making episodes, and stages of the policy-making process.

Halfmann shows that federalism initially confined abortion policy making in the United States to the subnational level. The result was prolonged and dispersed policy making that encouraged new constructions of the abortion issue in terms of women's rights. First, activists radicalized their demands after witnessing the disappointing results of early state-level reforms, and second, the prolonged process provided time and opportunity for the emerging feminist movement and civil liberties lawyers to join the debate and advocate abortion on demand as a right. By contrast, British and Canadian activists defined abortion as a medical necessity appropriately under the control of doctors and did not assert the rights of women to privacy or bodily autonomy. Abortion reforms occurred quickly, and closed out the issue before alternative constructions gained prominence. Britain and Canada allowed abortions only if doctors or hospital committees certified that pregnant women met requirements of medical or economic necessity, while the United States allowed pregnant women to obtain an early abortion for any reason as long as a doctor agreed to provide it. The United States, with a history of Puritanism and weak social policy, had established the most liberal abortion reform in the West.

After these reforms, sizable anti-abortion movements tried to roll them back in all three countries. Halfmann shows that American political parties were especially vulnerable to pressure from newly organized movements. Decentralized parties, candidate-centered elections, and weak party discipline provided multiple points of access; intra-party democracy allowed movements to help choose party leaders and policies; low-turnout elections enhanced the power of small, well-organized groups; expensive campaigns created demand for movements' money and labor; and coalitional parties included a broader array of social groups. In Britain and Canada, differences in these political contexts deflected the efforts of well-organized anti-abortion organizations. Parties and politicians successfully avoided the abortion issue, and abortions became more accessible as the result of increased public funding and reduced medical gatekeeping. In the United States, by contrast, the anti-abortion movement had a much larger impact. It moved abortion to the center of politics, and abortions became less accessible as the result of cuts in public funding, parental consent requirements, waiting periods, and mandatory anti-abortion counseling. Halfmann shows that American political parties were especially vulnerable to pressure from newly organized movements while British and Canadian parties were largely insulated from such pressure.

These analyses of the consequences of old-age and abortion movements reflect the suggestions above. They substitute the terms *political context* or *po-*

litical institutions for *political-opportunity*, and specify and clearly define the contextual factors that are relevant as well as the particular outcomes they are meant to explain. They also elaborate the mechanisms by which those factors affect outcomes; identify both short- and long-term factors; specify which factors apply to movements in general and which apply solely to the movements at hand; and suggest which processes may be limited to cases with circumscribed political parameters. The studies appraise theoretical claims over multiple and wide-ranging circumstances. While political-opportunity arguments typically focus on broad factors that comprise a still broader concept of political opportunity, and often make little effort to relate these factors to other work in political sociology and political science, these studies focus on narrower, more specific factors that have already been the subject of extensive social scientific analysis, such as underdemocratization, patronage parties, electoral systems, the separation of powers, federalism, and electoral systems.

Conclusion

Should we abandon or reform the political-opportunity concept and its allied theoretical claims? We call for abandoning the term, but harnessing part of the analytical impulse behind it. Reforming the *political opportunity* term is not possible and, it should be replaced by the term "political context." At the same time, we acknowledge that attention to political contexts is crucial for analyses of social movements, especially regarding their political campaigns. But we want more than a rebranding. Scholars of social movements must do better at relating relevant aspects of the political context, including the mechanisms of their effects, to specific aspects of social movements and their potential political consequences. The starting point is not the various vague concepts of the political-opportunity model, but aspects of the political context that have been conceptualized and theorized in depth within political sociology and political science. Scholars should also specify the scope of their claims and attempt to appraise them in as many different ways as possible. And one last thing: Next time you send out a paper making political contextual theoretical claims and the review comes back saying, "Aren't you talking about POS?" please say that you are not.

10 Sensing and Seizing Opportunities

How Contentious Actors and Strategies Emerge

**CHRISTIAN BRÖER AND
JAN WILLEM DUYVENDAK**

ONTENTIOUS ACTION can be depicted as a struggle between more or less established players, in a given field or arena, about some fixed desired goal. In the introduction to this volume, Jasper proposes to adopt this kind of strategic perspective: "We need to develop causal mechanisms that apply across many arenas. I think that a more strategic perspective, focusing on arenas and on players with ends and means, is the way to accomplish that." This contribution questions the essentialized character underlying strategic reasoning: are players established, arenas given, and goals fixed? By focusing on discursive opportunities, we propose to ask how players and goals emerge and develop under the influence of changing policy discourses. Specifically, we point to policy processes in which problems, solutions, and actors are defined and positioned. This process involves the shaping of emotions and cognitions (Bröer and Duyvendak 2009).

This chapter builds on recent theorizing about discursive opportunities. In line with Jasper's argument and critically reviewing our own earlier statements, we abandon the structure portion of the discursive opportunity structure concept. While we agree that "structure" might be a misleading concept, we still think that "opportunity" is a useful heuristic device. Changing policy discourses do open up new chances for mobilization. In that sense, they constitute an opportunity. To give one example: political recognition of rights for one ethnic group is easily followed by claims for similar rights from other groups or people claiming to form a group. This kind of opportunity falls halfway between the long-term rules of the game—often summarized as "opportunity structures," and the short-term "mistakes" that, according to Jasper, constitute opportunities proper.

In this chapter we will elaborate on discursive opportunity theory and point to mechanisms that shape activism, focusing on the field of policy making. The emergence of and changes in the field itself are not considered here (Goodwin and Jasper 1999/2004a, b; Verhoeven 2009).

Elsewhere we demonstrate the overall correlation of discursive opportunities and activism (Bröer 2006, 2008; Bröer and Duyvendak 2009). Here, the focus is on typical interactions. People learn how to feel and act when they focus on an issue, internalize its meaning, or take a critical stance on the basis of prior experiences. Mechanisms like these are explained and exemplified.

The findings presented here a part of a larger investigation into aircraft noise annoyance (Bröer and Wirth 2004; Bröer 2006, 2007, 2008; Kroesen and Bröer 2009). That research started with the observation that noise annoyance complaints and protest seem to react to noise annoyance policy, rather than the other way around. If policy discourse shapes problem perception and political (in)action, then we should see different noise "problems" in different policy settings. We found just this in a cross-country comparison of policy discourse and popular discourse on aircraft noise (in letters, complaints, inquiries, and interviews) in the Netherlands and Switzerland. These differences in perceptions of the problem matched differences in policy discourse. Furthermore, differences within each case were variations in the policy discourse. The qualitative research showed that people perceived the aircraft sound in a way that was consonant with the policy discourse or deviated only partly from it. A quantitative retest confirmed the earlier results (Kroesen and Bröer 2009).

Discursive Opportunities and Resonance

Discourse is a pattern in language use (Laclau and Mouffe 1985; Hajer 1995; Steinberg 1998; Howarth 2000; Wetherell et al. 2001; Yates et al. 2001; Howarth and Torfing 2005). It is not the content of one specific utterance or newspaper clipping. A policy discourse comprises opportunities and limitations for political action; it legitimizes certain concerns and forms of engagement and delegitimizes others.

Discourses, in our definition, convey meaning, whereas structure as such cannot do that. Discourses also contain cognition and emotion. Earlier we said that people mobilize "not only because they were informed about the possibilities, as Koopmans and Olzak would suggest . . . they conceived of these openings as real opportunities because they started to *feel* differently about their situation and their capacity to change it. Therefore, the regulation of feelings needs to be included in a discursive opportunity model" (Bröer and Duyvendak 2009, p. 353). A discourse then comprises "framing and feeling rules" (Hochschild 1979): what can be said, demanded, expected, and felt in a specific situation. This "selection," the dominance of a certain discourse, is its central political element.

These discourses are not translating structural characteristics of political systems, as POS theory would have it; the discourses themselves are providing opportunities or limitations to be sensed and seized. This relative autonomy of discursive opportunities is clearly stated by Koopmans (Koopmans and Statham 1999; Koopmans 2004; Koopmans and Olzak 2004). But his Discursive Opportunity Structure approach misses the wider political power of discourse and neglects the role of feelings. The dominance or hegemony of certain discourses escapes Koopmans' attention, perhaps because of his methodological orientation. Koopmans and coworkers mainly approach discourse as the content of media coverage. Instead, we consider discourse as the politically relevant pattern in both texts and practices. Discourse then shapes activism not only through the literal content of, for example, media messages, but more profoundly through what cannot be said or felt.

The first step toward mechanisms is the concept of *resonance*, used both in framing literature (Schudson 1989; Steinberg 1998; Benford and Snow 2000; Ettema 2005) and discourse research (Koopmans and Olzak 2004; Bröer and Duyvendak 2009). Resonance means echo or repercussion. Discourse resonance can take the form of consonance, which means a close resemblance between a dominant (policy) discourse and people's perception. Resonance can also mean dissonance: a partial rejection of and partial agreement with a dominant discourse. And of course, there may be no resonance of a dominant discourse at all, while people still strive for the recognition of an issue.

We have shown that a specific policy discourse resonates in the way citizens and activists experience an issue. For example, how people think and feel about aircraft noise and how they oppose it (see Box 1). Because aircraft noise policy is different in the Netherlands and Switzerland, one can observe different perceptions of noise, different methods of protest, and different kinds of social movement organization. Those differences cannot directly be related to vast concepts such as "political culture" or changes, for example, in government coalition, as in POS theory.

Resonance theory can be further clarified in comparison to the concept of strategic action, as in Jasper's opening statement, for example, and in comparison to Koopmans' evolutionary approach.

Emergence

A model of social movements as strategic action presupposes given players with certain goals. It has been stated many times that strategic action is bounded by lack of information, insight, time, and so on. But this is not the main point, since it only concerns the quality of the strategy. A more fundamental question is how players come to define their goals and themselves. And how do we explain that people cherish opposing goals? These goals are not given but have a sociological origin as well. Furthermore, in addition to goal-oriented action, we might assume that humans act on the basis of value orientation, on the basis of tradition or routine, and on the basis of emotion as well.

Our own constructivist model applies the idea of "action" to actors and strategies themselves: one has to analyze how these are socially constructed.

Koopmans (2005) generated insight by turning POS into an evolutionary model. Players slowly emerge in the long run in reaction to changing opportunities and in reaction to information about the mobilization efforts of other players. Koopmans proposes what we might call "the blind activist" model: through trial and error, actors unconsciously adjust their strategies to what is successful. This is a decidedly macrostructural model, contrary to the micro-model of Jasper, in which strategic action, players, and goals figure prominently.

While Koopmans opens up the possibility of analyzing changing goals and emerging players, he neglects reflexivity, which makes for a crucial difference between species evolution and cultural changes.

The evolutionary perspective considers discursive opportunities as information to which actors adapt, and if they don't adapt successfully they vanish. For the rest, the actors remain stable. Here, Koopmans' evolutionary approach misses a crucial difference between biological and cultural changes. In species evolution, changes in the environment do not directly affect the makeup of a living organism, only its life chances. But in the evolution of cultural forms, changes in the discursive field directly affect the present actors who are, in part, reflexive cultural beings. There is no clear divide between a movement actor and public discourse. Actors actively construct the public discourse through interpretation and by sending out information themselves. In the same process movement actors reflexively constitute themselves. Activists do not plainly read a message from a text and act accordingly, as the evolutionary perspective suggests. Instead, people bring a host of interpretations and experiences to the scene. In the interaction between a dominant discourse concerning a certain issue and prior experience, people form a subject position.

To give an example: in the process leading to the fall of the Berlin Wall in 1989, citizens of the former German Democratic Republic redefined themselves under the influence of changing political discourse, first as "We are the people" (Wir sind das Volk) and later into "We are one people" (Wir sind ein Volk). This was more than adaptation to a changing discourse: the actors themselves changed the public discourse and the stakes of the conflict simultaneously.

In contrast to Koopmans (2005, p. 21), who states that in an evolutionary perspective "actors' choices may ultimately reflect structural opportunities," we emphasize that actors themselves come about under the influence of discursive opportunities as they manifest themselves in the policy process. Here, we might agree with Foucault's notion of subjectivity as a product of discursive practices. But any discursive practice is only one of many in which humans engage or have engaged and which altogether shape their subjectivity. People actively define themselves in relation to a dominant discourse. The model of Koopmans (and Foucault in this respect) is too deterministic: the effect of a dominant discourse can be consonance but also dissonance. Or, people might not be affected at all.

A discourse, furthermore, is field or issue specific. In a process of learning, the feeling and framing rules of a discourse are internalized, perceived, used, challenged, or confronted with other rules. New discursive opportunities and limitations, altered under the influence of activism, can resonate in subsequent actions.

A discourse is never all-encompassing or closed because it contains internal possibilities for contradiction (evoking the external as necessary point of reference) and it can contradict other discourses. Again, these contradictions have to be perceived as such by people. They have to evaluate cognitively and/or emotionally a (potentially dominant) discourse. The result of that evaluation under the pressure of a field-specific discourse is a fragmentation of political subjectivity.

In sum, this is a constructivist model of social movements: we plead for an embedded and contextual understanding of actors, goals, and strategies. Opportunities play an important role, both in the genesis of political actors (their subjectivity) and in what they consider appropriate goals and strategies (in line with their framing and feeling rules).

We can demonstrate that there is a close affinity between a dominant policy discourse on a specific issue and people's perceptions of that issue. People's perceptions are formed through an active engagement with dominant feeling and framing rules. As usual, however, a causal argument is hard to make. It is possible to show that policy makers devise certain policies before they encounter large-scale protest. And it is possible to show that certain story-lines, metaphors, or frames are deliberately invented by experts. To establish a causal argument, a closer look at mechanisms is needed. One has to show how discursive opportunities might translate into human conduct.

Is This Framing?

In the literature on contentious action, "framing" is often portrayed as strategic action by given social movement organizations. The discussion on this and on related issues has already been documented (Benford 1997; Steinberg 1998; Benford and Snow 2000). Suffice to say that we hold the following assumptions.

First, in line with Goffman (1975) we hold that framing is always at least partly based on people's tacit assumptions about the world. Second, people actively and reflexively participate in framing. Third, framing of political issues extends beyond movement organizations. Following a Foucauldian approach we include the formation of meaning in discursive practices, and we especially include the mundane activities of policy making (Hajer 1995). An example of the latter is a complaint agency; once an authority installs a complaint agency concerning issue X, this tacitly signals to citizens that they are entitled to complain. X is reframed, and the question then arises if and how practices associated with the issue affect people's perception and identity and thereby chances for mobilization.

The mechanisms we will describe below to some extent involve reconfiguring frames of mind. Snow et al. (1986) coined the concept of "frame alignment" for this process, defined as "the linkage or conjunction of individual and SMO (social movement organization, CB/JWD) interpretive frameworks" (p. 467). More particularly, the authors introduced the following concepts:

1. Frame bridging: when two similar yet unconnected frames are combined by the activities of social movement organizations.

2. Frame amplification: when an existing frame of mind is strengthened or clarified by the activities of social movement organizations.

3. Frame extension: when the social movement organizations succeed in installing their frame in the minds of new people. Here, basic values are tapped, therefore there is some overlap with frame bridging.

4. Frame transformation: the implant of new values and meaning or the complete abandoning of old ideas (p. 473–74), similar to what Goffman calls conversion.

Frame alignment differs from our constructivist discourse model in several respects. First, frame alignment is about the efforts of movement organizations. Here we look at changes among potential activists. These changes are no solitary musings but part of policy implementation, organizational activities, discussions, confrontations, informational gatherings, and other discursive practices.

Second, the frame alignment model focuses on given movement organizations' activities, on their strategic framing efforts. We instead take meaning making and framing to be more dispersed processes. Since actors are constantly evolving, their goals are "under construction" and switching over time as well.

Third, the frame alignment approach focuses on cognitions. We include explicitly framing and feeling rules in our discourse model (see, for example, Jasper 1998; Flam and King 2005). A discourse is made up of what Arlie Hochschild (1979, 1983) calls *framing rules* and *feeling rules*. Framing rules refer to "the rules according to which we ascribe definitions or meanings to situations," and she defines feeling rules as "guidelines for the assessment of fits and misfits between feeling and situation" (1979, p. 566). Social processes affect the way potential activists experience their emotions. As Hochschild (1979, p. 567) puts it: "One can defy an ideological stance not simply by maintaining an alternative frame on a situation but by maintaining an alternative set of feeling rights and obligations."

At this point, we turn to the mechanisms that link changing discursive opportunities and potential activists.

Learning How to Feel and Act

The basic process of discourse resonance is learning how to think, feel, and act. Learning can go unnoticed, as in the theory of Koopmans, and it can be an evaluation and reflexive application of acquired framing and feeling rules. Learning comprises the shaping of cognitions and emotions.

When it comes to political action, learning can take different forms: focusing on an issue, internalizing its preconceived meaning, or converting (changing a point of view). These three processes (re)produce a discourse, leading to consonance, yet processes of critically evaluating and exploiting a discourse lead to dissonant positions. Last, we point to "avoiding" as a way of not dealing with a discourse. Below, we detail these processes and present empirical support.

Focusing

Our attention to a given issue is guided by prior experiences and current issue salience. Issues are more salient when they are "mediatized" or tackled in policy. A new issue gets attention if its importance is established by linking it to a recognized and important issue, a perceived cleavage, or dominant framing and feeling rules.

The degree to which meaning is preformed can differ. The meaning of Al Gore's *An Inconvenient Truth* and its effect on our attention are based on a range of existing symbols. In contrast, "9/11," at least in the first days, lacked much preformed meaning.

The focusing mechanism happens in small-scale interactions. You can test it yourself: tell your friends and family repeatedly about an issue you are interested in; they will report that, since talking to you, they have noticed the issue more often. This happened in our noise research too; people reported being more sensitive after the appointment for an interview was made.

Focusing is itself only a first step in the emergence of new actors and goals. It is necessary that the object of focus is defined in a certain way and that this definition is internalized.

Internalizing

If focusing is repeated, if the object of focus is defined in a certain way, and if these definitions are supported by practices, then a specific focus of attention will be internalized. Internalization is cumulative and especially strong when a policy discourse is dominant for a long period and becomes taken for granted. We present two examples of the internalization mechanism.

Noise annoyance due to aircraft sound shows a remarkable trend: less and less aircraft noise is needed to annoy people (Guski 2003; Bröer et al. 2005; Babisch et al. 2009), while no corresponding trend exists for cars or railways.

Moreover, the trend follows large-scale and partly successful noise annoyance policy. Thus, while several countries have succeeded in limiting aircraft sound exposure or holding it constant, people are increasingly annoyed by the sound. This difference between the quantified magnitude of exposure to a hazard and popular perception of the hazard is a well-known phenomenon in risk research. For example, few worried about air quality in Western Europe a hundred years ago, when it was much worse than now.

This paradox might be explained by the (successful) policy itself: a policy for aircraft noise sends a number of messages:

- There is a problem urgent enough to be addressed by (national) policy.
- Sound pressure is the main problem, noise has to be limited.
- People are victims of the noise load (and not, for example, the culprit)
- People have a right to feel annoyed.

We can see that noise policy contains framing rules and feeling rules. It contains a focus of attention (sound), a definition of a problem (noise load), an entitlement to certain feelings (annoyance), and the implication of a collective interest (silence). The way noise policy addresses people also configures them as "citizens" or "population" or "stakeholders." Literally, "stakes" are often part of the noise annoyance policy definition.

We have described elsewhere (Bröer and Duyvendak 2009) that this takes different forms in different contexts. The Dutch policy focuses on the general population, which leads people to define themselves as part of that population. The Swiss noise annoyance policy, on the contrary, defines citizens as local stakeholders. Consequently, attention is directed at the local effects of air-mobility, and mobilization is local or regional.

Noise policy legitimates existing and new complaints about noise. It reorganizes cognition (defines a problem as important) and emotion (legitimizes concern). A necessary condition is the visibility of the policy, and a mediating factor is implementation; the policy as implemented contains discursive opportunities and limitations.

In a process perspective, increasing noise annoyance can thus be understood as an unwanted "success" of noise policy; in various discursive practices, people have internalized the issue and react to noise on the basis of noise policy discourse.

Learning how to think and feel about an issue is an active process of involvement, but it can also go unnoticed. Previously, we have shown that noise complaints differ in the Netherlands and Switzerland. About one-fourth of the complaints are almost perfectly in line with the administrative and political demands of the complaint agencies. The Dutch agency asks citizens to report all noise events, which they readily do. In Switzerland, the complaint agency offers information about the cause of the noise, which is what many citizens ask for. Furthermore, the number of complaints follows calls for active involvement by policy makers and partly by oppositional groups. Next to these consonant complaints, we discuss below complaints in which people try to go against the administrative procedures.

Converting

Sometimes the process of learning is explicit, involving a noticeable switch from one set of feeling and framing rules to another. We present one example, in which the conversion leads a protest group to adopt the discourse of other groups and of the governmental noise policy.

In 1998, citizens of a small town near Zurich, Switzerland, started an organization called Committee Against Aircraft Noise. A general reduction of flight movements, they figured and claimed, would reduce or prevent noise exposure for all Swiss. The Committee targeted national noise policy. Around the same time, the Cantonal government changed its noise policy, starting a policy of redistributing flights. Redistribution was also meant to allow for further airport growth at Zurich Kloten. This policy was presented to all surrounding municipalities, involving citizens and stakeholders in extensive communication and consultation. Within a period of three years, about 50 new organizations were set up. In addition, most city councils and other political organizations entered the redistribution debate and a fierce discussion about "who gets what" ensued. Almost all groups and bodies argued for a different local distribution to protect their own areas. This discussion also affected the Committee Against Aircraft Noise. After extensive internal debates, the group stated that it was no longer feasible or strategically sound to strive for a national solution. They felt forced to plea for local noise protection, instead. They thus converted from a national or even universalist frame to a particularistic frame. More than merely a matter of cognition, the new, local-protection frame was also attractive because it offered a right to be concerned, in this case about the deterioration of one's "Heimat."

So far, we have isolated parts of a learning process (focusing, internalizing, and converting) in which a dominant discourse (framing and feeling rules) is gradually taken over by movement-activists-in-the-making. The last example, a movement organization's conversion, shows that discourse resonance does not happen in a vacuum. The new policy discourse first contradicted an existing discourse of activists. In the case of conversion, the contradiction was fully resolved. This comes close to Koopmans' gradual adaptation to discursive opportunities. In the ensuing discussion, however, we point to mechanisms in which these contradictions partly remain.

Using the Dominant Discourse

Activists often use the language and practices of a dominant policy to strive for their own goals and to oppose a policy. They might, for example, enter a committee to (try to) change its agenda. Discursively, the strategy of using a field has a "yes . . . but" structure. Hajer (1995) points to this as a "discursive paradox." One enters a field by agreeing and then adds divergent thoughts and feelings. Here, we want to point to the long-term consequences of this strategy: (1) actors themselves change through the internalization of dominant feeling and framing rules, and (2) actors support goals inherent in the dominant discourse. Three examples demonstrate how this works.

1. Friends of the Earth
In the Netherlands, environmental activists of Friends of the Earth (FoE) started to spearhead aircraft noise around 1994, roughly five years after the national government had reframed airport development as a matter of ecological modernization. Part of that policy was the introduction of noise limits and contours, intended to limit growth in this noise-polluting industry. In the beginning, learning about noise contours and decibels constituted a deliberate attempt to become an expert player in the field the policy had defined and then use that access to introduce other policy measures as well. Although things did not work out that way—FoE ultimately could not prevent the growth of Amsterdam's Schiphol Airport—the professionalization of the activist had other effects. In our interviews and contacts with them, activists had difficulties in approaching aircraft noise from a nonacoustic paradigm. Repeatedly, they suggested that any approach other than noise contours and acoustic limits would serve the interest of the industry. Sometimes they displayed anger about different approaches, which reveals the emotional value of the acquired position. Moreover, what started as an attempt to seize an opportunity became a taken-for-granted definition of a contested issue. The

adherence to the acoustic paradigm also strengthened the policy discourse activists wished to challenge.

2. Serial Complainers

Earlier we showed that the number and content of noise complaints closely followed changes in discursive construction of noise, as changes in policy legitimated concern and complaints. The widespread political attention for possible complaints made people focus on noise, and the government's responsiveness made it wise to participate by filing a complaint. The policy process in the Netherlands gave rise to serial complainers: people filing thousands of complaints per year. Such behavior is often full of contradictions and reflexivity. Citizens file a complaint while simultaneously trying to change the complaint procedure and policy. In a limited way, they follow the course of the activists of FoE: they learn how to complain professionally in order to enter the policy process. Let's take a look at one example of the thousands of complaint forms stored in the Netherlands (see Figure 10.1).

This person in 2000 addresses the complaint agency through a letter, although the agency also facilitates digital complaints. Letters tend to allow for more diverse ways to express criticism and discontent, and this one shows a typical mixture of administrative requirements, arguments, and emotional expressions.

After addressing the reader, the author opens with "Here we go again !!!!" referring to his earlier complaints, but also commenting on the procedure. The second sentence starts: "Once again, the period from 12-1-2000 till 27-1-2000 was motivation for Schiphol to choose Akersloot [the village] as a sightseeing spot for tourists and freight carriers, which is proven by the list below." He evaluates policy and expresses frustration. His tone suggests that complaining is ineffective, while at the same time he is making an effort to document the noise problem.

The list contains thirty flights, documented with date and time. This is exactly what the complaint agency asks for: time and date of noisy flights in order to file each date as a separate complaint. The handwritten line on the dates stems from the agency employee who filed these data. As an experienced complainer, this man knows the procedure. He knows that only the details of the complaints are recorded, yet he uses the complaint to add much more: the cynical "here we go again" and a scale for noisiness: "* = too much noise, ** = way too low and very noisy, *** = immediately remove from airspace." In the text line, he introduces the four-star category "**** = A number of planes (often the same ones !!!!!!!) are so way out of line that they should be taken out of airspace immediately and never allowed to come back."

Akersloot, 01/02/00

Geachte heer /mevrouw,

Daar gaan we weer !!!!
Ook in de periode van 12/01/00 tot en met 27/01/00 was voor Schiphol een reden om Akersloot uit te kiezen als een sight-seeing plaats voor de toeristen en vrachtvervoerders, zoals blijkt uit onderstaande lijst. Een lijst van data en tijden van de vliegtuigen die mijn rust verstoorden.

12/01/00	09.16 ***		21/01/00	09.55 ****
	11.00 ****(KLM!)			11.01 ****
	12.35 ****(USA!)			19.59 ****
15/01/00	00.06 ***		22/01/00	12.21 ***
	15.01 ***			19.32 ***
	16.56 ****		23/01/00	08.59 ****
16/01/00	07.57 ****			12.17 ***(KLM!)
	11.34 ****			12.29 ***(KLM!)
	12.10 ****		24/01/00	08.11 ****
	12.26 ***			08.53 ****
	14.39 ***			15.39 ***
18/01/00	17.06 ***		25/01/00	08.15 ****
19/11/00	12.11 ***			09.55 ****(KLM!)
	14.56 ***		27/01/00	07.41 ****
	23.43 ****			23.35 ****

2/2/00 mo

```
*    = te veel lawaai
**   = veel te laag en erg veel lawaai
***  = meteen uit het luchtruim verwijderen
```

Een aantal vliegtuigen(vaak dezelfde vliegtuigen!!!!!!!!) maakten het zo bont, dat ik vind dat zij terstond uit de lucht moeten worden gehaald en nooit meer mogen terugkomen. Deze vliegtuigen zijn herkenbaar bij de tijden met vier sterretjes(****). Ik constateer dat onze nationale 'trots' de KLM hierbij in de voorste linie aanwezig is(de KLM zou beter moeten weten, maar het is bekend dat deze vliegtuigmaatschappij een arrogante is!)

De heer ████
Binnengeest ██
1921 CP Akersloot

FIGURE 10.1 A Typical Letter of Complaint

SOURCE: From the archives of the Committee for Regional Consultation Schiphol.

There are more details, but the structure is evident: complainants use a standard procedure in standard and nonstandard ways at the same time. The letter contains arguments, recommendations, and a policy evaluation; at the same time, it contains anger and frustration (eighteen exclamation marks, considerable cynicism). The internal contradiction between using the complaint form and discontent about the procedure is one of the main features of the complaints procedure itself. It has been made so easy and almost obligatory to complain, while at the same time there is no clear or visible effect of complaints. Complainants who use the procedure for criticizing it are nonetheless supporting it at the same time. Facilitating mass complaining has locked some citizens into this administrative procedure.

3. Soundnet

In 2003, two young Internet experts privately discussed the "situation at Schiphol," angry about authorities' claim that the current sound measurement devices were the best available. The young technicians figured they could come up with a cheaper and, most of all, more democratic alternative, which would also generate new types of information.

Instead of a small number of sophisticated measuring devices run by the airport and government, they imagined a network of inexpensive microphones at people's houses linked through the Internet. By so doing, an average of measurement errors could be gauged and people would be provided with their own technical tools. The solution was so simple, they argued, that any child could do it. Hence, their logo of the first few years showed a child measuring noise by holding up a microphone.

This move was immediately successful because it appealed to three basic features of the public debate: (1) the amount of measured noise is the biggest problem, (2) people should participate in the policy process, (3) the authorities' statistics should not be trusted. Now, whereas statements 1 and 2 can be found in the dominant policy discourse, statement 3 establishes a dissonant or critical position: "yes . . . but."

Soon households and local communities were participating in the program called Soundnet. Gradually it turned into a commercial enterprise with a sophisticated technical apparatus. In the same period governmental noise statistics were made public and refined. Above all, this intervention stressed the dominance of the acoustic and technical approach to noise. However, while it enhanced people's capacities to document their immediate acoustic situation, it did not contribute to a different understanding of the problem.

· · ·

The three preceding examples, highlighting the experiences of Friends of the Earth, serial complainers, and Soundnet, all illustrate people's tendency to use dominant discursive practices within a field, and to strive for different goals. They first enter the discursive field referring to nondominant, often opposing discourses, then typically employ a "yes . . . but" structure in their arguments in order to engage in discursive struggle. This partial agreement allows for a critical distance and for emotional expression. At the same time, people become emotionally and cognitively attached to the dominant discourse. In all three examples, the countermoves support the very field one is trying to change.

Avoiding

In the face of a dominant policy discourse, people may try to avoid the issue altogether (Eliasoph 1997). Typically, the argumentative and emotional form is "no . . . but." People may withdraw into the private sphere, as did some of our interviewees who started by complaining or working for a social movement organization, but soon enough saw that they could not stand up against other parties. Typically, they evoked other socially available discourses to back up their position. Also, people tended to exaggerate the issue-specific discourse in order to distance themselves from it. As in the process of "using" a discourse, we clearly see the active and reflexive capacity of people.

A different kind of avoidance is visible with the Dutch organization, Acoustic Environment Protection Foundation. This group is not directly concerned with aircraft noise but with acoustic pollution in general, in a clear departure from the dominant political discourse that organizes the noise problem according to sources. The foundation claims that unwanted sound is a form of violence, while barely addressing the dominant noise discourse. It presents a cultural critique of noise as an unwanted part of modernity (Bijsterveld 2008) and technology. The foundation intentionally seeks support from specific groups of citizens rather than governmental or scientific entities, and its supporters include well-known artists and academics. Although it has a fundamental approach to noise, it actively avoids dealing with established noise problems related to traffic or neighborhoods.

Avoidance is partly a critique, and partly the construction of an alternative discourse altogether.

Conclusion

In response to thoughtful criticisms of political opportunity structures (Goodwin and Jasper 1999/2004a, b), we propose to abandon structuralist and other deterministic explanations of contentious action. More specifically, we address discursive opportunities. However, rejecting structuralist explanations does not necessarily imply a turn to voluntaristic approaches of collective action. We agree with Jasper and others that we have to take seriously actors' strategic considerations regarding goals and strategies, and we plea for an embedded and contextual understanding of these actors, their goals and strategies. In this constructivist understanding, opportunities still play an important role, both in the genesis of political actors (their subjectivity) and in what they consider appropriate goals and strategies (in line with their framing and feeling rules). Based on our research into noise policies in Switzerland and the Netherlands, we show variation in people's responses to discursive opportunities (from consonance to dissonance to no response at all). This variation can be explained by a series of mechanisms: focusing, internalizing, converting, using the dominant discourse, and avoiding. This is not meant as an exhaustive list of mechanisms, but as the principle mediating ones we came across in our analysis of, on the one hand, the policy process regarding aircraft noise and the discursive opportunities provided and, on the other hand, the development of contentious actors and their various goals and strategies.

Admittedly, we have stretched the concept of opportunity here. But, a (policy) discourse presents opportunities much the same way as professional jargon (terminology, language) does. Professional jargon is able to illuminate certain aspects of the world, while neglecting others. Policy discourse, like any other, works much the same way. Fortunately, people can turn this disciplining effect into an object of contention itself.

11 Eventful Protest, Global Conflicts

Social Mechanisms in the Reproduction of Protest

DONATELLA DELLA PORTA

P OLITICAL OPPORTUNITIES influence social movements, but they
are also changed by them. While early analyses of political opportunity structures considered them as exogenous, too deeply rooted to be
changed by social movement themselves, later research and theoretical reflection stressed the capacity of movements to produce changes in their environment as well as to frame opportunities advantageously. I would like to move
forward by looking at the ways in which events change structures by transforming the relations among actors. Protest, to various degrees, triggers cognitive and affective mechanisms that change the very definition of the self and
others, enhancing capacities to act. Interest and identities are endogenous to
social movements: not just conditions for their emergence but effects of their
action. In the language Jasper introduces in the introduction, this contribution
shows that protest creates players, rather than just responding to conditions.
The subject and its dispositions and desires are in fact created in action, rather
than existing before it.

Social movement studies have traditionally stressed conflict as a dynamic
element in societies. The European tradition sees new social movements as
potential carriers of a new central conflict in postindustrial societies, or at
least of an emerging constellation of conflicts. In the American tradition, the

Portions of this chapter have been adapted from *Distinktion. Scandinavian Journal of Social Theory* 17 (2008): 27–46.

resource mobilization approach reacted to a then-dominant conception of conflicts as pathologies. From Michael Lipsky (1969) to Charles Tilly (1978), the first systematic works on social movements developed within traditions that had stressed the importance of conflicts for power, in society, and in politics. In fact, a widely accepted definition of social movements mentions conflict as a central element in their conceptualization (della Porta and Diani 2006, p. 21).

Social movements are conflictual not only because of their stakes, but because of their forms. Protest has been considered the main repertoire of action—or even the modus operandi—of social movements. Not only do rational actors mobilize above all when and where they perceive the possibility of success (Tarrow 1994), but their strategies are also influenced by the reactions of authorities; the opening of channels of access moderates the forms of protest, while their closing down induces radicalization (della Porta 1995). In the 1990s, this instrumental view of protest was also linked to the spread of an image of a "protest society," with a sort of "conventionalization" of once-unconventional forms of action (della Porta and Reiter 1998; Meyer and Tarrow 1998). Widespread images occur of "movements without protest" (della Porta and Diani 2004), and, in parallel, of protest without movements. A sort of normalization—or routinization—of protest is certainly part of the picture of contemporary political conflicts in Western European societies.

Another part of the picture started to become more visible in 1999, with the protest in Seattle against the WTO Millennium Round, and grew after the attack on the Twin Towers in 2001. This is an image of political conflicts expressed on the street through mass rallies or direct action in what might be considered a new cycle of protest (della Porta 2007b; 2009a). Beyond describing some forms of action that (through countersummits and social forums) emerged in this cycle of protest, I shall address the more general issue of contemporary conflict by considering the emergent character of protest itself, by looking at the mechanisms that tend to reproduce protest in action.

Notwithstanding the relevance of protest events for social movements, they have been mainly studied as aggregated collective action (such as in protest cycles). In social movement studies, protest has in fact been mainly considered as a "dependent variable" and explained on the basis of political opportunities and organizational resources. In this analysis I want instead to stress the effects of protest on the social movement itself, inspired by the historical sociologist William H. Sewell, by focusing on what I would call "eventful protest." This differs from "teleological temporality," which explains events on the basis of abstract transhistorical processes "from less to more" (urbanization, industrialization, and the like), and from "experimental temporality," comparing different historical paths (revolution versus nonrevolution, democracy versus nondemocracy). "*Eventful temporality* recognizes the power of events in history" (Sewell 1996, p. 262). Sewell defines events as a "relatively rare subclass of happenings that *significantly transform structure*," and an eventful conception of temporality as "one that takes into account the transformation of structures by events" (p. 62; emphasis added). Especially during cycles of protest, some contingent events tend to affect the given structures by fuelling mechanisms of social change: organizational networks develop, frames are bridged, and personal links foster reciprocal trust. In this sense, some protest events constitute processes during which collective experiences develop through the interactions of different individual and collective actors. The event has a transformative effect, in that "events transform structures largely by constituting and empowering new groups of actors or by re-empowering existing groups in new ways" (p. 271). Some protest events put in motion social processes that "are inherently contingent, discontinuous and open ended" (p. 272).

"Eventful temporality" implies "transformative events." As McAdam and Sewell observed, "no narrative account of a social movement or revolution can leave out events. . . . But the study of social movements or revolutions—at least as normally carried out by sociologists or political scientists—has rarely paid analytic attention to the contingent features and causal significance of particular contentious events such as these" (2001, p. 101). The two scholars call for attention to the way in which events "become turning points in structural change, concentrated moments of political and cultural creativity when the logic of historical development is reconfigured by human action but by no means abolished" (p. 102). Moments of concentrated transformations have been singled out especially in those highly visible events that end up symbolizing entire social movements, such as the taking of the Bastille for the French Revolution, or the Montgomery Bus Boycott for the U.S. civil rights movement. These represent important turning points. According to David Hess and Brian Martin (2006), "A transformative event is a crucial turning point for a social movement that dramatically increases or decreases the level of mobilization" (p. 249).

In my conception of eventful protest, I share the focus on the internal dynamics and transformative capacity of protest, looking however at a broader range of events than those included under the label of transformative protest.

My assumption is that protests have cognitive, affective, and relational impacts on the very movements that carry them out and that some forms of action or specific campaigns have a particularly high degree of eventfulness. Through these events, new tactics are experimented with, signals about the possibility of collective action are sent (Morris 2000), feelings of solidarity are created, organizational networks are consolidated, and sometimes public outrage at repression develops (Hess and Martin 2006).

In this contribution, I look at the transformative capacity of protest more than at the characteristics of prominent events. Protest will be the independent variable; I shall look not at what produces protest, but at the by-product of protest itself. In more general terms, I would suggest that the contemporary sociological reflection on conflicts as producers of social capital, collective identity, and knowledge could balance the negative vision of conflicts as disruptive of social relations, an analysis that can emerge from an exclusive focus on the most extreme forms of political violence.

I will reflect in particular on what makes protest eventful. As mentioned previously, in most social movement literature protest events have been analyzed as the "dependent variable," with an attempt to explain their size and form on the basis of macro, contextual characteristics. Recently, two different theoretical developments have brought about a shift in perspective. One is a growing attention to the cultural and symbolic dimension of social movements (Goodwin, Jasper, and Polletta 2001; Flam and King 2006). The other is a more dynamic vision of protest, with attention paid to the causal mechanisms that intervene between macrocauses and macroeffects (McAdam, Tarrow, and Tilly 2001).

Even if protest is a resource that groups sometimes utilize to pressure decision makers, it should not be viewed in purely instrumental terms (Taylor and van Dyke 2004). During the course of a protest both time and money are invested in risky activities, yet resources of solidarity can often be created (or recreated). Many forms of protest "have profound effects on the group spirit of their participants," since "in the end there is nothing as productive of solidarity as the experience of merging group purposes with the activities of everyday life" (Rochon 1998, p. 115). Protest promotes a sense of collective identity, a condition for collective action (Pizzorno 1993). For workers, strikes and occupations represent not only instruments for collective pressure but also arenas in which a sense of community is formed (Fantasia 1988), and the same occurs during the occupation of schools and universities by students (Ortoleva 1988), or in squatted youth centers. In social movements the means used are closely tied to the desired ends: "Tactics represent important routines, emotionally and morally salient in these people's lives" (Jasper 1997, p. 237). I look at the capacity of protest events to produce relations, by facilitating communication as well as affective ties.

Together with attention to contingency and emotional effects, I reflect on processes that stress the role of temporality. In macroanalyses, causal mechanisms have been linked to systematic process analysis (Hall 2003), and "causal reconstruction" that "seeks to explain a given social phenomenon—an event, structure or development—by identifying the process through which it is generated" (Mayntz 2004, p. 238). Adapting Renate Mayntz's definition (p. 241), we might consider mechanisms as concatenation of generative events linking macrocauses (such as contextual transformation) to aggregated effects (cycle of protest) through transformation at the individual and organizational levels. Mechanisms refer therefore to intermediary steps between macroconditions and macro-outcomes. With more or less awareness, some research on social movements has gone beyond causal macro-macro inferences, looking at the mechanisms that link the macro and the micro (Coleman 1986), such as the construction of identity (Melucci 1996), the processes of networking (Diani 1995), framing (Snow et al. 1986), and the escalation of action-strategies (della Porta 1995). My analysis will build upon this literature by distinguishing *cognitive* mechanisms, with protest as an arena of debate; *relational* mechanisms, which bring about protest networks; and *emotional* mechanisms, through the development of feelings of solidarity "in action."

Research on contemporary protest events, especially around issues of global justice and democracy from below, will illustrate my argument. In section two, devoted to countersummits, I refer to interviews with representatives of social movement organizations conducted in Italy (della Porta and Mosca 2007). In section three, to illustrate the social forum process, I present some results of a study on the European Social Forums (ESFs), based on an analysis of organizational documents as well as a survey of their activists (della Porta 2009a). Finally, section four looks at direct action, drawing upon a case study on the protest campaign against the construction of a high-speed railway in Northern Italian Val di Susa (della Porta and Piazza 2008). Although relational, cognitive, and emotional consequences of protest on protestors are relevant to all three forms of protest, long-lasting transnational campaigns seem particularly apt to illustrate relational processes; open arenas for debates (such as social forums) to discuss the cognitive effects of protest; and direct action to analyze the role of emotions in mobilization. In the concluding remarks, I reflect on the conditions for the development of "eventful protests" in contemporary societies, linking them to a new cycle of protest, with strong transnational characteristics.

Networking in Action:
How Protest Produces Relations

European Marches targeted the EU Summits in Amsterdam, Cologne, and Nice, promoting a social dimension of Europe by protesting against the EU-sponsored employment strategies, because of their emphasis on "flexible" (precarious) jobs, and developing an Alternative Charter of Fundamental Rights. Initially launched by organizations of unemployed and critical unions, they became increasingly multi-issue and succeeded in sensitizing the activists of the institutionalized trade union confederations, developing into a systematic contestation of EU Summits through parallel countersummits in the same place as the official meetings. The European Marches have been defined as an early example of the formation of a flexible network addressing social issues at the European level (Mathers 2007, p. 51). This long-lasting and intense form of protest (inspired, in part, by the Hunger Marches of the 1930s) illustrates the growth of formal and informal networks "in action." The countersummits in particular involved a growing number of social movement organizations, networking networks of activists that had developed specific campaigns on EU issues. Along with the European Marchers were mobilized environmentalists active on Genetically Modified Organisms, NGOs promoting a social vision of Europe, and pacifist organizations protesting against the wars in ex-Yugoslavia and the Middle East. It was during the (often long-lasting) preparation of these events that interactions developed between different actors mobilized on different issues and in different countries. In this sense, protests created social capital (in Bourdieu's understanding of it as relational capital) of a particular type.

During this long campaign, successful networking steadily increased the number of organizations involved, as well as their diversity by countries of origin and main focus of concern. The first march was promoted by activists from two French organizations—Agir ensemble Contre le Chômage (AC!), and the rank-and-file union Solidaires, Unitaires, Démocratiques (SUD)—that had begun to focus on the wider European dimension during the mobilization of the French unemployed in the mid-1990s (della Porta 2008). According to the "thick description" of the campaign provided by Andy Mathers (2007), the first meeting of twenty-five representatives of organizations promoting a European March was held in Florence, on the occasion of an EU Summit in June 1996. In November of that year, forty participants from eight countries met in Paris, in what an activist describes as "a climate of co-operation. . . . There were people from different ideological positions and they entered into a dialogue and found a form of working together" (Mathers 2007, p. 57). After the success of the rally in Amsterdam in 1997, about one hundred people from eleven countries met in Luxembourg, in October 1997, and formed a European Marches network, de-fined as a loose network of groups that functioned by consensus.

With the organization of the countersummits, the mobilization extended to involve different types of actors at different territorial levels. During the preparation of the first march, "the various committees that sprung up to sup-port the marches at European, national, and local levels were notable for the plurality of participating organizations and for generating a discernable spirit of goodwill for the project" (p. 56). The following countersummits saw the participation not only of various—including mainstream—unions but also of associations of unemployed, immigrants, "alterglobalist" environmental-ists such as ATTAC, progressive and left-wing parties, communists and an-archists, Kurdish and Turkish militants, women's collectives, and Basque and Corsican autonomists. At the turn of the millennium, a similar convergence of different social and political actors developed at the local and national levels through processes of "contamination in action" (for the local level, della Porta and Mosca 2005; for the national level, della Porta 2007b). Protest produced relations between once-disconnected individuals and groups, and networking developed "in action."

Networking "in action" is instrumentally important in increasing the in-fluence of each organization and individual. Coordinations and umbrella or-ganizations emerged with the pragmatic aim of facilitating mobilization, and then helped develop inclusive norms (Andretta 2006). The logic of the network as an instrument for the coordination of activity facilitates the involvement of different political actors. Especially in the beginning, the networks kept together mainly through an emphasis on mobilization for concrete goals. In the European Marches, coordinated action was promoted above all for being instrumentally useful. According to an activist, "the concept of the European Marches Network has always been to say that even if there are tensions, it is necessary to find the spaces where we can work together" (Mathers 2007, p. 56).

The same "instrumental" reasoning seems to have been at the basis of coalition building in other campaigns. In the words of an Italian activist:

> One of the more important and useful things of the last years' experience is the fact that network-logic has been concretely affirmed . . . we were already active on some issues, but we were alone. By clarifying that it is better working together, that this is an additional resource, and that this logic is more useful for the people to whom you want to bring results: this idea starts to be affirmed. I think that one of the most positive aspects of this logic is precisely this reflection on the networks (cited in della Porta and Mosca 2007, p.11).

Beyond this instrumental aim, the preparation of common protest campaigns is also seen as intensifying relations between participants. The European Marches "produced new personal and collective identities amongst the unemployed, as well as new representations of them as an international and internationalist social and political force" (Mathers 2007, p. 87). This had a cognitive dimension. The marches developed social ties primarily by facilitating an exchange of knowledge, as relations with other activists induced cognitive changes. Alongside an increase in the number of organizations involved, and the structuring of the protest network, the definition of what was at stake also changed during the protest campaign, from a focus on unemployment to a broader range of EU policies and the participation of activists from various movements:

> [A]n important element of the marches was the opportunity they provided for sharing personal experiences of unemployment, for experiencing a sense of fellowship through sharing elements of everyday life such as food and entertainment, and for collectively tackling common practical and political problems. These sharing of common experiences and common problems helped to establish a sense of camaraderie amongst the marchers and in some cases friendships developed that were cemented through exchange visits and contact by mail between the continental events (Mathers 2007, p. 90).

During the long march, the activists met with participants in local struggles related to employment issues, such as dockers from Liverpool and Renault workers from Vilvoorde. In the words of an activist, "what was extraordinary about this first march were the networks that formed out of it. That's to say that the people who crossed over Europe gave their addresses to the people who they came in contact with and since then have been corresponding amongst themselves" (Mathers 2007, p. 90).

Transnational networks also allow the construction of transnational identities through the recognition of similarities across countries. In a scale-shift process (Tarrow 2005; Tarrow and McAdam 2004), during transnational campaigns activists begin to identify as part of a European or even global subject. Italian activists involved in transnational protest campaigns stressed the growing dialogue between leaders (or spokespersons) of different organizations as an effect of better reciprocal understanding: "after several years of developing common actions, you meet in the same movement, talk, you start understanding each other, you find codes of communication, methods for resolving problems . . . in the different mobilizations you meet different organized and non-organized actors with whom you had nothing to share before . . . there you start to enter into dialogue and to discover that you can do things together" (SF2, cited in della Porta and Mosca 2007; here and below, abbreviations refer to interviews: SF = social forum; IVS = Val di Susa). This reciprocal understanding is also considered by activists of various recent protest campaigns as pushing toward multi-issue claims: overlapping membership as well as participation in organizational coalitions have indeed been seen as preconditions for the spreading of innovative ideas (see, for example, Meyer and Whittier [1994] on the women's and peace movements). As an Italian activist stressed when talking about the Social Forum process, common campaigns link different issues while they mobilize: "we took part in networks following the principle that associations must avoid . . . hyper-specialization that de-localizes them; our principle is that they must re-localize and root themselves in their own cities, in their own territory, be loved by the people around them, build contacts, etc." (SF20, cited in della Porta and Mosca 2007).

At the personal level, participation in protest campaigns helps develop reciprocal knowledge and thus trust "in action." From this point of view, during the European Marches informal networks were created along with more formalized ones. As an activist stated, "In France in '97 I followed the activists for one week and we became friends. . . . With some people you become friends and then it becomes normal to see them and to call them and to ask them what they are doing? And to say 'we are doing this, why don't you come?'" (Mathers 2007, p. 90).

Emotions also play an important role. Friendship ties are often facilitated by the playfulness of the protest. Although speaking a language of anger (mentioned in several of the slogans), activists of the marches remember action as parties, festivals, and holiday events. "Collective action also enabled the unemployed to emerge out of the misery and solitude of everyday life and share in an episode of collective existence and solidarity that was on occasion a joyful experience" (ibid.). Solidarity ties can also be intensified by more negative yet highly emotional experiences, such as police repression (see also § 4): the countersummits were also eventful because of the frequent encounters with the police. Rank-and-file members see common campaigns as enabling a mutual familiarity that favors the construction of shared objectives, as knowledge allows them to overcome prejudice. As an Italian interviewee notes: "we have also got to know each other and to soften some attitudes, and there is trust and respect for every representation within the committee" (SF11, cited in ibid.). Marching allows the individuals to acquire a social position, as well as linguistic and technical skills.

The creation of mutual knowledge, trust, and friendship through protest is nothing new. In his research on labor conflicts, Rick Fantasia (1988) challenged the widespread idea of a lack of class-consciousness among U.S. workers. By looking at intense moments of protest (such as strikes and occupations), he developed the concept of a "culture of solidarity," as a more dynamic substitute for "static" class consciousness. The preparation of some symbolically relevant protest events often takes long months. This was evident in the history of events commemorating the First of May, which played a key role in the labor movement. In countries such as Italy, France, and Germany, relations often developed between the labor movements and other social movements during the long preparations, often up to a year, of the Labor Day demonstrations. What makes networking particularly relevant in contemporary movements, together with the already mentioned plural background of their activists, is the transnational level of the action. The European Marches, the European Preparatory Assemblies for the European Social Forum, as well as the meetings to prepare the EuroMayday represent moments of reciprocal knowledge among activists coming from different countries and backgrounds (Doerr and Mattoni 2007).

Arenas for Conversation:
How Protest Produces Cognitive Processes

The Social Forums have been an innovative experiment promoted by the global justice movement. Distinct from a countersummit, which is mainly oriented toward public protest, the Social Forum is a space of debate among activists. The format of the social forum epitomizes the cognitive processes that develop within protest events as arenas for encounter. Also present in many previous forms of protest was the cognitive dimension of protest events as spaces for exchanges of knowledge and ideas.

The charter of the World Social Forum defines it as an "open meeting place," and indeed the basic feature of a social forum is the concept of an open and inclusive public space. Participation is open to all civil society groups, barring those advocating racist ideas or employing terrorist means, and political parties that advocate these ideas. Its functioning involves hundreds of workshops and dozens of conferences (with invited experts), and testifies to the importance given at least in principle to the production and exchange of knowledge. In fact, the World Social Forum has been defined as "a market place for (sometime competing) causes and an 'ideas Fair' for exchanging information, ideas and experiences horizontally" (Schoenleitner 2003, p. 140). Writing on the European Social Forum in Paris, sociologists Agrikoliansky and Cardon (2005, p. 47) stressed its pluralistic nature:

> Even if it re-articulates traditional formats of mobilisations, the form of the "forum" has properties that are innovative enough to consider it as a new entry in the repertoire of collective action. . . . An event like the ESF in Paris does not indeed resemble anything already clearly identified. It is not really a conference, even if we find a program, debates and paper-givers. It is not a congress, even if there are tribunes, militants and *mots d'ordre*. It is not just a demonstration, even if there are marches, occupations and demonstrations in the street. It is neither a political festival, even if we find stands, leaflets and recreational activities. The social forums concentrate in a unit of time and space such a large diversity of forms of commitment that exhaustive participation in all of them is impossible.

What unifies these different activities is the aim of providing a meeting space for the loosely coupled, huge number of groups that form the archipelagos of the global justice movement. Its goals include enlarging the number of individuals and groups involved, but also laying the ground for a broader mutual understanding. Far from aiming at eliminating differences, the open debates should help to increase awareness of each other's concerns and beliefs. The purpose of networking-through-debating was in fact openly stated already at the first ESF in Florence, where the declaration of the European social movements reads: "We have come together to strengthen and enlarge our alliances because the construction of another Europe and another world is now urgent."

Social forums aspire to the creation of knowledge, through the construction of spaces where communication between groups with very different organizational forms, issue focus, and national background can develop free from the immediate concerns for decision of strategies and actions. Although this is not new, the internal heterogeneity and the transnational nature of these mobilizations give a special character to this search. Cognitive exchanges develop during various forms of protest, used by various movements. The assemblies have developed as (more or less) formalized and ritualized spaces of encounter and debate. Marches have usually ended with speeches of a more or less ideological content. What seems to make cognitive exchanges especially relevant for the Global Justice Movement in general, and the social forums in particular, is the positive value given to the openness toward "the others."

In this sense, social forums belong to emerging forms of action that stress plurality and inclusion. Similar forms of protest that favor cognitive "contamination" (or cross-fertilization) are the "solidarity assemblies," a series of meetings where multiple and heterogeneous organizations active on similar issues are called to participate with their particular experiences, or the "fairs of concrete alternatives," whose aim is to link together various groups that developed alternatives to the market economy ranging from fair trade to environmental protection (della Porta and Mosca 2007).

The exchanges that take place during forums are usually less ideological than informative, aimed at the construction of an alternative specialized knowledge. For instance, in campaigns against airports, roads, bridges, or high-speed railways, a main activity of protesters is the collection, elaboration, and diffusion of information on the projects, based on technical knowledge obtained through dialogue with experts and internalized through the participation in the protest of counterexperts (economists, engineers, urban planners, and so on) (della Porta and Piazza 2008). If technical information has a legitimizing effect on the elaboration and implementation of public policies (Lewanski 2004), technical counterknowledge is considered a fundamental resource for those who protest. Beyond this instrumental use, knowledge can also transform the form and content of the protest, as the various actors who participate in the protest tend to adopt a specialist language. And in the course of mobilization, activists appropriate, transform, and transmit technical knowledge.

Solidarity in Action: How Protest Creates Communities

The deputy police commissioner glimpsed local politicians: my councilor and I were wearing the national flag. It was not the first time that the State turned on itself, but this time it was strange because it was the deputy commissioner that gave me orders to evacuate the streets in five minutes. The police would have passed through anyway! At this point I began to call other politicians, various other people, asking them to come and join us. We are fortunate that we know the mountains well, the paths and mule tracks. After ten minutes the deputy commissioner returned to ask us what we had decided, and I replied that we would not move and would defend our territory. At this point the police advanced with their shields above their heads. We conducted an entirely pacific resistance, with our hands in the air; we were retreating because we could not stand such a conflict, until behind us came reinforcements from everywhere, which helped us to resist the advance. So many people arrived that the police had to stop, and despite pushing us to the side, they were unable to move us. This went on until late in the evening, it was a very tough confrontation, from seven in the morning till eight in the evening, until the deputy commissioner, in agreement with the president of the Mountainous Community, suspended their activities. At that point we decided to leave, as the police themselves were doing. That same night the police occupied the area (IVS7, cited in della Porta and Piazza 2008).

This is the chronicle, in the words of the Mayor of a village in the Val di Susa (Italian Alps), of a very eventful protest in the campaign against the construction of a high-speed railway on his territory: the so-called "battle of Seghino" on October 31, 2006. The evolution of local conflicts around large infrastructure projects often sees an escalation toward more disruptive forms of protest, as more moderate actions have failed to break the perceived "brick wall" of the authorities (della Porta 2004). Mass demonstrations are also accompanied by direct actions such as blocking roads or railway lines that, although excluding violence, still represent a challenge to the state in terms of public order. A radicalization of conflict is particularly evident in Val di Susa, around a classic mechanism of interaction in the street with the enforcers of the law, which also attains a strong symbolic value. The escalation in the conflict with the police, centered around the occupation of the building site, which both sides were seeking to control, is a source for growing solidarity and increasing identification with the protest. The eventfulness of protest emerges especially through the development of strong emotional ties, and with them of a sense of belonging to a community.

As mentioned earlier, protest repertoires are often chosen, or at least justified ex post facto, as instrumentally useful. Despite the risk of stigmatization, direct action is perceived by protesters as an instrument that raises the visibility of a protest ignored by the mass media. In the case described above, even beyond the valley "the attacks by the police earned the sympathy of those who knew nothing of the TAV [high speed train] . . . for them it was counterproductive because it gave us added visibility and prompted a democratic spirit that went beyond the TAV conflict, because in a democratic country certain things should not be done" (IVS3).

Beyond the instrumental dimension linked to increased visibility, an important effect of direct action on the closer circles of protestors is the strengthening of motivations through the development of feelings of solidarity and belonging. If emotions had long been looked on with suspicion (not only in social movement studies, but in political sociology and political science at large), attention to their role has recently (re)emerged. The emotional intensity of participation in protest events as passionate politics has been stressed (Goodwin, Jasper, and Polletta 2001; Aminzade and McAdam 2001) together with the role of subversive "counteremotions" in cementing collective identities (Eyerman 2005). Research has pointed to the mobilizing capacity of "good" emotions (such as hope, pride, and indignation), and the movements' work on potentially dangerous emotions (such as fear or shame) (Flam 2005). Reciprocal emotions (such as love and loyalty, but also jealousy, rivalry, and resentment) have especially important effects on movement dynamics. The role of dramaturgy, narrative, and rituals in intensifying commitment has been investigated for protest events in general (as the effect of an "emotional liberation," see Flam 2005) as well as for specific critical emotional events. All these elements emerge in our narratives.

Direct actions tend in fact to produce intense emotional effects. In Val di Susa, the activists underline the positive effects of direct action, as a moment of growth in solidarity with the local population. Stressing the emotional effects of some moments of escalation around the site where the work for the high-speed trains had to begin, accounts by the protesters in Val di Susa help single out some "emotional chains" that are produced in action.

First, the interaction with the police around occupied spaces produces the spread of *injustice* frames (Gamson 1990), often mentioned by protesters as a source of consensus in the population and a way to strengthen the collective identification with the community. In Val di Susa, the intervention of the police to clear the site occupation became the symbol of an unfair attitude toward those who were protesting peacefully, the military occupation of the area "being seen as an arrogance that nobody could justify" (IVS4). As local activists observe, "the explosion of the movement (and nobody expected a participation of this strength) occurred from the 31st of October onwards, the days in which the violence of the government sent the troops into the valley" (IVS2); "at the site occupation there were always 100–200 people during the day. When it looked likely to be cleared out then 2000–3000 people arrived, staying throughout the night to defend our position" (IVS11).

Participation becomes more intense when faced with a perceived external aggression, described by activists as an act of war against a peaceful community. In the words of one activist, this perceived aggression forces the community to "join the front line":

> People appeared in very large numbers on a week-day, they didn't go to work but went to the site occupation instead, believing that there was no use just in talking, but that they should join the front-line. They all appeared with banner and flags. In Bruzolo, when the police were confronting the crowd, we joined in with our household utensils to defend ourselves. We are not afraid of anybody; we want to defend our territory in a peaceful way. Maybe you will laugh at us, but the battle is long (IVS5).

The same sense of injustice emerges in the narratives on the dispersal of the site occupation by the police forces. In the recollection of one activist,

> they destroyed the books of the university students who were studying (after all this was time taken away from daily activities) throwing them in a bonfire. And when people were forced to leave the fields, the police went round with the No TAV banners as if they were a symbol of conquest . . . and they also had the cheek to destroy the food supplies that were needed to live in the camp . . . old people were beaten and they stopped the ambulances from coming. An old man stayed an hour slumped on the floor, because they never even let the stretchers in (IVS10).

Beyond the Val di Susa case, injustice frames produced "in action" have been central in the development of the global justice movement, particularly when linked to interventions by the police that are considered as all the more unjust, given the nonviolent forms of action chosen by the activists. In the protest against the WTO in Seattle and in those against the G8 Summit in Genoa, the images of the police brutalities against peaceful demonstrators produced emotional shocks not only among the demonstrators, but also among others who later on identified with the protesters (della Porta, Andretta, Mosca, and Reiter 2006).

Together with injustice, *arrogance* is a main narrative frame that emerges in reaction to the presence of the police in Val di Susa, described as the "militarization of the valley": the "final drop that makes the glass spill over"; while the successive mobilization is the "reaction against arrogance: the moment in which they made false moves with arrogance, and even trickery, there was a popular reaction, from everybody not just militants" (IVS4). Its consequences are often recalled as an act of violence on the territory and its inhabitants. The arrogance of a power that violates the very principle of democracy is often stressed with regard to the transnational demonstrations, when demonstrators are rejected at the borders, kept at distance from international summits, preventively arrested, and charged by the police. Images of the police forces, militarily equipped and aggressively deployed to protect a handful of powerful leaders from the large number of citizens ("You G8, we 8 billion" was the slogan of the Genoa protest) is often communicated by the movement media as illustrating this arrogance.

The perceived arrogance of the enemy can, however, discourage from collective action if it is not accompanied by *anger*. If repression, increasing the costs of collective action, can discourage protest, it may also reinforce the processes of identification and solidarity (della Porta and Reiter 2006). In the perception of the activists, the police brutality in Val di Susa produced indignation: "the people started to get angry; there was no way of stopping them: they occupied roads and highways (the people, not the associations), they would have stayed day and night until the government gave a signal . . . from the 1st of November till the 6th of December it went ahead like this, then on the 6th they used force, beating old people. Two days later people shouted 'let's take back the land' and 100,000 people descended and took it back" (IVS5). Anger is also mentioned by those marching against unemployment.

What makes anger a mobilizing emotion is its connection with a feeling of *empowerment*, which comes from the experiences of successful moments of direct action. Remaining in Val di Susa, the reconquest of Seghino (the place where the works were due to begin) is narrated as an epic return. In the words of one interviewee, the police charges mark the start of the time of fighting: "The morning after in the valley there was a massive strike. The workers left their factories, the teachers never entered the schools while the parents never took their children there, and everyone went to occupy the valley, which remained so for 3 days. It was the time of the revolt, which culminated in the 8th of December with the re-conquest of the field. It was wonderful." The memories of the police blockade at Mompatero are added to the observation that "even the meek in front of injustice are capable of rebellion and will not turn back, because they understand it is a question of pride and dignity. This was the most important thing" (IVS10).

A feeling of *belonging* therefore develops on the street (or in the case of Val di Susa, on the occupation sites). The activists in Val di Susa talked of a process of identification with the community, which stemmed from the experiences of conflict with the police forces coming from outside, but also from encounters with fellow citizens in the spaces that the protest had created. In the words of an interviewee, the community is built in action:

> Our identity began to strengthen itself from June, when the government tried to initiate the works. That summer people began to stay at the site from morning till night, people from the same town became friends although only acquaintances before.... *The people became a community* ... the site occupation became a social event and this cemented an identification between territory and citizen which is quite exceptional. Then the events of Venaus obviously emphasized the solidarity in these difficult situations. People ended up in hospital from police beatings, and a sense of community had been created (IVS8 emphasis added).

It is through long and intense actions, such as the site occupation, that in the activists' narrative, the "people" became a "community." The struggles around the No TAV site occupations of 2005 were seen as a moment of growth of the mobilization, not only in numerical terms but also in terms of identification with the protest. In the words of activists, the site occupation had "great emotional force," "a shared intimacy," "wonderful as well as striking for the behavior of the people; the diversity of those present; and the sense of serenity" (Sasso 2005, p. 61). In their narrative, the site occupation is remembered as a serene but intense experience that reinforced feelings of mutual trust: "When on the night of 5–6 December the police forces went to occupy the land at Venaus . . . there was a wonderful encampment under the falling snow, fires burning, children and dogs playing. There were pots full of food, young people from all over Italy—because at that point we became the focus and hope for a series of struggles" (IVS10).

More generally, some forms of direct action (such as protest camps or occupations) are eventful insofar as they affect the daily lives of the participants by creating free spaces. The site occupations in Val di Susa are described as places of strong socialization, "real homes built on this territory, which became focal points—a wonderful thing. In the summer there were scores of people that came to talk and socialize, allowing feelings of solidarity to grow with the awareness that this struggle was for everyone" (IVS11). Participation in the protest is seen as gratifying in itself, as it becomes part of everyday life: "Throughout the whole summer there were 50–100 people that occupied three places in the valley (Borgone, Bruzolo, Venaus). In the morning, you went to get a coffee at the site occupation and not at the bar. If you wanted an alternative dinner you went to the site occupation, where you might also listen to a concert" (IVS5).

Allowing for frequent and emotionally intense interactions, the site occupations were perceived as an opportunity for reciprocal identification, based on mutual recognition as members of a community: "This is the story of an unwitting revolution, says a young man, in these days we also changed, lost our prejudices and struck up friendships. People met each other that previously would have had little occasion to . . . we met, listened and found that we shared a common destiny" (Sasso 2005, pp. 62–63). In the site occupations "you got to know people *through the struggle*, you recognized each other" (IVS10 emphasis added). In this sense the action itself constitutes a resource of mutual solidarity and reciprocal trust, which allows the capacity to withstand later moments of intense conflict.

These site occupations also represent arenas of discussion and deliberation, places to experiment with a different form of democracy. They are described as participatory and allow for the development of individual creativity. In the words of one activist: "Everything began from these site occupations, a wonderful form of participatory democracy where people from below could have their say: They could coin a slogan, a new banner, invent a new march, a new message" (IVS5). The site occupations thus become political laboratories that produced interaction and communication. The struggle is perceived as "a moment of incredible growth, because very often it is difficult to act concretely, as we utter beautiful words on the world we want, the contradictions we want to eliminate. Here we threw ourselves into the game, we experimented on the things we said" (IVS1).

The experience of the site occupation thus transcends the opposition to high-speed trains. The occupied sites become places in which "all the small problems which must be confronted daily are resolved through discussion, with spontaneous assemblies, with mutual trust and a complicity which reinforces the sense of solidarity" (IVS1). In the words of one activist, "the site occupations were places inhabited by a different kind of life, where you could eat for free because money no longer had any value . . . it was a collective hope and when they responded with militarization the people rebelled" (IVS10).

In sum, the intense emotionality of protest affects protestors themselves. The protest itself produces resources instead of just using them for collective action. If protest tends to be emotionally intense, it is especially so in direct action, given the risks involved and the higher emotional attachments. The recent mobilizations on global justice have seen a return to direct action, after a period in which more moderate forms had been dominant. Direct actions have been widespread in various waves of protest, testifying to the intensity of the activists' commitment as well as challenging State control of territory. In such actions the risk of arrest testifies to the conviction that something had to be done about a decision considered profoundly unjust, even at the risk of high personal cost. The accounts of the struggle in Val di Susa indicate that participation in direct action is often rewarded by the creation of strong feelings of solidarity and identification in a community. In the intense moments of protest, activists do not seem to be guided by instrumental reasoning, but instead by a normative imperative to act against what is perceived as an unbearable injustice. A second characteristic of recent uses of direct action is the attempt to create free zones in which alternative forms of life can be experimented with. The Zapatistan experience is an influential example for global justice activists (Olesen 2003), in particular (and not by chance) for the squatted centers, which also focus on the construction of alternative space.

Conclusion

I have singled out relational, cognitive, and affective mechanisms that develop through protest events. Although protest is used every day by the most varied people, it is still a type of event that tends to produce effects, not only on public authorities or public opinion, but also (possibly mainly) on the movement actors themselves. I have looked at protest as an independent variable, but the effects I was interested in were especially those on the actors who participated. I suggested these effects are all the more visible in some specific forms of protest that require long preparatory processes, in which different groups come together (such as transnational campaigns), stress the relevance of communication (such as social forums), and are particularly intense from the emotional point of view (such as symbolic and physical struggles around the occupied sites in Val di Susa). These kinds of protest are especially "eventful": they have a relevant cognitive, relational, and emotional impact on participants and beyond participants. Long-lasting events (or chains of events, such as campaigns), inclusive communicative arenas, and free-spaces are forms of protest that seem particularly apt to create relational, cognitive, and emotional effects on protestors. I would not contend that these forms of protest are new, but I think it could be useful to further reflect upon the specific contextual conditions that make *eventful protests* more widespread.

Conclusion

Are Protestors Opportunists? Fifty Tests

JEFF GOODWIN

T HE IDEA that "political opportunities" are a necessary precondition for collective political contention has been common sense to social movement analysts for thirty years (McAdam 1982; McAdam, McCarthy, and Zald 1996a; Tarrow 1998a). Yet key questions about the causal relationship between political opportunities and the emergence of political contention remain, in part because current research on contention largely takes the form of single case studies (Crist and McCarthy 1996). Little research has systematically examined the impact of a *common* set of political opportunities; instead, authors have conceptualized such opportunities in either an idiosyncratic or post hoc fashion, hindering the cumulative acquisition of knowledge about the importance of specific kinds of opportunities. This volume has examined ten case studies in some depth, but I now wish to extend our effort to a more extensive sample.

Among the key questions that have been neglected or poorly answered in the literature are the following: Are political opportunities a significant causal factor in the emergence of *most* social movements, revolutions, and other forms of political contention? Does political contention emerge when opportunities expand? Are political opportunities *necessary* for the emergence of political contention? Are opportunities more important for the emergence of political conflict in democratic or in authoritarian political contexts? Are they more important for the emergence of some types of movements, or for the occurrence of some types of contention, than others? And which types of opportunities or combination of opportunities are most important for the emergence of political contention and for specific types of contention?

This chapter begins to address these questions, utilizing a fifty-case data set that draws upon the research of more than forty scholars and research assistants, including the authors of the essays collected in this volume. (The analyst of each of the fifty cases is indicated in Appendix A.) This is the largest and most diverse data set yet employed, as far as I am aware, to assess the importance of political opportunities for the emergence of various types of political conflict in different political settings. These data, set forth in Appendix A, indicate among other things whether four specific political opportunities were a significant causal factor in each of the fifty cases of social movements, rebellions, revolutions, or cultural movements. These four political opportunities were taken from Doug McAdam (1996, pp. 26–29), who himself synthesized them from the existing literature (see Tarrow 1994, pp. 85–89). These opportunities are (1) increasing popular access to the political system, (2) elite divisions or conflicts, (3) the presence of elite allies, and (4) declining state repression. The hypothesis, of course, is that one or more of these opportunities is a necessary precondition for the emergence of social movements.

The Data

Before turning to the findings, a few words about the data. These fifty cases are in no sense a random sample of political contention. Random sampling of movements and rebellions is presently impossible and likely to remain so for the foreseeable future. It would require an authoritative list of all instances of movements, rebellions, and revolutions that have occurred or been attempted in a given time frame or place. No such list exists, even for the United States during the past few decades—the country and era that have been most closely scrutinized by scholars of social movements. For this reason, I have not applied standard statistical tests to the data, which are best viewed as provisional and suggestive—and as a provocation, I hope, for further comparative research in this vein. That said, I believe these data do have important implications for political-opportunity analysis and for the analysis of political contention more generally.

While the cases in the data set were not randomly selected, they were intentionally chosen to include a wide range of cases, starting with the better known (and better studied) cases of recent U.S. social movements. The sample reaches beyond political contention in the democratic capitalist societies of Western

Europe and North America to include many cases in the poorer, dependent, and frequently nondemocratic societies of Latin America, Africa, Asia, and the former Soviet bloc. Nearly half of the cases (21) occurred in the latter societies, and more than a third of the cases (18) arose in the context of an authoritarian political regime. Moreover, in addition to the social movements on which scholars of political contention have tended to focus, the sample also includes types of contention for which the causal mechanisms associated with political opportunities also presumably matter, such as rebellions, revolutions, and cultural movements. The sample includes some of the most important movements and revolutions of the past two centuries as well as numerous cases of contention that are less well known and, by most standards, of less historical importance, in order to broaden the research findings about how movements develop.

The cases of political contention in Appendix A are listed in rough chronological order. The year(s) given for each case generally refers to the year(s) when that case of contention clearly appeared or emerged *qua* collective contention, rather than to its entire historical trajectory. (The focus in this chapter is on the relationship between political opportunities and the emergence of contention; I do not address the relationships between opportunities and longer-run movement dynamics, movement forms and strategies, movement decline, or the consequences of movements.) Although the cases span more than two centuries (since 1789), all but four occurred during the twentieth century, particularly the second half. Twelve emerged before or during the Second World War; the other thirty-eight occurred afterward.

The general political context in which each case of contention arose is also given in Appendix A. This variable is introduced in order to see whether political opportunities matter more (or less) if the context in which contention occurs is democratic or authoritarian. Accordingly, I have categorized the cases into four general political contexts: DEM (democratic); DEM/NON (democratic with certain nondemocratic features, such as key groups that lack civil rights); NON/DEM (nondemocratic with democratic features, such as semicompetitive elections or limited civil and political rights); and NON (nondemocratic, which subsumes totalitarian, post-totalitarian, single-party, military, and personalist dictatorships). These are fairly crude distinctions, and a more differentiated schema of political regimes could as easily be employed, but this is unnecessary for the limited purposes of this study.

I have also roughly categorized each case into three general types of political contention: REB (rebellions and revolutions, which seek to displace existing political authorities and/or pursue their goals violently or coercively); REF (re-form movements, which make demands on but do not seek to displace existing government authorities or other power holders, generally nonviolently); and CUL (cultural movements, which challenge dominant cultural codes or norms or the beliefs and values of specific groups). The purpose here is to see whether political opportunities matter more or less depending upon how groups gen-erally contend with other groups, including but not limited to state officials. These categories represent ideal types that may combine in empirical cases; in such instances, I have listed two (or even all three) types in the order in which the case best approximates these types. For example, I have described the U.S. "homophile" movement of the 1950s (case 13 in Appendix A; also Chapter 7) as primarily a reform movement, but with elements of a cultural movement (hence, "REF/CUL"). Again, one could apply a more differentiated and fine-grained analytical schema to the data, but this is unnecessary for our present, limited purposes.

The key data indicate whether McAdam's four political opportunities were judged to be causally significant for the emergence of each case of contention. In Appendix A, a "1" in one of the four columns under "political opportuni-ties" indicates that a causal mechanism related to that opportunity was found to be clearly important by the analyst of the movement; a "0" indicates that no such mechanism was judged important. Each case, accordingly, can be sum-marized by a four-digit string of numbers that indicates which of the four op-portunities, in the order listed above, were causally significant. The civil rights movement in Mississippi (case 17; also Chapter 5), for instance, can be sum-marized by the numerical string "0110," which indicates that elite divisions and elite allies (but not the other two opportunities) were important for the emergence of this movement. The Iranian Revolution of 1978–79 (case 31), to take another example, can be summarized by "0000," which indicates that none of the four opportunities factored in the emergence of that revolutionary movement.

The coding of political opportunities necessarily rests upon a number of interpretive judgments by the analysts involved in this project—judgments about not only when a given case of contention can be said to have arisen or emerged, but also how exactly McAdam's list of political opportunities should be operationalized and (not least) whether there is convincing evi-dence that one or more political opportunities were causally significant. There are, at present, no agreed-upon techniques for addressing the last two issues in particular. (The precise instructions provided to researchers are given in Appendix B.)

The broadly interpretive as opposed to technical nature of researchers' findings about political opportunities is another reason for treating these data as tentative and suggestive rather than definitive. Scholars evaluating the same empirical facts may reach very different conclusions about the importance of political opportunities for any given case of political contention. It is inevitable that the "intercoder reliability" of the findings about political opportunities must be judged relatively low for this project, as several researchers noted to me, because the concepts and causal mechanisms associated with political-opportunity analysis are often only vaguely defined or specified and because there is no consensus about how to operationalize these mechanisms for empirical analysis (see Meyer and Minkoff 1997).

Two other data categories are included in Appendix A: (1) additional pertinent information, listed under "Notes," including evidence for political-opportunity mechanisms other than those emphasized by McAdam as well as evidence for "contracting" political opportunities (or what might be conceptualized as "threats"), and (2) the monographs, chapters or journal articles utilized by analysts as the principal source(s) for making a determination about the relevance of specific political opportunities.

Findings

Are political opportunities a causal factor in the emergence of most social movements, revolutions, and other forms of political contention? Does political contention emerge in a context of "expanding" opportunities?
Our data suggest that political opportunities are indeed a causal factor of some significance in most cases of political contention. One or more political-opportunity was a factor in the emergence of 31 of our 50 cases of contention (62 percent). When cultural movements—which do not fit all definitions of social movements or political contention—are removed from the sample, political opportunities are a factor in about two-thirds (67.4 percent) of the remaining cases (see Table C.1, indicating the number of cases that correspond to each of the sixteen possible combinations of the four political opportunities).

Surprisingly, "contracting" opportunities—specifically, declining access to the polity and/or intense or increasing repression—were important factors in many of these cases. In the 31 cases for which political opportunities mattered,

TABLE C.1 Patterns of Political Opportunities

	All cases	All cases except cultural (or primarily cultural) movements
	n=50	n=43
ABCD		
0000	19	14
0110	11	10
0010	4	4
0100	4	3
1110	3	3
1111	3	3
0111	1	1
0101	1	1
0011	1	1
1100	1	1
1010	1	1
0001	1	1
1000	0	0
1001	0	0
1101	0	0
1011	0	0

Percentage of cases in which political opportunities were judged causally important:

All cases	All cases except cultural (or primarily cultural) movements
62.0 (n=31)	67.4 (n=29)

KEY: A=increasing access to the political system; B=elite divisions or conflicts; C=elite allies; D=declining repression.

contracting opportunities were important in more than a third (n=12). In other words, the emergence of contention in these cases was partly a result of simultaneously expanding *and* contracting political opportunities. Thus, well under half of the cases of contention in our sample (19 of 50, or 38 percent) emerged in a context of exclusively expanding political opportunities (19 of 43, or 44 percent of the cases, if we exclude cultural and primarily cultural movements).

Are political opportunities necessary for the emergence of political contention?
As noted at the outset, many analysts of social movements explicitly or implicitly suggest that expanding political opportunities are necessary, albeit not sufficient, for the emergence of social movements and kindred forms of political
contention. According to McAdam, McCarthy, and Zald, political opportunities are a "necessary prerequisite" to movements and revolutions because they
"render the established political order more vulnerable or receptive to challenge" (1996a, p. 8). Tarrow suggests that "changes in political opportunities
and constraints create the *most important* incentives for initiating new phases
of contention" (1998b, p. 7; emphasis added). Our data suggest that such claims
are exaggerated. As Table C.1 indicates, a significant proportion of the cases of
contention in our sample—nearly four in ten—did not occur due to political
opportunities. Even when cultural movements are removed from the sample,
nearly a third of the remaining cases arose because of factors other than political opportunity. The set of cases for which political opportunities were not
important includes several powerful movements and revolutions, including the
anti-Vietnam War movement in the United States, the Iranian Revolution of
1978–79, and the Chinese democracy movement of 1989.

   Our data suggest another reason to reject the notion that political opportunities are necessary for the emergence of contention: in many cases in which
they were causally important, it is difficult to claim that contention would not
have occurred on a large scale in their absence. Indeed, any number of factors
may encourage or facilitate contention without being strictly obligatory or indispensable. Consider the debate between James Jasper and Christian Smith
regarding the U.S. Central America peace movement of the 1980s (Chapter 8).
Smith argues, convincingly in my view, that this movement would not have
been as large and effective as it was without elite allies in Washington (specifically in the U.S. Congress). Yet Jasper is equally convincing in his claim that
elite allies were not a significant factor behind the initial emergence of this
movement and that considerable protest against the Reagan administration's
policies in Central America would have occurred even if Congress had unanimously supported those policies. As Smith himself notes, "the majority of the
activists [in the peace movement] became involved because they believed it
was the right and necessary thing for them to do, *whatever the outcome*, and
not primarily because they calculated that the probable consequences of their
individual participation warranted their involvement and justified the costs
it would entail" (Smith 1996, p. 195; Smith's emphasis). Thus, even if one

agrees with Smith that elite allies were a significant political opportunity for the growth of this movement, it does not follow that they were necessary for its emergence.

Or consider the nativist and anti-slavery "Know Nothing" movement in the United States of the mid-1850s. Tyler Anbinder's (1992) outstanding study demonstrates that elite allies (of a sort) were an important factor in the explosive growth of this movement in 1854. Specifically, Anbinder notes that many Protestant ministers in rural areas "used the Know Nothings as a means to exert political influence. Not all ministers supported Know Nothingism, but the impression that many religious leaders sympathized with its goals helped the Know Nothings attract members outside of nativism's traditional urban strongholds" (1992, pp. 49–50). Anbinder is equally clear, however, that the movement had a substantial urban base and was attractive primarily because it provided an anti-slavery alternative to the dominant Whig and Democratic parties. The movement would certainly have been very powerful, accordingly, perhaps even in rural areas, with or without the help of Protestant ministers (although whether these ministers should count as "elite allies" external to the movement is a serious question).

Political opportunities, in sum, are not always necessary for the emergence of political contention, even when they contribute to it in some significant way.

Are political opportunities more important for the emergence of political conflict in democratic or in nondemocratic political contexts?

The data strongly suggest that political opportunities are much more likely to matter for the emergence of political contention in nondemocratic than in democratic societies. In democracies, one or more political opportunity was a causal factor in the origins of contention in less than half of the cases (40.9 percent); in nondemocratic contexts, by contrast, political opportunities were important in more than four-fifths (83.3 percent) (see Table C.2). We find the same pattern in "mixed" political contexts. Political opportunities were causally significant in only 41.7 percent of the cases of contention that emerged under democratic regimes with or without important nondemocratic features; by contrast, political opportunities mattered in 80.8 percent of the cases of contention that arose under nondemocratic regimes with or without important democratic elements.

These findings bear out the hypothesis that *changing* political opportunities are likely to matter less for the emergence of political contention in democracies than under authoritarian regimes because the former tend, by definition,

TABLE C.2 Patterns of Political Opportunity in Different Political Contexts

	All cases	DEM	DEM/NON	NON/DEM	NON
	n=50	n=22	n=2	n=8	n=18
ABCD					
0000	19	13	1	2	3
0110	11	3	0	4	4
0010	4	1	0	0	3
0100	4	2	0	1	1
1110	3	1	1	0	1
1111	3	1	0	1	1
0111	1	0	0	0	1
0101	1	0	0	0	1
0011	1	0	0	0	1
1100	1	0	0	0	1
1010	1	1	0	0	0
0001	1	0	0	0	1
1000	0	0	0	0	0
1001	0	0	0	0	0
1101	0	0	0	0	0
1011	0	0	0	0	0

Percentage of cases in which political opportunities were judged causally important:

All cases	DEM	DEM/NON	NON/DEM	NON
62.0	40.9	50.0	75.0	83.3
	DEM + DEM/NON		NON/DEM + NON	
	41.7		80.8	

SOURCE: Derived from Appendix A. KEY: DEM=democratic; DEM/NON=democratic with important nondemocratic features; NON/DEM=nondemocratic with some democratic features; NON=nondemocratic (see text for explanation).

to tolerate many types of nonviolent political contention. Democracies are "structurally open," so to speak, to a variety of forms of contention. Under democracies, accordingly, the outbreak of contention is as likely to be a result of suddenly imposed (or perceived) grievances or fears, moral shocks, new collective identities, and/or the development of social ties and organizations among aggrieved populations as of changing political opportunities. By contrast, political opportunities are likely to matter more under authoritarian regimes for the simple reason that many forms of protest are routinely repressed under such regimes. Given their tendency to rely upon force and threats, authoritarian regimes generally need to be "shaken up" in some fashion before people will undertake risky protest. Those fighting for citizenship rights need openings that those who already have such rights do not (Jasper 1997).

There is an irony to these findings. Political opportunity and political-process theorists have been criticized for developing their ideas about contention exclusively from the histories of Western European and North American societies, neglecting the experiences of the Third World. Some have implied that political-opportunity theory is less applicable—or even inapplicable—to the Third World because of this alleged Eurocentric bias. Our findings indicate, however, that political-opportunity analysis is actually more illuminating of contention outside of Europe and North America to the extent that authoritarian regimes historically have been more prevalent in poorer and dependent Third World societies.

Are political opportunities more important for the emergence of some types of movements or conflict than for others?

Table C.3 indicates the prevalence of the various patterns of political opportunities for each of the three general types of contention in the sample. I have given each type of contention a loose and a strict definition for this purpose. The former (summed in column 1) includes all cases that fit each type in some significant manner. For example, the findings about political opportunities for the U.S. homophile movement (case 13) are included under the loose definition of cultural movements, even though this was primarily a reform movement. By contrast, only "pure" cases of each type are included under the strict definition (summed in column 2). Thus, the findings for the Cuban Revolution (case 14), for example, are included under the strict definition of rebellions and revolutions (column 2) as well as under the loose definition of this type of contention (column 1).

Political opportunities tend to matter most for the emergence of rebellions and revolutions, loosely defined (90.9 percent of all such cases), and to matter least for cultural moments, strictly defined (0 percent), with reform movements falling in between. Interestingly, political opportunities were important for the emergence of fewer than half the reform movements, strictly defined (46.2 percent).

Rebellions and revolutions tend to occur under, and typically against, authoritarian regimes, whereas reform movements tend to occur under democratic regimes—and the emergence of contention, as we have just seen, is more

TABLE C.3 Patterns of Political Opportunity by Type of Contention

	All cases		REB		REF		CUL	
	(1)	(2)	(1)	(2)	(1)	(2)	(1)	(2)
	n=50	n=43	n=22	n=16	n=28	n=13	n=18	n=4
ABCD								
0000	19	14	2	2	13	7	10	4
0110	11	10	6	3	7	4	2	0
0010	4	4	3	3	1	0	1	0
0100	4	3	4	1	2	0	2	0
1110	3	3	2	2	1	0	1	0
1111	3	3	1	1	2	1	1	0
0111	1	1	1	1	0	0	0	0
0101	1	1	0	0	1	1	0	0
0011	1	1	1	1	0	0	0	0
1100	1	1	1	1	0	0	0	0
1010	1	1	0	0	1	0	1	0
0001	1	1	1	1	0	0	0	0
1000	0	0	0	0	0	0	0	0
1001	0	0	0	0	0	0	0	0
1101	0	0	0	0	0	0	0	0
1011	0	0	0	0	0	0	0	0

Percentage of cases in which political opportunities were judged causally important:

	All cases		REB		REF		CUL	
	(1)	(2)	(1)	(2)	(1)	(2)	(1)	(2)
	62.0	69.8	90.9	87.5	53.6	46.2	44.4	0.0

KEY: REB=rebellion or revolution; REF=reform movement; CUL=cultural movement.
(1)=loose definition; (2)=strict definition. See text for explanation.

dependent upon changing political opportunities under authoritarianism than in democracies. Contention tends to be channeled into rebellious and revolutionary forms under authoritarian regimes, whereas it is more likely to be reformist under democracies. In other words, political opportunities would seem to matter more for rebellions and revolutions than for reform movements because the former are more likely to occur under (and against) authoritarian regimes. In fact, as Table C.4 indicates, 88.9 percent of the rebellions and revolutions in our sample (or cases judged to be primarily rebellions or revolutions, with secondary attributes of other types) emerged under *nondemocratic*

TABLE C.4 Types of Contention in Different Political Contexts

Political context

Type of contention	DEM or DEM/NON	NON or NON/DEM	Total (row)
REB (or primarily REB)	2 (10.5%) (11.1%)	16 (66.7%) (88.9%)	18 (100%)
REF (or primarily REF)	17 (89.5%) (68.0%)	8 (33.3%) (32.0%)	25 (100%)
Total (column)	19 (100%)	24 (100%)	43

KEY: DEM=democratic; DEM/NON=democratic with important nondemocratic features; NON=nondemocratic; NON/DEM=nondemocratic with some democratic features; REB=rebellion or revolution; REF=reform movement. See text for explanation.

regimes (or undemocratic regimes with important democratic features); two-thirds (66.7 percent) of the cases in the sample that emerged in authoritarian or primarily authoritarian contexts (excluding cultural movements, strictly defined) took the form of rebellions or revolutions or contention that was primarily rebellious or revolutionary. By contrast, about two-thirds (68 percent) of the reform movements in our sample (or cases judged to be primarily reform movements, with secondary attributes of other types) arose within democratic contexts with or without authoritarian features); 89.5 percent of the cases in the sample that emerged in democratic or primarily democratic contexts (excluding cultural movements, strictly defined) took the form of reform movements or movements primarily reformist in orientation.

That political opportunities did not matter for the emergence of any of the cultural movements, strictly defined, should not be taken to mean that opportunities are never important for cultural movements. This finding may simply reflect the fact that all of the "pure" cultural movements in our sample arose under democratic or primarily democratic regimes. Our sample also includes three cases of contention that were judged to be primarily, but not exclusively, cultural in orientation. One of these cases arose in a democratic context, while the other two arose in nondemocratic contexts—and one or more political opportunities did matter for both of the latter cases (cases 5 and 7). In short, while much more research is needed, it seems that political opportunities may be quite important for the emergence of cultural as well as other types of movements under authoritarian regimes.

Which type of opportunities, or combination of opportunities, is most important for the emergence of political contention and for specific types of contention?
The dominance of the case-study approach in scholarship on social movements, revolutions, and other forms of political contention, as well as the variety of specifications of political opportunities that have been employed by scholars, has made it difficult to discern exactly which political opportunities matter most for contention generally or for specific forms of contention. Three configurations of political opportunities account for 61 percent of all cases (n=31) in which one or more opportunity was causally significant. In more than a third (n=11), the combination of elite conflicts and elite allies helped to bring about contention; in another quarter (n=8), either elite allies alone or elite conflicts alone were an important factor in the emergence of contention. In other words, elite conflicts, elite allies, or the combination of these two factors were causally significant in well over half the cases of contention in which opportunities mattered.

The importance of elite divisions and elite allies for contention can be gleaned from the final line of the table in Appendix A, which indicates that each of these opportunities was a significant factor in 24 of the 50 cases in the sample. In fact, there is only one case in our entire sample, among those for which opportunities mattered, in which neither elite divisions nor elite allies played an important role: the "velvet revolution" of 1989 in Czechoslovakia.

By contrast, the other two political opportunities proved much less important for the emergence of contention. Increasing access to the political system was an important factor in only 8 of the 50 cases, and declining repression was a significant factor in only 7 cases. By comparison, decreasing access to the polity was important in at least 3 cases, and intense or increasing repression was significant in at least 9 cases. Thus, the relationship between these two factors and the emergence of contention is often the opposite of the hypothesized relationship. When these factors matter at all, in other words, access to the polity and repression seem to have a curvilinear relationship to the emergence of contention.

The importance of elite divisions and elite allies holds across both political contexts and types of contention. Whether the political context was democratic or authoritarian, elite conflict, elite allies, and (especially) the combination of these factors were the most prevalent configurations of political opportunities, when opportunities mattered (see Table C.2). Similarly, when political opportunities mattered, elite conflict, elite allies, and the combination of these factors were the three most prevalent patterns of political opportunities across all types of political contention (see Table C.3). (A partial exception to this generalization is the finding that the combination of all four opportunities was important for reform movements more frequently than elite divisions or elite allies alone, although it was less frequent than the combination of elite divisions and allies.)

The importance of both elite allies and elite conflicts may be overstated in these data. The very notion that elite allies may be important for contention implies that only nonelites can be the principal agents of contentious politics or protest: elites may form alliances with campaigns and mobilizations of various sorts, but may not, apparently, serve as ordinary, rank-and-file participants, activists, or leaders in contentious mobilizations. The assumption here—erroneous in my view—seems to be that no elites would ever need to engage directly in "extrainstitutional" politics because they already have, perhaps by definition, access to political authorities. Our data, however, include a number of movements, rebellions, and revolutions in which elites (in the sense of comparatively wealthy individuals) comprised a significant or even the major share of participants. In many of these cases, however, my sense is that the analysts for this project seem to have decided, for this very reason, that "elite allies" provided a political opportunity for contention. Yet this is illogical, to say the least. Political contention that primarily or substantially involves particular elites may certainly emerge in part because of support from other elites. Yet elites who are themselves directly contending with other groups, or with the state, are surely not allying with themselves. This apparent confusion, which stems from a questionable theoretical assumption, may have produced an exaggerated sense of the importance of elite allies in our data set. Some of the chapters in this volume support my suspicion, using what I consider an overly generous definition of "elite allies."

The importance of elite divisions may also be overstated in our data. As a number of the analysts in this project suggested to me, it is often possible to find such divisions ex post facto. Whether these divisions were a cause or consequence of contention, however, is not always easy to determine. Moreover, exactly *who* needs to act upon perceptions of elite divisions for one to conclude that they were a necessary or even significant incentive for, or trigger of, protest is not clear. A few key leaders of a movement or rebellion? A sizeable minority of the participants in a particular case of contention? Most such participants? It is all too easy for researchers to conclude that elite conflicts were a significant cause of contention based on their own perceptions of such conflicts or on the ex post facto statements of a few individuals.

To confound matters more, Jasper suggests in the Introduction that it is often difficult to distinguish elite allies from elite division. When elites join insurgents or protestors, this alliance demonstrates elite division. But that division need not have existed before the elites made the choice to break away out of sympathy, indignation, or calculated advantage. The fully polarized, structural model of elites versus nonelites characterizes relatively few countries, as several of our authors point out. In sum, while our data reveal the strikingly consistent importance for much contention of elite divisions and elite allies, in a variety of political contexts and for various types of contention, further comparative research is required to determine for certain whether the causal mechanisms associated with these particular political opportunities come into play with such frequency.

Other Political Opportunities

The analysts involved in this project were asked to note whether any political opportunities not included in McAdam's list were important for the emergence of political contention (see Appendix B). Two such opportunities were reported.

The first set of mechanisms may be labeled "popular allies" for short. In one case—the Nicaraguan peasant movement under the dictator Somoza (see Chapter 2)—contention emerged partly because of various forms of assistance from popular organizations (trade unions, social movement organizations, etc.) and/or social circles and individuals who would not seem to qualify as "elite" allies. Indeed, more than one researcher for this project noted that it is far from clear just who qualifies as an elite. Middle-class individuals, or just the very wealthy? What about influential writers, intellectuals, and professional people? Local politicians, or only very powerful political leaders? Tarrow, for his part, emphasizes the potential importance of what he calls "influential allies" (1994, p. 88; 1998a, pp. 79–80), but this simply raises the question in a new form: What is "influence," and who has it?

Rather than simply expanding McAdam's list of opportunities to include "popular" as well as "elite" allies—a crude distinction at best—we might do better by differentiating the causal mechanisms by which external allies of whatever sort encourage or facilitate contention by other groups. Alliances with some groups (e.g., politicians and military officers) may encourage contention because such people directly wield state power; these are the sorts of allies, of course, that most movements ultimately strive to enlist or create. Alliances with other groups or individuals ("friends in court" and other political brokers, for example) may encourage protest because such people are known or believed to have access to political authorities. Still other allies—and not necessarily "elites"—may provide contenders with money and other material resources (such as printing presses, fax machines, guns, or safe houses). Other people (religious leaders, for example) may provide moral legitimacy or a sense of righteousness to contenders. And still others may channel activists and militants (with their strategic know-how and commitment, among other traits) into the struggles of contending groups. Thus, external allies may encourage contention through a variety of mechanisms that analysts need to be clear about.

The other causal mechanism that emerged from this research might be labeled "newly sympathetic government (or executive)." In several instances (cases 10, 20, and 24), political activists and ordinary people perceived that the government had become sympathetic to their concerns. They were encouraged to mobilize out of a belief that authorities would react favorably to organized pressure from below. This belief typically resulted from the statements of certain political leaders prior to their ascension to power or from the apparently sympathetic fashion in which certain politicians treated the demands of other contentious groups.

These types of mechanisms reflect a more strategic perspective in contrast to McAdam's structural vision. A variety of players are capable of making numerous blocking or enabling moves, or none, in interaction with each other, yet they need not be defined as elite or insurgent from the start. These moves include statements as well as coercion, providing resources, attracting media attention, intervening in courts, and more. Future research should be sensitive to more strategic mechanisms as well as those structural ones emphasized by McAdam.

Alternative Paths to Contention

According to political-process theory, the basic causal story of the emergence of contention reads something like this: political contention (riots, rebellions, movements, and the like) occurs in part because, and when, the opening or expansion of political opportunities—that is, perceived structural changes in the polity—convinces aggrieved people with some social ties or organization (but not necessarily vast material resources) that disruptive collective action is likely to bring about certain benefits or goods. As Tarrow puts it, "contentious politics is triggered when changing political opportunities and constraints create incentives for social actors who lack resources on their own" (Tarrow 1998a, p. 2).

Political contention is frequently triggered in just this way, although, as we have noted, it also often arises when political opportunities are simultaneously expanding and contracting. Furthermore, the research for this project suggests at least three other general scenarios through which contention may arise, none of which necessarily depends upon even the partial opening or expansion of political opportunities.

First, contenders in many cases simply do not seem to make a determination that any particular moment is especially opportune for protest, because of structural shifts in the polity or for some other reason; rather, people are so outraged or shocked by a situation that they feel morally obligated to protest immediately, regardless of the chances for success and at times despite the high risks associated with some forms of protest. In these cases, it is moral shock, intense anger, or other emotions that trigger contention (Jasper 1997). We see this in Amy Risley's discussion of human rights activists in Argentina and James Jasper's discussion of the U.S. Central America peace movement, as well as abolitionism (Young 2001) and anti-racist movements (Warren 2010). Middle-class people in liberal democracies seem especially likely to assume or simply take for granted that protest (at least the nonviolent type) is possible at any time.

Second, much contention occurs in response to contracting political opportunities, often in contexts characterized by intense or increasing repression. In this scenario, contention is animated by intense frustration with politics as usual or fear of imminent harm in the absence of resistance or rebellion. Contention in such cases is triggered by fear and loathing of the status quo. Indeed, much contention is primarily defensive in nature, a kind of survival strategy. We see this scenario played out in the case of the Communist Party in Alabama during the 1930s (case 9), the U.S. homophile movement during the 1950s (case 13), the Soweto uprising in South Africa in 1976 (case 29), and the Zapatista rebellion of 1994 in Chiapas, Mexico (case 49).

Finally, people sometimes engage in contentious collective action out of general concern but without the conviction that the time for protest is right. They may participate hesitatingly and be quick to retreat—precisely in order to test whether authorities will tolerate their behavior and listen to their demands. Authorities' reactions are never entirely predetermined. In this scenario, which is not unusual in authoritarian settings, political opportunities are not seized so much as incrementally discovered or created by protest; such opportunities do not obviously precede protest, but are revealed by it, and they are sometimes rapidly shut down for just this reason. We see this scenario played out in the Chinese democracy movement of 1989 (case 43) and to some extent in the revolutions in East Germany (case 44) and Czechoslovakia (case 45) later that same year.

These alternative paths to contention are of more than scholarly interest. The research summarized in this chapter suggests that political activists, organizers, and ordinary folk with an interest in contentious action need not bide their time waiting for the opportune moment for action. It indicates that opportune moments for collective action may occur more frequently than many theorists of political contention realize. Contention is often borne of an optimism generated by political openings, but it may also arise from moral outrage, disgust with the status quo, simple frustration with politics as usual, fears for the future, and/or the courage to confront intransigent rulers.

Conclusion

Is the glass half empty or half full? Any balanced assessment of the political opportunities concept must recognize both its strengths and its limitations for explaining the onset of political contention. On the positive side, some of the causal mechanisms associated with the concept have been shown to account, in part, for the emergence of a variety of forms of contention in different political settings. Elite divisions and elite allies seem especially important for contention, although, as noted, their importance may be overstated in our own data set.

On the other hand, the importance of political opportunities should not be exaggerated, as has been the tendency in much recent theorizing about contention. Either political opportunities do not matter significantly for the emergence of contention, or they only matter in conjunction with political repression, threats, declining access to the state, and, more generally, the closing down of political space. The widespread assumption among scholars that political opportunities are *necessary* for the emergence of contention is clearly mistaken.

The research summarized in this chapter and this volume hopefully sheds light upon the place of political opportunities in the emergence of many important and interesting cases of political contention and in the emergence of contention generally. On the one hand, opportunities are a key part of strategic engagement between challengers and authorities, and we need the right analytic tools for understanding them. On the other hand, McAdam's four opportunities may no longer be the most promising ones. Instead, the authors in this volume have pointed to more nuanced, microlevel, and strategic mechanisms that will do the same work better, with less confusion. This is the essence of scientific progress: crude, vague concepts are replaced by more refined, concrete ones, for which the former have been mere placeholders.

Appendix A: Fifty Cases of Political Contention

Case	Political context	Type	Political opportunities: A	B	C	D	Notes	Principal source(s)	Analyst
1. Peasant subsistence revolts (France), 1789–93	NON	REB	1	1	0	0	largely defensive	Markoff 1996	J. Goldstone (see Chapter 1)
2. Antiseigneurial revolts (France), 1789–93	NON	REB	1	1	1	1		Markoff 1996	J. Goldstone (see Chapter 1)
3. Counterrevolutionary revolts (France), 1789–93	NON	REB	1	1	1	0	largely defensive	Markoff 1996	J. Goldstone (see Chapter 1)
4. U.S. anti-vice (Comstock) campaigns, 1870s–1880s	DEM	REF/ CUL	0	1	1	0	substantial participation	Beisel 1997	N. Eliasoph, P. Lichterman
5. Malawi's Watch-tower movement, 1908	NON	CUL/ REB	0	1	1	0	declining access to polity	Fields 1985	M. Chaves
6. Ireland's Easter Rising, 1916	NON/ DEM	REB	0	0	0	0	fear of imminent represion	Ward 1980; Caulfield 1995/1963	G. Sawicki
7. Zambia's Watchtower movement, 1917	NON	CUL/ REB	0	1	0	0	increasing repression	Fields 1985	M. Chaves
8. "Second" Ku Klux Klan, early 1920s	DEM	REF/ CUL	1	0	1	0		Blee 1991	R. McVeigh
9. U.S. Communist movement (Alabama), 1930s	NON/ DEM	REF/ CUL	0	0	0	0	intense repression	Kelley 1990	J. Gerteis
10. U.S. Townsend (pension) movement, 1930s	DEM	REF	0	0	0	0	executive viewed as sympathetic	Amenta and Zylan 1991	E. Amenta
11. U.S. Alcoholics Anonymous, late 1930s, early 1940s	DEM	CUL	0	0	0	0		Kurtz 1988	K. Albright

KEY: Political context: DEM=democratic; DEM/NON=democratic with important nondemocratic features; NON/DEM=nondemocratic with some democratic features; NON=nondemocratic. Type of political contention: REB=rebellion or revolution; REF=reform movement; CUL=cultural movement; types are listed in ascending order of importance for combined types. Political opportunities: A= increasing access to the political system; B=elite divisions or conflicts; C=elite allies; D=declining repression; the number "1" indicates that a causal mechanism implied by the factor or variable is clearly important, if not necessary; "0" indicates that no such causal mechanism seems important.

Case	Political context	Type	Political opportunities:				Notes	Principal source(s)	Analyst
			A	B	C	D			
12. U.S. radical pacifism, early 1940s	DEM	REF/ REB/ CUL	0	1	0	0		Tracy 1996	S. Rosenbloom
13. U.S. homophile movement, early 1950s	DEM/ NON	REF/ CUL	0	0	0	0	increasing repression	D'Emilio 1983	A. Green (see Chapter 7)
14. Cuban Revolution, 1952–1959	NON	REB	0	1	1	0	declining access to polity	Paterson 1994	E. Linger
15. Nicaraguan peasant movement, 1955–1961	NON	REF	0	1	0	1	popular allies	Gould 1990	A. Pereira (see Chapter 2)
16. U.S.-Cuba solidarity movement, 1959–1961	DEM	REF/ CUL	0	0	0	0		Gosse 1993	S. Risley
17. U.S. civil rights movement (Mississippi), 1962	NON/ DEM	REF	0	1	1	0		Payne 1995	F. Polletta (see Chapter 5)
18. U.S. Anti-Vietnam War movement, 1964–65	DEM	REF	0	0	0	0		DeBene- detti 1990	K. Moore
19. U.S. farm- workers movement (Calif.), 1960s	DEM	REF	0	1	1	0	state govt. opposed to movement; federal govt. neutral	Jenkins and Perrow 1977; Jenkins 1985	D. Mattingly
20. U.S. women's movement, 1960s	DEM	REF/ CUL	1	1	1	0	govt. seen as sympa- thetic	Costain 1992	J. Skretny (see Chapter 6)
21. Shanghai workers' movements, 1966	NON	REB	0	0	1	1	strong local elite opposition	Perry and Li 1997	G. Yang
22. U.S. Nichiren Shoshu Buddhist Movement, late 1960s	DEM	CUL	0	0	0	0		Snow 1993	G. Ho

Case	Political context	Type	Political opportunities:				Notes	Principal source(s)	Analyst
			A	B	C	D			
23. U.S. gay liberation movement, late 1960s–early 1970s	DEM	REF/CUL	1	1	1	1		D'Emilio 1983	A. Green (see Chapter 7)
24. U.S. prostitutes' rights movement, early 1970s	DEM	REF/CUL	0	0	1	0	govt. seen as sympathetic	Jenness 1993	S. Byrd
25. U.S. anti-nuclear movement, early 1970s	DEM	REF	0	0	0	0		Jasper 1990; Joppke 1993	J. Jasper
26. Salvadoran guerrilla movement, 1970s	NON	REB	0	1	1	0	intense repression	Pearce 1986	L. Ladutke
27. U.S. pro-life movement (Calif.), 1973-	DEM	REF	0	0	0	0	"moral shock" led to mass self-recruitment	Luker 1984	S. Shapiro
28. Ethiopian Revolution, 1974	NON	REB	0	1	1	1		Keller 1988	E. Harsch
29. Soweto uprising (S. Africa), 1976	NON	REB	0	0	1	0	increasing repression	Marx 1992	R. Krabill
30. Argentine human rights movement, late 1970s	NON	REF	0	0	0	0		Brysk 1994	A. Risley (see Chapter 3)
31. Iranian Revolution, 1978–79	NON	REB	0	0	0	0		Arjomand 1988; Parsa 1989	C. Kurzman
32. Brazilian farm-workers movement, 1979–1985	NON/DEM	REF	1	1	1	1		Pereira 1997	J. Hammond (see Chapter 4)
33. Hezbollah movement (Lebanon), early 1980s	NON/DEM	REB	0	1	1	0	external elite allies; increasing repression by external actors	Jaber 1997	E. Naughton

Case	Political context	Type	Political opportunities:				Notes	Principal source(s)	Analyst
			A	B	C	D			
34. U.S. animal rights movement, 1980s	DEM	REF/CUL	0	0	0	0		Jasper and Nelkin 1992	J. Jasper
35. U.S. Central America peace movement, 1980s	DEM	REF	0	0	0	0		Smith 1996a	J. Jasper (see Chapter 8)
36. Miskitu rebellion (Nicaragua), 1980s	DEM/NON	REB	1	1	1	0	external elite allies	Hale 1994	Y. Sarikaya
37. Chilean shantytown protests, mid-1980s	NON	REF/REB	0	1	1	0	intense repression	Schneider 1995	J. Olaya
38. Anti-Marcos movement (Philippines), mid-1980s	NON/DEM	REB/REF	0	1	1	0	increasing repression	Thompson 1995	K. Schock
39. U.S. postpartum depression movement, 1980s	DEM	CUL/REF	0	0	0	0	decreasing access to polity; some elite support following emergence	Taylor 1996	N. Beisel
40. U.S. AIDS activism (ACT UP), 1980s	DEM	REF/CUL	0	0	0	0	triggered by anti-gay Supreme Court decision	Gould 2009	D. Gould
41. Mexico's new left party (FDN/PRD), 1986–1989	NON/DEM	REF	0	1	1	0	access decreasing for key elites; electoral fraud in 1988	Bruhn 1997	T. Wada
42. U.S. "hip-hop" movement, late 1980s	DEM	CUL	0	0	0	0		Rose 1994	C. Bonastia
46. U.S. mytho-poetic men's movement, early 1990s	DEM	CUL	0	0	0	0	some elite partici-pants	Schwalbe 1996	S. Shapiro

Case	Political context	Type	Political opportunities:				Notes	Principal source(s)	Analyst
			A	B	C	D			
47. U.S. Christian anti-gay movement, early 1990s	DEM	REF	0	1	1	0		Bull and Gallagher 1996	T. Fetner
48. U.S. militia movement, mid-1990s	DEM	REB/ REF	0	1	0	0		Stern 1996	D. Stemen
49. Zapatista rebellion (Chiapas, Mexico), 1994	NON/ DEM	REB	0	1	0	0	intense repression	Collier 1994; Harvey 1995	M. Kang
50. Taliban movement (Afghanistan), 1994–1996	NON	REB	0	0	1	0		Maley 1998	E. Naughton
Total	n=50		8	24	24	7			

Appendix B: Instructions to Analysts

Please note whether, on the eve of the movement's emergence, there is evidence for:

1. Increasing popular access to the political system. Specifically, is protest viewed by challengers as more likely to succeed or to be treated more seriously by authorities because protesters have gained some access to the political system, as opposed to very little or none at all?
2. Unstable elite alignments or elite competition (such as electoral instability, inter- or intra-party competition, or state-elite conflict). Specifically, do challengers believe that protest may be less risky and more effective or influential because elites (political, economic, cultural and/ or religious) have divided in some way?
3. The presence of elite allies who encourage or facilitate protest. Specifically, are certain elites strategically supporting particular challengers because these elites are contending with other elites or for some other (for example, ideological) reason?
4. Declining state repression against opponents. Specifically, do challengers believe that protest is less risky and/or more likely to be effective or influential because state repression is declining?

Also, is there evidence for expanding political opportunities other than these four? Specifically, have other changes or events occurred in the political environment that have made protest less costly to challengers and have apparently increased its likelihood of making a difference? (Please list and describe.)

Possible answers to these questions: (1) yes, (2) no, (3) just the opposite, (4) contradictory trends are evident, or (5) not discussed by the author.

• • •

Note: This list of political opportunities is taken from Doug McAdam, "Conceptual Origins, Current Problems, Future Directions," in *Comparative Perspectives on Social Movements,* edited by McAdam, McCarthy, and Zald (Cambridge University Press, 1996), pages 23–40, which you may want to review closely (especially pages 26–29). See also the similar discussion in Sidney Tarrow, *Power in Movement* (Cambridge University Press, 1994), pages 85–89.

REFERENCE MATTER

Contributors

EDWIN AMENTA is a professor of sociology at the University of California, Irvine. He is the author most recently of *When Movements Matter: The Townsend Plan and the Rise of Social Security* and *Professor Baseball*.

CHRISTIAN BRÖER is assistant professor of sociology at the University of Amsterdam. He publishes on the relation between political processes and people's perception, concerning health, risk, and noise.

ALISON BRYSK is the Mellichamp Chair in Global Studies at the University of California, Santa Barbara. She is the author of *The Politics of Human Rights in Argentina, From Tribal Village to Global Village, Human Rights and Private Wrongs*, and *Global Good Samaritans*.

ANNE N. COSTAIN is professor of political science and director of the Women and Gender Studies Program at the University of Colorado, Boulder. She was coeditor with Simone Chambers of *Deliberation, Democracy, and the Media*. Her current work examines recurring social movements in the United States focusing on historical movements opposing racism and sexism.

JOHN D'EMILIO is a professor of history and of women's and gender studies at the University of Illinois at Chicago. Among his many books, *Sexual Politics, Sexual Communities* and *Lost Prophet: Bayard Rustin and the Quest for Peace and Justice in America* both won the Stonewall Book Award for nonfiction.

DONATELLA DELLA PORTA is professor of sociology at the European University Institute. Recent publications include *Social Movements and Europeanization; Another*

Europe; Democracy in Social Movements; Voices from the Valley, Voices from the Street; The Global Justice Movement; Globalization from Below; Social Movements: An Introduction (2nd ed.); and *Transnational Protest and Global Activism.*

JAN WILLEM DUYVENDAK is professor of sociology at the University of Amsterdam. He publishes on social movements, multiculturalism, and topics of belonging. His most recent book is *The Politics of Home.*

JACK A. GOLDSTONE is the Virginia E. and John T. Hazel Professor of Public Policy at George Mason University. He is the author of *Revolution and Rebellion in the Early Modern World,* awarded the 1993 Distinguished Scholarly Research Award of the American Sociological Association, and nine other books, of which his latest are *Why Europe? The Rise of the West 1500–1850* and *Political Demography: Identities, Change, and Conflict.*

JEFF GOODWIN teaches sociology at New York University. His books include *No Other Way Out* and a number of coedited volumes, including *The Contexts Reader, Passionate Politics,* and *The Social Movements Reader.*

JEFFREY L. GOULD is the James H. Rudy Professor of History at Indiana University. From 1995 to 2008, he was director of the Center for Latin American and Caribbean Studies. His books include *To Rise in Darkness, To Lead as Equals, El Mito de Nicaragua Mestiza y la Resistencia Indígena, To Die in This Way, The Twentieth Century: A Retrospective,* and *Memorias de Mestizaje.* Gould codirected and coproduced the documentary, *Scars of Memory: El Salvador, 1932.*

ADAM ISAIAH GREEN teaches sociology at the University of Toronto. His research has been supported by the Canadian Institute of Health Research, the Canadian Foundation for AIDS Research, and the SSHRC.

DREW HALFMANN is an assistant professor at the University of California, Davis. His research focuses on the politics of health and social policy with an emphasis on reproductive policy and health inequalities.

JOHN L. HAMMOND is the author of *Fighting to Learn: Popular Education and Guerrilla War in El Salvador* and *Building Popular Power: Workers' and Neighborhood Movements in the Portuguese Revolution.* He teaches sociology at Hunter College and at the Graduate Center, City University of New York.

JAMES M. JASPER's books include *Nuclear Politics, The Animal Rights Crusade,* coauthored with Dorothy Nelkin, *The Art of Moral Protest, Restless Nation,* and *Getting Your Way,* which develops a sociological language for talking about strategic action. He now teaches at the Graduate Center of the City University of New York.

JOHN MARKOFF is Distinguished University Professor of Sociology, History, and Political Science at the University of Pittsburgh and Investigador Doctor in the Departamento de Geografía, Historia, y Filosofía, Pablo de Olavide University (Seville). He is the author of *Waves of Democracy: Social Movements and Political Change* and coeditor (with Verónica Montecinos) of *Economists in the Americas: Convergence, Divergence, and Connection.*

ANTHONY W. PEREIRA is professor of Brazilian studies and director of the Brazil Institute at King's College London. He is the author of *Political (In)justice: Authoritarianism and the Rule of Law in Brazil, Chile, and Argentina* and is currently engaged in research on police and public security reform in Brazil.

FRANCESCA POLLETTA is a professor of sociology at the University of California, Irvine. She studies social movements, experiments in radical democracy, and culture in politics. She is the author of *It Was Like a Fever: Storytelling in Protest and Politics* and *Freedom Is an Endless Meeting: Democracy in American Social Movements,* and editor, with Jeff Goodwin and James M. Jasper, of *Passionate Politics.*

AMY RISLEY received her Ph.D. in government from the University of Texas at Austin. She is currently assistant professor of international studies at Rhodes College. Her research on civil society, social movements, gender and politics, and human trafficking has appeared in *International Feminist Journal of Politics, The Latin Americanist,* and several edited volumes.

JOHN D. SKRENTNY is professor of sociology at the University of California, San Diego. His research focuses on the intersection of public policy, law, and inequality. He is the author of *The Minority Rights Revolution* and *The Ironies of Affirmative Action,* and the editor of *Color Lines: Affirmative Action, Immigration and Civil Rights Options for America.*

CHRISTIAN SMITH is the William R. Kenan, Jr. Professor of Sociology, Director of the Center for the Study of Religion and Society, and Founding Director of the Center for Social Research at the University of Notre Dame.

References

Adut, Ari. 2005. "A Theory of Scandal: Victorians, Homosexuality, and the Fall of Oscar Wilde." *American Journal of Sociology* 111: 213–48.

———. 2008. *On Scandal*. New York: Cambridge University Press.

Agrikoliansky, Eric, and Dominique Cardon. 2005. "Un programme de débats: forum, forms et formats." In *Radiographie du movement altermondialiste*, edited by Eric Agrikoliansky and Isabelle Sommier. Paris: la Dispute.

Alexander, Jeffrey C. 1982. *Theoretical Logic in Sociology*. Vol. 1: *Positivism, Presuppositions, and Current Controversies*. Berkeley: University of California Press.

Almeida, Paul D. 2003. "Opportunity Organizations and Threat-Induced Contention: Protest Waves in Authoritarian Settings." *American Journal of Sociology* 109: 345–400.

Amenta, Edwin. 2006. *When Movements Matter: The Townsend Plan and the Rise of Social Security*. Princeton, NJ: Princeton University Press.

Amenta, Edwin, Drew Halfmann, and Michael P. Young. 1999. "The Strategies and Contexts of Social Protest: Political Mediation and the Impact of the Townsend Movement in California." *Mobilization* 4: 1–23.

Amenta, Edwin, and Michael P. Young. 1999a. "Democratic States and Social Mobilization: Theoretical Arguments and Hypotheses." *Social Problems* 46: 153–68.

———. 1999b. "Making an Impact: The Conceptual and Methodological Implications of the Collective Benefits Criterion." In *How Social Movements Matter: Theoretical and Comparative Studies on the Consequences of Social Movements*, edited by Marco Giugni, Doug McAdam, and Charles Tilly. Minneapolis: University of Minnesota Press.

Amenta, Edwin, Neal Caren, Elizabeth Chiarello, and Yang Su. 2010. "The Political Consequences of Social Movements." *Annual Review of Sociology* 36: 287–307.

Amenta, Edwin, Neal Caren, and Sheera Joy Olasky. 2005. "Age for Leisure? Political Mediation and the Impact of the Pension Movement on U.S. Old-Age Policy." *American Sociological Review* 70: 516–38.

Amenta, Edwin, and Yvonne Zylan. 1991. "It Happened Here: Political Opportunity, the New Institutionalism, and the Townsend Movement." *American Sociological Review* 56: 250–65.

Aminzade, Ron, and Doug McAdam. 2001. "Emotions and Contentious Politics." In *Silence and Voice in Contentious Politics*, edited by Ron Aminzade, Jack Goldstone, Doug McAdam, Elizabeth Perry, William Sewell, Sidney Tarrow, and Charles Tilly. New York: Cambridge University Press.

Anaya Muñoz, Alejandro. 2009. "Transnational and Domestic Processes in the Definition of Human Rights Policies in Mexico." *Human Rights Quarterly* 31: 35–58.

Anbinder, Tyler. 1992. *Nativism and Slavery: The Northern Know Nothings and the Politics of the 1850s*. New York: Oxford University Press.

Andretta, Massimiliano. 2007. "Democrazia in Azione. Modelli Decisionali e Ideali Democratici degli Attivisti Globali." In *La Sociatà in Movimento*, edited by Fabio de Nardis. Rome: Editori Riuniti.

Araj, Bader, and Robert J. Brym. 2009. "Opportunity, Culture, and Agency." *International Sociology* 25: 842–68.

Arjomand, Said. 1988. *The Turban for the Crown: The Islamic Revolution in Iran*. New York: Oxford University Press.

Armony, Ariel C. 2004. *The Dubious Link: Civic Engagement and Democratization*. Stanford, CA: Stanford University Press.

Babisch, W., et al. 2009. "Annoyance Due to Aircraft Noise Has Increased over the Years—Results of the HYENA Study." *Environment International* 35: 1169–76.

Bailly, Jean-Sylvain. 1821. *Mémoires de Bailly*. Paris: Baudoin.

Becker, Susan D. 1981. *The Origins of the Equal Rights Amendment: American Feminism Between the Wars*. Westport, CT: Greenwood Press.

Beisel, Nicola. 1997. *Imperiled Innocents: Anthony Comstock and Family Reproduction in Victorian America*. Princeton, NJ: Princeton University Press.

Benford, Robert D. 1997. "An Insider's Critique of the Social Movement Framing Perspective." *Sociological Inquiry* 67: 409–30.

Benford, Robert D., and David A. Snow. 2000. "Framing Processes and Social Movements: An Overview and Assessment." *Annual Review of Sociology* 26: 611–39.

Bijsterveld, Karin. 2008. *Mechanical Sound: Technology, Culture and Public Problems of Noise in the Twentieth Century*. Cambridge, MA: MIT Press.

Blee, Kathleen M. 1991. *Women of the Klan: Racism and Gender in the 1920s*. Berkeley: University of California Press.

Bloom, Jack M. 1987. *Class, Race, and the Civil Rights Movement: The Changing Political Economy of Southern Racism*. Bloomington: Indiana University Press.

Bob, Clifford. In press. *Globalizing the Right-Wing: Conservative Activism and World Politics*. New York: Cambridge University Press.

Bonner, Michelle. 2007. *Sustaining Human Rights: Women and Argentine Human Rights Organizations*. University Park: Pennsylvania State University Press.

Boudreau, Vincent. 1996. "Northern Theory, Southern Protest: Opportunity Structure Analysis in Cross-National Perspective." *Mobilization* 1: 175–89.

———. 2004. *Resisting Dictatorship: Repression and Protest in South East Asia.* New York: Cambridge University Press.

Bousquet, Jean-Pierre. 1983. *Las Locas de la Plaza de Mayo.* Buenos Aires: Fundación Para la Democracia en Argentina.

Bouvard, Marguerite Guzmán. 1994. *Revolutionizing Motherhood: The Mothers of the Plaza de Mayo.* Wilmington, DE: SR Books.

Brinks, Daniel. 2003. "Informal Institutions and the Rule of Law: The Judicial Response to State Killings in Buenos Aires and São Paulo in the 1990s." *Comparative Politics* 36: 1–20.

Brockett, Charles. 1991. "The Structure of Political Opportunities and Peasant Mobilization in Central America." *Comparative Politics* 23: 253–74.

———. 1995. "A Protest-Cycle Resolution of the Repression/Popular Protest Paradox." In *Repertoires and Cycles of Collective Action,* edited by Mark Traugott. Durham, NC: Duke University Press.

———. 2005. *Political Movements and Violence in Central America.* New York: Cambridge University Press.

Bröer, Christian. 2006. *Beleid vormt overlast, hoe beleidsdiscoursen de beleving van geluid bepalen* (Policy annoyance, how policy discourses shape the experience of aircraft sound). Amsterdam: Aksant.

———. 2007. "Aircraft Noise and Risk Politics." *Health Risk & Society* 9: 37–52.

———. 2008. "Private Trouble, Policy Issue, How Policy Discourses Shape Our Experience of Aircraft Sound." *Critical Policy Studies* 2: 93–117.

———, and Jan Willem Duyvendak. 2009. "Discursive Opportunities, Feeling Rules, and the Rise of Protests against Aircraft Noise." *Mobilization* 14: 337–56.

Bröer, Christian, and Katja Wirth. 2004. "Mehr Belästigung bei gleichem Pegel, Wieso Flugzeuggeräusche heute möglicherweise lästiger sind als vor 40 Jahren." *Zeitschrift für Lämbekämpfung* 4: 118–22.

Bröer, Christian, et al. 2005. "Veränderung der Lärmbelästigung im zeitlichen Verlauf." *Umweltmedizin in Forschung und Praxis* 10: 105–112.

Bruhn, Kathleen. 1997. *Taking on Goliath: The Emergence of a New Left Party and the Struggle for Democracy in Mexico.* University Park: Pennsylvania State University Press.

Brysk, Alison. 1993. "From Above and Below: Social Movements, the International System, and Human Rights in Argentina." *Comparative Political Studies* 26: 259–85.

———. 1994. *The Politics of Human Rights in Argentina: Protest, Change, and Democratization.* Stanford, CA: Stanford University Press.

———. 1995. "Hearts and Minds: Bringing Symbolic Politics Back In." *Polity* 25: 559–85.

———. 2000. *From Tribal Village to Global Village: Indian Rights and International Relations in Latin America.* Stanford, CA: Stanford University Press.

Bull, Chris, and John Gallagher. 1996. *Perfect Enemies: The Religious Right, the Gay Movement, and the Politics of the 1990s.* New York: Crown.

Burgerman, Susan. 2001. *Moral Victories: How Activists Provoke Multilateral Action.* Ithaca, NY: Cornell University Press.

Burstein, Paul. 1985. *Discrimination, Jobs, and Politics.* Chicago: University of Chicago Press.

———. 1998. "Interest Organizations, Political Parties, and the Study of Democratic Politics." In *Social Movements and American Political Institutions,* edited by Anne N. Costain and Andrew S. McFarland. Lanham, MD: Rowman & Littlefield.

Calhoun, Craig. 1994. *Neither Gods nor Emperors: Students and the Struggle for Democracy in China.* Berkeley: University of California Press.

Carson, Clayborne. 1986. "Civil Rights Reform and the Black Freedom Struggle." In *The Civil Rights Movement in America,* edited by Charles Eagles. Jackson: University Press of Mississippi.

Caulfield, Max. 1995/1963. *The Easter Rebellion.* Boulder, CO: Roberts Rinehart.

CELS (Centro de Estudios Legales y Sociales). 1997. *Informe sobre la situación de los derechos humanos en la Argentina 1996.* Buenos Aires: CELS.

Chamberlin, William. 1965. *The Russian Revolution 1917–1921,* 2 volumes. New York: Grosset and Dunlap.

Chauncey, George. 1994. *Gay New York: Gender, Urban Culture, and the Making of the Gay Male World, 1890–1940.* New York: Basic Books.

Chelala, César. 1993. "Women of Valor: An Interview with Mothers of the Plaza de Mayo." In *Surviving Beyond Fear: Women, Children, and Human Rights in Latin America,* edited by Marjorie Agosín. Fredonia, NY: White Pine Press.

Chorev, Nitsan. 2007. *Remaking U.S. Trade Policy.* Ithaca: Cornell University Press.

Clemens, Elisabeth S. 1997. *The People's Lobby: Organizational Innovation and the Rise of Interest Group Politics in the United States, 1890–1925.* Chicago and London: University of Chicago Press.

Cloward, Richard A. 1959. "Illegitimate Means, Anomie, and Deviant Behavior." *American Sociological Review* 24: 164–76.

Coleman, James. 1986. "Microfoundations and Macrosocial Theory." In *Approaches to Social Theory,* edited by S. Lindenberg, J. S. Coleman, and S. Nowak. New York: Russell Sage.

Collier, George A., with Elizabeth Lowery Quaratiello. 1994. *Basta! Land and the Zapatista Rebellion in Chiapas.* Oakland, CA: Institute for Food and Development Policy.

CORREPI (Coalition Against Police and Institutional Repression). 1995. Boletín Especial (July).

Costain, Anne N. 1992. *Inviting Women's Rebellion: A Political Process Interpretation of the Women's Movement.* Baltimore, MD: Johns Hopkins University Press.

———, Richard Braunstein, and Heidi Berggren. 1997. "Framing the Women's Movement." In *Women, Media, and Politics,* edited by Pippa Norris. New York: Oxford University Press.

Crist, John, and John McCarthy. 1996. "If I Had a Hammer: The Changing Methodological Repertoire of Collective Behavior and Social Movement Research." *Mobilization* 1: 87–102.

Crossley, Nick. 2002. *Making Sense of Social Movements*. Buckingham: Open University Press.

DeBenedetti, Charles. 1990. *An American Ordeal: The Antiwar Movement of the Vietnam Era*. Syracuse, NY: Syracuse University Press.

della Porta, Donatella. 1995. *Social Movements, Political Violence and the State*. New York: Cambridge University Press.

———. 2004. "Multiple Belongings, Flexible Identities and the Construction of Another Politics." In *Transnational Protest and Global Activism*, edited by Donatella della Porta and Sidney Tarrow. Lanham, MD: Rowman & Littlefield.

———. 2007a. "Global Activists: Conceptions and Practices of Democracy in the European Social Forums," paper presented at the Annual Joint Sessions of the European Consortium for Political Research, Helsinki, May 2007.

———. 2007b. *The Global Justice Movement in Cross-national and Transnational Perspective*. New York: Paradigm.

———. 2008. "The Protest on Unemployment: Forms and Opportunities." *Mobilization* 13: 277–95.

della Porta, Donatella, Massimiliano Andretta, Lorenzo Mosca, and Herbert Reiter. 2006. *Globalization from Below*. Minneapolis: University of Minnesota Press,

della Porta, Donatella, and Mario Diani. 2004. *Movimenti senza protesta? L'ambientalismo in Italia*. Bologna: Il Mulino.

———. 2006. *Social Movements: An Introduction*. Malden, MA, and Oxford: Blackwell.

della Porta, Donatella, and Lorenzo Mosca. 2007. "In Movimento: 'Contamination' in Action and the Italian Global Justice Movement." *Global Networks: A Journal of Transnational Affairs* 7: 1–27.

della Porta, Donatella, and Gianni Piazza. 2008. *Voices of the Valley, Voices of the Straits: How Protest Creates Community*. Oxford: Berghahn Books.

della Porta, Donatella, and Herbert Reiter. 1998. "Introduction: The Policing of Protest in Western Democracies." In *Policing Protest*, edited by Donatella della Porta and Herbert Reiter. Minneapolis: University of Minnesota Press.

———. 2006. Conclusions. In *The Policing of Transnational Protest*, edited by Donatella della Porta, Abby Peterson, and Herbert Reiter. Aldershot: Ashgate.

della Porta, Donatella, and Sidney G. Tarrow, eds. 2004. *Transnational Protest and Global Activism*. Lanham, MD: Rowman & Littlefield.

———. 2007. *The Global Justice Movement: Cross-national and Transnational Perspectives*. Boulder, CO: Paradigm.

D'Emilio, John. 1983. *Sexual Politics, Sexual Communities: The Making of a Homosexual Minority in the Unites States, 1940–1970*. Chicago: University of Chicago Press.

Diani, Mario. 1995. *Green Networks*. Edinburgh: Edinburgh University Press

Dittmer, John. 1994. *Local People: The Struggle for Civil Rights in Mississippi*. Urbana: University of Illinois Press.

Dobbin, Frank. 2009. *Inventing Equal Opportunity*. Princeton, NJ: Princeton University Press.

Doerr, Nicole, and Mattoni, Alice. 2007. "The Euromayday Parade against Precarity: Cross National Diffusion and Transformation of the European Space 'From Below.'" Paper presented at the 8th Annual Conference of the European Sociological Association. Caledonian University, Glasgow.

Dyrberg, Torben Bech. 1997. *The Circular Structure of Power: Politics, Identity, Community*. London: Verso.

Edsall, Thomas Byrne, and Mary Edsall. 1991. *Chain Reaction: The Impact of Race, Rights and Taxes on American Politics*. New York: W. W. Norton.

Eliasoph, Nina. 1997. "'Close to Home': The Work of Avoiding Politics." *Theory and Society* 26: 605–47.

Elster, Jon. 1999. *Alchemies of the Mind*. New York: Cambridge University Press.

Einwohner, Rachel L. 2003. "Opportunity, Honor, and Action in the Warsaw Ghetto Uprising of 1943." *American Journal of Sociology* 109: 650–75.

Eisinger, Peter K. 1973. "The Conditions of Protest Behavior in American Cities." *American Political Science Review* 67: 11–28.

Emirbayer, Mustafa, and Jeff Goodwin. 1994. "Network Analysis, Culture, and Problem of Agency." *American Journal of Sociology* 99: 1411–54.

Ettema, James S. 2005. "Crafting Cultural Resonance." *Journalism* 6: 131–52.

Evans, Sara M. 1979. *Personal Politics: The Roots of Women's Liberation in the Civil Rights Movement and the New Left*. New York: Knopf.

———. 1989. *Born for Liberty: A History of Women in America*. New York: Free Press.

Eyerman, Ron. 2005. How Social Movements Move: Emotions and Social Movements. In *Emotions and Social Movements*, edited by Helena Flam and Debra King. London: Routledge.

Faderman, Lillian. 1991. *Odd Girls and Twilight Lovers*. New York: Penguin Books.

Fantasia, Rick. 1988. *Cultures of Solidarity: Consciousness, Action, and Contemporary American Workers*. Berkeley: University of California Press.

Felson, Marcus. 1994. *Crime and Everyday Life*. Thousand Oaks, CA: Pine Forge.

Fields, Karen E. 1985. *Revival and Rebellion in Colonial Africa*. Princeton, NJ: Princeton University Press.

Fillieule, Olivier. 1997. *Stratégies de la Rue*. Paris: Presses de Sciences-Po.

———. 2005. "Requiem pour un Concept: Vie et Mort de la Notion de Structure des Opportunités Politiques." In *La Turquie Conteste*, edited by Gilles Dorronsoro. Paris: CNRS Editions.

Fisher, Jo. 1989. *Mothers of the Disappeared*. Boston: South End Press.

Flacks, Richard. 2004. "Knowledge for What? Thoughts on the State of Social Movement Studies." In *Rethinking Social Movements: Structure, Meaning, and Emotion*, edited by Jeff Goodwin and James M. Jasper. Lanham, MD: Rowman & Littlefield.

Flam, Helena. 2005. "Emotions' Map: A Research Agenda." In *Emotions and Social Movements*, edited by Helena Flam and Debra King. New York: Routledge.

————, and Debra King, eds. 2005. *Emotions and Social Movements*. New York: Routledge.

Foweraker, Joe. 1995. *Theorizing Social Movements*. Boulder, CO: Pluto Press.

Francisco, Ronald. 1995. "The Relationship between Coercion and Protest: An Empirical Evaluation in Three Coercive States." *Journal of Conflict Resolution* 39: 263–81.

Franco, Jean. 1992. "Gender, Death and Resistance: Facing the Ethical Vacuum." In *Fear at the Edge: State Terror and Resistance in Latin America*, edited by Juan E. Corradi, Patricia Weiss Fagen, and Manuel Antonio Garretón. Berkeley: University of California Press.

Freeman, Jo. 1975. *The Politics of Women's Liberation*. New York: David McKay.

French, John D. 1992. *The Brazilian Workers' ABC: Class Conflict and Alliances in Modern São Paulo*. Chapel Hill: University of North Carolina Press.

Friedan, Betty. 1974/1963. *The Feminine Mystique*. New York: Dell.

————. 1991. *"It Changed My Life": Writings on the Women's Movement*. New York: W.W. Norton.

Friedman, Elisabeth Jay, and Kathryn Hochstetler. 2002. "Assessing the Third Transition in Latin American Democratization: Representational Regimes and Civil Society in Argentina and Brazil." *Comparative Politics* 35: 21–42.

Frymer, Paul, and John David Skrentny. 1998. "Coalition-Building and the Politics of Electoral Capture during the Nixon Administration: African Americans, Labor, Latinos." *Studies in American Political Development* 12: 131–61.

Gamson, William. 1990. *The Strategy of Social Protest*, 2nd ed. Belmont, CA: Wadsworth.

————. 1992. *Talking Politics*. New York: Cambridge University Press.

————, and David S. Meyer. 1996. "Framing Political Opportunity." In *Comparative Perspectives on Social Movements: Political Opportunities, Mobilizing Structures, and Cultural Framings*, edited by Doug McAdam, John D. McCarthy, and Mayer N. Zald. New York: Cambridge University Press.

Ganz, Marshall. 2004. "Why David Sometimes Wins: Strategic Capacity in Social Movements." In *Rethinking Social Movements: Structure, Meaning, and Emotion*, edited by Jeff Goodwin and James M. Jasper. Lanham, MD: Rowman & Littlefield.

————. 2009. *Why David Sometimes Wins*. New York: Oxford University Press.

Garton Ash, Timothy. 1990. *The Magic Lantern: The Revolution of '89 Witnessed in Warsaw, Budapest, Berlin, and Prague*. New York: Random House.

Gates, Leslie C. 2009. "Theorizing Business Power in the Semiperiphery: Mexico 1970–2000." *Theory and Society* 38: 57–95.

Gelb, Joyce, and Marian Palley. 1987. *Women and Public Policies*. Princeton, NJ: Princeton University Press.

Gitlin, Todd. 1980. *The Whole World Is Watching*. Berkeley: University of California Press.

Goffman, Erving. 1975. *Frame Analysis: An Essay on the Organization of Experience*. Harmondsworth: Penguin.

Goldstone, Jack. 1991. *Revolution and Rebellion in the Early Modern World*. Berkeley: University of California Press.

———. 2004. "More Social Movements or Fewer? Beyond Political Opportunity Structures to Relational Fields." *Theory and Society* 33: 333–65.

———. 2011. "The Social Origins of the French Revolution Revisited." In *Releasing the Deluge: The Origins of the French Revolution*, edited by Dale van Kley and Thomas Kaiser. Stanford, CA: Stanford University Press.

———, and Charles Tilly. 2001. "Threat (and Opportunity): Popular Action and State Response in the Dynamics of Contentious Action." In *Silence and Voice in the Study of Contentious Politics*, edited by Ronald R. Aminzade, Jack A. Goldstone, Doug McAdam, Elizabeth J. Perry, William H. Sewell, Jr., Sidney Tarrow, and Charles Tilly. New York: Cambridge University Press.

Goodwin, Jeff, and James M. Jasper. 1999/2004a. "Caught in a Winding, Snarling Vine: The Structural Bias of Political Process Theory." *Sociological Forum* 14: 27–54. Reprinted in *Rethinking Social Movements: Structure, Meaning, and Emotion*, edited by Jeff Goodwin and James M. Jasper. Lanham, MD: Rowman & Littlefield.

———. 1999/2004b. "Trouble in Paradigms." *Sociological Forum* 14: 107–25. Reprinted in *Rethinking Social Movements: Structure, Meaning, and Emotion*, edited by Jeff Goodwin and James M. Jasper. Lanham, MD: Rowman & Littlefield.

———. 2006. "Emotions and Social Movements." In *Handbook of the Sociology of Emotions*, edited by Jan E. Stets and Jonathan H. Turner. New York: Springer.

———, eds. 2004. *Rethinking Social Movements: Structure, Meaning, and Emotion*. Lanham, MD: Rowman & Littlefield.

Goodwin, Jeff, James M. Jasper, and Francesca Polletta. 2000. "The Return of the Repressed: The Fall and Rise of Emotions in Social Movement Theory." *Mobilization* 5: 65–84.

———,, eds. 2001. *Passionate Politics: Emotions and Social Movements*. Chicago: University of Chicago Press.

Goodwin, Jeff, and Steven Pfaff. 2001. "Emotion Work in High-Risk Social Movements: Managing Fear in the U.S. and East German Civil Rights Movements." In *Passionate Politics*, edited by Jeff Goodwin, James M. Jasper, and Francesca Polletta. Chicago: University of Chicago Press.

Gosse, Van. 1993. *Where the Boys Are: Cuba, Cold War America and the Making of a New Left*. London: Verso.

Gould, Deborah B. 2009. *Moving Politics: Emotion and ACT UP's Fight Against AIDS*. Chicago: University of Chicago Press.

Gould, Jeffrey L. 1990. *To Lead as Equals: Rural Protest and Political Consciousness in Chinandegea, Nicaragua, 1912–1979*. Chapel Hill: University of North Carolina Press.

———. 1998. *To Die in This Way: Nicaraguan Indians and the Myth of Mestizaje, 1880–1965*. Durham, NC: Duke University Press.

Graham, Hugh Davis. 1990. *The Civil Rights Era: Origins and Development of National Policy*. New York: Oxford University Press.

Guenther, Katja M. 2009. "The Impact of Emotional Opportunities on the Emotion Cultures of Feminist Organizations." *Gender and Society* 23: 337–62.

Guski, Rainer. 2003. "Status, Tendenzen und Desiderate der Lärmwirkungsforschung." *Zeitschrift für Lärmbekämpfung* 49: 219–32.

Hajer, Maarten H. 1995. *The Politics of Environmental Discourse: Ecological Modernization and the Policy Process.* Oxford: Clarendon Press.

Hale, Charles R. 1994. *Resistance and Contradiction: Miskitu Indians and the Nicaraguan State, 1894–1987.* Stanford, CA: Stanford University Press.

Halfmann, Drew. 2011. *Doctors and Demonstrators: How Political Institutions Shape Abortion Law in the United States, Britain and Canada.* Chicago: University of Chicago Press.

Hall, Peter. 2003. "Aligning Onthology and Methodology in Comparative Research." In *Comparative Historical Research in the Social Sciences*, edited by James Mahoney and Dietrich Rueschemeyer. New York: Cambridge University Press.

Harrison, Cynthia. 1988. *On Account of Sex: The Politics of Women's Issues, 1945–1968.* Berkeley: University of California Press.

Harvey, Neil. 1995. "Rebellion in Chiapas: Rural Reforms and Popular Struggle." *Third World Quarterly* 16: 39–73.

Hawkins, Darren G. 2002. *International Human Rights and Authoritarian Rule in Chile.* Lincoln: University of Nebraska Press.

Hess, David, and Brian Martin. 2006. "Repression, Backfire, and the Theory of Transformative Events." *Mobilization* 11: 249–67.

Hilgartner, Stephen, and Charles L. Bosk. 1988. "The Rise and Fall of Social Problems: A Public Arenas Model." *American Journal of Sociology* 94: 53–78.

Hipsher, Patricia L. 1998. "Democratic Transitions as Protest Cycles: Social Movement Dynamics in Democratizing Latin America." In *The Social Movement Society*, edited by David S. Meyer and Sidney Tarrow. Lanham, MD: Rowman & Littlefield.

Hochschild, Arlie R. 1979. "Emotion Work, Feeling Rules and Social Structure." *American Journal of Sociology* 85: 551–75.

———. 1983. *The Managed Heart: Commercialization of Human Feeling.* Berkeley: University of California Press.

Hoff, Joan. 1994. *Nixon Reconsidered.* New York: Basic Books.

Howarth, David R. 2000. *Discourse.* Buckingham: Open University Press.

———, and Jacob Torfing. 2005. *Discourse Theory in European Politics: Identity, Policy, and Governance.* New York: Palgrave Macmillan.

Huntington, Samuel P. 1981. *American Politics: The Promise of Disharmony.* Cambridge, MA: Harvard University Press.

Jaber, Hala. 1997. *Hezbollah: Born with a Vengeance.* New York: Columbia University Press.

Jasper, James M. 1990. *Nuclear Politics: Energy and the State in the United States, Sweden, and France.* Princeton, NJ: Princeton University Press.

———. 1992. "Three Nuclear Controversies." In *Controversy*, edited by Dorothy Nel-kin, 3rd ed. Thousand Oaks, CA: Sage.

———. 1997. *The Art of Moral Protest: Culture, Biography, and Creativity in Social Movements*. Chicago: University of Chicago Press.

———. 1998. "The Emotions of Protest: Affective and Reactive Emotions in and Around Social Movements." *Sociological Forum* 13: 397–424.

———. 2004. "A Strategic Approach to Collective Action." *Mobilization* 9: 1–16.

———. 2006. *Getting Your Way*. Chicago: University of Chicago Press.

———, Mitchel Y. Abolafia, and Frank Dobbin. 2005. "Strategy and Structure on the Exchanges: A Critique and Conversation about Making Markets." *Sociological Forum* 20: 473–87.

Jasper, James M., and Dorothy Nelkin. 1992. *The Animal Rights Crusade: The Growth of a Moral Protest*. New York: Free Press.

Jasper, James M., and Jane Poulsen. 1993. "Fighting Back: Vulnerabilities, Blunders, and Countermobilization by the Targets in Three Animal Rights Campaigns." *Sociological Forum* 8: 639–57.

———. 1995. "Recruiting Strangers and Friends: Moral Shocks and Social Networks in Animal Rights and Anti-Nuclear Protest." *Social Problems* 42: 493–512.

Jenkins, J. Craig. 1995. "Social Movements, Political Representation, and the State: An Agenda and Comparative Framework." In *States and Social Movements*, edited by J. Craig Jenkins and Bert Klandermans. Minneapolis: University of Minnesota Press.

———, and Charles Perrow. 1977. "Insurgency and the Powerless: Farm Worker Movements in the U.S." *American Sociological Review* 42: 429–68.

Jenness, Valerie. 1993. *Making It Work: The Prostitutes' Rights Movement in Perspective*. New York: Aldine de Gruyter.

Johnson, Eric J., Colin F. Camerer, Sankar Sen, and Talia Rymon. 2002. "Detecting Failures of Backward Induction." *Journal of Economic Theory* 104: 16–47.

Joppke, Christian. 1993. *Mobilizing Against Nuclear Energy: A Comparison of Germany and the United States*. Berkeley: University of California Press.

Kay, Herma Hill. 1988. *Sex-Based Discrimination: Text, Cases and Materials*, 3rd ed. St. Paul, MN: West Publishing.

Keck, Margaret E., and Kathryn Sikkink. 1998. *Activists beyond Borders: Advocacy Networks in International Politics*. Ithaca, NY: Cornell University Press.

Keller, Edmond J. 1988. *Revolutionary Ethiopia: From Empire to People's Republic*. Bloomington: Indiana University Press.

Kelley, Robin D. G. 1990. *Hammer and Hoe: Alabama Communists During the Great Depression*. Chapel Hill: University of North Carolina Press.

Khagram, Sanjeev, James V. Riker, and Kathryn Sikkink, eds. 2002. *Restructuring World Politics*. Minneapolis: University of Minnesota Press.

Khawaja, Mawan. 1993. "Repression and Popular Collective Action: Evidence from the West Bank." *Sociological Forum* 8: 47–71.

King, Gary, Robert Keohane, and Sidney Verba. 1994. *Designing Social Inquiry: Scientific Inference in Qualitative Research*. Princeton, NJ: Princeton University Press.

Kirk, Marshall, and Hunter Madsen. 1989. *After the Ball: How America Will Conquer Its Fear and Hatred of Gays in the '90s.* New York: Doubleday.

Kitschelt, Herbert P. 1986. "Political Opportunity Structures and Political Protest: Anti-Nuclear Movements in Four Democracies." *British Journal of Political Science* 16: 57–85.

Klein, Ethel. 1984. *Gender Politics: From Consciousness to Mass Politics.* Cambridge, MA: Harvard University Press.

Koopmans, Ruud. 1995. *Democracy from Below.* Boulder, CO: Westview.

———. 1997a. "Dynamics of Repression and Mobilization." *Mobilization* 2: 149–64.

———. 1997b. "Political. Opportunity. Structure. Some Splitting to Balance the Lumping." *Sociological Forum* 14: 93–105.

———. 2004. "Movements and Media: Selection Processes and Evolutionary Dynamics in the Public Sphere." *Theory and Society* 33: 367–91.

———. 2005. "The Missing Link between Structure and Agency: Outline of an Evolutionary Approach to Social Movements." *Mobilization* 10: 19–35.

———, and Susan Olzak. 2004. "Discursive Opportunities and the Evolution of Right-Wing Violence in Germany." *American Journal of Sociology* 110: 198–230.

Koopmans, Ruud, and Paul Statham. 1999. "Political Claims Analysis: Integrating Protest Event and Political Discourse Approaches." *Mobilization* 4: 203–21.

Kriesi, Hanspeter. 1996. "The Organizational Structure of New Social Movements in a Political Context." In *Comparative Perspectives on Social Movements: Political Opportunities, Mobilizing Structures, and Cultural Framings,* edited by Doug McAdam, John D. McCarthy, and Mayer N. Zald. New York: Cambridge University Press.

———. 2004. "Political Context and Opportunity." In *The Blackwell Companion to Social Movements,* edited by David A. Snow, Sarah A. Soule, and Hanspeter Kriesi. Malden, MA: Blackwell.

———, Ruud Koopmans, Jan Willem Duyvendak, and Marco Guigni. 1995. *New Social Movements in Western Europe: A Comparative Analysis.* Minneapolis: University of Minnesota Press.

Kroesen, Maarten, and Christian Bröer. 2009. "Policy Discourse and People's Internal Frames on Declared Aircraft Annoyance: An Application of Q-methodology." *Journal of the Acoustical Society of America* 126: 195–207.

Kuran, Timur. 1995. *Private Truths, Public Lies: The Social Consequences of Preference Falsification.* Cambridge, MA: Harvard University Press.

Kurtz, Ernest. 1988. *A.A.: The Story.* San Francisco: Harper and Row.

Kurzman, Charles. 1998. "Organizational Opportunity and Social Movement Mobilization: A Comparative Analysis of Four Religious Movements." *Mobilization* 3: 23–49.

Laclau, Ernesto, and Chantal Mouffe. 1985. *Hegemony and Socialist Strategy.* London: Verso.

Lawson, Stephen F. 1976. *Black Ballots: Voting Rights in the South, 1944–1969.* New York: Columbia University Press.

———. 1991. "Freedom Then, Freedom Now: The Historiography of the Civil Rights Movement." *American Historical Review* 96: 456–71.

Lewanski, Rodolfo. 2004. Il Discorso della Protesta. In *Comitati di Cittadini e Democrazia Urbana*, edited by Donatella della Porta. Rubbettino: Soveria Mannelli.

Lipsky, Michael. 1969. *Protest in City Politics: Rent Strikes, Housing and the Power of the Poor.* Chicago: Rand MacNally.

Loveman, Mara. 1998. "High-Risk Collective Action: Defending Human Rights in Chile, Uruguay, and Argentina." *American Journal of Sociology* 104: 477–525.

Luker, Kristin. 1984. *Abortion and the Politics of Motherhood.* Berkeley: University of California Press.

Machiavelli, Nicolo. 1965/1521. *The Art of War.* New York: Da Capo.

Maier, Charles S. 1997. *Dissolution: The Crisis of Communism and the End of East Germany.* Princeton, NJ: Princeton University Press.

Mainwaring, Scott, and Eduardo Viola. 1984. "New Social Movements, Political Culture, and Democracy: Brazil and Argentina in the 1980s." *Telos* 61: 17–52.

Maley, William, ed. 1998. *Fundamentalism Reborn? Afghanistan and the Taliban.* New York: New York University Press.

Mansbridge, Jane. 1986. *Why We Lost the ERA.* Chicago: University of Chicago Press.

Markoff, John. 1996. *The Abolition of Feudalism: Peasants, Lords, and Legislators in the French Revolution.* University Park: Pennsylvania State University Press.

Marx, Anthony W. 1992. *Lessons of Struggle: South African Internal Opposition, 1960–1990.* New York: Oxford University Press.

Mathers, Andy. 2007. *Struggling for Another Europe.* Aldershot: Ashgate.

Mathieu, Lilian. 2009. "Secteurs." In *Dictionnaire des Mouvements Sociaux*, edited by Olivier Fillieule, Lilian Mathieu, and Cécile Péchu. Paris: Sciences Po.

Mavidal, Jérôme, and Emile Laurent, eds. 1862. *Archives parlementaires de 1787 à 1860.* 1st ser. Paris: Librairie Administrative de Paul Dupont.

Mayntz, Renate. 2004. "Mechanisms in the Analysis of Social Macro-Phenomena." *Philosophy of the Social Sciences* 34: 237–59.

McAdam, Doug. 1982. *Political Process and the Development of Black Insurgency, 1930–1970.* Chicago: University of Chicago Press.

———. 1989. "The Biographical Consequences of Activism." *American Sociological Review* 54: 744–60.

———. 1995. "'Initiator' and 'Spin-Off' Movements: Diffusion Processes in Protest Cycles." In *Repertoires and Cycles of Collective Action*, edited by Mark Traugott. Durham, NC: Duke University Press.

———. 1996. "Conceptual Origins, Current Problems, Future Directions." In *Comparative Perspectives on Social Movements: Political Opportunities, Mobilizing Structures, and Cultural Framings*, edited by Doug McAdam, John D. McCarthy, and Mayer N. Zald. New York: Cambridge University Press.

———. 1998. "On the International Origins of Democratic Political Opportunities." In *Social Movements and American Political Institutions*, edited by Anne N. Costain and Andrew S. McFarland. Lanham, MD: Rowman & Littlefield.

McAdam, Doug, John D. McCarthy, and Mayer N. Zald. 1996a. "Introduction: Op-
portunities, Mobilizing Structures, and Framing Processes—Towards a Synthetic,
Comparative Perspective on Social Movements." In *Comparative Perspectives on
Social Movements: Political Opportunities, Mobilizing Structures, and Cultural
Framings*, edited by Doug McAdam, John D. McCarthy, and Mayer N. Zald. New
York: Cambridge University Press.

———, eds. 1996b. *Comparative Perspectives on Social Movements*. New York: Cambridge University Press.

McAdam, Doug, and William H. Sewell. 2001. "It's about Time: Temporality in the
Study of Social Movements and Revolutions." In *Silence and Voice in the Study
of Contentious Politics*, edited by Ronald Aminzade et al. New York: Cambridge
University Press.

McAdam, Doug, Sidney Tarrow, and Charles Tilly. 2001. *Dynamics of Contention*.
New York: Cambridge University Press.

McCarthy, John D., and Mayer N. Zald. 1977. "Resource Mobilization and Social
Movements: A Partial Theory." *American Journal of Sociology* 82: 1212–41.

McFarland, Andrew S. 1987. "Interest Groups and Theories of Power in America."
British Journal of Political Science 17: 129–47.

Melucci, Alberto. 1996. *Challenging Codes: Collective Action in the Information Age*.
New York: Cambridge University Press.

Merton, Robert K. 1959. "Social Conformity, Deviation, and Opportunity Structures." *American Sociological Review* 24: 177–89.

———. 1995. "Opportunity Structure: The Emergence, Diffusion, and Differentia-
tion of a Sociological Concept, 1930–1950s." In *Advances in Criminological Theory: The Legacy of Anomie Theory*, edited by Freda Adler and William S. Laufer.
New Brunswick, NJ: Transaction.

Meyer, David S. 1990. *A Winter of Discontent*. New York: Praeger.

———. 1997. "Contentious Politics in the United States after World War II." Paper
presented at the annual meeting of the American Political Science Association,
August 1997, Washington, DC.

———. 1999. "Tending the Vineyard: Cultivating Political Process Research." *Sociological Forum* 14: 79–92.

———. 2004. "Protest and Political Opportunities." *Annual Review of Sociology* 30:
125–45.

———, and Debra C. Minkoff. 2004. "Conceptualizing Political Opportunity." *Social
Forces* 82: 1457–92.

Meyer, David S., and Suzanne Staggenborg. 1996. "Movements, Countermovements,
and the Structure of Political Opportunity." *American Journal of Sociology* 101:
1628–60.

Meyer, David S., and Sidney Tarrow, eds. 1998. *The Social Movement Society*. Lanham,
MD: Rowman & Littlefield.

Meyer, David S., and Nancy Whittier. 1994. "Social Movement Spillover." *Social Problems* 41: 277–98.

Mische, Ann. 2008. *Partisan Politics: Communication and Contention across Brazilian Youth Activist Networks*. Princeton, NJ: Princeton University Press.

Moghadam, Valentine M., and Elham Gheytanchi. 2010. "Political Opportunities and Strategic Choices: Comparing Feminist Campaigns in Morocco and Iran." *Mobilization* 15: 267–88.

Molotch, Harvey. 1970. "Oil in Santa Barbara and Power in America." *Sociological Inquiry* 40: 131–44.

Moore, Will H. 2000. "The Repression of Dissent: A Substitution Model of Government Coercion." *Journal of Conflict Resolution* 44: 107–28.

Morris, Aldon D. 1984. *The Origins of the Civil Rights Movement: Black Communities Organizing for Change*. New York: Free Press.

———.2000. "Charting Futures for Sociology: Social Organization." *Contemporary Sociology* 29: 445–54.

———. 2004. "Reflections on Social Movement Theory: Criticisms and Proposals." In *Rethinking Social Movements: Structure, Meaning, and Emotion*, edited by Jeff Goodwin and James M. Jasper. Lanham, MD: Rowman & Littlefield.

———, and Carol McClurg Mueller, eds. 1992. *Frontiers in Social Movements Theory*. New Haven, CT: Yale University Press.

Murray, Pauli, and Mary O. Eastwood. 1965. "Jane Crow and the Law: Sex Discrimination and Title VII." *George Washington Law Review* 34: 232–56.

Murray, Stephen. 1996. *American Gay*. Chicago: University of Chicago Press.

Navarro, Marysa. 1989. "The Personal Is Political: Las Madres de Plaza de Mayo." In *Power and Popular Protest*, edited by Susan Eckstein. Berkeley: University of California Press.

Nepstad, Sharon Erickson. 2004. *Convictions of the Soul: Religion, Culture, and Agency in the Central America Solidarity Movement*. New York: Oxford University Press.

———, and Christian Smith. 2001. "The Social Structure of Moral Outrage in Recruitment to the U.S. Central America Peace Movement." In *Passionate Politics*, edited by Jeff Goodwin, James M. Jasper, and Francesca Polletta. Chicago: University of Chicago Press.

Nonet, Philippe. 1969. *Administrative Justice*. New York: Russell Sage Foundation.

Noonan, Rita K. 1995. "Women Against the State: Political Opportunities and Collective Action Frames in Chile's Transition to Democracy." *Sociological Forum* 10: 81–111.

Norden, Deborah. 1996. *Military Rebellion in Argentina: Between Coups and Consolidation*. Lincoln: University of Nebraska Press.

Oberschall, Anthony. 1996. "Opportunities and Framing in the Eastern European Revolts of 1989." In *Comparative Perspectives on Social Movements*, edited by Doug McAdam et al. New York: Cambridge University Press.

O'Donnell, Guillermo. 1994. "Delegative Democracy." *Journal of Democracy* 5: 55–69.

———, and Philippe Schmitter. 1986. *Transitions from Authoritarian Rule: Tentative Conclusions about Uncertain Democracies*. Baltimore, MD: Johns Hopkins University Press.

Olesen, Thomas. 2003. *International Zapatismos: The Construction of Solidarity in the Age of Globalization.* London: Zed Books.

Olivier, Johan. 1991. "State Repression and Collective Action in South Africa, 1970–84." *South African Journal of Sociology* 22: 109–17.

Ondetti, Gabriel. 2008. *Land, Protest, and Politics: The Landless Movement and the Struggle for Agrarian Reform in Brazil.* University Park: Pennsylvania State University Press.

Opp, Karl-Dieter. 2009. *Theories of Political Protest and Social Movements.* London: Routledge.

———, Peter Voss, and Christiane Gern. 1995. *Origins of a Spontaneous Revolution: East Germany, 1989.* Ann Arbor: University of Michigan Press.

Ortoleva, Peppino. 1988. *Saggio sui Movimenti del 68 in Europa e in America.* Rome: Editori Riuniti.

Osa, Maryjane. 2001. "Mobilizing Structures and Cycles of Protest: Post-Stalinist Contention in Poland, 1954–59." *Mobilization* 6: 211–31.

———, and Cristina Corduneanu-Huci. 2003. "Running Uphill: Political Opportunity in Non-democracies." *Comparative Sociology* 2: 605–29.

Osa, Maryjane, and Kurt Schock. 2007. "A Long, Hard Slog: Political Opportunities, Social Networks and the Mobilization of Dissent in Non-Democracies." In *Research in Social Movements, Conflicts and Change* 27, edited by Patrick G. Coy. Bingley, UK: Emerald Group Publishing.

Oxhorn, Philip. 1994. "Where Did All the Protesters Go? Popular Mobilization and the Transition to Democracy in Chile." *Latin American Perspectives* 21: 49–68.

Parsa, Misagh. 1989. *The Social Origins of the Iranian Revolution.* New Brunswick, NJ: Rutgers University Press.

Paterson, Thomas. 1994. *Contesting Castro: The United States and the Triumph of the Cuban Revolution.* New York: Oxford University Press.

Payne, Charles M. 1995. *I've Got the Light of Freedom: The Organizing Tradition and the Mississippi Struggle.* Berkeley: University of California Press.

Pearce, Jenny. 1986. *Promised Land: Peasant Rebellion in Chalatenango, El Salvador.* Nottingham: Russell Press.

Pereira, Anthony W. 1997. *The End of the Peasantry: The Rural Labor Movement in Northeast Brazil, 1961–1988.* Pittsburgh: University of Pittsburgh Press.

Perrow, Charles. 1984. *Normal Accidents: Living with High-Risk Technologies.* New York: Basic Books.

Perry, Elizabeth J., and Li Xun. 1997. *Proletarian Power: Shanghai in the Cultural Revolution.* Boulder, CO: Westview.

Pion-Berlin, David. 1987. "Military Breakdown and Redemocratization in Argentina." In *Liberalization and Redemocratization in Latin America*, edited by George Lopez and Michael Stohl. Westport, CT: Greenwood Press.

Piven, Frances Fox. 2006. *Challenging Authority: How Ordinary People Change America.* Lanham, MD: Rowman & Littlefield.

———, and Richard Cloward. 1977. *Poor People's Movements.* New York: Pantheon.

———. 1983. "Toward a Class-based Realignment of American Politics: A Movement Strategy." *Social Policy* 14: 2–14.

Pizzorno, Alessandro, ed. 1993. *Le Radici della Politica Assoluta e Altri Saggi*. Milan: Feltrinelli.

Polletta, Francesca, and James M. Jasper. 2001. "Collective Identity and Social Movements." *Annual Review of Sociology* 27: 283–305.

Powdermaker, Hortense. 1968. *After Freedom*. New York: Atheneum.

Ramos, Howard. 2008. "Opportunity for Whom? Political Opportunity and Critical Events in Canadian Aboriginal Mobilization, 1951–2000." *Social Forces* 87: 795–823.

Rhode, Deborah. 1989. *Justice and Gender*. Cambridge, MA: Harvard University Press.

Riordan, William L. 1963. *Plunkitt of Tammany Hall: A Series of Very Plain Talks on Very Practical Politics*. New York: Dutton.

Ringmar, Erik. 1996. *Identity, Interest and Action: A Cultural Explanation of Sweden's Intervention in the Thirty Years War*. New York: Cambridge University Press.

Risley, Amy. 2006. "Framing Violence: Argentina's Gender Gap." *International Feminist Journal of Politics* 8: 581–611.

Robnett, Belinda. 1997. *How Long? How Long? African-American Women in the Struggle for Civil Rights*. New York: Oxford University Press.

Rochon, Thomas R. 1998. *Culture Moves: Ideas, Activism, and Changing Values*. Princeton, NJ: Princeton University Press.

Rogin, Michael. 1987. *Ronald Reagan, the Movie and Other Episodes in Political Demonology*. Berkeley: University of California Press.

Rojas, Fabio. 2007. *From Black Power to Black Studies*. Baltimore, MD: Johns Hopkins University Press.

Rose, Tricia. 1994. *Black Noise: Rap Music and Black Culture in Contemporary America*. Hanover, NH: Wesleyan University Press/University Press of New England.

Rucht, Dieter. 1996. "The Impact of National Contexts on Social Movement Structures: A Cross-Movement and Cross-National Comparison." In *Comparative Perspectives on Social Movements*, edited by Doug McAdam et al. New York: Cambridge University Press.

Rule, James. 1988. *Theories of Civil Violence*. Berkeley: University of California Press.

Rupp, Leila J., and Verta Taylor. 1987. *Survival in the Doldrums: The American Women's Rights Movement, 1945 to the 1960s*. New York: Oxford University Press.

Santoro, Wayne A., and Gail M. McGuire. 1997. "Social Movement Insiders: The Impact of Institutional Activists on Affirmative Action and Comparable Worth Policies." *Social Problems* 44: 503–19.

Sasso, Chiara. 2005. *No Tav. Cronache dalla Val di Susa*. Naples: Intra Moenia.

Scammon, Richard, and Ben Wattenberg. 1970. *The Real Majority*. New York: David McKay.

Schirmer, Jennifer. 1989. "Those Who Die for Life Cannot Be Called Dead: Women and Human Rights Protest in Latin America." *Feminist Review* 32: 3–28.

Schneider, Cathy Lisa. 1995. *Shantytown Protest in Pinochet's Chile*. Philadelphia: Temple University Press.

Schock, Kurt. 1999. "People Power and Political Opportunities: Social Movement Mobilization and Outcomes in the Philippines and Burma." *Social Problems* 46: 355–75.

Schoenleitner, Guenther. 2003. "World Social Forum: Making Another World Possible?" In *Globalizing Civic Engagement: Civil Society and Transnational Action*, edited by John Clark. London: Earthscan.

Schudson, Michael. 1989. "The Sociology of News Production." *Media Culture & Society* 11: 263–82.

Schwalbe, Michael. 1996. *Unlocking the Iron Cage: The Men's Movement, Gender Politics, and American Culture*. New York: Oxford University Press.

Scott, James C. 1985. *Weapons of the Weak: Everyday Forms of Peasant Resistance*. New Haven, CT: Yale University Press.

Sewell, William H. 1996. "Three Temporalities: Toward an Eventful Sociology." In *The Historic Turn in the Human Sciences*, edited by Terence J. McDonald. Ann Arbor: University of Michigan Press.

Shapiro, Gilbert, and John Markoff. 1998. *Revolutionary Demands: A Content Analysis of the Cahiers de Doléances of 1789*. Stanford, CA: Stanford University Press.

Silver, Beverly J. 2003. *Forces of Labor*. New York: Cambridge University Press.

Skocpol, Theda. 1979. *States and Social Revolutions: A Comparative Analysis of France, Russia and China*. Princeton, NJ: Princeton University Press.

———. 1992. *Protecting Soldiers and Mothers*. Cambridge, MA: Harvard University Press.

Skrentny, John David. 1996. *The Ironies of Affirmative Action: Politics, Culture, and Justice in America*. Chicago: University of Chicago Press.

———. 1998. "State Capacity, Policy Feedbacks and Affirmative Action for Blacks, Women and Latinos." *Research in Political Sociology* 8: 279–310.

———. 2002. *The Minority Rights Revolution*. Cambridge, MA: Harvard University Press.

———. 2006. "Police-Elite Perceptions and Social Movement Success: Understanding Variations in Group Inclusion in Affirmative Action." *American Journal of Sociology* 111: 1762–815.

Smith, Christian. 1991. *The Emergence of Liberation Theology: Radical Religion and Social Movement Theory*. Chicago: University of Chicago Press.

———, ed. 1996a. *Disruptive Religion: The Force of Faith in Social Movement Activism*. New York: Routledge.

Smith, Christian. 1996b. *Resisting Reagan: The U.S. Central American Peace Movement*. Chicago: University of Chicago Press.

———. 2003. *Moral, Believing Animals: Human Personhood and Culture*. New York: Oxford University Press.

Snow, David A. 1993. *Shakubuku: A Study of the Nichiren Shoshu Buddhist Movement in America, 1960–1975*. New York: Garland Publishing.

————, et al. 1986. "Frame Alignment Processes, Micromobilization and Movement Participation." *American Sociological Review* 51: 464–81.

Snow, David A., Sarah A. Soule, and David M. Cress. 2005. "Identifying the Precipitants of Homeless Protest across 17 U.S. Cities, 1980 to 1990." *Social Forces* 83: 1183–210.

Steinberg, Marc W. 1998. "Tilting the Frame: Considerations on Collective Action Framing from a Discursive Turn." *Theory and Society* 27: 845–72.

Stern, Kenneth S. 1996. *A Force upon the Plain: The American Militia Movement and the Politcs of Hate.* New York: Simon and Schuster.

Stinchcombe, Arthur. 1983. *Economic Sociology.* New York: Academic Press.

Sugrue, Thomas J. 1996. *Origins of the Urban Crisis.* Princeton, NJ: Princeton University Press.

————. 1998. "The Tangled Roots of Affirmative Action." *American Behavioral Scientist* 41: 886–97.

Tarrow, Sidney. 1983. "Struggling for Reform." *Western Studies Paper No. 15.* Ithaca, NY: Cornell University Paper Series.

————. 1988. "National Politics and Collective Action: Recent Theory and Research in Western Europe and the United States." *Annual Review of Sociology* 14: 421–40.

————. 1994. *Power in Movement: Social Movements, Collective Action and Politics.* New York: Cambridge University Press.

————. 1996. "States and Opportunities: The Political Structuring of Social Movements." In *Comparative Perspectives on Social Movements,* edited by Doug McAdam, John D. McCarthy, and Mayer N. Zald. New York: Cambridge University Press.

————. 1998a. *Power in Movement: Social Movements and Contentious Politics,* 2nd ed. New York: Cambridge University Press.

————. 1998b. "'The Very Excess of Democracy': State Building and Contentious Politics in America." In *Social Movements and American Political Institutions,* edited by Anne N. Costain and Andrew S. McFarland. Lanham, MD: Rowman & Littlefield.

————. 1999. "Paradigm Warriors: Regress and Progress in the Study of Contentious Politics." *Sociological Forum* 14: 71–79.

————. 2005. *The New Transnational Contention.* New York: Cambridge University Press.

Tarrow, Sidney, and Doug McAdam. 2004. "Scale Shift in Transnational Contention." In *Transnational Protest and Global Activism,* edited by Donatella della Porta and Sidney Tarrow. Lanham, MD: Rowman & Littlefield.

Taylor, George V. 1967. "Non-Capitalist Wealth and the Origins of the French Revolution." *American Historical Review* 72: 469–96.

Taylor, Verta. 1996. *Rock-a-by Baby: Feminism, Self-Help, and Postpartum Depression.* New York: Routledge.

————, and Nella van Dyke. 2004. "'Get Up, Stand Up': Tactical Repertoires of Social

Movements." In *The Blackwell Companion to Social Movements*, edited by David A. Snow, Sarah H. Soule, and Hanspeter Kriesi. Malden, MA, and Oxford: Blackwell.

Thompson, Mark R. 1995. *The Anti-Marcos Struggle: Personalistic Rule and Democratic Transition in the Philippines*. New Haven, CT: Yale University Press.

Tilly, Charles. 1964. *The Vendée*. Cambridge, MA: Harvard University Press.

———. 1978. *From Mobilization to Revolution*. Reading, MA: Addison-Wesley.

———. 1986. *The Contentious French*. Cambridge, MA: Harvard University Press.

———. 1992. *Coercion, Capital, and European States, AD 990–1992*. Cambridge, UK: Blackwell.

———. 1995. *Popular Contention in Great Britain, 1758–1834*. Cambridge, MA: Harvard University Press.

———. 1997. "Parliamentarization of Popular Contention in Great Britain, 1758–1834." *Theory and Society* 26: 245–73.

———. 1999. "Wise Quacks." *Sociological Forum* 14: 55–61.

———. 2008. *Contentious Performances*. New York: Cambridge University Press.

———, ed. 1975. *The Formation of National States in Western Europe*. Princeton, NJ: Princeton University Press.

Tocqueville, Alexis de. 1955. *The Old Regime and the French Revolution*. New York: Doubleday.

Touraine, Alain. 1981. *The Voice and the Eye: An Analysis of Social Movements*. New York: Cambridge University Press.

Tracy, James. 1996. *Direct Action: Radical Pacifism from the Union Eight to the Chicago Seven*. Chicago: University of Chicago Press.

Underdown, David. 1987. *Revel, Riot, and Rebellion*. Oxford: Oxford University Press.

Verhoeven, I. 2009. *Burgers tegen beleid (Citizens against policy)*. Amsterdam: Aksant.

Vovelle, Michel. 1993. *La découverte de la politique: Géopolitique de la Révolution française*. Paris: la Découverte.

Ward, Alan J. 1980. *The Easter Rising: Revolution and Irish Nationalism*. Wheeling, IL: Harlan Davidson.

Warren, Mark R. 2010. *Fire in the Heart: How White Activists Embrace Racial Justice*. New York: Oxford University Press.

Wetherell, Margaret, Simeon J. Yates, and Stephanie Taylor. 2001. *Discourse Theory and Practice: A Reader*. London: Sage.

Wilson, James Q. 1980. "The Politics of Regulation." In *The Politics of Regulation*, edited by James Q. Wilson. New York: Basic Books.

Wolf, Eric R. 1969. *Peasant Wars of the Twentieth Century*. New York: Harper.

Wolford, Wendy. 2010. *This Land Is Ours Now*. Durham, NC: Duke University Press.

Wood, Elisabeth Jean. 2001. "The Emotional Benefits of Insurgency in El Salvador." In *Passionate Politics*, edited by Jeff Goodwin, James M. Jasper, and Francesca Polletta. Chicago: University of Chicago Press.

———. 2003. *Insurgent Collective Action and Civil War in El Salvador*. New York: Cambridge University Press.

Wright, Thomas. 2007. *State Terrorism in Latin America: Chile, Argentina, and International Human Rights.* Lanham, MD: Rowman & Littlefield.

Yates, Simeon, Margaret Wetherell, and Stephanie Taylor. 2001. *Discourse as Data: A Guide for Analysis.* Thousand Oaks, CA: Sage.

Young, Michael P. 2001. "A Revolution of the Soul: Transformative Experiences and Immediate Abolition." In *Passionate Politics*, edited by Jeff Goodwin, James M. Jasper, and Francesca Polletta. Chicago: University of Chicago Press.

Index

Bröer, Christian, 32
Brown, Rap, 176
Brown, Willie, 185, 193
Brownell, Herbert, 145
Bruhn, Kathleen, 298
Brym, Robert J., 17, 26-27
Brysk, Alison, 30, 297; on agency, 104,
    105; on consciousness-raising, 106;
    on economistic models, 93, 98,
    105-6; on grievances, 105, 106; on
    identity formation, 93, 98-99, 105; on
    international pressure, 95, 96, 105-6;
    on mobilizing messages, 111; on Other-
    identification, 106; *The Politics of Human
    Rights in Argentina*, 86-93, 98-99, 104-8,
    109, 111; on symbolic politics, 87, 92,
    105-6, 110
Bull, Chris, 299
Burgerman, Susan, 106
Burma, 102
Burstein, Paul, 170, 178
Bush, George H. W., 205, 208, 209
Byrd, S., 297

Canada: abortion in, 237, 238
Cardon, Dominique, 266
Caren, Neal, 236
Carmichael, Stokely, 176
Carson, Clayborne, 136
Carter, Jimmy, 95, 96, 206, 209, 214, 222
Caulfield, Max, 295
Causes: causal mechanisms, 9-10, 9n, 78, 79,
    113, 150-51, 194-97, 200, 202, 209-10,
    212-13, 230, 235, 240, 245, 260, 277-
    78, 279, 280-82, 284-92, 294, 295-300;
    cognitive mechanisms, 260, 265-67,
    274-75; determinism and free will, 3;
    emotional mechanisms, 9n, 260-61,
    268-75; political opportunities as, 279,
    280-84; relational mechanisms, 260,
    261-65, 274-75; vs. consequences, 16-18,
    18n6, 19
Central America peace movement, 29, 31-32,
    110, 203-23, 293, 298; origins of, 205-7,
    283; Pledge of Resistance, 205, 220; and
    political opportunity structures, 205,
    207-17, 218-23; Sanctuary movement,

203, 205, 206, 207, 220; Witnesses for
    Peace, 205, 220
Chamberlin, William, 51
Chamorro, Pedro Joaquín, 61, 80
Chauncey, George, 195
Chaves, M., 295
Chávez, Hugo, 104
Chelala, César, 97
Chiapas: Zapatista rebellion of 1994, 274,
    293, 299
Chiarello, Elizabeth, 236
Chile, 109; shantytown protests in, 298
Chinese democracy movement of 1989, 283,
    293
choices, 9n, 17, 22-23, 27. *See also* rational
    choice theory; strategic choices
Chorev, Nitsan, 22
citizenship rights movements, 27
civil rights movement, 133-41, 210, 237;
    activist networks during, 142-45, 148,
    149, 151; McAdam on, 6-7, 27, 30, 134-
    35, 137-38, 139, 140, 142, 147-48, 153,
    157, 175; in Mississippi, 133-37, 138-39,
    144, 146-47, 149, 150-51, 152, 280, 296;
    Montgomery Bus Boycott, 258; and
    political opportunity structures, 30-31,
    136-38, 151-52, 153, 217; relationship
    to gay and lesbian rights movements,
    188, 193-94, 199, 202; relationship to
    women's movement, 156, 157, 160, 168-
    71, 174, 175-77, 178, 180; repression
    of, 133-34, 135, 136, 138-41, 143, 145,
    146, 148, 149-51, 152, 212, 216; role of
    federal government in, 141, 142, 144-
    45, 146, 147, 148-49, 152, 180; White
    Citizens' Council (WCC) during, 133,
    134, 139, 141, 143, 144. *See also* National
    Association for the Advancement of
    Colored People (NAACP)
Clarenbach, Kathryn, 161, 163
Clarksdale, Miss., 134, 138-39
class, 13, 30, 75, 76-77, 127, 152; and
    Marxism, 14, 15; relational class identity,
    62, 69, 78, 79, 81, 82, 186, 195; white
    planters in Mississippi, 133, 137-38, 140-
    41, 148, 149, 151; working class, 63, 64,
    68, 73, 79, 93, 189, 216. *See also* elites

There is room for critique of the PP model, but it should not be abandoned altogether. The NIC movement is an example of a movement that the PP can be applied to and it works well like the womens mvmnt, depended on CRM

Not to be discounted but account would benefit from theoretical perspective (fr raming)

cites numerous examples that could be bolstered / reinforced by theory